BAJA RV CAMPING

LAURA MARTONE

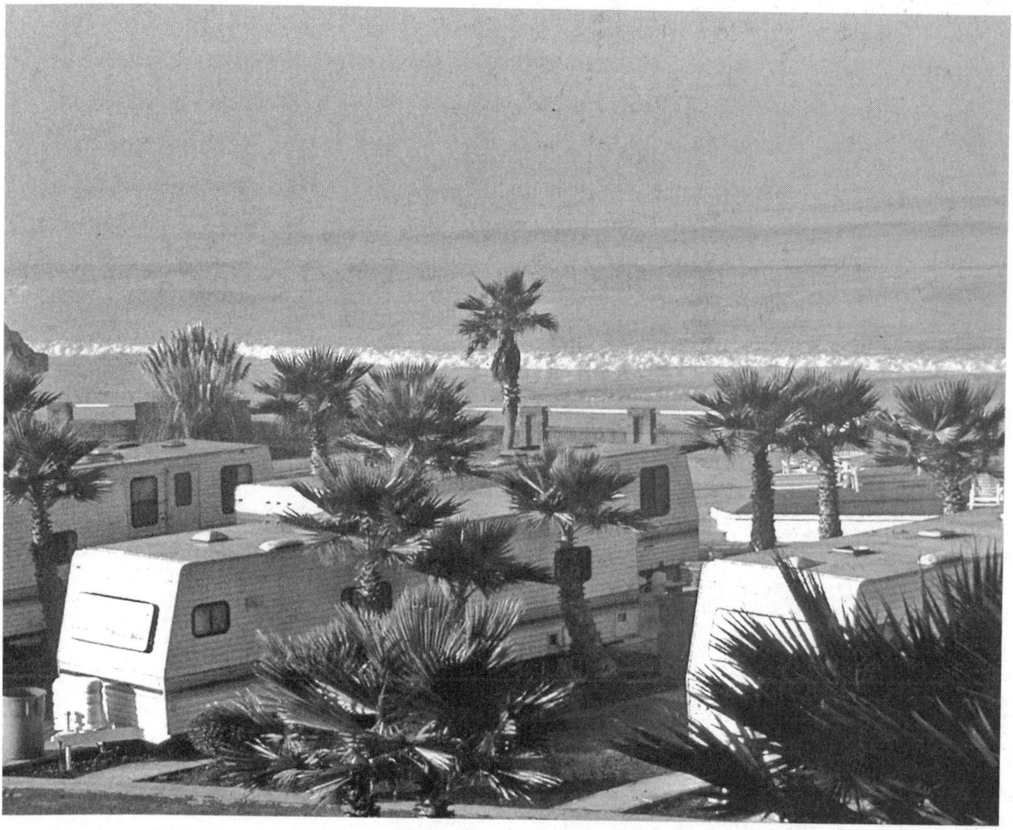

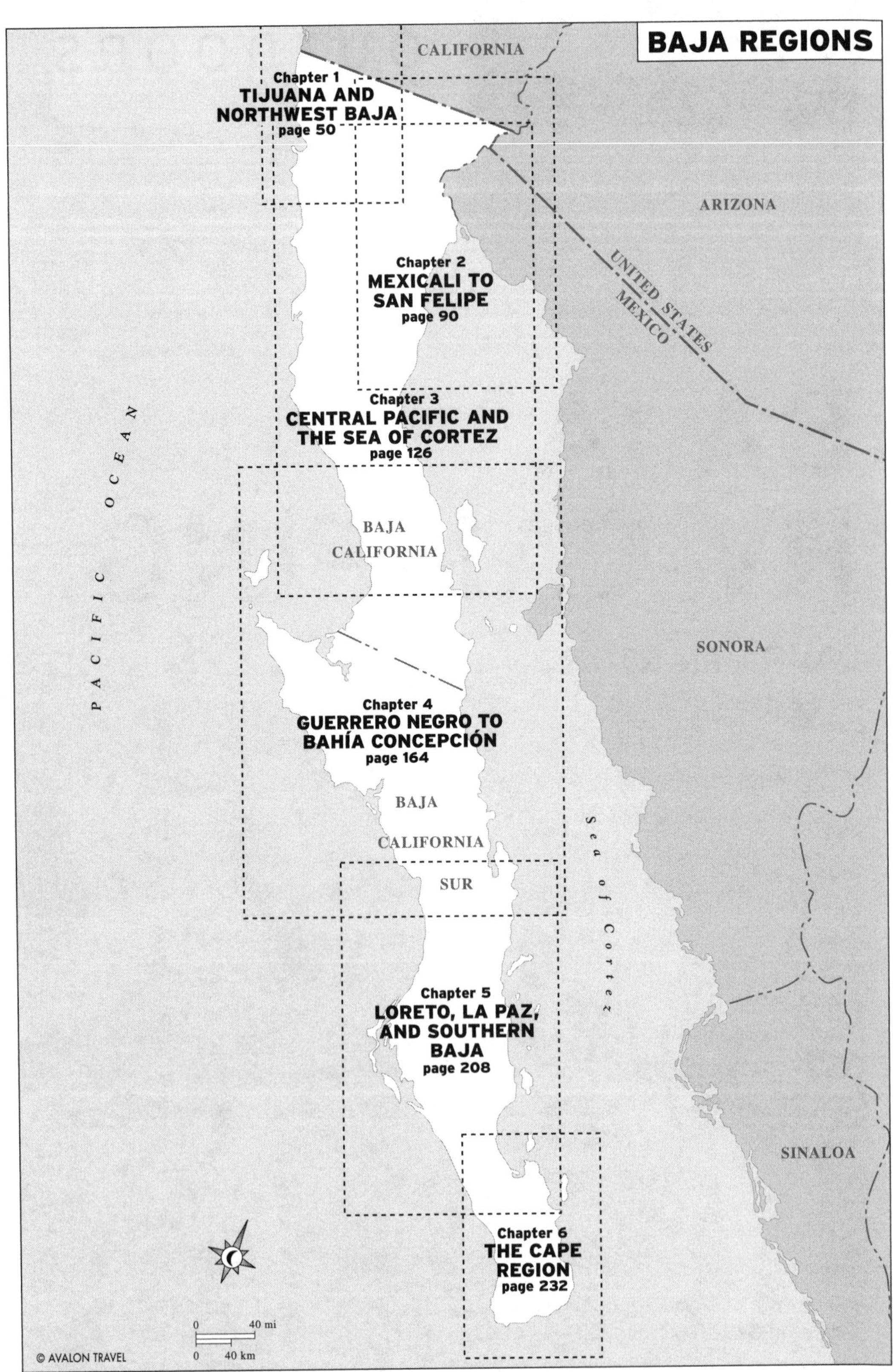
BAJA REGIONS
CALIFORNIA
Chapter 1
TIJUANA AND NORTHWEST BAJA
page 50
ARIZONA
Chapter 2
MEXICALI TO SAN FELIPE
page 90
UNITED STATES
MEXICO
Chapter 3
CENTRAL PACIFIC AND THE SEA OF CORTEZ
page 126
PACIFIC OCEAN
BAJA CALIFORNIA
SONORA
Chapter 4
GUERRERO NEGRO TO BAHÍA CONCEPCIÓN
page 164
BAJA CALIFORNIA SUR
Sea of Cortez
Chapter 5
LORETO, LA PAZ, AND SOUTHERN BAJA
page 208
SINALOA
Chapter 6
THE CAPE REGION
page 232
0 40 mi
0 40 km
© AVALON TRAVEL

Contents

How to Use This Book

ABOUT THE CAMPGROUND PROFILES

The campgrounds are listed in a consistent, easy-to-read format to help you choose the ideal camping spot. If you already know the name of the specific campground you want to visit, or the name of the surrounding geological area or nearby feature (town, national or state park, forest, mountain, lake, river, etc.), look it up in the index and turn to the corresponding page. Here is a sample profile:

Each campground in this book begins with a brief overview of its setting. The description typically covers ambience, information about the attractions, and activities popular at the campground.

RV sites, facilities: This section notes the number of campsites for tents and RVs and indicates whether hookups are available. Facilities such as restrooms, picnic areas, recreation areas, laundry, and dump stations will be addressed, as well as the availability of piped water, showers, playgrounds, stores, and other amenities. The campground's pet policy and wheelchair accessibility are also mentioned here.

Reservations, fees: This section notes whether reservations are accepted, and provides rates for tent sites and RV sites. If there are additional fees for parking or pets, or discounted weekly or seasonal rates, they will also be noted here.

Directions: This section provides mile-by-mile driving directions to the campground from the nearest major town or highway.

Contact: This section provides an address, phone number, and website, if available, for the campground. Unless otherwise noted, all phone numbers listed in this book are based in Mexico.

ABOUT THE ICONS

The icons in this book are designed to provide at-a-glance information on activities, facilities, and services available on-site or within walking distance of each campground.

- Hiking trails
- Biking trails
- Swimming
- Fishing
- Boating
- Canoeing and/or kayaking
- Hot or cold springs
- Wildlife
- Pets permitted
- Playground
- Wheelchair accessible
- RV sites
- Tent sites

MAP SYMBOLS

Expressway	80 Interstate Freeway	Airfield
Primary Road	101 U.S. Highway	Airport
Secondary Road	21 State Highway	City/Town
Unpaved Road	66 County Highway	Mountain
Ferry	Lake	Park
National Border	Dry Lake	Pass
State Border	Seasonal Lake	State Capital

ABOUT THE SCENIC RATING

Each campground in this guide has been designated a scenic rating on a scale of 1 to 10, with 10 being the highest possible rating. The scenic rating measures only the overall beauty of the campground and environs; it doesn't take into account noise level, facilities, available activities, etc.

INTRODUCTION

Author's Note

Nestled between the U.S.-Mexico border, the aquamarine waters of the Pacific Ocean, and the sparkling Sea of Cortez lies an extraordinary stretch of land that Spanish conquistadors once thought was an island brimming with gold. Despite the eventual discovery that this so-called island was, in fact, a peninsula, the region has remained a metaphorical isle of sorts. Separated from the Mexican mainland, Baja is a unique jewel—with its own distinct history, scenery, and cuisine—and a completely different language, culture, and economy than that of its northern neighbor.

For nearly a decade, I've traveled often to Baja, staying in tents or small RVs and observing the shifting sands of time—as favorite campgrounds in San Felipe and Los Cabos have given way to condominium developments and resident-only trailer parks. Despite such changes, I remain utterly fascinated with the stark beauty, year-round sunshine, and sheer diversity of this strange, budget-friendly paradise. Through this guide, I hope to share my passion and insight with other like-minded RV travelers.

Divided into two states—Baja California (or Baja Norte) and Baja California Sur (or Baja Sur, for short)—the peninsula has long been a favorite haunt for surfers, deep-sea anglers, RV caravans, and other outdoor enthusiasts from around the globe, especially since the creation of the paved Carretera Transpeninsular (Highway 1) in the early 1970s. Though not the kind of multilane interstate prevalent throughout the United States, this two-lane highway certainly facilitates traveling the 1,061-mile (1,707-km) distance between the border and the cape. Still, despite this handy thoroughfare, most *turistas* see little more than the crowded bars of Tijuana and the high-class resorts of Cabo San Lucas, a popular stop for fly-in visitors and international cruise ships.

Few foreigners seem to venture into the peninsula's rough-hewn interior—a tapestry of eclectic regions that have long resisted the permanent influence of conquistadors, missionaries, miners, and developers. Many seasoned travelers agree that crossing the peninsula via RV offers a truly rewarding experience. It's certainly cheaper, more comfortable, and less stressful than flying, and riding in your own home-on-wheels sure beats moving between hotel rooms.

No matter where you're headed, an RV is a terrific base from which to explore an array of recreational and cultural diversions, from diving amid the *arrecifes de coral* near Cabo Pulmo to touring the 19th-century edifices of quaint Santa Rosalía. Along the way, you might even meet some new folks, learn a few new skills, and find rejuvenation in nature. With an RV, you and your companions have the freedom to flit from village to village at your own pace—or stay, as many full-time RVers do, in one spot for an entire season. Despite its long-time status as the "forgotten peninsula," Baja offers a wide spectrum of RV accommodations, from primitive oceanside campgrounds to full-service resorts with wireless Internet access.

At once festive and tranquil, the Baja peninsula is the ideal locale for an RV vacation—whether for a few days or for weeks on end. Depending on your schedule, budget, and energy level, you'll be treated to a myriad of sights—from the vineyards of Valle de Guadalupe to the well-preserved Misión de San Ignacio de Kadakaamán to the bustling towns of Ensenada and La Paz. Via RV, you can reach much of what Baja has to offer—including pristine *playas,* remote *desiertos,* saltwater *bahías,* freshwater *lagunas,* mangrove *esteros,* snowcapped *montañas,* and seaside *pueblos*—places that can make you feel as though you've slipped into a time warp, where modern-day stresses seem improbable.

Despite its relatively compact size, Baja presents something for every kind of RV traveler. Amateur historians will be enchanted by the ruins of old Spanish *misiones* and the ancient *pinturas rupestres* within the Sierra de San Francisco. Shoppers will delight in the variety of accessible bargains—from the furniture of Playas de Rosarito to the glasswork of Cabo San Lucas. Gourmands will relish the margaritas, fish tacos, fresh *langosta,* and multi-ethnic cuisine—often available at inexpensive prices. Festival lovers, meanwhile, can flock to year-round events, including Carnaval celebrations, chili cook-offs, sportfishing tournaments, and art and music fiestas.

Wildlife enthusiasts can observe waterfowl amid the marshes of Bahía San Quintín or view migrating *ballenas gris* in the Laguna Ojo de Liebre. Anglers will find numerous fruitful spots in this water-lover's playground, from the Islas de Todos Santos to Bahía de los Ángeles. Expert climbers can savor incredible views from the top of Picacho del Diablo, Baja's highest mountain, and even stargazers will be intrigued by the nearby observatory in the Parque Nacional Sierra de San Pedro Mártir. In addition, the peninsula lures hikers, equestrians, bicyclists, boaters, surfers, swimmers, snorkelers, kayakers, golfers, off-road drivers, and those that simply want to relax on a quiet, breezy beach with an engrossing book and a clear view of the sunset.

Whether you're driving an RV from Southern California or crossing the ferry from Mexico, it helps to have a guidebook tailor-made for RV travelers, written by someone who's intimately aware of the RV lifestyle and the perils of Baja travel—from facing a busted towing vehicle to running low on *gas butano.* Intended as the ultimate bible for RV novices and veterans alike, this comprehensive directory provides all the necessary information (such as ambience, facilities, nearby attractions, and directions) for 185 campgrounds that welcome overnight RVers. In addition, you will find tips to help you plan, execute, and enjoy your RV camping trip across Baja—regardless of your interests, RV experience, vehicle type, familiarity with Mexico, and intended length of stay. In a practical, easy-to-read format, this guide presents RV camping checklists, health and safety advice, camping etiquette, information about regional flora and fauna, as well as tips about visiting a foreign country.

Perhaps it's difficult to summarize Baja's essence with just one guide; it's certainly impossible to experience it all in just one visit. Luckily, other nomads have explored and written about this complex place, so you'll find a number of Baja-related books—from field guides to novels. RV travelers, however, have distinct needs, which are specifically addressed in this book. Not only will it assist you in navigating the Baja peninsula and selecting a suitable campground, it will also help you locate the best fishing spots, the best beaches, the best cultural sites—in short, the best of Baja. It will enable you to discover (or rediscover) this amazing peninsula, cultivate your own perspective of its exuberant people, and learn to expect the unexpected. Then perhaps, like me, you'll find yourself returning again and again.

Just remember that Baja is an ever-evolving entity, where real-estate development has encroached upon prime oceanfront spots, where campgrounds can close as suddenly as new ones open, and where road conditions can change with the weather (especially during *chubasco* season), so it's possible that even the most meticulously researched book can lead you astray at times. While up-to-date maps and guides are necessary tools, it's equally critical that you consult local residents before heading into the wilderness. Breaking down or getting stuck in the sand is no fun, especially in an isolated place.

So, with that warning, turn the page, plan your route, pack up your gear, and hit the road for high adventure (or quiet reflection) on the Baja peninsula . . .

Best RV Parks and Campgrounds

Can't decide where to stay on the Baja peninsula? Here are the picks for the best RV parks and campgrounds in 10 different categories.

Best for Beaches

Baja Seasons Beach Resort, RVs, Villas, & Motel, Tijuana and Northwest Baja, page 59

Playas del Sol, Mexicali to San Felipe, page 101

Playa Punta Estrella, Mexicali to San Felipe, page 114

San Antonio del Mar Beach, Central Pacific and the Sea of Cortez, page 135

El Pabellón Trailer Park, Central Pacific and the Sea of Cortez, page 144

Playa La Gringa, Central Pacific and the Sea of Cortez, page 155

Playa El Requesón, Guerrero Negro to Bahía Concepción, page 201

Playa Balandra, Loreto, La Paz, and Southern Baja, page 223

Kurt-n-Marina, Loreto, La Paz, and Southern Baja, page 227

Playa Los Cerritos, The Cape Region, page 235

Club Cabo Inn and Camp Cabo, The Cape Region, page 236

Playa Norte RV Park, The Cape Region, page 248

Best for Boating

Campo Playa RV Park, Tijuana and Northwest Baja, page 65

Villarino RV Park & Camping, Tijuana and Northwest Baja, page 73

Club de Pesca RV Park, Mexicali to San Felipe, page 111

Villa Vitta Hotel Resort, Central Pacific and the Sea of Cortez, page 156

Hotel Serenidad, Guerrero Negro to Bahía Concepción, page 191

Rivera del Mar RV Park, Loreto, La Paz, and Southern Baja, page 209

Tripui Vacation Park and Hotel Tripui, Loreto, La Paz, and Southern Baja, page 214

RV Casa Blanca, Loreto, La Paz, and Southern Baja, page 222

Vagabundos del Mar Trailer Park, The Cape Region, page 239

Martin Verdugo's Beach Resort, The Cape Region, page 245

Best for Diving

Rancho La Bufadora, Tijuana and Northwest Baja, page 77

Puerto Santo Tomás Resort, Central Pacific and the Sea of Cortez, page 129

Daggett's Campground, Central Pacific and the Sea of Cortez, page 154

Playa Santispac, Guerrero Negro to Bahía Concepción, page 194

Loreto Shores Villas y RV Park, Loreto, La Paz, and Southern Baja, page 211

Tripui Vacation Park and Hotel Tripui, Loreto, La Paz, and Southern Baja, page 214

Playa El Tecolote, Loreto, La Paz, and Southern Baja, page 224

Club Cabo Inn and Camp Cabo, The Cape Region, page 236

Cabo Pulmo Campground, The Cape Region, page 243

Martin Verdugo's Beach Resort, The Cape Region, page 245

El Cardonal's Hide-a-Way, The Cape Region, page 250

Best for Fishing

Estero Beach Hotel/Resort, Tijuana and Northwest Baja, page 67

Club de Pesca RV Park, Mexicali to San Felipe, page 111

Papa Fernández Restaurant and Camping, Mexicali to San Felipe, page 119

Guillermo's Sportfishing, Hotel, & Restaurant, Central Pacific and the Sea of Cortez, page 157

Campo Rene, Guerrero Negro to Bahía Concepción, page 174

Hotel Serenidad, Guerrero Negro to Bahía Concepción, page 191

Loreto Shores Villas y RV Park, Loreto, La Paz, and Southern Baja, page 211

Tripui Vacation Park and Hotel Tripui, Loreto, La Paz, and Southern Baja, page 214

Villa Serena RV Park, The Cape Region, page 241

Martin Verdugo's Beach Resort, The Cape Region, page 245

East Cape RV Resort, The Cape Region, page 246

El Cardonal's Hide-a-Way, The Cape Region, page 250

Best for Golf

Popotla Trailer Park, Tijuana and Northwest Baja, page 55

Baja Seasons Beach Resort, RVs, Villas, & Motel, Tijuana and Northwest Baja, page 59

Playa Salsipuedes, Tijuana and Northwest Baja, page 60

Estero Beach Hotel/Resort, Tijuana and Northwest Baja, page 67

Rancho Ojai, Tijuana and Northwest Baja, page 81

Big RV's Camp, Mexicali to San Felipe, page 98

Pete's Camp, Mexicali to San Felipe, page 99

Playa Juncalito, Loreto, La Paz, and Southern Baja, page 213

Vagabundos del Mar Trailer Park, The Cape Region, page 239

Villa Serena RV Park, The Cape Region, page 241

Best for Hiking

Campo No. 5, Tijuana and Northwest Baja, page 76

Rancho Ojai, Tijuana and Northwest Baja, page 81

Rancho Sordo Mudo RV Park, Tijuana and Northwest Baja, page 84

Parque Nacional Constitución de 1857, Tijuana and Northwest Baja, page 86

Guadalupe Canyon Hot Springs & Campground, Mexicali to San Felipe, page 94

Las Cañadas Campamento, Central Pacific and the Sea of Cortez, page 127

Parque Nacional Sierra de San Pedro Mártir, Central Pacific and the Sea of Cortez, page 136

Parque del Palmerito, Central Pacific and the Sea of Cortez, page 148

Ricardo's Rice and Beans RV Park, Guerrero Negro to Bahía Concepción, page 175

Rancho Verde RV Park, The Cape Region, page 251

Best for Historic Sites

Rancho Mal Paso RV Park, Tijuana and Northwest Baja, page 58

Guadalupe Canyon Hot Springs & Campground, Mexicali to San Felipe, page 94

Balneario El Palomar, Central Pacific and the Sea of Cortez, page 130

Posada Don Diego RV Park & Restaurant, Central Pacific and the Sea of Cortez, page 140

Old Mill Motel and RV Park, Central Pacific and the Sea of Cortez, page 142

Lonchería Sonora, Central Pacific and the Sea of Cortez, page 148

Malarrimo Restaurant, Motel y RV Park, Guerrero Negro to Bahía Concepción, page 169

Ricardo's Rice and Beans RV Park, Guerrero Negro to Bahía Concepción, page 175

RV Park Las Palmas, Guerrero Negro to Bahía Concepción, page 182

Hacienda de la Habana, Guerrero Negro to Bahía Concepción, page 187

El Moro Motel and RV Park, Loreto, La Paz, and Southern Baja, page 210

El Litro Trailer Park, The Cape Region, page 233

Best for Horseback Riding

Baja Seasons Beach Resort, RVs, Villas, & Motel, Tijuana and Northwest Baja, page 59

Estero Beach Hotel/Resort, Tijuana and Northwest Baja, page 67

Villarino RV Park & Camping, Tijuana and Northwest Baja, page 73

Hacienda Santa Verónica RV Resort, Tijuana and Northwest Baja, page 83

Rancho Los Manzanos, Central Pacific and the Sea of Cortez, page 135

Rivera del Mar RV Park, Loreto, La Paz, and Southern Baja, page 209

Club Cabo Inn and Camp Cabo, The Cape Region, page 236

Vagabundos del Mar Trailer Park, The Cape Region, page 239

Playa Norte RV Park, The Cape Region, page 248

Rancho Verde RV Park, The Cape Region, page 251

Best for Surfing

Alisitos K-58 Surf Camp, Tijuana and Northwest Baja, page 57

Playa Salsipuedes, Tijuana and Northwest Baja, page 60

Playa Saldamando, Tijuana and Northwest Baja, page 61

Villa de San Miguel, Tijuana and Northwest Baja, page 62

Coyote Cal's, Central Pacific and the Sea of Cortez, page 133

Punta San Jacinto Campground, Central Pacific and the Sea of Cortez, page 138

Punta Santa Rosalillita, Central Pacific and the Sea of Cortez, page 160

Scorpion Bay, Loreto, La Paz, and Southern Baja, page 216

Playa San Pedrito, The Cape Region, page 234

Playa Los Cerritos, The Cape Region, page 235

Best for Wildlife Viewing

Parque Nacional Constitución de 1857, Tijuana and Northwest Baja, page 86

Guadalupe Canyon Hot Springs & Campground, Mexicali to San Felipe, page 94

Parque Nacional Sierra de San Pedro Mártir, Central Pacific and the Sea of Cortez, page 136

Parque del Palmerito, Central Pacific and the Sea of Cortez, page 148

Daggett's Campground, Central Pacific and the Sea of Cortez, page 154

Mario's Tours and Restaurant, Guerrero Negro to Bahía Concepción, page 167

Malarrimo Restaurant, Motel y RV Park, Guerrero Negro to Bahía Concepción, page 169

Laguna Ojo de Liebre Campground, Guerrero Negro to Bahía Concepción, page 171

Campo Rene, Guerrero Negro to Bahía Concepción, page 174

Ecoturismo Kuyimá, Guerrero Negro to Bahía Concepción, page 181

Tripui Vacation Park and Hotel Tripui, Loreto, La Paz, and Southern Baja, page 214

El Cardonal's Hide-a-Way, The Cape Region, page 250

RV Travel Tips

Baja is a fascinating destination, a place that's unquestionably part of the Mexican culture and yet isolated from the rest of the world—a place with unique trends, diversions, regulations, and considerations. Hopefully, the following information and advice will assist you in having a safe, smooth, and memorable RV journey to this once "forgotten peninsula."

BAJA TRENDS

Despite the laid-back character of many Baja villages and the seemingly untouched nature of the peninsula's vast deserts, mountain ranges, and forests, parts of Baja are snared in an ever-evolving state of development. In recent decades, technological improvements like paved roadways and Internet access have made it increasingly easier for foreign visitors to live, work, and play here. Real-estate developers, full-time RVers, and outdoor enthusiasts are among the many folks who have discovered the winning aspects of this magnificent, rough-hewn jewel—and have tried to make it their own. Consider the following trends.

Internet

It's hard to imagine the days when travel was possible without the Internet. In any given day, with the help of a computer and a modem, you can research Baja's native flora, book sportfishing charters, monitor the day's best surfing spots, view the menu of a Los Cabos restaurant, review the proposed route of an RV caravan, apply for Mexican automotive insurance, and perform a host of other duties. Access to your own laptop can make such tasks even more convenient, especially since several of Baja's RV parks offer some form of wireless Internet access. Internet cafés in towns like Ensenada and Loreto, as well as the presence of Internet-ready computers in many campground offices, make it difficult to stay out of touch for long—even in a place as seemingly remote as Baja. Just remember that not all websites are updated regularly. Always consult local residents or contact businesses directly before making any travel plans.

Real Estate

White-sand beaches, swaying palm trees, crystalline waters, and gorgeous sunsets are some of Baja's finest jewels. The sad truth is that, in recent years, many people have discovered these natural riches—including real-estate developers from the United States, Mexico, and beyond. While the influx of foreign money from condominium developments, golf courses, and posh resorts is beneficial for some people in Baja, it's unfortunate to think that the overdeveloped nature of Cabo San Lucas has spread to other parts of the peninsula. For RVers, real-estate trends, sudden land sales, and permanent housing needs have meant the closure or redevelopment of several favorite campgrounds. In San Felipe, for instance, the once-popular El Dorado Ranch RV Park closed its doors to overnight RVers to make way for condos and golf greens. In places like Mulegé, Todos Santos, La Paz, and Cabo San Lucas, many campgrounds have become permanent-only trailer parks—usually because annual leases are more reliable and more lucrative than seasonal ones. Luckily, though, as old parks close, new ones (like the Paraiso del Mar RV Resort north of Los Barriles) continue to open—though perhaps not at quite the same rate.

Full-Time RV Travel

Although increasing gasoline prices in the United States and other countries have caused a slight downshift in the RV industry as of late, many Americans and Canadians still embrace the full-time RV lifestyle. Not all of these full-timers are retirees either; younger couples have begun to discover the joys of living and working in their very own homes-on-wheels.

BAJA'S PEOPLE

The Baja California peninsula is divided into two Mexican states – Baja California and Baja California Sur – though it's often less confusing to refer to them as Baja Norte and Baja Sur, respectively. Both states are defined by a diverse geography, ranging from islands to beaches to deserts to mountains to forests to coastal marshes, lagoons, and bays.

Established in 1952 as the 29th state of Mexico, the northern half, Baja Norte, definitely contains the larger overall population of the two. While the 2005 census estimated Baja Norte's population at 2.84 million people, there are probably over 3 million inhabitants nowadays, the majority of which dwell within the two border cities of Tijuana and Mexicali, the state capital. The region's demographics consist of *mestizos* (those of Spanish and American Indian descent); immigrants from other parts of Mexico; East Asians; Middle Easterners; indigenous Cachanilla Indians; U.S. expatriates; and large immigrant populations from Central America. The following list contains the populations of Baja Norte's major cities and notable towns, based on the 2005 census and 2007 estimates:

- **Tijuana** – 1.48 million
- **Mexicali** – 856,000
- **Ensenada** – 375,000
- **Tecate** – 91,000
- **Playas de Rosarito** – 73,300
- **San Felipe** – 25,000
- **San Quintín** – 20,000
- **Colonia Vicente Guerrero** – 10,600
- **San Vicente** – 3,500
- **El Rosario** – 3,500
- **Bahía de los Ángeles** – 600
- **Santo Tomás** – 400

Baja Sur, which became Mexico's 31st state in 1974, has a population of roughly 512,000, according to the 2005 census; the demographics consist of native Mexicans (many from the mainland) as well as immigrants, most notably U.S. expatriates. Its largest city, La Paz, is also the state capital. The following list contains the populations of Baja Sur's major cities and notable towns, based on the 2005 census and 2007 estimates:

- **La Paz** – 215,500
- **Cabo San Lucas** – 56,800
- **San José del Cabo** – 48,500
- **Ciudad Constitución** – 37,300
- **Guerrero Negro** – 12,000
- **Loreto** – 10,300
- **Santa Rosalía** – 9,800
- **San Ignacio** – 4,000
- **Mulegé** – 4,000
- **Todos Santos** – 4,000
- **Vizcaíno** – 2,350
- **Los Barriles** – 600
- **Cabo Pulmo** – 111

Baja, despite the lack of standard amenities in many camping areas, attracts quite a number of these permanent nomads. Perhaps it helps that full-time RVers usually have a solid handle on living in a self-contained manner; knowing how to conserve water, propane, and electricity and how to take advantage of nearby laundries, post offices, stores, and other establishments when you can will help you better enjoy staying in Baja. After all, while full-service resorts, such as the Estero Beach Hotel/Resort near Ensenada, do exist, the majority of Baja's campgrounds offer little more than basic toilets, lukewarm showers, and inconsistent electricity—but, wow, what amazing views!

Snowbirds

For many years, warm, sunny destinations like Baja have lured those escaping the cold winters of their hometowns. Called snowbirds, winter Texans, and other such affectionate terms, these seasonal travelers will often journey via RV to a favored getaway location and stay there through the entire winter. Such practices are common

LEAVE NO TRACE ETHICS

As much as RV travelers relish Baja's great outdoors, it's surprising how often visitors leave behind evidence of their stay. Happily, the concept of ecotourism – traveling with a conscience – has gained momentum in recent decades, and the old guideline "take only photographs; leave only footprints" is just as critical today, especially in places like Baja, where preserving the Mexican culture, conserving natural resources, protecting wildlife, and ensuring a safe, healthy experience for present and future visitors is paramount. Whether you're touring the ruins of a former Spanish mission or diving within the Parque Marino Nacional Cabo Pulmo, it's important to make as little impact on your surroundings as possible. Here are some guidelines to keep in mind:

Plan in Advance

- Familiarize yourself with the area that you aim to visit, including any restrictions. If you're planning, for instance, a trip to see the ancient *pinturas rupestres* (cave paintings) within the Sierra de San Francisco, you must secure a permit from the Instituto Nacional de Antropología e Historia (www.inah.gob.mx) and review a list of regulations intended to preserve these fragile relics.
- Prepare for extreme weather, uneven terrain, and potential hazards so as to minimize your impact on backcountry resources. Do not underestimate aspects like heat, altitude, pack weight, physical condition, and trail difficulty. Be especially careful during Baja's unpredictable *chubasco* season (June-October), when hurricanes can wash out roads and trails.
- Pack all appropriate equipment, including a compass, a GPS, and a first-aid kit, and bring current maps of the area you plan to explore. In this way, you can eliminate the need to mark trails with rocks, paint, and other potentially damaging elements.
- If possible, visit Baja during the off-season, when crowds are less likely. In most areas, the high season is winter, when "snowbirds" have come to escape colder places elsewhere.
- Visit protected areas in small groups – a guideline that ecotourism organizations such as Malarrimo's in Guerrero Negro regularly practice.
- Understand the skill level of everyone in your group (and plan accordingly) so as to avoid unnecessary emergencies.
- Bring food that does not require cooking (and, therefore, campfires), and repackage any unused food to minimize waste.
- Bring plenty of water (one gallon per person per day) and a filtration system to avoid contracting any harmful microorganisms from water in the wilderness.

Travel with Care

- Whenever possible, hike on established trails, especially in places like the Parque Nacional Sierra de San Pedro Mártir. Do not take shortcuts across switchbacks, walk through fragile meadows, or overturn rocks, because such practices can lead to trail erosion.
- Camp on durable surfaces such as rock, gravel, or dry grass, and try not to alter the area.
- Do not disturb areas prone to erosion, such as the sand dunes around Guerrero Negro.
- Protect riparian areas and avoid water contamination by camping at least 200 feet (61 meters) from lakes and streams.
- In popular areas, concentrate use on existing trails and campsites, walk within the center of all trails, and establish small campsites where vegetation is absent.
- In pristine areas, disperse use to prevent the creation of new trails and campsites.
- Utilize lightweight stoves and lanterns in lieu of campfires.
- Where campfires are permitted, use established fire rings or barbecue grills, and keep the fires small. Use only deadwood from the ground; do not clear away brush, reshape the earth, or build fire rings.

- When you're finished with the campfire, make sure that all wood and coals are burned to ash, then extinguish the fire completely and scatter the cool ashes.

Preserve the Landscape

- Examine, but do not touch, Baja's artifacts, cultural landmarks, and historic structures – such as the former mining sites, pre-Columbian *pinturas rupestres*, and old Spanish *misiones* that populate the peninsula.
- Do not destroy or deface trees, shrubs, or any other natural or cultural features.
- Do not build structures or dig trenches.
- Do not introduce or transport nonnative plant or animal species.
- Leave rocks, plants, wildflowers, and other natural resources as you find them.
- When diving in Baja, take care not to damage underwater formations, especially fragile ones like the *arrecifes de coral* near Cabo Pulmo. Human contact can kill living coral.

Respect the Wildlife

- Observe wildlife from a distance; do not follow or approach any wild animal, no matter how innocuous it might seem.
- Never feed wild animals. Doing so puts you in danger, damages their health, alters their natural behavior, and exposes them to predators.
- Protect wildlife (and yourself) by storing food rations and trash several feet from your campsite – for instance, secured within boulder cracks or suspended in trees.
- When you go hiking or backcountry camping, leave your pets in the RV. Dogs, in particular, can annoy other travelers, harass wildlife, pollute campsites, pass harmful diseases to other animals, and get hurt or lost in the wilderness.
- Avoid wildlife during sensitive times, such as mating or nesting season. In the case of licensed whale-watching trips in places like Laguna Ojo de Liebre, follow your guides' instructions and do not attempt to touch the whales or their offspring.
- Do not disturb fragile estuaries, especially those that are home to migratory birds and waterfowl – such as the marshes surrounding Bahía San Quintín.

Pack out Waste

- If you pack it in, then pack it out. Before leaving a campsite or rest area, search for any trash; place all refuse, from bottles to orange peels, in plastic bags; and toss said bags into proper trash receptacles at your journey's end. Do not burn, bury, or scatter trash in campgrounds or the wilderness.
- To properly dispose of solid human waste, pick a spot at least 200 feet (61 meters) from any trails, streams, and camping areas; dig an 8-inch (20-cm) hole; deposit the waste; and cover the hole with soil, sand, or duff, blending it into the surroundings. Excrement near lakes or streams can damage water quality and lead to an increase in harmful microorganisms.
- Pack out all toilet paper, hygiene products, and used diapers.
- To wash yourself, clothing, or dishes, carry water 200 feet (61 meters) away from streams or lakes, use small amounts of biodegradable soap, and disperse strained dishwater.

Consider Other Visitors

- Respect other visitors and protect the quality of their experience.
- Be courteous and yield to others on the trail.
- Step to the downhill side of the trail when encountering pack mules.
- Camp away from trails and other visitors.
- Avoid making loud noises.

Part of this copyrighted information has been reprinted with permission from the Leave No Trace Center for Outdoor Ethics (www.LNT.org, 303/442-8222 or 800/332-4100 from the U.S.).

on the Baja peninsula, where places like Bahía Concepción (which boasts a dozen primitive campgrounds with unparalleled views) have become the semipermanent winter homes of many happy snowbirds—couples and families alike, who develop lifelong friendships with one another and feel a sense of security with such like-minded nomads so near.

Back-Road Driving

Baja California offers a wealth of interesting and challenging back roads, which can range from wide, graded routes to narrow, corrugated tracks that only a handful of RVs (most notably, high-clearance, four-wheel-drive pickup campers) can negotiate. In recent years, more and more RV travelers have come to Baja if for no other reason than to explore the quaint fish camps, historic Spanish missions, ghost towns, lonely deserts, botanical wonders, coastal lagoons, and isolated peninsulas that lie at the end of such rugged routes. If you do intend to engage in some memorable (if bone-jarring) back-road driving during your Baja adventure, remember to consult local residents before venturing forth. Storms, real-estate development, and other factors can alter road conditions at any time.

It's important, too, to bring a reliable, up-to-date map on your journey, but even then, you cannot always trust that a road that appears to be graded and well maintained will indeed be so upon your arrival. Before attempting such remote areas as the Península Vizcaíno, make sure that your vehicle is in good condition; don't forget to check things like shock absorbers, tire pressure, and emergency provisions (for making vehicle repairs and surviving the wilderness for a while). It's also advisable to travel in pairs (as in a pair of RVs), because you might have to save each other in the case of a breakdown or worse.

Recreational Activities

As the world continues to shrink in size, and places once thought of as remote become more and more civilized, an increasing number of outdoor enthusiasts have come to appreciate the wealth of recreational activities that Baja's diverse landscapes promote. While many RVers travel to Baja for its shops, cantinas, wineries, and festivals, many more come to pursue a variety of outdoor diversions, including fishing, golf, hiking, horseback riding, water sports, and wildlife viewing.

Fishing

Although the heyday of fishing in the offshore waters of Baja California—when famous folks like Ernest Hemingway made fruitful journeys into the Sea of Cortez—took place over six decades ago, fishing is still a popular activity here. While you can bring your own boat to comb the waters surrounding this incredible peninsula, plenty of sportfishing outfits are available to lead you to the finest fishing grounds. Consider well-respected guides like Sergio's Sportfishing Center in Ensenada (www.sergios-sportfishing.com) or The Fishermen's Fleet in La Paz (www.fishermensfleet.com). Refer to the *Resources* section for additional outfitters and reference materials, and remember to secure a valid Mexican fishing license prior to your trip.

Golf

For years, golf has been a main attraction for those coming to Baja, RV travelers included. Several championship golf courses exist on the peninsula, including a few designed by legendary golf pro Jack Nicklaus himself. While some of the golf courses are members-only, most welcome the public. The highest concentrations of courses are at either end of the peninsula—with at least four between Tijuana and Ensenada and even more in the Los Cabos region. For more information, refer to www.golfbaja.com.

Horses, Hikes, and Bikes

While most travelers consider Baja to be a water-lover's playground, the peninsula actually offers a wealth of sightseeing opportunities for landlubbers, too. Many campgrounds, such as Rancho Ojai near Tecate, offer trails that are ideal for hiking, bicycling, and, sometimes,

golfers at sunset

horseback riding. If that sounds a little too tame, you can always engage in a wilderness hike in one of Baja Norte's two national parks, participate in a 50-mile (80-km) bicycle race from Rosarito to Ensenada (www.rosarito ensenada.com), or take a mule-packing trip into the Sierra de San Francisco (www.kuyima .com). Just remember to do your research ahead of time; it's important to bring the proper gear, the right clothing, and any other necessities (such as water and sunscreen).

Water Sports

It goes without saying that most RV travelers come to Baja for the water. The fact that, in many RV parks and campgrounds, the ocean-front spots are the first to be occupied is a fairly telling sign. Swimming, surfing, snorkeling, scuba diving, kayaking, boating, and kite-boarding are all favored pastimes here. Surfing is especially popular on the Pacific side, where the waves are wilder, while kayakers tend to favor the calmer waters of the Sea of Cortez. Snorkelers and scuba divers will find a wealth of underwater attractions along the fringes of Baja, especially near the Punta Banda peninsula, Cabo San Lucas, and the Parque Marino Nacional Cabo Pulmo. Windsurfers, meanwhile, prefer the wintertime winds that prevail near La Ventana. Even Jet Skis and water skis are prevalent in Baja, especially in resort areas like Los Cabos.

Wildlife at Play

Many RV enthusiasts travel to the Baja California peninsula to immerse themselves in nature—and, by extension, the native flora and fauna. Hikers will be treated to the sight of all manner of strangely shaped cacti, colorful lizards, birds of prey, and desert bighorn sheep in places like the Valle de los Cirios and Parque Nacional Sierra de San Pedro Mártir. Bird-watchers will find a variety of bountiful spots to view migratory birds in action—such as the marshes around Bahía San Quintín and Estero El Coyote, which are particularly rewarding. Those who favor marine animals will relish seeing dolphins in the surf, sea lions near Ensenada, and sea turtles in Bahía de los Ángeles, but, of course, the peninsula's primary wildlife-watching pastime occurs every winter, from December to April.

During that time, migrating California *ballenas gris* (gray whales) journey from the frigid waters of Alaska to the warmer lagoons of Baja, such as the Laguna Ojo de Liebre and Laguna San Ignacio, where they begin the mating season, give birth to their calves, and start to raise their young. Licensed *panga* (fishing boat) operators, hired by individuals or ecotourism companies like Ecoturismo Kuyimá (www.kuyima.com), take eager visitors into these protected lagoons to watch these magnificent cetaceans at play.

Just remember: Whether you're viewing desert creatures, waterfowl, or gray whales, try never to disturb the animals; watch them from a distance, and you will both benefit from the experience.

RED TAPE

Unfortunately, Baja's not all sun, sand, and sea. There are some important facts that you need to know to cross the U.S.-Mexico border safely, legally, and without hassle. Topics like customs regulations, insurance requirements, passports, permits, and contraband—learned over the course of nearly a decade of RV travel on the Baja peninsula—have been distilled to their essence and discussed here.

Border Crossings

Although RVers can reach the Baja California peninsula by hopping aboard a ferry from the Mexican mainland, most travelers come via the international border that separates the United States from Mexico. Baja California has six international border crossings: two in Tijuana, one in Tecate, two in Mexicali, and one in Algodones. All of these stations are open to vehicles as well as pedestrians. While travelers headed to Mexico can usually avoid long delays by crossing during off-hours (such as well after the morning rush), prolonged waits are frequently encountered when exiting Mexico and passing through U.S. Customs.

In addition, there is a border crossing between San Luis, Arizona, and San Luis Río Colorado, Sonora. Although not as popular among travelers bound for Baja, this station can also be used to cross from the United States to Mexico and onto the Baja peninsula itself. One terrific aspect about this crossing, as well as the six in Baja, is that you won't be forced to secure a temporary vehicle permit, as international visitors must do throughout the rest of Mexico. In fact, the only reason you'll need such a permit while in Baja is if you're planning to take a ferry from Santa Rosalía or La Paz to the Mexican mainland.

The seven border crossings, listed below, are presented as they appear on a typical road map, from west to east.

San Ysidro

Situated just north of downtown Tijuana, the San Ysidro border crossing—incidentally, the busiest international border crossing in the world—sits at the southern terminus of U.S. I-5 and I-805 in Southern California. It's open 24 hours daily. Northbound motorists should expect to wait more than two hours to cross on summer weekends and perhaps 20 minutes during midday and late-night hours on weekdays.

Otay Mesa

The border crossing at Otay Mesa—which is open 6 A.M.–10 P.M. daily—is positioned 6 miles (9.7 km) east of San Ysidro and directly east of the Tijuana airport. It typically handles passenger vehicles, including RVs, as well as all the commercial trucking traffic in the San Diego–Tijuana region. Although crossing times can be shorter here than in San Ysidro, northbound motorists should still expect to wait a solid hour on busy summer weekends. To reach this border crossing from San Diego, take California Highway 905 (from I-5 or I-805) and drive roughly 6.2 miles (10 km) to the border.

Tecate

There's no doubt that the Tecate crossing is off the beaten track. Given that it lies roughly 36 miles (57.9 km) from San Diego and 30 miles (48.3 km) west of Tijuana, a long highway drive is usually required on both sides of the border to reach it. But many travelers prefer this crossing over San Ysidro and Otay Mesa; for one thing, it's considerably less crowded than the other two. This small crossing is open 6 A.M.–11 P.M. daily.

CALEXICO

Adjacent to downtown Mexicali, this is the primary border crossing for Calexico and Mexicali, Baja Norte's state capital. Situated at the southern end of California Highway 111, the Calexico station is open 24 hours daily. During busy periods, crossing times can sometimes exceed an hour, especially for those headed north into California.

CALEXICO EAST

As with Otay Mesa, this station is located 6 miles (9.7 km) east of the area's main border crossing (Calexico in downtown Mexicali) and handles all of the commercial trucking traffic in the region. Open 6 A.M.–10 P.M. daily, Calexico East experiences much shorter waiting times than the downtown crossing. Another obvious advantage to this station is that you can avoid driving through the center of Mexicali, which could otherwise slow you down on your way to San Felipe or elsewhere. To reach this border crossing from California, take Highway 111 toward Calexico, head east on Highway 98 for 7.2 miles (11.6 km), turn south onto Highway 7, and follow the signs for the car crossing. You'll first reach the U.S. border station, shortly followed by the Mexican one.

ALGODONES

The farthest border crossing from Tijuana is sandwiched within the northeastern corner of Baja California, just south of California and not far west of the Arizona state line. From Yuma, Arizona, you can take I-8 West for 9.8 miles (15.8 km) to Highway 186, where you'll turn south and head toward the U.S.-Mexico border. Waiting times are fairly short at this small crossing, which is open 6 A.M.–8 P.M. daily.

SAN LUIS RÍO COLORADO

Located about 24 miles (38.6 km) south of Yuma, Arizona, this 24-hour border crossing is often less busy than the six that allow passage directly into Baja. From here, you can easily navigate through San Luis Río Colorado, follow Sonora State Highway 40 to the smaller town of Coahuila, connect with Baja California State Highway 4, and head west toward Highway 5 (México 5), the interstate that leads north to Mexicali or south to San Felipe.

Customs

Crossing the U.S.-Mexico border into Baja isn't nearly as frightening as you might have been led to believe, especially if you research the process ahead of time, bring along all the necessary documents, and leave all contraband at home. RVers—especially those with a lot of interior room, several storage bins, and enough space for sundry recreational items, like boats, kayaks, motorcycles, and the like—tend to bring a great deal more "stuff" with them than travelers in small cars and jeeps. That said, they also tend to undergo more searches, most notably at the border.

If you treat the Mexican border authorities with courtesy and cooperation, they will usually overlook non-duty-free items—even if you exceed per-person restrictions such as the 20-pack limit on cigars and cigarettes, 3.2-quart (3-liter) liquor/wine limit, and odd film-roll limit of 12. However, they won't overlook firearms (which must be accompanied by a Mexican hunting permit), ammunition and certain knives (for which fines and detainment are possible), medicine (which must be prescribed by a doctor), illegal drugs (which are just plain illegal), and food—specifically, produce, plants, and seeds. If any of your food items present a potential agricultural risk, Mexican authorities will confiscate them. For more information about Mexican customs regulations, visit http://travel.state.gov or http://portal.sre.gob.mx/usa.

Insurance

Although you might be the sort of international traveler who likes to live dangerously, never paying attention to details like insurance when venturing to places such as Europe and the Caribbean, you should know that U.S. automotive insurance policies are, in fact, completely invalid in Mexico; Mexican officials will not recognize such policies. While carrying Mexican automotive insurance is not required for entry into the country, it would be very dangerous for you to drive through Baja without it. In addition, it is highly recommended that you purchase medical and/or travel insurance as well.

Medical

Although residents of Africa and South America are required to have documented yellow fever vaccinations before entering Baja, American, Canadian, European, and Asian travelers have no such health restrictions. Regardless, anything can happen during your stay in Mexico—from food poisoning to boating accidents to wild animal attacks. So, although it is not required, it behooves you to have some form of medical insurance or travel insurance (which should include medical coverage) in order to protect yourself and your assets while traveling abroad. SafeMex Travel Insurance & Assistance (www.safemex.com) is a good place to start for such protection.

Although Baja may be part of a Third World nation, there are full-service hospitals in all of the major cities and towns, such as Tijuana, Ensenada, Mexicali, Guerrero Negro, Santa Rosalía, Ciudad Constitución, La Paz, and Cabo San Lucas. Medical and dental services abound as well, and Mexican pharmacies usually offer a greater variety of over-the-counter medications than their U.S. counterparts. Just remember that all hospitals and medical/dental offices will expect you to pay your bill in full before leaving the premises; be sure to save the receipt in order to pursue insurance reimbursement after your trip to Baja.

Automobile

Before embarking upon your RV trip to Baja California, you must first purchase automobile insurance suitable for travel in Mexico. Most U.S.-based insurance policies are not valid in Baja and will, therefore, not cover you in the case of a collision. Without proper insurance, you could also face jail time following an accident—an inauspicious way to begin your trip to another country.

Since Mexican authorities will only recognize policies issued by companies that are licensed to sell automobile insurance in Mexico, it's imperative that motorists purchase separate insurance policies for their RVs, tow vehicles, motorcycles, and the like before crossing the U.S.-Mexico border. In addition, you should carry proof of your insurance (as well as current vehicle registration) whenever you're behind the wheel. Take some time to review your policy before the start of your trip, so that you will be prepared in the case of an accident.

If you are unfortunate enough to experience an automobile accident while in Mexico, be sure to follow the written instructions that your insurance provider issued at the time of your purchase. It's important to note that most (if not all) Mexican-authorized insurance providers expect you to report and file any insurance claims prior to leaving Mexico. In addition, your policy could be declared null and void if an unauthorized motorist was found to be driving your vehicle at the time of the accident—or if drugs or alcohol were involved.

You can apply at several Mexican-authorized insurance agencies on both sides of the border at Tijuana, Tecate, and Mexicali. Before doing so, however, you should compare prices and coverage details among several different companies. If you plan to stay in Baja for several weeks or more, consider purchasing long-term insurance (for six months or a year) versus short-term insurance (at a daily or weekly rate), which can be considerably more expensive in the long run.

Once you've made a selection, you can expect to receive your policy as soon as the application has been accepted. Please refer to the *Resources* section, where you will find contact information (including websites) for several different insurance providers. Even the Automobile Club of Southern California (www.aaa-calif.com) offers affordable Mexican automotive insurance; it takes just a few minutes to apply online.

Legal Protection

To protect yourself and your assets, you shouldn't skimp on your automotive insurance policy. Besides full coverage (which includes collision, fire, theft, liability, etc.), you should purchase some form of legal aid as well—which can be helpful if an accident results in incarceration. Ask your automotive insurance provider if they cover such things as fines, court costs, bail bond premiums, and attorney fees.

Passports and Visas

At one time, U.S. and Canadian citizens merely needed an identification card to cross into Mexico. Soon, this will no longer be the case. Although Mexico's National Immigration Institute attests that passports are not required to enter Baja, you will, by June 2009, need a passport to re-enter the United States, per the requirements of the U.S. Department of Homeland Security. No matter what your country of origin, you must have a valid driver's license to successfully drive your RV or towing vehicle across the border. If you are a U.S. citizen and do not have a current passport, get one as soon as possible—well in advance of your intended trip to Baja. The recent policy changes have caused a severe increase in the wait times for passport applications.

Although U.S. and Canadian citizens are not required to secure a visa before traveling in Baja, they might have to apply for a tourist card (also called a tourist permit). All foreign nationals arriving in Baja California by land, staying less than 72 hours, and planning to go no farther than Ensenada via Highway 1 (México 1) or San Felipe via Highway 5 (México 5) do not need a tourist card. If, however, you plan to stay longer than three days or travel south of Ensenada for any length of time (which you should want to do!), you will have to obtain a tourist card at the U.S.-Mexico border.

Since you can no longer purchase a tourist card in Ensenada or at the border between Baja Norte and Baja Sur, you will need to obtain one from the Mexican immigration office at the border. Because of the crowded nature of most U.S.-Mexico border crossings, many RVers choose to spend the night at a California-based park near the border just prior to their trip to Baja. In that way, you can walk across the border, purchase your tourist card, head back to your RV, and get an early start the next morning. To make it an even easier process, you can purchase tourist cards from authorized U.S. agents, such as the Discover Baja Travel Club (www.discoverbaja.com), which offers such permits to their members for $29 each. Note that it's a little cheaper (about $22) if you procure it directly from the immigration office.

To purchase a tourist card from the immigration office, you must present a valid passport or driver's license (with a picture) and explain how long you plan to be in Mexico (if you are in Baja for less than a week, you will not have to pay for the card). It's better to overestimate the length of time you intend to stay in Baja, so that unexpected delays or extensions won't cause you problems later. Unfortunately, travelers who overstay the time limit on their tourist cards will be subject to a fine.

After applying for the card, you will have to pay for it at a nearby bank (either at the border crossing or within the border town itself), where it will be validated with a stamp. Note that, even if you purchase the tourist permit from a company like Discover Baja, you will have to get it stamped at an immigration office. The maximum length for a tourist card is 180 days, and the permit can be used for multiple entries. Just remember that you will need to return your tourist permit to a Mexican immigration office prior to its expiration date. For more information about immigration requirements, visit http://travel.state.gov or http://portal.sre.gob.mx/usa.

Licenses and Permits

Passports, driver's licenses, and tourists cards aren't the only permits required during your stay in Baja. If you plan to go fishing or take a private boat with you, you might need to secure a Mexican fishing license and boat permit as well.

Any nonresident alien (16 years or older) must possess a valid Mexican Sportfishing License before fishing from a boat in Mexican waters—whether it's a private boat or sportfishing charter. The license covers all types of fishing (including underwater spearfishing), and you must carry it with you whenever you are on board a fishing boat. Although foreign nationals are not actually required to have a current Mexican fishing license when fishing from the shore, you should probably purchase one anyway—if only to avoid any unnecessary grief from local police and other officials. You can obtain a nontransferable fishing license (whether daily, weekly, monthly, or annual) through a local fishing or tackle store, a Mexican insurance dealer, or the Mexico Department of Fisheries office in San Diego: 2550 5th Avenue, Suite #101, San Diego, CA 92103, tel. 619/233-4324 (U.S.). Be aware of any daily bag limits and other regulations, and remember that it is illegal to sell, trade, or exchange your catch. The capturing of sea turtles, sea anemones, coral, and other protected marine life is strictly forbidden by Mexican law, and all fish must be declared when returning to the United States.

A boat permit is not required unless you plan to fish from the boat. If there are any fishing paraphernalia or fish parts on board, however, you will be required to get a permit for the boat as well as a fishing license for every person on board. Remember that you will need your current vehicle registration form (for the boat) in order to apply for a permit.

Besides fishing licenses and boat permits, you might also need a motorized vehicle permit. A temporary vehicle permit is not required if you are only driving your RV within Baja and parts of Sonora. If, however, you plan to take a ferry from Santa Rosalía or La Paz, you will need to obtain a vehicle permit at the ferry ticket office prior to boarding the ferry. To get a vehicle permit, you must provide a separate driver's license for each motorized vehicle. In other words, one licensed driver cannot register both a motor home and tow vehicle; you will need two drivers for this purpose. The only wrinkle is that the name on each driver's license must match the name on the related vehicle registration and credit card (for payment). After paying a fee of around $30, you will receive an official packet, and a sticker will be placed on your front window (which can be removed only by a Mexican border official upon your return to the United States).

Illegal Items

Although it's important to bring items like current driver's licenses, valid passports, up-to-date vehicle registration, proof of Mexican auto insurance, and tourist cards when crossing the U.S.-Mexico border, it is almost *more* critical that you refrain from bringing any firearms, ammunition, or illicit drugs along for the ride. It is, in fact, illegal for any non-Mexican resident to possess a gun without first securing a special Mexican hunting permit, which must be obtained through licensed Mexican hunting guides or the Mexican consulate. Given the number of military roadblocks and inspection stations that you'll encounter in Baja (especially if you do much driving on the Transpeninsular Highway), you are bound to be stopped and have your vehicle searched at least once (if not multiple times). Firearms, ammunition, certain knives, and illicit drugs are the primary items for which officials are looking, and if they find such contraband, you will surely face some hefty fines, not to mention a rather lengthy stay in a Mexican prison.

Returning to the United States

Crossing the U.S.-Mexico border from the south is a bit trickier than traveling from California to Baja. For one thing, according to the U.S. Department of Homeland Security, you will soon be required to show a valid passport upon re-entering the United States. In addition, you will need to declare any purchases made in Baja. Each individual can import, without paying a duty, the following goods: $800 for gifts and personal articles, which includes 50 pounds (22.7 kg) of food, 1.1 quart (1 liter) of alcohol, 100 cigars, and 200 cigarettes. Customs officials will probably search your RV refrigerator and confiscate certain fruits, vegetables, and nuts (even fruit and meat purchased in the United States will be confiscated). If you have any further questions, visit the U.S. Customs and Border Protection website, www.customs.ustreas.gov. These items are prohibited:

- Avocados
- Cuban cigars
- Eggs
- Endangered species
- Illegal drugs
- Okra
- Pork and poultry
- Potatoes

TRAVELING IN MEXICO

Before crossing the U.S.-Mexico border or reaching Baja via a ferry from the Mexican mainland, there are a few facts that you should know about planning your RV trip to this foreign land. Your Baja adventure will unfurl a lot smoother if you're familiar with the region's seasons, accommodations, time zones, communications, and currency ahead of time. It's equally critical that you're prepared for possibilities such as toll roads, limited supplies, and vehicle breakdowns, not to mention the unique needs of your traveling companions. The following information will aid in such preparations.

When to Come

With ever-present breezes along the coast, mild temperatures for much of the year, and daylong sunshine in most places, Baja is definitely a year-round destination. Still, choosing when to come depends on many factors, not the least of which are health, comfort, danger, and interests.

For instance, if you're prone to heat exhaustion, you might want to avoid visiting places like San Felipe and Cataviña during the summer months, when both tend to be brutally hot. If you're escaping a wintertime landscape in the north, you might opt for a comfortably warm place like La Paz (as opposed to chilly Rosarito Beach in northwest Baja Norte, a popular stop for summertime vacationers). To avoid hurricanes, wind damage, and flash floods, you should probably avoid the southern half of Baja Sur during *chubasco* season (early June to late October), when tropical storms are highly probable.

Of course, interests make a difference, too. If you'd like to join a whale-watching excursion in the Laguna Ojo de Liebre, Laguna San Ignacio, or Bahía Magdalena, you should come sometime in January, February, or March, when the whales' breeding season reaches its zenith. Likewise, windsurfers will find the best conditions in winter; in fact, some La Ventana–area campgrounds are really only active from October to April. Fishing, on the other hand, tends to be more promising (and more popular) in the summertime. Lastly, you might consider shaping your trip around one of the peninsula's many annual holidays, festivals, and celebrations, such as spirited Cinco de Mayo (May 5) in the spring, Ensenada's Fiesta de la Vendimia (Wine Harvest Festival) in August, and spooky Día de los Muertos (Day of the Dead) in the fall.

How to Get Here

As with most places, the Baja peninsula can be reached in one of three ways: by air, by sea, or by land. Since this guide focuses on RV camping, airplanes and cruise ships are barely mentioned. The primary mode of transportation, therefore, is motorized vehicle—which could mean many things to an RVer. After all, recreational vehicles come in a multitude of shapes and sizes, from 45-foot (13.7-meter) motor homes with multiple slide-outs to a pickup truck with a pop-up, cab-over camper. The real question is how you plan to enter and traverse

MAJOR HOLIDAYS AND EVENTS

While Baja offers vast tracts of soul-cleansing wilderness, it's also known for its festive annual occasions. In fact, many RV travelers plan their trips around the peninsula's major holidays and events, from Carnaval parades to seafood fiestas. The following list presents a sampling of the celebrations you can expect to encounter year-round:

January

- **Día de los Santos Reyes** – the end of the Christmas season (January 6), also called Three Kings' Day or the Epiphany, when Mexicans traditionally exchange presents
- **Festival de Arte** – a weeklong arts festival in Todos Santos, which highlights folk dancing, turtle conservation, and Mexican artwork (late January or early February)

February

- **Día de la Candelaria** – a Candlemas feast of processions and bullfights, which commemorates the day that the infant Jesus was presented at the Jerusalem temple (February 2)
- **Día de la Constitución** – an official holiday (February 5) that commemorates Mexico's 1917 Constitution (still in use today)
- **Día de la Bandera** – a national parade of Mexican flags (February 24)
- **Carnaval** – a celebration of music, food, and parades during the week before Lent (early February to early March), popular in Ensenada, San Felipe, and La Paz

March

- **AgroBaja** – Mexico's only farming and fishing exhibition, which takes place in early March in Mexicali (www.agrobaja.com)
- **San Felipe 250** – an off-road race in San Felipe during mid-March (www.score-international.com)
- **Spring Break** – a rowdy tradition for U.S. college students, usually celebrated in Ensenada, San Felipe, and Cabo San Lucas in mid- to late March
- **Semana Santa** – Holy Week (Palm Sunday to Easter Sunday in March or April), popular in San Felipe as a Mexican beach holiday

April

- **Rosarito-Ensenada Fun Bicycle Ride** – a bicycle race in mid-April (www.rosaritoensenada.com)
- **Newport to Ensenada Yacht Race** – a boating race in late April (www.nosa.org)

May

- **Día del Trabajo** – Mexico's Labor Day (May 1)
- **Cinco de Mayo** – a holiday that commemorates the French defeat during the battle of Puebla de los Ángeles in 1862 (May 5)

June

- **Día de la Marina Nacional** – a celebration of the Navy in San Felipe (June 1)

Baja via RV. Should you rent an RV, join an RV caravan, hop a ferry from the Mexican mainland, or simply cross the border on your own and take the toll road?

RV Rentals

If you don't possess a motor home, travel trailer, or pickup camper of your own, the next best option is to rent an RV from a reputable company in the United States or Canada. Unfortunately, most RV rental companies forbid travelers to use their vehicles south of the U.S.-Mexico border. Two outfitters, however—Cruise America and El Monte RV—allow such international travel. Refer to the *Resources* section for contact information, and remember that, unless the company offers Mexican automotive insurance and/or participation in a Mexican auto

© MEXICO TOURISM BOARD

August

- **Fiesta de la Vendimia** – a grape harvest festival in the wine-producing Valle de Guadalupe and in nearby Ensenada (early to mid-August)

September

- **Fiesta de la Independencia** – a celebration of independence from Spain in 1821 (September 16)
- **Rosarito-Ensenada Fun Bicycle Ride** – a bicycle race in late September (www.rosaritoensenada.com)

October

- **Fiestas del Sol** – a three-week exposition of agriculture and industry and a celebration of music, dance, art, and regional cuisine in Mexicali
- **Día de la Raza** – a commemoration of Columbus's discovery of the New World and the founding of the *mestizo* people (October 12)
- **Fiesta de Langosta (Lobster Festival)** – a food-filled celebration in Puerto Nuevo to kick-start the lobster season (mid-to-late October; www.puertonuevolobster.com)

November

- **Día de Todos los Santos** – All Saints' Day (November 1), when people visit cemeteries to pay their respects to deceased loved ones
- **Día de los Muertos** – the Day of the Dead (November 2), a continuation of the previous day's festivities, particularly colorful in Tijuana
- **Feria del Camarón** – a shrimp festival in San Felipe (early November)
- **Festival Internacional de la Cerveza** – an annual mid-November beer festival in Tijuana (www.tjbeerfest.com)
- **Baja 1000** – an annual off-road race in Ensenada (mid-to-late November; www.score-international.com)

December

- **Día de Nuestra Señora de Guadalupe** – a colorful celebration in Tecate honoring the Virgin of Guadalupe, Mexico's patron saint (December 12)
- **Día de la Navidad** – Christmas Eve (December 24) and Christmas Day (December 25)
- **Fin de Año** – New Year's Eve (December 31)
- **Whale-watching Season** – from December to April, a prime time to view migrating *ballenas gris* (gray whales) in coastal lagoons along the Pacific coast

club, you will be responsible for procuring such services on your own.

RV Caravans

If you've never traveled to Baja via RV before, or you're a little unsure about venturing into this strange land alone, you might consider participating in an RV caravan. Traveling with a large group of RVs will promise camaraderie and ensure more safety on the road; others will, after all, be present to assist you in the case of vehicle breakdowns or automobile accidents, and thieves are less likely to target such a large group. Still, many RVers don't like being beholden to an official itinerary, which leaves little time for exploring off the beaten path. In addition, delays are more probable, because others can suffer breakdowns and

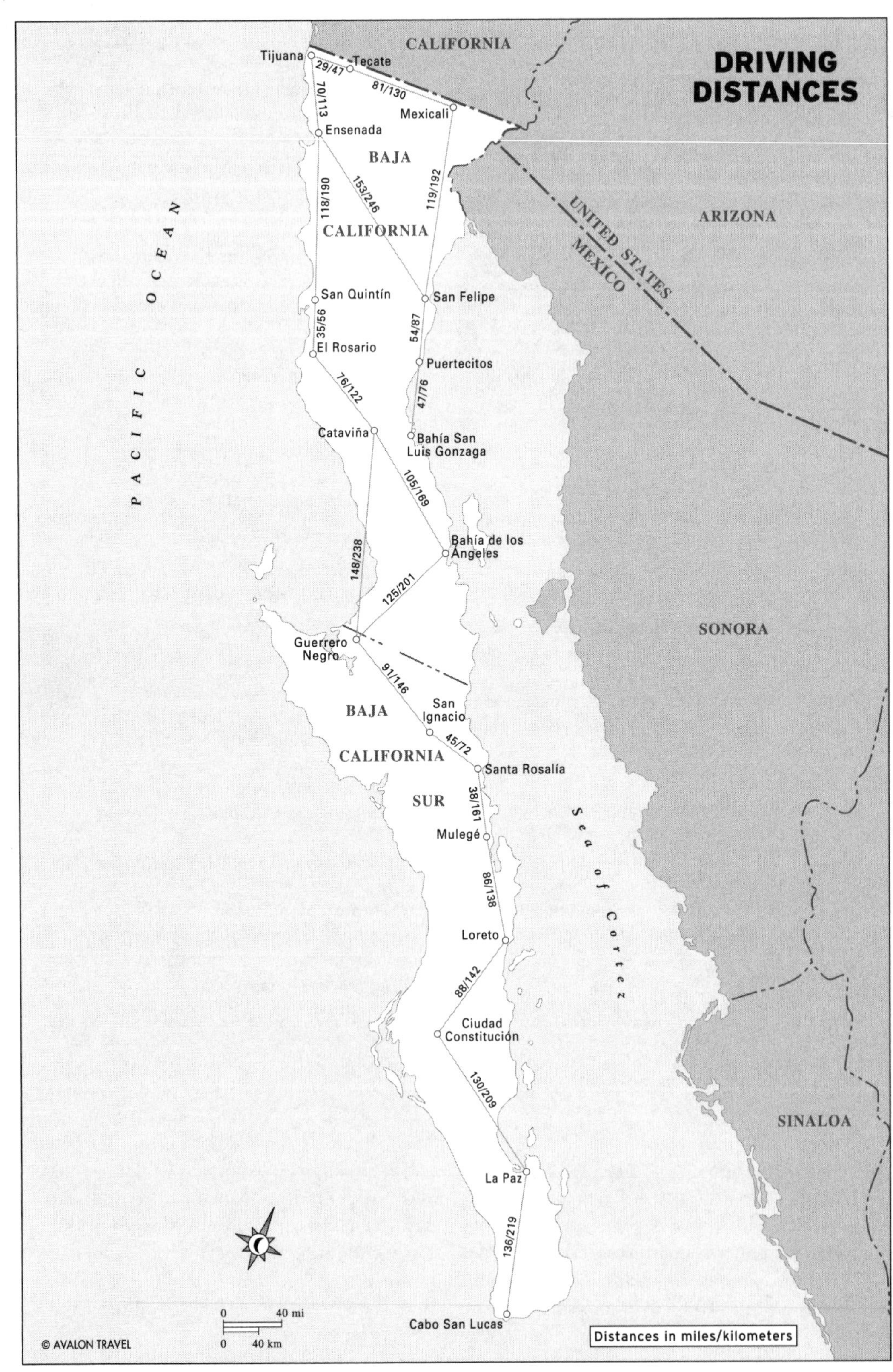
DRIVING
DISTANCES
CALIFORNIA
ARIZONA
SONORA
SINALOA
UNITED STATES
MEXICO
BAJA
CALIFORNIA
BAJA
CALIFORNIA
SUR
PACIFIC OCEAN
Sea of Cortez
Tijuana
Tecate
Mexicali
Ensenada
San Quintín
El Rosario
San Felipe
Puertecitos
Cataviña
Bahía San
Luis Gonzaga
Bahía de los
Ángeles
Guerrero
Negro
San
Ignacio
Santa Rosalía
Mulegé
Loreto
Ciudad
Constitución
La Paz
Cabo San Lucas
29/47
81/130
70/113
118/190
153/246
119/192
35/56
54/87
47/76
76/122
105/169
148/238
125/201
91/146
45/72
38/161
86/138
88/142
130/209
136/219
0 40 mi
0 40 km
Distances in miles/kilometers

accidents, too. Moreover, RV caravans tend to dominate campgrounds, especially given the small size of most Baja destinations, so if you're not part of a caravan, you might resent the increased noise and activity that such large groups encourage. Luckily, it's fairly easy to find out which campgrounds cater to caravans; for instance, Playa Norte RV Park, north of Los Barriles, actually offers a dedicated area for caravans, separate from the rest of the park.

Ask others about their caravan experiences and do some research on your own. It might not be a bad way for a tentative first-timer to test out Baja. Several clubs and companies offer such group treks into the "forgotten peninsula"—refer to the list in the *Resources* section.

Ferries

While most RV travelers enter Baja via one of the border crossings along the California state line, it is also possible to access the peninsula from the Sea of Cortez coast. Ferries regularly leave the Mexican mainland, from ports like Guaymas and Mazatlán, and deposit passengers and their vehicles in Santa Rosalía and La Paz, respectively. If you plan to take the ferry service from Baja to the Mexican mainland, remember that you will first need to register for a temporary vehicle permit, which you can do at the ferry office. Refer to these websites for more information: www.ferrysantarosalia.com and www.bajaferries.com.

Toll Roads

Be aware that Baja has a few toll roads, including Highway 1-D, a north–south route that connects Tijuana and Ensenada; Highway 2-D, a west–east route that links Tijuana, Tecate, El Hongo, and La Rumorosa; and the bypass route from San José del Cabo to Los Cabos International Airport. While driving on these roads, watch for the signs that indicate an upcoming toll plaza, and have the requisite fee for your vehicle type ready.

Where to Stay

The RV accommodations in Baja certainly run the gamut, from primitive campgrounds in the middle of the central desert to full-service RV resorts in Cabo San Lucas. While you should not expect luxurious amenities in most of these spots, do not be surprised to find full hookups, swimming pools, restaurants, and other similar delights—including reasonable proximity to sights and attractions such as whale-watching lagoons, historic missions, and golf courses. Be aware that, although this guide lists 185 campgrounds, divided into six different regions, the peninsula offers a wealth of other boondocking options, too—just consult local residents for such possibilities. When selecting a park or campground, consider factors like location, cost, facilities, maneuverability, and safety—after all, some places are more appropriate for groups of RVs, not those traveling alone.

Boondocking

Primitive camping (also called dry camping, dry docking, or boondocking) is a popular activity in Baja, often because there is no official campground available near otherwise advantageous places, such as terrific surf breaks. Boondocking is possible in a wide array of areas, including wineries on Highway 3 (México 3) and remote fish camps along both coasts. Many of the campgrounds listed in this guidebook, such as several on the Punta Banda peninsula, are intended for boondocking only, with little in the way of facilities and often nothing in the way of utility hookups. In order to have a safe, memorable boondocking experience, you should make sure that your RV is self-contained, meaning that you have your own water supply, toilet, generator, and so forth. In addition, it's usually not safe to park alone in isolated boondocking areas; try to travel in pairs or groups if at all possible. When in doubt about the status of a seemingly welcoming boondocking area—such as the beaches north and south of San Felipe—consult local residents just to be sure.

RV CAMPING ETIQUETTE

No matter where you park your RV for the night, you're bound to encounter some inconsiderate neighbors at times. Try not to be one of them. Although some of Baja's campgrounds and RV parks (especially the more organized and better staffed ones) have rules regarding issues like fireworks, noise, trash disposal, pet behavior, and the like, some managers are too ill-equipped or too reluctant to enforce them. Whether you're staying in a primitive campground on the Punta Banda peninsula or a full-service resort in Cabo San Lucas, be considerate of other campers and respect their right to peace and safety.

Here are just a few etiquette guidelines to keep in mind:

Cleanliness

- Keep your campsite tidy – do not tie unsightly items to trees, shrubs, or boulders; avoid the use of clotheslines; bring in towels and swimsuits once they have dried; and store toys and tools when not in use.
- Never, under any circumstances, litter. Dispose of all garbage in proper trash bins. If the campground has no such bins, pack out all of your trash and dispose of it when next you encounter a trash receptacle. Do not leave your trash outside the RV, where it will attract insects and wild animals. When you're packing up to leave the campground, double-check to ensure that you have left no trash behind.
- Always clean up your pet's droppings and dispose of them in a proper trash bin.
- If a dump station is available, use it as often as needed. Take care not to spill any gray water (such as dishwater) or black water (raw sewage) on the ground.
- Where fires are permitted, use existing fire rings or barbecue grills. When leaving the area, put out the fire completely, disperse the cool ashes, and clean all debris from the space.

Conservation

- Do not disturb or feed wildlife in the area. Feeding wild animals will only make them less wary of humans, which can lead to dangerous consequences.
- Where campfires are permitted, use only purchased firewood or charcoal. Do not use wood from the surrounding area without management's permission.
- Water (especially hot water) is a premium commodity in Baja, so practice conservation by avoiding long showers, using

FACILITIES

For the most part, the nicest RV parks in Baja tend to be situated within highly populated areas, such as Ensenada and Cabo San Lucas. In such places, you'll probably find full hookups, swimming pools, laundry rooms, and other communal facilities. But many of Baja's campgrounds have very few amenities; often pit toilets and convenient beach access are the most you're likely to receive.

To effectively plan your Baja vacation (or long-term stay), it's important to know what, if anything, an RV park or campground provides in addition to an overnight parking spot. Is there a hot tub or a game room? Are the showers hot? Is there any *sombra* (shade) from the *sol* (sun), or are all the spaces out in the open? These questions and many more are addressed within each campground profile in this guide.

One thing to note, however, is the matter of waste disposal. During the course of your RV trip in Baja, you'll note that few campgrounds have both sewer hookups and dump stations—in fact, most have either only one of these options or none at all, which can be terribly inconvenient for long-term campers. In areas where no sewer facilities are available (such as the campgrounds that line the western shore of Bahía Concepción), some tenants have as little water as necessary for washing dishes and clothes, and shutting off any running faucets.

Consideration

- Keep your radio and television at an unobtrusive volume. Not everyone will appreciate your programming tastes.
- Do not disturb your neighbors with the use of excessively noisy generators, air conditioners, and the like, especially in cramped campgrounds.
- Leave your firearms at home, as it is altogether illegal to bring them into Baja. Avoid practices that are forbidden by most campgrounds, such as the use of fireworks and loud all-terrain vehicles.
- Observe standard quiet hours (9 P.M.–9 A.M.), and advise your visitors to stifle unnecessary noise, especially at night.
- Supervise your children at all times – for their safety as well as for the comfort of others.
- Always keep your pets on a leash, and walk them only where it is allowed. Never tie up your pets alongside your vehicle while you're away; either bring them with you or leave them inside the RV. Be aware that barking or aggressive dogs are usually forbidden – and cause for eviction in most places.
- Do not take shortcuts (whether via foot or vehicle) across occupied campsites.
- If alcohol is allowed in the campground, do not use it to excess in public.
- Check the park rules before doing mechanical repairs, oil changes, and the like.
- If there is a laundry on the premises, do not leave your clothes in the washer or dryer after the cycle ends. Remove your clothes promptly and fold them in the designated area (which could be back at your RV).
- If there are bathrooms on-site, try not to track in mud or sand from the outside. Inform the management when supplies (such as paper towels and toilet paper) are running low.
- Many primitive campgrounds in Baja have little more than pit toilets or flush toilets with marginal plumbing. In such rural areas, it is not acceptable to put used toilet tissue in the toilet bowl; rather, you must dispose of the tissue in available wastebaskets or, if no such wastebaskets exist, pack the used tissue with your own trash.
- Wash dishes in the appropriate place – which is often not inside the restrooms.
- Park boats and extra vehicles in the designated area.

resorted to the following choices: using available restroom and washing facilities whenever possible, relieving themselves in the wilderness, or digging a deep hole and covering it with a plank in order to accommodate their sewer lines (certainly the most irresponsible, environmentally damaging option).

The best solution, however, is to purchase a portable waste tank (which can range in capacity from 12 to 35 gallons/45 to 132 liters) from a camping store in the U.S., such as Camping World. While staying in Baja, you should try to conserve space in your built-in holding tank and portable tank, being careful how much gray water (from showers, washing dishes, and the like) and black water (raw sewage) you produce. Definitely use outside facilities (such as restrooms and washing stations) whenever possible, and never pass up a chance to use a campground's dump station. If you're not staying in the campground itself, you should offer to pay for the service.

Reservations and Rates

Many campgrounds in Baja accept reservations for overnight camping. Probably just as many do not. In some cases—most notably with primitive, unstaffed campgrounds—there's no contact information with which you could even make a reservation. Nearly every single RV park

CAMPGROUND NAMES

While traveling in Baja, you will often encounter discrepancies in the names of streets, restaurants, and, especially, campgrounds. Tourists and local residents might in fact refer to a single locale in several different ways, which could prove confusing for first-time visitors. Sometimes, the names are simply variations on a theme, as with Alisitos K-58 Surf Camp (in the *Tijuana and Northwest Baja* chapter), which has been alternately called Campo Alisitos or Alisitos K-58 Surf Point Camping. At other times, a campground might have altogether different names, such as Lakeside RV Park in San Ignacio (in the *Guerrero Negro to Bahía Concepción* chapter), which is also known as Don Chon's.

To alleviate any potential confusion, the campground profiles in this guide have included alternate monikers where appropriate. But, as always, if you're ever in doubt about the name of a place, simply consult the locals. You'll find that most Baja residents are friendly and helpful – especially if you try asking them in Spanish first.

or campground listed in this book welcomes walk-in guests.

Each campground profile indicates whether or not that particular place accepts reservations. Rates (usually based on double occupancy) and other fees are listed as well. Taxes are typically included within each rate.

RV Restrictions

Unlike campgrounds and RV parks in the United States, most places in Mexico have no age restrictions regarding recreational vehicles. In other words, you're welcome to park overnight in most of the 185 destinations listed in this guide, regardless if you're staying in a 2008 Winnebago Itasca Latitude motor home or a converted 1975 Volkswagen van camper.

The only restrictions you might encounter involve length and clearance. Many of Baja's campgrounds (especially those in San Felipe) have short spaces, narrow roadways, and tight turns, making it difficult for any rig longer than 30 feet (9.1 meters) to maneuver. In other areas, such as San Ignacio, obstacles like palm trees can make it hard on big rigs, too. In addition, some campgrounds are situated down lengthy, washboard-like roads—routes that lengthy motor homes, unwieldy travel trailers, and low-clearance vehicles will find impossible to negotiate. When in doubt about the space available in a park or the status of an entrance road, consult local residents or, if possible, check it out on foot before continuing. It never pays to be stubborn or impatient in Baja; otherwise, you might find yourself in a tight parking jam—sometimes in the middle of nowhere.

Supplies

To enhance your RV trip to Baja, it's important to understand the supplies that you'll not only need during your journey but also be able to procure in Baja's major towns and small villages. Although it's important to be prepared for anything, it's also possible to be too prepared. Given all the nooks and crannies that most RVs contain, it's tempting to fill up every blessed space available—but sometimes this can encourage waste and cramped quarters, and oftentimes you'll end up bringing something (such as produce) that will be confiscated by Mexican border officials anyway. For a comprehensive list of necessary equipment, refer to the *RV Camping Checklist* in the *Traveling in Mexico* section of this chapter.

Food and Water

One terrific aspect of staying in an RV is the immediate access to a kitchen. While it's fun (and advisable) to sample the fare of Mexican cantinas, *loncherías,* and restaurants during your Baja adventure, it's equally nice knowing that you'll save money by preparing your own meals in your own motor home, travel trailer, van, or pickup camper. Luckily, you'll find convenient *supermercados* (supermarkets, such as Gigante or CCC) in several of Baja's major cities, including Tijuana, Rosarito, Ensenada, Mexicali, Ciudad Constitución, La Paz, and Cabo San Lucas. In addition, towns and villages along the peninsula offer a host of smaller *mercados,* such as *abarroterías* (grocery stores), *carnicerías* (butcher shops), *fruterías* (produce stores), *panaderías* (bakeries), *pescaderías* (fish markets), and *tortillarías* (tortilla shops).

When you're not dining in a nearby restaurant, you should consider preparing authentic Baja dishes—if only to experience the Mexican culture at its fullest. For a wealth of ideas, you can refer to the cookbooks listed in the *Resources* section or visit Jim Peyton's Lo Mexicano website (www.lomexicano.com).

Given the presence of such stores as those listed above, it's not necessary to bring all ingredients with you from the United States. For one thing, certain items (such as produce) will be confiscated at the border; officials at the Baja Sur state line do not even allow the passage of apples, avocados, citrus fruits, and potatoes from Baja Norte. Besides, with a little effort and a lot of time, you can find pretty much everything you'll crave in Baja, including fresh seafood, lean meats, and unusual fruits. It is advisable, however, to pack items like dried spices, canned goods, and specialty foods, such as no-calorie sweeteners, low-fat condiments, and your favorite imported beer—things that can be more expensive or harder to find in Mexico.

It is critical that you bring *agua purificada* (purified water) with you, as well as a water filtration system (for the RV plumbing as well as potential backpacking trips). Although you will be able to find *agua purificada* as well as safe-to-use *hielo* (ice) in Baja, it's important to start your journey with a decent supply. You need to be very careful about the matter of drinking water in Mexico, because most foreign nationals are not equipped to handle the potentially damaging effects of such untreated water. When in doubt, drink bottled water and order sodas without ice (even in a seemingly reputable restaurant). You should also avoid washing your produce in tainted water.

Fuel

Depending on the size, type, and condition of your RV, you'll need a variety of fuels during your Baja vacation. First and foremost, you'll require a full tank of gasoline or diesel fuel—both of which are available in most Pemex stations across the peninsula. Pemex is, in fact, the only brand of automotive fuel sold in Mexico, and the gasoline is offered in two grades: Magna unleaded, which is available at all stations, and Premium unleaded, which is difficult to find in remote areas and usually only available in stations between the U.S. border and Ensenada or in the Cape Region between La Paz and Cabo San Lucas. As a word of caution, you should fill up your fuel tank whenever you can, because supply conditions are subject to sudden changes. In some places, such as the 200-mile (322-km) stretch between El Rosario and Guerrero Negro, you're unlikely to find any functioning fuel pumps at all, and in other spots, such as Bahía de los Ángeles, you might have to wait a while for a refueling tanker to arrive.

In addition to 12-volt batteries, self-contained rigs often rely on gasoline-powered generators and *gas butano* (propane) tanks to power lights, water pumps, televisions, microwaves, air conditioners, heating systems, and the like. To enhance your living conditions—especially in the primitive, facility-free campgrounds that abound in Baja—you should fill up your propane tanks immediately prior to entering Baja. Although *gas butano* is available in Baja, supplies are sparse beyond the major cities, so as with gasoline, fill up on propane whenever you can. Other fuels that you should store in abundance include mini-propane tanks for use with camp stoves as well as the charcoal, firewood, lighter fuel, and propane required for some barbecue grills. Extra batteries are also a must—be sure that you have an assortment of types for all your electronic needs, including

RV CAMPING CHECKLIST

Important References and Paperwork

- Auto Club of Mexico membership (www.mexicanautoservices.com)
- Automotive/RV manuals
- Baja guidebooks, field guides, and other Mexico-related reading materials
- Mexican auto insurance information
- Mexican fishing licenses and boat permits
- Money (pesos, travelers checks, and credit cards)
- Passport, driver's license, and other identification
- Prescriptions
- Spanish phrasebook
- Temporary vehicle permits (for ferries to Mexico)
- Tourist cards
- Up-to-date maps of the region
- Vehicle registration (for RVs, towing vehicles, motorcycles, boats, etc.)

Personal Items

- Cold-weather clothing (such as jackets, sweaters, and mittens)
- Feminine hygiene products
- Hats to block the sun
- Hiking boots and sneakers
- Insect repellent
- Pants (lightweight for hot weather, thicker weave or denim for cold weather)
- Prescription and over-the-counter medication
- Rain gear (such as ponchos and hooded raincoats)
- Sandals or flip-flops (for the beach and the bath house)
- Shirts (short-sleeve for hot weather, long-sleeve for cold weather)
- Shorts
- Soap and shampoo
- Sunglasses
- Sunscreen and lip balm
- Swimsuits
- Toiletries
- Towels and washcloths
- Underwear and socks
- Water shoes

Basic Supplies

- Baling wire
- Batteries of all types
- Blankets, comforters, pillows, and sheets
- Cell phones and walkie-talkies
- Cleaning rags and supplies
- Compass
- Electrical outlet tester and indoor/outdoor outlet adapters
- First-aid kit (for cuts, burns, abrasions, insect stings, etc.)
- Flashlights (one per person) with extra batteries
- Generator (if your RV has no built-in unit)
- Hatchet/small ax and folding shovel
- Laundry bag and detergent
- Lighters with extra fuel
- Matches in waterproof container
- Multitool device and pocketknife
- Netting for awning area (to impede flying insects)
- Nylon cord
- Propane tanks (filled)
- Rug or mat (for the entryway)
- Scissors
- Sewer and water hoses (as long as possible)
- Spray lubricant
- Tape measure
- Tissue and toilet paper
- Tool kits for the car, RV, boat, bicycles, etc. (see *Automotive Supplies and Tools*)
- Voltmeter
- Weather-alert radio

Kitchen Gear

- Bakeware (such as oven-safe pans)
- Barbecue utensils (such as tongs and spatulas)
- Bottle/can opener
- Broom and dustpan
- Cooking utensils
- Cookware, such as stovetop pots and pans
- Cutlery and eating utensils
- Cutting board and mixing bowls
- Dishes, bowls, and glasses (preferably plastic)
- Dish towels, sponges, and scrub brush
- Dishwashing soap

- Food (preferably dry goods, specialty items, and limited produce, due to Mexican customs regulations)
- Garbage bags, food-storage bags, and aluminum foil
- Mop and bucket
- Oven mitts
- Paper towels
- Portable stove and propane bottles
- Purified water (in bottles or gallon jugs) and iodine tablets
- Stove fuel
- Wastebasket
- Water filters, spare water pump, and collapsible plastic water jug (with a spigot)

Automotive Supplies and Tools

- Alligator-clip test leads
- Automotive fluids (oil, transmission fluid, radiator coolant, brake fluid, etc.)
- Boards, rope, a shovel, and chains (in case your wheels get stuck in the sand)
- Brake-adjusting tool
- Chisel
- Claw hammer
- Cleaning tool for battery terminals
- Crowbar
- Drive pins
- Duct and electrical tape
- Extra car battery and jumper cables
- Flat-tire sealer
- Fuel can and extra fuel
- Hacksaw
- Hand file
- Hex key set
- Jacks (appropriate for your vehicle)
- Nails, screws, nuts, and bolts
- Plastic ties
- Pliers (needle-nose, vise-grip, etc.)
- Putty knife scraper
- Red flag to signal motorists during an emergency
- Screwdriver set (with slotted and Phillips heads)
- Siphoning hose
- Spare parts such as air/oil/gas filters, belts, clamps, fuses, hitch balls, hoses, spark plugs, and wheel bearings
- Spare set of keys (for RV, vehicle, motorcycle, boat, etc.)
- Spare tires (appropriate for your specific RV, trailer, towing vehicle, etc.)
- Spark plug tool
- Spool of copper wire
- Steel wool
- Tire gauge
- Tire-inflating compressor
- Tow cable, rope, and bungee cords
- 12-volt test light
- Wire cutters
- Wire stripping/crimping tool
- Wrenches (lug, crescent, distributor, monkey, pipe, socket, etc.)

Optional Supplies

- Baby food, diapers, or other kid necessities
- Barbecue grill
- Bicycles and bicycle pump
- Binoculars for bird-watching
- Biodegradable soap for backpacking trips
- Board games, playing cards, etc.
- Boat with trailer
- Canoe, kayak, or inflatable boat with paddles
- Extra propane
- Firewood or charcoal
- Fishing rods and tackle (including hooks, swivels, sinkers, lures, and fillet knives)
- Folding table and chairs
- Golf clubs
- GPS (global positioning system)
- Ice chest
- Lantern (with extra batteries)
- Laptop computer with modem, network cables, and wireless card
- Magazines, books, and notebooks
- Motorcycles on trailer
- Pet food and supplies
- Portable waste tank
- Radio or stereo (battery-powered)
- Sink plug
- Sleeping bags
- Snorkeling and scuba-diving gear
- Still camera (with extra flashes, filters, batteries, film, or memory cards)
- Sun shower
- TV satellite dish or wiring to connect to park's cable television
- Two-person tent, ground tarpaulin, sleeping pads, and canteens for backpacking trips
- Video camera (with extra batteries, adapters, tape stock, etc.)
- Waste bags for pet droppings

lanterns, flashlights, cameras, radios, laptops, cell phones, walkie-talkies, and GPS devices.

Travel Safety

Nothing can ruin a trip faster than being ill prepared for driving conditions and considerations in Mexico. To have a successful journey, it's important to ensure that your vehicle is in top working order before leaving the United States. Once in Baja, you should drive with the utmost care, obey speed limits and traffic laws, know what to do in the case of a breakdown, be prepared for poor road conditions (including soft sand), and prepare yourself for the inevitable roadblock.

Never drive on the highway (or on any road, for that matter) at night. In the dark, you will be less equipped to deal with unexpected road

ROAD SAFETY TIPS

Despite the presence of modern cities like Tijuana, Mexicali, Ensenada, and Cabo San Lucas – where gasoline stations, repair shops, and supply stores are available – most of Baja is an isolated, service-free place, especially along remote back roads and the 220-mile (354-km) stretch of Highway 1 (México 1) between El Rosario and the Baja Sur state line. So, it behooves you to ensure that your vehicle (whether a motor home, van camper, or pickup truck) is in top-notch condition before crossing the U.S.-Mexico border. To prepare for a safe, memorable trip across the Baja peninsula, review the following pre-trip services and on-the-road tips.

Before Your Trip

- Join the Auto Club of Mexico (www.mexicanautoservices.com), the only emergency roadside assistance and international towing service designed specifically for Americans and Canadians traveling or living in Baja California and Mexico. In a pinch, the Auto Club can change a flat tire, provide emergency gasoline, unlock car doors, recharge batteries, and tow your vehicle to a service station in Mexico or back to the United States.
- Purchase Mexican automotive insurance and familiarize yourself with the policy before crossing the border (refer to the *Resources* section for insurance options).
- Consider joining an RV caravan or club (refer to the *Resources* section for contact information). Driving with others can enhance your Baja experience and provide some on-the-road safety, especially in case of a breakdown. Of course, mechanical problems with other rigs can also cause delays for you.
- Get a full tune-up, a front-end alignment, an oil change, a lube job, and an air/gas/oil filter change for your motor home or towing vehicle immediately prior to your trip.
- Make sure that all belts, brake pads, car batteries (and terminals), hoses, lights, pumps, shock absorbers, tires, and wiper blades are in stellar condition, because Baja's heat can be detrimental to such vital parts. In addition, check your turn signals, tighten your wheel lug nuts, and be sure your spare tires are properly inflated.
- Use a reliable map of Baja (such as AAA's fold-out road map) to plan your route, noting the classification of each road – whether it's a paved highway meant for all vehicles, an unpaved road suitable for smaller RVs, or a washboard track intended for high-clearance, four-wheel-drive vehicles only.
- Leave behind any firearms or nonprescription narcotics, both of which are illegal for visitors to Mexico.

During Your Trip

- Drive slowly and carefully. Roads in Baja, even the Transpeninsular Highway (Highway 1), are often narrow and poorly maintained.
- Obey all signs, traffic laws, and speed limits. International-style signs are frequently used for stops, parking, one-way roads,

hazards, narrow passages, and aggressive truck drivers. Also, it's simply not a safe time for you to be stranded on the road. Security patrols are infrequent then, and thieves and other marauders are more likely to prowl around after hours.

To prepare your vehicle and yourself for the journey, refer to the *Road Safety Tips* sidebar.

Specialized Travel

When traveling with companions who might have special needs—such as pets, children, disabled individuals, and senior citizens—it's important to prepare for inevitable situations and modify your travel plans accordingly.

Pets, for instance, are allowed in nearly every campground listed in this guide, but it's

rest areas, gas stations, attractions, and the like, but some signs (especially nonvisual ones written in Spanish) can be confusing for the first-time visitor. When in doubt about the meaning of a sign, refer to the list of common Mexican signs in the *Resources* section of this guide.

- Remember that all speed-related signs are expressed in kilometers (not miles), which can make a big difference in determining whether or not you're speeding.
- Consult local residents about road conditions before heading to your next stop.
- Monitor the engine temperature – especially in hot weather, on rough roads, and during uphill climbs – to avoid overheating in the middle of nowhere.
- Check the car battery, fluids, oil level, and tire pressure on a regular basis.
- Avoid driving at night if at all possible.
- Try not to drive more than 200 miles (322 km) in a given day. Too much driving can cause excessive fatigue for you and unnecessary strain for your vehicle.
- When you encounter an official roadblock or inspection station, be courteous to the personnel and cooperate if they choose to search your vehicle.
- On Highways 1-D and 2-D, have your fees ready for the toll plazas.
- Fill up your gas tanks when you have the chance. In Baja, service stations are sometimes few and far between.
- If you do experience a breakdown in a remote region, do not hesitate to contact the Auto Club of Mexico (if you're a member). You can also rely on the Ángeles Verdes (Green Angels), a free highway service that offers helpful, bilingual mechanics, equipped with first-aid kits, radio communication, basic supplies, small automotive parts (at a reasonable cost), and tourist information. You can expect to see them along Highway 1 at least twice daily. Tipping them is customary.
- In case of a breakdown, do not abandon your vehicle, because this will invite thieves. If you're unable to reach help via phone, try to flag down a passing motorist and ask him/her to send a mechanic or tow truck from the next town.
- If you require a particular part to repair your vehicle, try to procure it yourself. Otherwise, you might be waiting for several weeks for the part to arrive via a repair shop.
- If you have a minor automotive accident in Mexico, some Mexican residents might suggest that you try to come to an arrangement with the other party, without involving the police, but it's best to follow the written instructions of your insurance carrier. Usually, you have to report an accident before leaving Mexico in order to receive any reimbursement for services and repairs.
- Because of Baja's inconsistent voltage, you should check your vehicle batteries often while staying in a full-hookup campground – if only to avoid problems once you hit the road again.

See *Traveling in Mexico* in this chapter for a comprehensive checklist of what to pack. Preparation and planning are essential steps in ensuring safety.

important to understand the pet-related rules for each location. Typically, you are asked to keep your pets on a leash at all times, walk them in designated areas, control their behavior so as not to disturb or endanger others, and always pick up after them.

Children, meanwhile, are permitted in every campground in this guide; however, they must be supervised at all times. Most of these parks and campgrounds have limited staff and no lifeguards on duty, so it's especially important that you monitor your children around swimming pools and beaches.

Unfortunately, disabled individuals will find few wheelchair-accessible facilities on this side of the U.S.-Mexico border. In fact, many of the more primitive campgrounds have unsuitable terrain—such as sand and uneven lots—for wheelchairs. When in doubt, call ahead or consult local residents.

Another form of specialized travel involves a woman traveling alone. While it's admirable for an independent woman to explore the world on her own, it's simply not advisable in a Third World nation like Mexico. While Baja tends to be a safer place than the mainland, there are still too many things that can go wrong, especially while camping alone in an isolated place. If you must travel alone, stick to daytime driving and busy campgrounds.

For those RVers who enjoy turning their getaways into volunteer vacations, consider contacting the following organizations:

- Grupo YMCA Ciudad de México (www.ymca.org.mx)
- Los Médicos Voladores (The Flying Doctors, www.flyingdocs.org)
- Red Casas del Migrante (www.migrante.com.mx)
- The Flying Samaritans (www.flyingsamaritans.org)

Time Zones

In spite of Baja's compact size, the peninsula is divided into two time zones. Baja Norte, the northern state, adheres to *hora oficial del Pacífico* (Pacific standard time), similar to California. Baja Sur, meanwhile, is situated within the *hora oficial de las montañas* (mountain standard time) zone, similar to Colorado. It's especially important that you remember this when driving from the north to the south. If you fail to move your clocks and watches ahead one hour, you will undoubtedly be late for something—perhaps even a whale-watching excursion south of Guerrero Negro.

Communications

Typically, a foreign visitor will get along just fine without knowing how to speak Spanish. Still, Baja residents appreciate an effort to speak their language, no matter how inept the attempt. Bring a Spanish phrasebook with you—you might need it to decipher the Mexican road signs, though many of them are listed in the back of this book (where you'll also find a phrasebook).

Regarding other forms of communication, email access and public pay phones are available in major towns and even some campgrounds. In fact, many campgrounds offer wireless Internet access in lieu of (or in addition to) an Internet-linked computer in the office. Although telephone service is improving in Baja, it can still be expensive to make an international call; purchasing a phone card will make it easier and often cheaper to call home.

Remember that, unless otherwise noted in parentheses, all phone numbers in this guide are based in Mexico. If you're calling any phone number from the United States, remember to dial "1" before the area code of any U.S. number (unless you happen to be within the same area code), "011-1" before the area code of any Canadian number, and "011-52" before the area code of any Mexican number. From Canada, you must dial "1" before any Canadian area code (unless you happen to be within the same area code), "001-1" before any U.S. area code, and "011-52" before any Mexican area code. If you're calling a phone number from a Mexico-based phone, you must dial "001" before any

U.S. or Canadian area code and "01" before any Mexican area code (unless you happen to be within the same area code).

Currency

To be prepared for any monetary situation in Baja, you should bring credit cards, travelers checks, U.S. dollars, and some pesos (converted in the United States) with you. While some campgrounds, restaurants, and other establishments will accept major credit cards (and sometimes even personal checks, especially for reservations), you should be prepared for cash-only transactions at all times. Primitive campgrounds, for example, will only accept cash (often pesos or dollars will suffice). Try to find out what the requirements are ahead of time, so that you can stop at a bank in a nearby town and convert dollars to pesos, if necessary. For up-to-date currency conversions, visit www.xe.com.

RV LIFESTYLE

There's nothing quite like traveling in your own home-on-wheels, especially in a rugged destination like Baja California, where you'll certainly appreciate having immediate access to some of the comforts and conveniences to which you may be accustomed. Eschewing planes and cruise ships and traveling via RV instead can be a truly liberating experience, immersing you in the Mexican culture and allowing you to fully experience the exuberant people, old-fashioned villages, historic landmarks, and natural wonders that define this magical place. To maximize your trip across the Baja peninsula, it's helpful to understand the features of your particular RV as well as the supplies you'll need to make your day-to-day, far-from-home existence a bit easier.

RVs come in many shapes and sizes, from lengthy motor homes to midsized travel trailers to compact van campers. No matter what kind of vehicle you possess, however, you should understand how everything operates, including sewage and water hoses, propane tanks, the electrical system, and appliances (such as the stove, refrigerator, and air conditioner). Having an RV manual that's written specifically for your model is a must. It's critical, too, that your recreational vehicle be in tip-top shape prior to embarking upon your trip. Be sure to check that all appliances and water-filtration systems are working and that you have the requisite equipment and supplies—in case of an emergency. Refer to the *Road Safety Tips* sidebar in the *Traveling in Mexico* section of this chapter.

To make your RV trip even more convenient, make sure that you pack efficiently. Bring clothes and footwear for a variety of weather conditions and activities, including rain gear, hiking boots, wetsuits, etc. Also pack necessities such as plastic dishware, unbreakable cookware, cleaning supplies, plastic storage bags, etc. Refer to the *RV Camping Checklist* in the *Traveling in Mexico* section of this chapter.

CLIMATE AND WEATHER PROTECTION

RV camping on the Baja peninsula can reward you with a plethora of memorable experiences—whether watching kaleidoscopic sunsets over the Mar de Cortés, spying a solitary eagle amid snowcapped *montañas* in the Parque Nacional Sierra de San Pedro Mártir, drifting among majestic *ballenas gris* in the Laguna San Ignacio, snorkeling alongside Cabo Pulmo's rare *arrecifes de coral* only steps from your RV, catching killer waves along Punta San Miguel in the Océano Pacífico, exploring the botanical oddities that abound within the Valle de los Cirios, swapping stories with an old-timer in Tecate's central plaza, or sipping margaritas in Sammy Hagar's infamous Los Cabos–area cantina. But, while you can expect coastal breezes and unimpeded sunshine most of the time, Baja's climate isn't always as desirable as the travel brochures claim.

In general, temperatures tend to be higher at lower elevations, in southern towns, and along the Sea of Cortez coast. For your own safety, well-being, and comfort, though, you should anticipate and prepare for a wide range

BAJA'S AVERAGE TEMPERATURES

Weather on the Baja peninsula is typically warm and pleasant year-round; snowbirds especially relish the months of November through May, when areas along the Sea of Cortez and south of the Paralelo 28° are warm and dry. The sun shines most of the time in Baja, though you should be prepared for chilly winters in Rosarito, brutally hot summers in Cataviña, and tropical storms and hurricanes during *chubasco* season (early June to late

JAN.	FEB.	MAR.	APR.	MAY	JUNE
TIJUANA					
46-68° (8-20°)	48-69° (9-21°)	50-68° (10-20°)	53-70° (12-21°)	57-70° (14-21°)	60-73° (16-23°)
SAN FELIPE					
67-81° (19-27°)	68-82° (20-28°)	72-84° (22-29°)	74-85° (23-29°)	77-89° (25-32°)	78-90° (26-32°)
LORETO					
53-73° (12-23°)	54-76° (12-24°)	55-80° (13-27°)	57-85° (14-29°)	60-88° (16-31°)	65-93° (18-34°)
LA PAZ					
52-74° (11-23°)	53-77° (12-25°)	56-81° (13-27°)	58-81° (14-27°)	61-89° (16-32°)	66-94° (19-34°)
CABO SAN LUCAS					
54-76° (12-24°)	55-74° (13-23°)	56-77° (13-25°)	58-81° (14-27°)	61-86° (16-30°)	66-89° (19-32°)

of weather—from extreme dry heat in places like Cataviña to sudden tropical storms and hurricanes during *chubasco* season (June–October). Although the seasonal transitions are fairly mild here, you should pack clothes suitable for cold, heat, rain, and sun. Light jackets are often necessary to protect against wintertime winds during whale-watching excursions in the coastal lagoons. You might also encounter cold weather (sometimes even snow) atop mountains such as those within the Sierra de San Pedro Mártir range. To avoid overheating in desert-type areas or on the beaches in summer, you should bring light clothes, such as shorts and swimsuits, and protect against the sun by using sunscreen, sunglasses, and a wide-brimmed hat, and by drinking plenty of water. Remember to bring ponchos, raincoats, and umbrellas, especially

October). In general, temperatures tend to be higher at lower elevations, in southern towns, and along the Sea of Cortez coast.

The following month-by-month charts illustrate the average daily low and high temperatures for different areas of Baja (with the Fahrenheit temperatures listed first, followed by the Celsius conversions):

JULY	AUG.	SEPT.	OCT.	NOV.	DEC.
TIJUANA					
64-76° (18-24°)	65-78° (18-26°)	64-79° (18-26°)	58-76° (14-24°)	50-72° (10-22°)	45-69° (7-21°)
SAN FELIPE					
78-92° (26-33°)	77-92° (25-33°)	76-91° (24-33°)	74-87° (23-31°)	72-83° (22-28°)	69-81° (21-27°)
LORETO					
72-95° (22-35°)	74-94° (23-34°)	74-93° (23-34°)	67-89° (19-32°)	62-82° (17-28°)	57-76° (14-24°)
LA PAZ					
75-96° (24-36°)	77-95° (25-35°)	75-94° (24-34°)	68-90° (20-32°)	63-83° (17-28°)	58-77° (14-25°)
CABO SAN LUCAS					
73-94° (23-34°)	75-96° (24-36°)	75-95° (24-35°)	68-90° (20-32°)	63-83° (17-28°)	58-77° (14-25°)

during the rainy season, and keep abreast of weather reports at all times; if a hurricane is headed toward Baja, get to high ground and shelter immediately. Flash floods in Baja's many *arroyos* have been known to kill people.

SAFETY AND FIRST AID

When you later reflect upon your Baja experience, you don't want to focus on the cactus needles, spider bites, poisonous snakes, contaminated water, heat exhaustion, wrong turns, and inconvenient thefts you could have avoided. To keep your trip to Mexico on a safe, healthy track, adhere to the guidelines in this section.

Plants

While hiking amid the botanical oddities that abound in remote *desiertos* (deserts) like the

Valle de los Cirios or Desierto de Vizcaíno, be careful where you step (and where you place your hands). The needles of a cactus plant, for instance, are a lot sharper than you might imagine. In addition, while you can eat plants like the prickly pear cactus (minus the needles, of course), you should refrain from digesting any tempting berries, flowers, plants, and the like without first consulting local residents and expert field guides. Refer to the *Resources* section for helpful titles.

Insects and Invertebrates

Annoying creatures, such as gnats, mosquitoes, wasps, ants, spiders, and scorpions, abound in Baja. Typically, you can expect to encounter mosquitoes in humid places, such as alongside the Río Mulegé, and gnats often swarm amid coastal *esteros* (marshes). The central *desierto* is home to many varieties of ants and spiders, not to mention poisonous scorpions. Just be careful where you walk and be sure to bring two items wherever you go: insect repellent to ward off the flying bugs and a first-aid kit in case the repellent doesn't work. It's helpful to be familiar with any potentially harmful arachnids, especially in remote areas; if you do get bitten by a poisonous spider or a scorpion, you should seek proper medical treatment immediately.

Wildlife

While in Baja, you will probably spy a variety of wildlife, including marine mammals, birds, snakes, coyotes, deer, and other such creatures. To avoid animal attacks, always pay attention to where you're swimming or hiking. If you do encounter a snake or wild animal, keep your distance. Never, under any circumstances, attempt to feed the wildlife. Though dolphins or small birds might appear to be friendly and eager for a snack, they are still unpredictable entities, with impulses of their own. Besides, feeding them will only make them less wary of humans and less likely to seek out their own sustenance.

pelicans and gulls along Baja's rocky coast

Water Pollution

Unless you're relying on bottled water, it is never advisable to drink water without treating it first. This includes any streams that you might encounter while hiking in the wilderness. Always bring iodine tablets, charcoal water filters, and other such paraphernalia to remove any potentially harmful parasites, such as giardia, which can cause severe diarrhea and other extreme intestinal reactions.

Sometimes, it can be equally harmful for you to swim or bathe in contaminated water. On occasion, official warnings are issued regarding the water quality along the Pacific coast (in Southern California and northern Baja). Heed these warnings; if you swim in such polluted water, toxins may penetrate your pores and make you very sick indeed.

First Aid

Not only is it critical that you bring a well-stocked first-aid kit with you to Baja, but it is also important that you defend against the common health-related pitfalls of outdoor activity. The sun is a primary cause for concern, especially on a peninsula that experiences more than its fair share of sunny days. Although sunscreen will help to prevent sunburn (a painful condition that, if experienced often, can cause long-term problems for your skin), you must apply it often (and liberally). Prolonged sun exposure, high temperatures, and little water consumption can also cause dehydration, which can lead to heat exhaustion—a harmful condition whereby your internal cooling system begins to shut down. Symptoms may include clammy skin, weakness, vomiting, and abnormal body temperature. In such instances, you must lie down in the shade, remove restrictive clothing, and drink some water.

If you do not treat heat exhaustion promptly, your condition can worsen quickly, leading to heatstroke (or sunstroke)—a dangerous condition whereby your internal body temperature starts to rise to a potentially fatal level. Symptoms can include dizziness, vomiting, diarrhea, abnormal breathing and blood pressure, headache, cessation of sweating, and confusion. If any of these occur, you must be taken to a hospital as soon as possible; in the meantime, your companions should move you into the shade, remove your clothing, lower your body temperature with damp sheets, cool water, or fans, and try to give you some water to drink, if you're able.

Besides accidents, insect bites, animal attacks, and extreme weather, heat is probably the biggest health concern in Baja. You might not think, in fact, that hypothermia—a condition whereby the body temperature begins to lower to a dangerous level—is possible here, but it is. Being cold and wet for an extended period of time, such as during a rainstorm or in higher elevations, can be fatal. Try to keep warm and dry at all times. If you start to shiver, slur your speech, stumble, or feel drowsy, do not fall asleep. Instead, find some shelter, get into dry clothes, try to move around, and eat a quick-energy snack.

Navigational Tools

If you stick to the main highway, you might need little more than a reliable map to navigate the Baja peninsula. But if you have any intention of exploring the central desert, the mountainous backcountry, or other remote parts of Baja, it is imperative that you bring a compass and GPS (global positioning system) with you. Always travel with others, especially when venturing into the wilderness, and try to plan your route ahead of time. Consult local residents before heading into a remote area, and inform someone else of your intentions—in case you don't return when scheduled.

Cell Phones

Although a cell phone can be a necessary tool, especially in an emergency situation, there are at least two drawbacks to bringing one into the Baja wilderness. First, you're not necessarily guaranteed a signal. Second, if your telephone service provider is based outside Mexico, your rates might be astronomical. If in doubt, contact your provider prior to the trip.

Security

Perhaps the biggest reason that RV enthusiasts in the United States and Canada avoid traveling in Baja is their concern for personal safety. Between the Mexican mainland's bad reputation with international kidnappings, the drug-enforcement problems along the U.S.-Mexico border, and the horrible stories that national media outlets have reported regarding thefts and assaults on tourists in Baja, it's a wonder that anyone decides to head down. Reports of banditos, language barriers, water issues, horrendous roads, corrupt cops, and the like might, at times, be based in reality—but visiting Baja is often a much less daunting experience, where friendly neighbors and helpful Mexicans are more typically the standard.

To protect yourself and your belongings, however, try to follow these simple precautions:

- Before leaving for Baja, install a dead-bolt on your door—and perhaps an alarm system as well.
- Do not boondock alone; always try to camp with others, especially in isolated places.
- Do not leave your RV unattended on the side of the road; it's better to park it in a campground first, and then go exploring.
- Never leave valuables outside the RV or in plain view on your car seat.
- In case of an accident, do not abandon your vehicle, because this will invite thieves.
- Once night has come, do not open your door to an unfamiliar knock without first peeking through the window blinds or curtains to see who it is.

TIJUANA AND NORTHWEST BAJA

© RANCHO OJAI

BEST RV PARKS AND CAMPGROUNDS

Beaches
Baja Seasons Beach Resort, RVs, Villas, & Motel, **page 59**

Boating
Campo Playa RV Park, **page 65**
Villarino RV Park & Camping, **page 73**

Diving
Rancho La Bufadora, **page 77**

Fishing
Estero Beach Hotel/Resort, **page 67**

Golf
Popotla Trailer Park, **page 55**
Baja Seasons Beach Resort, RVs, Villas, & Motel, **page 59**
Playa Salsipuedes, **page 60**
Estero Beach Hotel/Resort, **page 67**
Rancho Ojai, **page 81**

Hiking
Campo No. 5, **page 76**
Rancho Ojai, **page 81**
Rancho Sordo Mudo RV Park, **page 84**
Parque Nacional Constitución de 1857, **page 86**

Historic Sites
Rancho Mal Paso RV Park, **page 58**

Horseback Riding
Baja Seasons Beach Resort, RVs, Villas, & Motel, **page 59**
Estero Beach Hotel/Resort, **page 67**
Villarino RV Park & Camping, **page 73**
Hacienda Santa Verónica RV Resort, **page 83**

Surfing
Alisitos K-58 Surf Camp, **page 57**
Playa Salsipuedes, **page 60**
Playa Saldamando, **page 61**
Villa de San Miguel, **page 62**

Wildlife Viewing
Parque Nacional Constitución de 1857, **page 86**

Although much of Baja's central peninsula seems fairly remote, rarely seen, and seldom touched, the same cannot be said about the northwest corner of Baja California, which includes the bustling towns of Tijuana, Tecate, Rosarito, and Ensenada. The region's proximity to the magnificent Pacific Ocean and the U.S.-Mexico border has made it a popular getaway for countless Southern Californians. Despite recent passport requirements (and occasional assaults on tourists), so many Americans make a regular practice of packing up the car and hopping across the border for a spontaneous weekend in Baja that this part of Mexico's treasured peninsula almost feels like an extension of the Golden State.

Considered to be one of the world's busiest border crossings, the passage between San Ysidro, California, and Tijuana, Mexico, is often chaotic for motorists, so, if you only require a glimpse of Mexican culture, you might want to stow your RV in one of San Diego's lovely parks, take the light-rail Blue Line Trolley to the border, and use your feet (or a taxicab) to explore Mexico's fourth-largest city. But for those hoping to experience the "real" Baja, don't fret. Crossing the border via RV and staying in a Mexican campground could be the start of a rewarding adventure, and RVers can pursue a variety of activities in northwest Baja Norte.

In Tijuana, shoppers can bargain for jewelry, leather goods, and pottery at the Mercado de Artesanías and along the famous Avenida Revolución and Avenida Constitución. Cultural spectators will relish a wide range of sights, from live concerts at the Frontón Palacio Jai Alai, to famous characters at the *museo de cera* (wax museum), to ballet performances at the Centro Cultural Tijuana. Those who embrace the nightlife will find plenty of restaurants, bars, and discotheques, and even sportsmen will be entertained here – Tijuana boasts a seasonal *plaza de toros* (bull ring), a *canódromo* (greyhound racetrack), a *campo de béisbol* (baseball stadium), and an 18-hole *campo de golf*.

Beyond this crowded metropolis, however, a plethora of unique experiences awaits. Movie lovers can tour the historic Rosarito Beach Hotel, a Spanish Colonial–style resort from the mid-1920s that once hosted Hollywood luminaries like Orson Welles and Rita Hayworth. Just south of town, cinema buffs can explore the behind-the-scenes process at Xploration, an extension of Baja Studios, where original sets, props, and costumes from the blockbuster film *Titanic* are on display. Farther south, gourmands can dine on fried *langosta* (lobster) in Puerto Nuevo near the coast, while wine connoisseurs can tour the vineyards of the Valle de Guadalupe.

In Ensenada, a major port town, you'll find a number of handicraft shops, art galleries, supermarkets, and restaurants. English is so prevalent that American citizens, especially first-timers to Mexico, often feel quite comfortable here. Besides shopping and dining, visitors also enjoy the town's other delights, including the peninsula's largest *pescadería* (fish market), the sea lions that congregate just offshore, the waterspout at La Bufadora, and several annual events, from wine festivals to bike races.

Although the road from Tijuana to Ensenada is probably the busiest route on the entire peninsula, there are actually six border crossings between the United States and Baja California. For a more laid-back, authentic ambience than that of Tijuana, visit the neighboring border town of Tecate and marvel at the workings of the Cervecería Cuauhtémoc Moctezuma, home of the popular Tecate beer.

Outdoor enthusiasts won't be disappointed either. In northwest Baja Norte, you can stroll below the dramatic cliffs south of Playas de Rosarito, surf the waves of Punta San Miguel, and board a fishing charter or whale-watching boat in Bahía de Todos Santos. Golfers will find a handful of courses between Tijuana and Ensenada, including the 18-hole Real del Mar Golf Resort and the three nine-hole courses of Bajamar Ocean Front Golf Resort. There's even a national park in this region, the 28,000-acre (11,330-hectare) Parque Nacional Constitución de 1857, nestled within the Sierra de Juárez and featuring Laguna Hanson, a shallow, picturesque lake surrounded by pine forests, granite boulders, and rustic cabins.

The RV parks in this diverse region are just as varied as the attractions. Depending on your budget and taste, you'll find everything from luxurious, resort-style campgrounds to low-key, primitive spots beside the Pacific Ocean. Many places in northwest Baja, such as fish camps on the Punta Banda peninsula as well as wineries and recreation areas along Highway 3 (México 3), even allow overnight boondocking; just consult local residents for such possibilities, as they can change suddenly due to weather conditions and management whims.

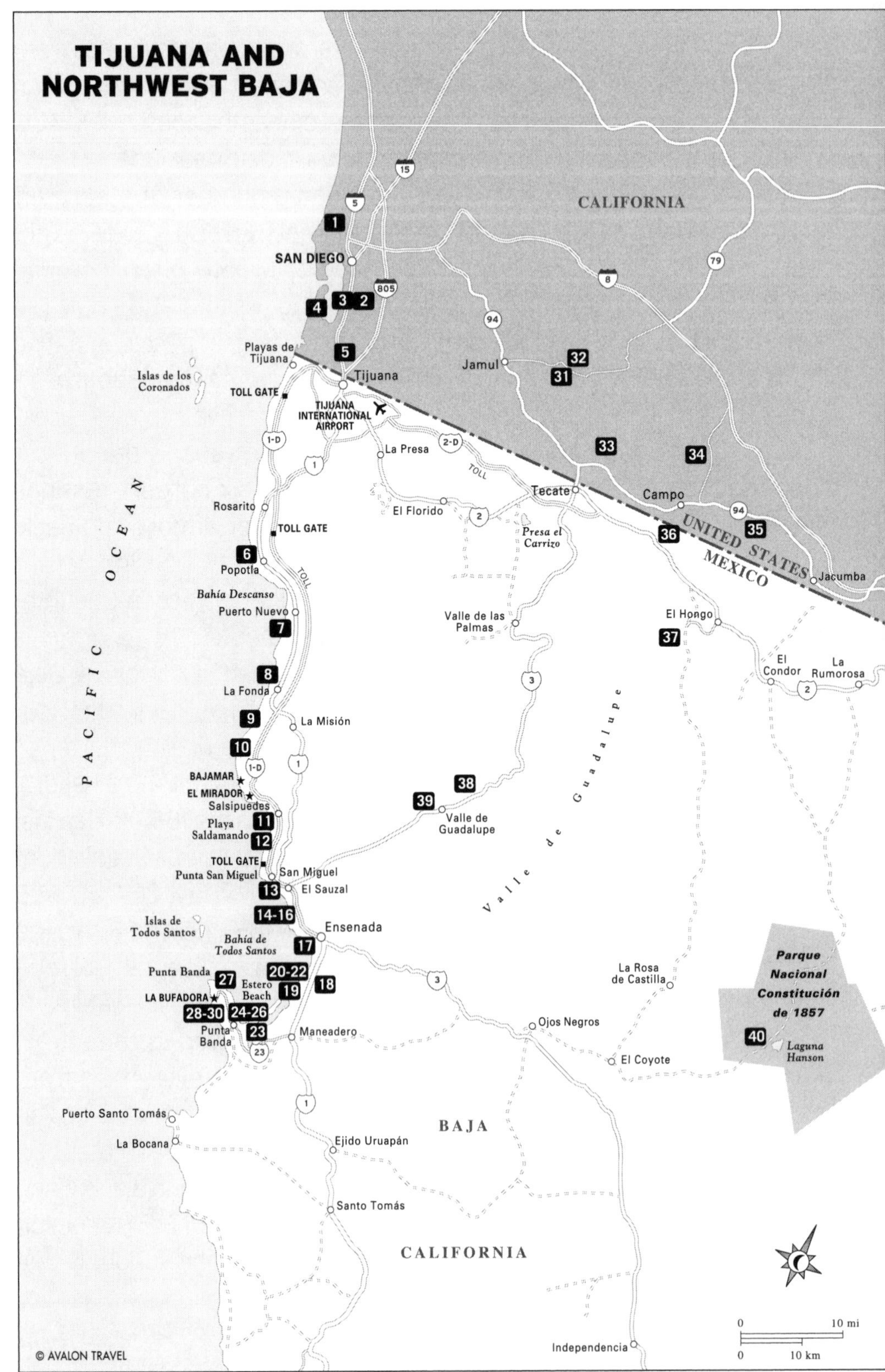
TIJUANA AND NORTHWEST BAJA
CALIFORNIA
SAN DIEGO
Playas de Tijuana
Islas de los Coronados
Tijuana
TOLL GATE
TIJUANA INTERNATIONAL AIRPORT
La Presa
TOLL
Jamul
Tecate
Campo
Jacumba
UNITED STATES
MEXICO
El Florido
Presa el Carrizo
Rosarito
TOLL GATE
TOLL
Popotla
Bahía Descanso
Puerto Nuevo
PACIFIC OCEAN
La Fonda
La Misión
Valle de las Palmas
El Hongo
El Condor
La Rumorosa
Valle de Guadalupe
BAJAMAR
EL MIRADOR
Salsipuedes
Playa Saldamando
TOLL GATE
Punta San Miguel
San Miguel
El Sauzal
Islas de Todos Santos
Bahía de Todos Santos
Ensenada
Punta Banda
LA BUFADORA
Estero Beach
Punta Banda
Maneadero
La Rosa de Castilla
Ojos Negros
El Coyote
Parque Nacional Constitución de 1857
Laguna Hanson
Puerto Santo Tomás
La Bocana
Ejido Uruapán
BAJA CALIFORNIA
Santo Tomás
Independencia
0 10 mi
0 10 km
© AVALON TRAVEL

1 CAMPLAND ON THE BAY

Scenic Rating: 10

in the Mission Bay Park area of San Diego

See map page 50

San Diego offers an assortment of RV parks and campgrounds, each of which can serve as a home base for day trips to Tijuana or as a place to prepare you, your guests, and your vehicle for the long trip down the Baja peninsula. This park, which offers plenty of room for RV caravans, is one of the finest in the San Diego area—and also one of the most expensive.

Situated on Fiesta Bay in Mission Bay Park and accented with palm trees and vibrant bird-of-paradise flowers, this lovely destination is close to SeaWorld and just a few minutes' drive from the Mexican border. So, while you can certainly distract yourself with this bustling park's myriad activities, including bicycling, boating, fishing, swimming, volleyball, bird-watching, and sightseeing, you'll appreciate its proximity to Baja, which is literally just a trolley-ride away.

RV sites, facilities: The park offers a wide variety of nearly 600 spaces, including primitive (with a fire ring, a picnic table, and no hookups), limited (with water and electricity, but no sewage), standard (with full hookups and phone service), preferred (with full hookups, plus options such as grass, phone service, and pull-through driveways), bay view (with full hookups and clear views of Mission Bay), beachfront (with full hookups and direct beach access), and super site (with full hookups, privacy, bay view, hot tub, washer, dryer, and gas grill). Other amenities include wireless Internet access, cable television (at all but the primitive sites), public restrooms and telephones, wheelchair-accessible restrooms, hot showers, dump stations, a coin laundry, recycling bins, trash receptacles, a propane tank and air pump, storage areas for RVs and boats, and shuttle bus service to area attractions. On the premises, you'll also find swimming pools and spas, a market, an amphitheater, a park, two dog walk areas, a volleyball court, a game room, a barbecue stand and ice cream parlor, a fishing jetty, and a marina with boat slips and boat, bike, skate, and quad rentals. In addition, there's handy access to the beach, bay, and nearby wildlife sanctuary. Children, pets, and lengthy RVs (up to 40 feet/12.2 meters long) are welcome; tents are allowed in designated areas. Supplies can be purchased throughout San Diego.

Reservations, fees: Reservations are recommended, especially during the busy summer season. You can reserve a space up to two years in advance; however, there is a $25 fee for cancellations, and a full refund is only possible with proper notice (24 hours in winter, 48 hours in summer, and 72 hours for holidays). Depending on the type of space, prices range $38–284 daily in winter, $40–374 daily in summer, $260–1,110 weekly (in winter only), and up to $1,195 monthly (from early September to July 1). Cash (U.S. dollars) and major credit cards are accepted. The park, which is open all year, charges additional fees for dogs, golf carts, extra guests and vehicles, boats, trailers, RV storage, and boat slips, and there are minimum-stay requirements for summer weekends and holidays.

Directions: From I-5 South in San Diego, California, take Exit #23 (Balboa Avenue/Garnet Avenue), continue along Mission Bay Drive, and turn right onto Garnet Avenue. Continue west for a half mile (0.8 km) until Garnet Avenue becomes Balboa Avenue. Turn left onto Olney Street, then left again onto Pacific Beach Drive. The park is on the right, beside Fiesta Bay. From I-5 North, take Exit #23B, turn left onto Garnet Avenue (Balboa Avenue), cross Mission Bay Drive, and follow the above directions to the park entrance.

Contact: Campland on the Bay, 2211 Pacific Beach Drive, San Diego, CA 92109, tel. 800/422-9386 (U.S.), www.campland.com. For more information about the San Diego trolley system, including route maps and schedules, visit www.transit.511sd.com.

2 SAN DIEGO METRO KOA

Scenic Rating: 9

in Chula Vista, California

See map page 50

Chula Vista is practically just a hop, a skip, and a jump away from Tijuana, and this spacious campground serves as a terrific base for a quick jaunt across the border. In fact, many RV caravans use this park as a starting point for their journeys into Baja.

The location is, after all, perfect. The park itself is well designed, with attractive landscaping, paved roadways, and a slew of amenities. With three freeways so close, you're also not far from San Diego's main attractions, including SeaWorld, Balboa Park, the San Diego Zoo, several golf courses, and numerous beaches. If you have a little time before your Baja trip, feel free to explore your environs, or just enjoy KOA's hospitality. In the summertime, especially, you'll experience an assortment of family-friendly activities, from hayrides and outdoor movies to all-you-can-eat pancake breakfasts.

RV sites, facilities: In addition to a tent-camping area, this gated park has over 200 RV sites, with full hookups (including 50-amp electric service), wireless Internet access, and basic cable television. Each space can accommodate lengthy rigs (up to 65 feet/19.8 meters long). Cabins, an event pavilion, and a communal kitchen are also available. Amenities include hot showers, a coin laundry, a dump station, a heated swimming pool and hot tub, a playground, a basketball court, a dog-walking area, a market, pay phones, propane fuel, and shuttle service to the Blue Line Trolley (to Tijuana). Children and pets are welcome. Supplies can be purchased throughout San Diego.

Reservations, fees: Given the park's popularity, reservations are indeed necessary. RV spaces here are pricier ($39–57 daily) than those of most Baja-area campgrounds. For extra fees, you can pick up some firewood, rent a bicycle, or book a sightseeing tour. Cash (U.S. dollars) and major credit cards are accepted. The campground is open all year.

Directions: From I-5 or I-805, take the E Street exit in Chula Vista. From I-5, head east on E Street for 1.5 miles (2.4 km) and turn left (north) onto 2nd Avenue. From I-805, head west on E Street for 0.9 mile (1.4 km), turn right (north) onto 2nd Avenue, and drive 0.8 mile (1.3 km). The gated park is on the right side.

Contact: San Diego Metro KOA, 111 North 2nd Avenue, Chula Vista, CA 91910, tel. 619/427-3601 (U.S.) or 800/562-9877 (U.S.), fax 619/427-3622 (U.S.), www.koa.com/where/ca/05112. For more information about the San Diego trolley system, including route maps and schedules, visit www.transit.511sd.com.

3 CHULA VISTA RV RESORT

Scenic Rating: 10

in Chula Vista, California

See map page 50

Visitors headed for Mexico love this clean, quiet park for three important reasons: Its location beside the San Diego Bay promises gorgeous views and access to the adjacent marina; its proximity to Chula Vista (and San Diego itself) allows you to procure food, water, fuel, and other necessary supplies for your trip; and its private shuttle bus service can take you directly to the local stop for the Blue Line Trolley (to Tijuana). So, if you're a first-timer to the U.S.-Mexico border, you'll enjoy staying in this friendly, first-class park, where the scenery is rejuvenating, the facilities are top-notch, and the activities could keep you busy for days. Whether you enjoy swimming, boating, sightseeing, relaxing in a hot tub, or strolling along the waterfront, you'll find it all here. Just don't forget why you've really come: Tijuana's shops, cuisine, and area golf courses await.

RV sites, facilities: There are 237 back-in and pull-through sites with paved driveways, patios, and full hookups, including 30/50-amp electricity, water service, sewage access, and cable television. Separated from one another by landscaped shrubbery, the spaces can accommodate lengthy rigs (up to 45 feet/13.7 meters long), as well as slide-outs. Amenities include modern restrooms, hot showers, wireless Internet access, a pay phone, a coin laundry, propane service, meeting rooms, bike rentals, and pet areas. On the premises, you'll also find paved walkways along the waterfront, a general store (with a ladies' boutique), a heated swimming pool and spa, a picnic area with barbecue pits, an adjacent 552-slip marina with a boat launch and two on-site restaurants, and a convenient shuttle bus to central Chula Vista and the nearest Blue Line Trolley stop (to Tijuana). Children and leashed pets are welcome, though there is a two-pet maximum, and owners must pick up after them. Unfortunately, tents are prohibited, and there is no dump station. The staff is friendly and knowledgeable, and restaurants, groceries, and other attractions are conveniently close, in nearby Chula Vista and the San Diego area.

Reservations, fees: Given the park's popularity, reservations are highly recommended. RV spaces here are pricier than those of most Baja-area campgrounds. Depending on the season and the type of space (perimeter, interior, deluxe interior, telephone, pull-through, and premium), the daily fee is $45–59 in winter, $52–67 in summer. Weekly rates are $270–402 (plus a $10 electric fee each week), while monthly rates are $790–1,625 (plus metered electricity). Holiday rates are higher, but senior and Good Sam discounts are available. There are additional fees for pets ($1 daily, $6 weekly, and $20 monthly), extra people ($3 daily, $18 weekly, and $25 monthly), extra vehicles ($3 daily, $20 weekly, and $30 monthly), boat slips ($36–45 daily), and cancellations ($25 fee and deposit refund with 72-hour notice for daily rates). Cash (U.S. dollars) and major credit cards are accepted. The park is open all year.

Directions: From I-5 South, exit at J Street/Marina Parkway (Exit #7B) and turn right (west) onto Marina Parkway. From I-5 North, take the J Street/Marina Parkway exit (#7B) and turn left (west) onto Marina Parkway. Follow the curve of the road. When the parkway narrows into two lanes, turn left (west) onto Sandpiper Way and continue until you've passed the marina. The park is on the left side.

Contact: Chula Vista RV Resort, 460 Sandpiper Way, Chula Vista, CA 91910, tel. 619/422-0111 (U.S.) or 800/770-2878 (U.S.), fax 619/422-8872 (U.S.), www.chulavistarv.com. For more information about the San Diego trolley system, including route maps and schedules, visit www.transit.511sd.com.

4 BERNARDO SHORES RV PARK

Scenic Rating: 7

in Imperial Beach, California

See map page 50

Located within walking distance of the beach, this clean, well-maintained park is also conveniently close to stores and restaurants. In addition, it's not far from the bike path that runs north along the Silver Strand, beside San Diego Bay, to the Coronado peninsula, which is most notable for its historic Hotel del Coronado—a gorgeous, scarlet-hued, Victorian-style landmark that was immortalized in the 1958 comedy classic *Some Like It Hot.* Since 1888, "The Del" has welcomed numerous U.S. presidents, movie stars, and American legends, from Thomas Edison to Babe Ruth.

RV travelers also appreciate the park's proximity to the Tijuana River Valley Regional Park, not to mention to Tijuana itself. In fact, it's quite common for tourists to stow their RV in this U.S. park and hop aboard the Blue Line Trolley for a quick day trip to another country. Although the park specializes in long-term stays, temporary visitors are welcome. So, if you're at all nervous to stay overnight in Mexico, this is an ideal way to get your feet wet.

RV sites, facilities: There are 124 spaces in this gated RV resort. Each site has full hookups (with 30/50-amp electric service), telephone/fax hookups, a brick patio, enough space to park two extra cars, and landscaping that offers privacy from neighboring RVs. Most sites measure 35 by 50 feet (10.7 by 15.2 meters), while some are 70 feet (21.3 meters) long. Lengthy rigs (up to 45 feet/13.7 meters long) are welcome here. Amenities include clean bathroom facilities; automated gated access; a large, air-conditioned laundry facility (which utilizes electronic cards in lieu of coins); a recreation room; a horseshoe pit; propane delivery; and communal activities like games and barbecues. All facilities are wheelchair-accessible, and children and pets are welcome (one small pet, under 20 lb./9.1 kg, per space). Tent camping, however, is not allowed, and there is no dump station. Stores, restaurants, and gas stations are only a short drive away.

Reservations, fees: Reservations are accepted. Prices are steep—$50 per day, $280 per week, and $665 per month. Monthly RVers are also charged for metered electricity usage. Cash (U.S. dollars) and major credit cards are accepted. The park is open all year.

Directions: From I-5 North, take Exit #5A and turn left onto Palm Avenue/Highway 75. From I-5 South, take Exit #5A and turn right onto Palm Avenue/Highway 75. Continue for 1.9 miles (3.1 km) to Rainbow Drive. The park is on the right side of the road.

Contact: Bernardo Shores RV Park, 500 Highway 75, Imperial Beach, CA 91932, tel. 619/429-9000 (U.S.), fax 619/429-4870 (U.S.), bernardoshoresrv@aol.com. For more information about the San Diego trolley system, including route maps and schedules, visit www.transit.511sd.com.

5 LA PACIFICA RV RESORT

Scenic Rating: 7

in San Ysidro, California

See map page 50

Of all the San Diego–area RV parks and campgrounds, this is, by far, the most convenient one for travelers wishing to see Mexico. It's literally 2.5 miles (4 km) from the San Ysidro port of entry along the U.S.-Mexico border, so it's a marvelous place to park your RV while you hop the southbound Blue Line Trolley and spend the day in Tijuana. With its quiet ambience, shady trees, and tempting diversions, it's also a fine spot to relax before a month-long journey across the Baja peninsula.

RV sites, facilities: The park offers 179 RV sites, with full hookups (including 30/50-amp electric service, sewer access, and cable television) and plenty of room for lengthy RVs (up to 45 feet/13.7 meters long); many are even pull-through spaces, and some are shaded. On-site amenities consist of laundry facilities, clean restrooms, propane service, telephone and Internet access, a dump station, a convenience store, a meeting room, a heated swimming pool and spa, a picnic area, a playground, and barbecue pits. In addition, there is a clubhouse equipped with televisions, ping-pong tables, billiards, and a video/book library. Many of the facilities are wheelchair-accessible, and groups, children, pets, and tents are welcome. Not far away, you'll find stores, restaurants, RV repair service, boat rentals, fishing charters, miniature golf, scenic drives, wildlife viewing, horseback riding, historic attractions, spectator sports, and sightseeing in San Diego and Mexico.

Reservations, fees: Reservations are definitely recommended; they can be made via phone or through the website. RV spaces are $30 daily. Monthly rates (plus utilities) are also available. Cash (U.S. dollars) and major credit cards are accepted. The park is open all year.

Directions: Heading south on I-5, toward the U.S.-Mexico border, pass the Highway 905 junction, take Exit #2, and turn left onto Dairy Mart Road, then left again onto West San Ysidro Boulevard. From I-5 North, take Exit #2 and turn left onto West San Ysidro Boulevard. The park is on the left side, between the road and the interstate.

Contact: La Pacifica RV Resort, 1010 West San

Ysidro Boulevard, San Diego, CA 92173, tel. 888/786-6997 (U.S.), www.lapacificarvresort park.com. For more information about the San Diego trolley system, including route maps and schedules, visit www.transit.511sd.com.

6 POPOTLA TRAILER PARK

Scenic Rating: 6

south of Rosarito

See map page 50 **BEST**

Pleasant summers along the Pacific Ocean lure RV travelers and tent campers to this beachside park. Although mainly used as a residential facility for permanent trailers, the park does contain a separate area for temporary overnight guests. Luckily, the enclosed campground is near the ocean, adjacent to a lovely little beach. Naturally, most people come here to relax, swim, hike, fish, comb the shore, and watch passing birds, dolphins, and gray whales.

Besides such outdoor delights, however, and the nearby town of Rosarito, the other closest attraction is Baja Studios, located 3 miles (4.8 km) south of the La Paloma/Popotla/Calafia/Las Rocas exit on Highway 1. Originally built for the epic film *Titanic*, this 40-acre (16.2-hectare), self-contained, oceanfront production facility was, until recently, owned by one of America's top moviemakers, Fox Studios. Today, the facility—which includes a helipad, several soundstages, on-lot production offices, scenery shops, wardrobe rooms, and some of the world's largest filming tanks—is a Mexican-owned company. Tourists come here to experience Xploration, an amusement park set within this working studio, which offers a glimpse behind the scenes of modern moviemaking. Attractions include film sets (from movies like *Hello Dolly!* and *X-Men 3: The Last Stand*), prop rooms, interactive exhibits, a preview theater, and a museum containing the original sets, props, and costumes from the Academy Award–winning blockbuster film *Titanic*.

In recent years, the RV parks and campgrounds between Tijuana and Rosarito have been closing for various reasons. So, although Popotla lies south of Rosarito, it's the closest Mexican park to Tijuana's shops, restaurants, and nightlife as well as the area's two main golf clubs: the 18-hole Club Campestre de Tijuana in the heart of the city and the 18-hole Real del Mar Golf Resort & Country Club south of Tijuana.

RV sites, facilities: The park comprises 28 tent-camping sites and 11 back-in RV sites with full hookups (including 20-amp outlets), concrete pads, and ocean views. Although the sites can accommodate 40-foot (12.2-meter) motor homes and trailers (with slide-outs), the perpendicular position of the spaces to the access roads makes it challenging to maneuver lengthy rigs. Some of the spaces are situated along the bluff, while the rest are positioned on the beach below, near a small cove. Amenities include a swimming pool, a pay phone, a coin laundry, a bar and restaurant, and clean, tiled restrooms with flush toilets and hot showers. There is no dump station. Children and pets are welcome. The property is secured by a guarded gate and a perimeter fence. Some of the staff members speak English. You should obtain food, water, fuel, and other supplies in Rosarito, as there are no major stores within walking distance.

Reservations, fees: Reservations are accepted. RV sites cost $30 per night and $180 per week, while tent spaces cost $25 per night and $150 per week. Credit cards are not accepted; cash (Mexican pesos or U.S. dollars) is the preferred form of payment. The campground is open all year, though spaces are more often available during the winter season.

Directions: From Tijuana, drive south on Highway 1 (the free Tijuana–Ensenada road) and exit at Km 34, just south of Baja Studios. The campground is on the right, along the shore, roughly 3.5 miles (5.6 km) south of Rosarito.

Contact: Popotla Trailer Park, Km 34 de

la Carretera Libre Tijuana–Ensenada, Rosarito, Baja California, C.P. 22710, Mexico, tel. 661/612-1501 or 661/612-1502, fax 661/612-1503, or P.O. Box 431135, San Ysidro, CA 92143-1135. For more information about the Xploration theme park, visit www.xploration.com.mx. For further details about nearby golf courses, visit www.tijuanacountryclub.com (Club Campestre de Tijuana) or www.realdelmar.com.mx (Real del Mar Golf Resort & Country Club).

7 CANTAMAR DUNES

Scenic Rating: 7

south of Puerto Nuevo

See map page 50

Between Puerto Nuevo, Baja's self-proclaimed "lobster capital," and El Descanso, site of a historic cemetery as well as the ruins of a Dominican mission, lies an expanse of spectacular sand dunes, popular among off-road vehicle enthusiasts and the primitive-camping set. Although the beach is beautiful, it can be noisy at times, especially on summer weekends. If you're not a fan of motorcycle motors, you might not enjoy this beach. On less crowded occasions, however, the view can be stunning, and you can spend a pleasant afternoon watching shorebirds, wading in the ocean, or collecting the multicolored pieces of sea glass that pepper the coast.

Although RVers can appreciate this delightful setting, tent campers often find it easier to park here. In fact, unless you have a four-wheel-drive vehicle (such as a pickup truck with a cab-over camper), you probably shouldn't attempt the soft sand at all. No matter what sort of vehicle you have, however, you're advised to bring shovels, boards, chains, and rope with you; it's not uncommon for wheels to get stuck in the sand.

Be advised, too, that there's been some question lately as to the ownership of these dunes. Part of the beach is fenced and off-limits, so don't be surprised if the whole area is soon closed to the public. Long-time visitors have already begun recommending the dunes farther south, near El Descanso.

RV sites, facilities: There are no designated RV sites here—you can park wherever you like. Besides the sand and sea, however, there are few official amenities, save for a handful of dingy outhouses. Only small, self-contained RVs should park here, preferably in pairs or groups, as there's no drinking water, dump station, electricity, or security on the premises. Showers and laundry facilities are also unavailable. Children, pets, and tent campers are welcome, but the terrain is not suitable for wheelchairs. Stop along the highway or in the small village of Cantamar for food, water, fuel, and other supplies, as there are no stores nearby—although, at busier times (such as weekends in summer), you might find stands selling beverages and renting off-road bikes and all-terrain vehicles. Be sure to pack out all trash when you leave.

Reservations, fees: Given the primitive nature of this campground, reservations are not accepted; spaces are available on a first-come, first-served basis. There is a day-use fee of $5 per vehicle; overnight camping costs an additional $5 per night. Although there is often no one at the entry gate to collect the requisite fee (especially on weekdays in winter), you should have the money ready just in case. Credit cards are not accepted; cash (Mexican pesos or U.S. dollars) is the customary form of payment. For now, the beach is open all year.

Directions: From Puerto Nuevo, drive south on Highway 1 to Km 47. Continue for a quarter mile (0.4 km), exit the highway, and head west toward the ocean. Down the asphalt road, you will encounter a metal gate. If it's open, you can simply continue toward the beach; if it's closed and guarded, pay the requisite fee to pass.

Contact: Since there's no official contact person, mailing address, or phone number for the Cantamar Dunes, it's best just to drive toward the ocean and see which spots are available. For details about the Rosarito area, visit www.rosarito.org.

8 ALISITOS K-58 SURF CAMP

Scenic Rating: 7

northwest of La Misión

See map page 50 **BEST**

As the name suggests, this campground is especially popular among surfers, particularly on weekends and during the warm summer months. But, even if you don't ride the waves, you'll appreciate camping atop the scenic bluff. With the Pacific Ocean down below, there's no shortage of gorgeous sunsets. Amid such tranquil beauty, you'll be hard-pressed not to forget your cares for a while and find a bit of rejuvenation—whether physical, spiritual, or otherwise.

Once you've relaxed enough, you might want to experience some of the region's unique culture. About 11.4 miles (18.3 km) north along Highway 1, you can enjoy fresh, pan-fried *langosta* (lobster) in Puerto Nuevo, a tiny coastal village and the self-described "Lobster Capital of Baja," where you can find the town specialty in over 30 restaurants. Lobster season runs from October to March, and the town's annual Wine and Lobster Festival, which takes place in mid- to late October, is a terrific time to experience Mexican culture. Besides lobster dinners and samplings from nearby wineries, the event features mariachi music and folkloric dancers.

Roughly 23.7 miles (38.1 km) south of Alisitos, you'll encounter Highway 3, also known as the Ruta del Vino (Wine Route), which leads to a 14-mile (22.5-km) stretch of sumptuous wineries, from San Antonio de las Minas to Valle de Guadalupe and beyond. Some of the more popular wineries include Vinisterra, Monte Xanic, and L.A. Cetto, one of the largest and oldest in Mexico. Run by an Italian family, L.A. Cetto provides regional and global markets with affordable, high-quality wines, including their award-winning Petite Sirah, Nebbiolo, and Cabernet Sauvignon.

RV sites, facilities: There are no designated RV sites in this large open area—you can park wherever you like. The combination of ample space and easy access makes it possible to accommodate lengthy rigs (up to 45 feet/13.7 meters long). Besides the sand and sea, however, there are few amenities—just flush toilets, cold showers, limited security from the on-duty resident manager, and a paved access road down to the long, sandy beach. Only self-contained RVs and rugged tent campers should park here, preferably in pairs or groups, as there's no drinking water, dump station, or electricity on-site. Laundry facilities are also unavailable. Children and pets are welcome, but the terrain is not suitable for wheelchairs. Although there is a small shop (staffed with English-speaking employees) that offers limited camping and surfing supplies—plus a popular bar and restaurant, La Palapa de José, alongside the ocean—you'll need to pick up food, water, fuel, and other supplies in Rosarito, Ensenada, or nearby La Fonda. Remember to pack out all trash when you leave.

Reservations, fees: Reservations are not accepted; spaces are first-come, first-served. Given its primitive status, the campground is moderately priced at $16.50 per night for tents, $18 for travel trailers, and $22 for motor homes. Be aware that it's always more crowded on weekends and during holidays, when it's filled with surfers and tent campers from Tijuana. Credit cards are not accepted; cash (Mexican pesos or U.S. dollars) is the only acceptable form of payment. The campground and beach are open all year.

Directions: From Tijuana, drive south on Highway 1 (free Tijuana–Ensenada road) to the Alisitos/La Fonda exit at Km 59, 11.4 miles (18.3 km) south of Puerto Nuevo. The campground is on the right, along the shore. It's hard to miss the huge red "K-58" on the camp's water tank, which is visible from the highway. If you're heading south on Highway 1-D (the Tijuana–Ensenada Toll Road), take the La Misión/La Fonda exit at Km 65, turn right onto the free road, and head north. The Alisitos camp entrance will be on the left. Just drive through the security gate and find a space.

Contact: Alisitos K-58 Surf Camp, Km 59 de la Carretera Libre Tijuana–Ensenada, La Misión, Baja California, Mexico, tel. 646/155-0120. To contact La Palapa de José, call 646/155-0339; for more information about the Alisitos K-58 Board Shop, visit www.alisitosk58.com.

9 RANCHO MAL PASO RV PARK

Scenic Rating: 9

west of La Misión

See map page 50 BEST

Known by various names, this campground sits directly on the beach, just steps from the Pacific Ocean. With its mild waters, this particular stretch of the Baja coastline is perfect for swimmers and less popular with surfers. Families especially like to frequent the soft, white sand here, and imported soil allows for easy driving up to the high-tide line. The beach extends north and south of the camping area.

For many years, this was just a primitive campground, sharing the same beach as the fancier Baja Seasons Beach Resort to the south. Today, a modern new RV park has emerged. In fact, while the primitive camping area will remain on a solid, level space at the north end of the property, the new park promises a bit more luxury along the waterfront.

When you've tired of the area's main activities—notably swimming, sunbathing, beachcombing, hiking, fishing, and wildlife-watching—you might want to take a lesson in Baja's history. Luckily, the campground is close to the sacred ruins of two former Dominican missions: the Misión de El Descanso de San Miguelito, alongside an *arroyo* east of the town of El Descanso, and the Misión de San Miguel Arcángel de la Frontera, not far from the Río Guadalupe in La Misión. Although crumbling adobe walls are really all that's left of these two missions, they still make for an interesting visit—and a memorable photo opportunity.

RV sites, facilities: There are no designated RV sites in the primitive camping area—you can park wherever you like. The wide-open space, overlooking the beach, accommodates lengthy rigs (up to 45 feet/13.7 meters long). Besides the sand and sea, however, there are few amenities, just flush toilets, hot showers, and limited security from the resident owners. Only self-contained RVs and rugged tent campers should park here, as there's no drinking water, dump station, or electricity on-site. Children and pets are welcome, but the terrain is not suitable for wheelchairs. You'll need to pick up food, water, fuel, and other supplies in Rosarito, Ensenada, or La Misión, as no stores are in the immediate vicinity. Remember to pack out all trash when you leave.

South of the no-frills camping area, the new-and-improved RV park has 75 back-in, paved sites, accessible via paved roadways and equipped with full hookups (20/30/50-amp outlets, water service, and sewer access). These sites can also accommodate motor homes and travel trailers up to 45 feet (13.7 meters) in length. Amenities include a coin laundry and restroom buildings with hot showers.

Reservations, fees: Reservations are not accepted; spaces are first-come, first-served. Given its primitive status, the upper campground is moderately priced at $15 per night for RVs and tents. The new RV park costs $30 nightly. Credit cards are not accepted; cash (Mexican pesos or U.S. dollars) is the only acceptable form of payment. The campground and beach are open all year.

Directions: From Tijuana, drive south on Highway 1-D (Tijuana–Ensenada Toll Road), exit at Km 71—west of La Misión and just north of a pedestrian overpass—and head for the palm trees and trailers beside the ocean. Drive into the small compound, pay the fee, and either continue toward the beach or turn left (south) toward the new campground. From south of the La Misión area, in the northbound lanes of the highway, you cannot directly access Rancho Mal Paso. In fact, you'll have to drive north to the Alisitos exit and turn around to reach Playa La Salina.

Contact: Rancho Mal Paso RV Park, Playa La Salina, Km 71 de la Carretera Tijuana–Ensenada, Baja California, Mexico. Since there's no official phone number for the Rancho Mal Paso RV Park, it's best just to drive into the campground, talk to the owners, and see which spots are available. For details about the Rosarito area, visit www.rosarito.org.

10 BAJA SEASONS BEACH RESORT, RVS, VILLAS, & MOTEL

Scenic Rating: 9

south of La Misión

See map page 50 BEST

The Baja peninsula has a wide range of campgrounds—from primitive sites to full-blown resorts—and this is definitely one of the latter. With its prime location on a sprawling, splendid beach, this first-class property features a multitude of amenities for RV travelers, not to mention posh villas and a comfortable motel. Besides beach activities, such as swimming, beachcombing, kite-flying, and surf fishing, the park also offers miniature golf, volleyball, tennis, and horseback riding.

True golf enthusiasts can head 3 miles (4.8 km) south to the nearby Bajamar Ocean Front Golf Resort. Sometimes called the "Pebble Beach South of the Border," this spectacular resort presents three gorgeous nine-hole courses: the seaside Oceano, the rolling Lagos, and the challenging, desert-style Vista. In addition, this gated expanse of oceanfront property offers putting and chipping greens, a driving range, a Spanish Colonial–style hotel, an enormous clubhouse, and a network of cobblestone streets, accented by surrounding palm trees, rugged hills, and a rocky coastline.

RV sites, facilities: The fenced-in park consists of 140 back-in, full-hookup sites with 30/50-amp electricity, sewer and water access, concrete pads, satellite television, pleasant landscaping, and enough room for 45-foot (13.7-meter) rigs, which are popular here. Also available are motel rooms with ocean views and luxury, beachfront villas with multiple bedrooms and fully stocked kitchens. Facilities include saunas, a coin laundry, a swimming pool and spa, a camp store, and clean, tiled restrooms with flush toilets and hot showers. The 20,000-square-foot (1,860-square-meter) clubhouse features a recreation room, game room, reading room, full-service restaurant, and cantina lounge. Other amenities include two lighted tennis courts, a volleyball court, a horseshoe pit, a putting green, horse rentals, a guarded gate, a pay phone, an English-speaking staff, Internet access, 24-hour security, and paved access roads. There's no dump station, but purified water is available in the restaurant. Children and pets are welcome. Tents are also allowed, though most tent enthusiasts find it difficult to set up camp on the paved sites. Ask about RV storage, safe-deposit boxes, and transportation to Ensenada. Limited supplies are available in La Misión, to the north.

Reservations, fees: Given the park's popularity, reservations are recommended. Fees are extremely high by Baja's standards, and they vary greatly depending on the season and the area. In winter, interior sites cost $36 per night, while oceanfront sites cost $48 per night. In summer, interior sites cost $48 per night, while oceanfront sites cost $72 per night. Rates are higher during holidays. Weekly and monthly rates are also available. Cash (Mexican pesos or U.S. dollars) and major credit cards are accepted. The resort is open all year.

Directions: From La Misión, drive 3 miles (4.8 km) south on Highway 1-D (the toll road). Near the Km 72 marker, you'll see the park on your right, along a clear stretch of highway. Heading north, you'll notice the campground on your left, but you'll have to drive 4.1 miles (6.6 km) to the Alisitos exit, turn around, and retrace the miles on the southbound lanes.

Contact: Baja Seasons Beach Resort, RVs, Villas, & Motel, 1177 Broadway, Suite #4, PMB #329,

Chula Vista, CA 91911, tel. 646/155-4015 (Mexico) or 800/754-4190 (U.S.), fax 646/155-4019 (Mexico), reservacionesbs@yahoo.com.mx. For more information about the Bajamar Ocean Front Golf Resort, visit www.golfbajamar.com.

11 PLAYA SALSIPUEDES

Scenic Rating: 9

between La Misión and El Sauzal

See map page 50 **BEST**

Yet another in a string of public beaches that allow overnight camping, this spectacular shoreline is exceedingly popular with surfers, especially on summer weekends. The camping area is situated on a scenic bluff above the shore, but the beach itself, accessible via a steep trail, is rather rocky, though still gorgeous. Swimmers, beachcombers, hikers, kite-fliers, and sunbathers love it almost as much as the surfing set. The only drawback is the access road to the campground, which is so precipitous that you might have trouble ascending it once it's time to go home, especially if a rainstorm comes during your stay.

The name itself is a warning: *Salsipuedes* means "leave if you can" in Spanish. Although RVers can appreciate this lovely setting, tent campers, van owners, and those with four-wheel-drive pickup trucks often find it easier to park here. There's plenty of space for lengthy rigs, but, before heading in with a large motor home or unwieldy travel trailer, you should trek down to the bluff to see if you'll fit. If you do decide to stay, you'll find two different areas for overnight camping: on the wide-open bluff, with an unobstructed view of the Pacific Ocean and the surfers down below, or within a shady olive orchard set back from the edge. Be advised that, as with many coastal areas in Baja California, this one has recently been threatened by the possibility of development, so enjoy this primitive beauty while you can.

In addition to its obvious attributes for outdoor enthusiasts, Playa Salsipuedes is also not far from the Bajamar Ocean Front Golf Resort. Situated near Km 77.5 along the toll road between Rosarito and Ensenada, this upscale resort lies only 6.5 miles (10.5 km) north of the beachside campground. Here, you'll find a lovely hacienda-style hotel, a refreshing restaurant and bar, and, of course, three unique nine-hole golf courses along the dramatic oceanside cliffs that line this part of the Pacific coast.

RV sites, facilities: There are no designated RV sites here—you can park wherever you like. Besides the sand and sea, however, there are few amenities, just flush toilets, cold showers, and limited security, courtesy of the on-duty resident manager. Only self-contained RVs and rugged tent campers should park here, preferably in pairs or groups, as there's no drinking water, dump station, or electricity on-site. Laundry facilities and English-speaking employees are also unavailable. Children and pets are welcome, but the terrain is not suitable for wheelchairs. Stop in nearby Ensenada for food, water, fuel, and other supplies, as there are no stores nearby, and be sure to pack out all trash when you leave.

Reservations, fees: Reservations are not accepted; spaces are first-come, first-served. Given its primitive status, the campground is moderately priced at $7 per vehicle for day use and $10 per vehicle for overnight camping. Credit cards are not accepted; cash (Mexican pesos or U.S. dollars) is the only acceptable form of payment. The campground and beach are open all year.

Directions: From the U.S. border in Tijuana, drive 5.6 miles (9 km) west until you reach Highway 1-D (toll road). Continue south for another 49.1 miles (79 km) and exit at Km 88, where there is a well-marked Salsipuedes/Playa Saldamando sign. Carefully turn right onto the dirt road, pass through the entrance gate (past the usually empty gatehouse), and follow the steep, dusty slope for a half mile (0.8 km) toward the beach. Enter the compound (where the managers live), pay the camping fee, then head down another steep section to the bluff itself. From Ensenada, head north on the toll road, take the Salsipuedes/Playa Saldamando exit, and follow the above directions.

Contact: Playa Salsipuedes, Km 88 de la Carretera Escénica Tijuana–Ensenada (#1-D), Baja California, Mexico. Since there's no official phone number for Playa Salsipuedes, it's best just to drive into the campground, talk to the managers, and see which spots are available. For details about the Ensenada area, visit www.ensenada.com. For more information about the Bajamar Ocean Front Golf Resort, visit www.golfbajamar.com.

12 PLAYA SALDAMANDO

Scenic Rating: 8

northwest of El Sauzal

See map page 50 **BEST**

Pleasant all year long, this low-key oceanside campground (named after its friendly owner, George Saldamando) is exceptionally popular with surfers. Though it's nearly impossible for unwieldy travel trailers and lengthy motor homes to navigate the steep access road, the pleasure of dry docking on a fenced-in bluff above the ocean is well worth the effort. With advance notice, the owner will open a second gate for larger RVs. But regardless of how you get here, you'll appreciate the natural surroundings. Marked with white, painted rocks, the waterfront campsites line about a half mile (0.8 km) of sandy beaches and rocky coastline.

Besides surfing, popular activities include swimming, kayaking, snorkeling, and scuba diving. Visitors can also hike along the rocky coastline, where they might spy a lounging starfish or two. The surf fishing is excellent here; using mussels for bait, anglers can fish for sheephead, sea bass, and halibut directly from the rocks. In addition, you can watch dolphins every morning and migrating whales in winter. If you feel like venturing beyond the beach, you'll find several diversions in the region, from touring wineries to taste-testing pan-fried lobster in Puerto Nuevo. Just remember to return before the security gates are locked at night, usually at 10 P.M. Sunday–Thursday and at midnight on Friday and Saturday. Otherwise, you'll have to park your vehicle outside the property, at least until the gates reopen at 6 A.M.

RV sites, facilities: This primitive campground offers numerous delineated sites, though no hookups. Most spots are well separated from one another and have picnic tables, campfire rings, excellent views of the surfers below, and plenty of room for tents and small RVs. Clean restrooms, pit and flush toilets, and cold showers are available, but there is no laundry or dump station. Boogie boards, kerosene lanterns, and firewood can be rented or purchased, though groceries, fuel, and other supplies are only 10 miles (16.1 km) away, in Ensenada. Guests can also rent furnished trailers, with stoves, showers, and flush toilets. Resident guards, watch dogs, solar lights, a perimeter fence, and a single entrance road ensure security for campers. The staff speaks English and Spanish. Children and leashed pets are allowed, but fireworks, three-wheelers, noisy vehicles, drugs, and nude sunbathing are forbidden. Before arriving, you should stop in Rosarito or Ensenada for purified drinking water, as the water near the campground is not potable.

Reservations, fees: Reservations are required on holidays and recommended at other times. For up to four people per motor home or travel trailer, the sites cost $17 nightly; tent sites cost $15 nightly. The monthly rate for RVs is $300 (though criminal and credit record checks are performed prior to accepting monthly RV campers). There is a $3 charge for each extra person. Furnished trailers cost $30–40 per night. In addition, there are fees for firewood ($5 per bundle), kerosene lanterns ($3 per night), and boogie-board rentals ($5 per day). Credit cards are not accepted; cash (Mexican pesos or U.S. dollars) is the only acceptable form of payment. The campground and beach are open all year.

Directions: From the U.S. border in Tijuana, drive 5.6 miles (9 km) west until you reach Highway 1-D (toll road). Continue south for another 52.8 miles (85 km), watch for the final Playa Saldamando sign, and exit at Km 94, 3.7 miles (6 km) south of Playa Salsipuedes. Carefully turn right onto the dirt road and follow the precipitous slope of the mountainside toward a blue gate. If you're arriving during the daylight hours, continue through the open gate and down the road for about a mile (1.6 km), until you reach the bottom of the slope, where you'll see a stop sign, a "Honk for Service" sign, and a crossing arm on the left-hand side. An employee will greet you and give you a receipt for camping.

From Ensenada, take the toll road north, pass the campground, and drive approximately 3.7 miles (6 km) to the Salsipuedes/Playa Saldamando exit. As you pass beneath the bridge, stay to the right and take the southbound toll road to Km 94. Try to arrive early in the day, as the gate closes every night between 10 P.M. and midnight and doesn't open again until early morning.

Contact: Playa Saldamando, Km 94 de la Carretera Escénica Tijuana–Ensenada, Baja California, Mexico, or P.O. Box 15401, San Diego, CA 92175, tel. 619/857-9242 (U.S.), www.playasaldamando.com.

13 VILLA DE SAN MIGUEL

Scenic Rating: 6

west of El Sauzal

See map page 50 BEST

Punta San Miguel, probably the most prized surf break along the northern coastline of Baja California, lies just west of this campground, which is located on a plateau above the rocky beach. So, it's obviously a favorite among die-hard surfers; in fact, it's often teeming with them, especially in milder weather. Swimming and hiking are also popular activities here, and it's a pleasant base for trips to Ensenada's cultural diversions to the south as well as the Valle de Guadalupe's wineries to the east.

RV sites, facilities: There are 30 back-in, full-hookup (15-amp electricity, water, and sewer) sites on a large gravel parking lot beside the beach. Lengthy RVs (up to 45 feet/13.7 meters long) can easily traverse the entrance road and fit into the available spaces. Tent campers usually pitch their tents in front of the parking area; hundreds of them can fit there. Amenities include a pay phone, barbecue pits, a dump station, and a cement-block building with flush toilets and cold showers. These restrooms are often dirty and poorly maintained, but luckily there are better restrooms, with hot showers, above the beach area, where you'll also see some permanently situated RVs. Nearby, there's also a hopping bar and restaurant. Children and pets are allowed, and 24-hour guards provide a modicum of security. Little English is spoken here. Restaurants, grocery stores, laundry facilities, purified water, fuel, and other supplies are available in nearby Ensenada, 8 miles (12.9 km) southeast of the turnoff.

Reservations, fees: Reservations are accepted, though often spaces are first-come, first-served. RV and tent sites are $15–20 nightly. Weekly and monthly rates are also available. Credit cards are not accepted; cash (Mexican pesos or U.S. dollars) is the only acceptable form of payment. The beach and campground are open all year.

Directions: From the north, you can reach the campground via Highway 1-D (toll road) or Highway 1 (free road). In fact, the turnoff is just south of where the two highways meet, 60.9 miles (98 km) south of the U.S.-Mexico border. Driving south on the four-lane coastal road (1-D), you'll pass through the southernmost toll station (before Ensenada). Head south for another half mile (0.8 km), then exit at San Miguel near the Km 99 marker and head west toward the ocean. You'll encounter an entrance gate, where fees are collected and after which the road descends to the campground above the beach.

Contact: Villa de San Miguel, Km 99 de la

Carretera Tijuana–Ensenada, Apartado Postal #55, Ensenada, Baja California, C.P. 22760, Mexico, tel. 646/174-7948.

14 CALIFORNIA TRAILER PARK AND MOTEL

Scenic Rating: 6

in El Sauzal

See map page 50

At high tide, intermediate- and advanced-level surfers head for the breaking waves in front of this small motel and adjacent campground. The beach is lovely, but when the tide goes out, exposed rocks can impede surfers, swimmers, anglers, waders, and other lovers of the salty ocean. The motel itself is fairly average, but there are a few nondescript sites for RV and tent travelers, certainly adequate for overnight camping.

Considering the park's few amenities, there's little to do here but explore the coast and relish the scenery. But sumptuous wineries and seaside villages aren't far away. Of course, Ensenada is probably the most obvious destination. The town's jewelry boutiques, handicraft shops, art galleries, fish markets, lounging sea lions, festive cantinas, and annual events could keep you busy for days on end.

RV sites, facilities: There are eight back-in campsites beside the motel. The spaces can accommodate tents, vans, and 30-foot (9.1-meter) RVs. Most of the sites have paved pads, and all have 15-amp power outlets, water service, and sewage drains. Small restrooms offer flush toilets and cold showers. There is no laundry or dump station on the premises. Children and pets are welcome. The motel compound and RV park are secured by a perimeter fence. Restaurants, grocery stores, laundry facilities, purified water, fuel, and other supplies are available in nearby Ensenada, 5 miles (8 km) southeast of the motel.

Reservations, fees: Reservations are accepted, though often spaces are first-come, first-served. RV and tent sites cost $20 nightly. Weekly and monthly rates are also available. Credit cards are not accepted; cash (Mexican pesos or U.S. dollars) is the only acceptable form of payment. The campground is open all year.

Directions: Heading south on the four-lane Highway 1, you'll see the motel on the right-hand (ocean) side, between the Km 103 and Km 104 markers. From Ensenada, drive 5 miles (8 km) northwest to the Km 104 exit; the motel and campground are on your left, to the west.

Contact: California Trailer Park and Motel, Km 103.7 de la Carretera Tijuana–Ensenada, Apartado Postal #262, Ensenada, Baja California, C.P. 22800, Mexico, tel. 646/174-6033.

15 RAMONA BEACH RV PARK AND MOTEL

Scenic Rating: 5

in El Sauzal

See map page 50

Southeast of the California Motel lies another small structure, the Ramona Beach Motel, just north of which is a basic, though level, campground, situated atop a low bluff, with easy access to the beach. Despite its proximity to the magnificent Pacific Ocean, it isn't much to see. The facilities and spaces are rather old and poorly maintained. In fact, you might miss the property from the highway; it often has the air of abandonment, as though travelers and employees alike have vacated the premises. Usually, however, the campground is open for business; just inquire in the motel office, and make sure to choose a space with working hookups.

RV sites, facilities: There are 30 RV sites, 15 of which have pull-through access, concrete pads, and full hookups (including water, sewage, and 15-amp electricity), though the hookups are often not in working condition. The spaces are easily accessible and can accommodate large rigs (up to 40 feet/12.2 meters long). Basic motel rooms are also available. Other amenities include a small store inside the motel, security lights after dark, and a restroom building, tucked behind the motel office and housing both flush toilets and hot showers. There is no laundry or dump station on-site. Children, pets, and tent campers are welcome. Restaurants, grocery stores, laundry facilities, purified water, gas stations, and other supplies are available in nearby Ensenada, 5 miles (8 km) southeast of the motel.

Reservations, fees: Reservations are accepted. RV and tent sites cost $14 per night (for two people). Weekly and monthly rates are also available, and motel rooms cost $20 per night. Credit cards are not accepted; cash (Mexican pesos or U.S. dollars) is the only acceptable form of payment. The park is open all year.

Directions: Heading south on the four-lane Highway 1, you'll see the Ramona Beach Motel on the right-hand (ocean) side, near the Km 104 marker. The campground is adjacent to the motel. From Ensenada, drive 5 miles (8 km) northwest to the Km 104 exit; the motel and campground are on your left, southeast of the California Trailer Park and Motel.

Contact: Ramona Beach RV Park and Motel, Km 104 de la Carretera Tijuana–Ensenada, Apartado Postal #513, Ensenada, Baja California, C.P. 22800, Mexico, tel. 646/174-6045.

16 KING'S CORONITA RV PARK

Scenic Rating: 7

west of Ensenada

See map page 50

Ocean swimming is a popular pastime along this part of Baja's Pacific coastline. Lapping beside the nearby marina, the waters here are mild, warm, and lovely. The trailer park itself, though old, is well maintained and surrounded by beauty. Slender palm trees encircle the bluff upon which the campground sits, and a mountainous point lies in the distance, across the Bahía de Todos Santos. From here, you can watch the goings-on in the Ensenada port, one of the busiest on the entire peninsula. Cruise ships, fishing vessels, and whale-watching boats drift in and out of this active bay.

Since most of the park is filled with permanently located motor homes and trailers, travelers should call ahead for availability, especially during the busy summer months. Lengthy RVs can access the campground, though some spaces are smaller than others. Unfortunately, the few sites available to overnight travelers are situated away from the bluff, with less than ideal views of the ocean below. But boaters might especially favor this park, with both a marina and Ensenada's port so near.

RV sites, facilities: Although there are roughly 65 spaces in the park, most of them are occupied by permanent trailers. Only 10 of them, a mix of pull-throughs and back-ins, are available for temporary travelers. Each site has a concrete pad, full hookups (including water and sewage access, as well as 15-amp electricity), and enough space for large rigs (up to 40 feet/12.2 meters long). Cabins, trailer rentals, and boat storage are also available. Amenities include clean restrooms, flush toilets, hot showers, a coin laundry, tables, barbecue pits, and a playground. On-site guards provide limited security. Children, pets, and tent campers are welcome, and English-speaking staff members are present. There is no dump station. Restaurants, grocery stores, purified water, gas stations, and other supplies are available in nearby Ensenada, 3 miles (4.8 km) east of the park.

Reservations, fees: Given the small number of available spaces, reservations are recommended here. Sites are $20 per night (for up to four people). Weekly, monthly, and long-term rates are also available. Credit cards are not accepted; cash (Mexican pesos or U.S. dollars) is the only acceptable form of payment. The park is open all year.

Directions: Heading south on the four-lane Highway 1, you'll see the sign for King's Coronita on the right-hand (ocean) side, near the Km 107 marker, just west of where the road curves around Ensenada's waterfront. From downtown Ensenada, drive 3 miles (4.8 km) east to the Km 107 exit; the campground is on your left, on the north side of the Marina Coral.

Contact: King's Coronita RV Park, Km 107 de la Carretera Tijuana–Ensenada, Ensenada, Baja California, C.P. 22860, Mexico, tel. 646/174-4540, or P.O. Box 5515, Chula Vista, CA 91912.

17 CAMPO PLAYA RV PARK

Scenic Rating: 5

in Ensenada

See map page 50 **BEST**

Today, several large campgrounds exist along the coast between Ensenada and Punta Banda, but this is the only RV park located within the heart of Ensenada, making it an ideal base for your sightseeing adventures. Although numerous palm trees provide cool shade for RV and tent campers, this cozy park's location is definitely its best feature. From here, you're within convenient walking distance of an immigration office and several bars, restaurants, liquor stores, art galleries, and handicraft shops in downtown Ensenada. You're so close, in fact, that you can often hear music from the surrounding nightclubs until the wee hours on weekends.

To the east is a large Gigante supermarket, situated at the corner beside which Highway 1 veers sharply to the south. Also nearby is the town's lovely waterfront, where you can view lounging sea lions, board whale-watching trips in the winter, launch your own boat, or join fishing excursions any time of the year. Some of the most popular sportfishing outfits include Sergio's Sportfishing Center, Gordo's Fishing, and Botes Juanitos. Near the bay, you can also take a moment to examine a prominent, 12-foot-high (3.7-meter-high) landmark that consists of three famous busts (representing the Mexican heroes Benito Juárez, Venustiano Carranza, and Miguel Hidalgo y Castillo). While in Ensenada, you can choose to explore its cultural and culinary delights via foot, cab, or your own vehicle; it's entirely up to you.

RV sites, facilities: There are 50 full-hookup RV sites, with 15-amp electricity, water service,

the bustling streets of Ensenada

sewage drains, wireless Internet access, concrete patios, and cable television (including over 50 channels, many of which are English-language). Most of the sites are snug, yet shaded, pull-throughs that allow large RVs (up to 40 feet/12.2 meters long); others are rather small, with partial hookups. Amenities include a public pay phone, a coin laundry, and English-speaking employees. The restrooms are usually clean but poorly maintained; although they have flush toilets and hot showers, it might be best to bring only self-contained units into the park, especially since there's no dump station. The campground is secured by a front gate and a chain-link fence, but given the urban location, it's best to keep your belongings locked away at all times. Children, tent campers, and leashed pets are welcome. Although there's no camp store, the park is within walking distance of restaurants, groceries, gas stations, and other shops in downtown Ensenada.

Reservations, fees: Reservations are accepted, preferably via email, as long-distance phone calls will not be returned. RV sites (for motor homes and travel trailers) are $25 daily, $150 weekly, and $330 monthly. Tent sites, meanwhile, cost $18 daily, $108 weekly, and $240 monthly. The rates are fixed for two adults (and two children); extra guests cost $3 each per day. Credit cards are not accepted; cash (Mexican pesos or U.S. dollars) is the only acceptable form of payment. The park is open all year.

Directions: In Ensenada, street signs are often difficult to find (and people often disagree on the street names anyway), so relying on landmarks is often the best way to navigate the town. If you're entering Ensenada from the north on Highway 1, take the right fork (marked "Ensenada Centro") at Km 107, continue along Highway 1-D, then take the left fork at Km 109. At the stoplight, you'll see a Pemex gas station on the left. Follow the waterfront road for 1.2 miles (1.9 km), past the three-headed statue in the Plaza Cívica near the sportfishing piers. Keep an eye out for the naval base (and its enormous Mexican flag) on the right-hand side. Turn left at the stoplight, onto Calle Augustin Sanginés, and pass another Pemex gas station. After one block, turn left onto Boulevard Las Dunas. The trailer park is on your right.

Contact: Campo Playa RV Park, Boulevard Las Dunas & Calle Augustin Sanginés, Ensenada, Baja California, C.P. 22880, Mexico, tel. 646/176-2918 or 646/176-1504, campo_playa_sa@hotmail.com. For more information about fishing in the area, visit www.ensenada.com.

18 HOTEL JOKER AND RV PARK

Scenic Rating: 6

south of Ensenada

See map page 50

Halfway between Ensenada and Maneadero, this whimsical motel offers a festive setting for traveling families. In fact, the place seems to specialize in parties and events; there are playgrounds, barbecue pits, even a *piñata* area, intended for communal gatherings. RVers and tent campers are also welcome here, though there isn't much room for them these days, especially if the hotel is hosting a special event.

If the spaces are available, don't hesitate to stay here. After all, the location is terrific for curiosity-seekers; you're about as close to the cantinas and art galleries of Ensenada as you are to the rugged beauty of the Punta Banda peninsula, and the lovely beaches in between.

RV sites, facilities: The hotel has a large, grassy tent-camping area as well as three back-in RV sites with shady patios, barbecue pits, and full hookups, including 15-amp electricity and satellite television. The campsites are rather short and narrow, only suitable for rigs that are less than 24 feet (7.3 meters) long. All other vehicles will find it difficult to maneuver and park here. Facilities consist of a small swimming pool, a hot tub, a bar, a restaurant, two playgrounds, and clean (though older) restrooms with flush toilets and hot showers. Other amenities include a public pay phone, an English-speaking staff, and bottled water. There is no laundry or dump station. Security is provided by an on-site guard. Children and leashed pets are allowed. Although there's no camp store, the park isn't far from the groceries, gas stations, and other shops in downtown Ensenada.

Reservations, fees: Reservations are accepted. The nightly fee is $15. Modest hotel rooms are also available. Cash (Mexican pesos or U.S. dollars) and credit cards are accepted. The campground is open all year.

Directions: From the intersection of Avenida Reforma and Calle Augustin Sanginés in Ensenada, head south on Highway 1 for 3.8 miles (6.1 km). The Hotel Joker will be on the left (east) side of the road, just north of the Km 13 marker. From Maneadero, head north on Highway 1 and drive 1.4 miles (2.3 km) past the road that leads to Estero Beach. After passing the airport, you'll see the Hotel Joker on your right. The RV park entrance is on the side street to the north of the hotel. Just park outside, head to the hotel office, and ask about space availability.

Contact: Hotel Joker and RV Park, Km 12.5 de la Carretera Transpeninsular, Ejido Chapultepec, Ensenada, Baja California, Mexico, tel. 646/176-7201 or 646/177-5151, fax 646/177-4460, www.hoteljoker.com.

19 ESTERO BEACH HOTEL/RESORT

Scenic Rating: 10

south of Ensenada

See map page 50 **BEST**

Likely one of the most popular RV parks on the Baja peninsula—and certainly one of the finest that Mexico has to offer—this modern beachfront resort has the price tag to match its high-end status, but its luxurious amenities and assorted activities make it well worth the expense. Besides its equidistance from Ensenada's handicraft shops and fish market to the north and La Bufadora's impressive waterspout to the south, the four-star hotel and adjacent RV park offer enough diversions to keep travelers occupied for a week or more.

A favorite family-oriented destination since the 1950s, Estero Beach is a dichotomy—at once an ideal place to seek spiritual rejuvenation and a terrific spot to have an outdoor adventure. Host to annual sporting events, including tennis and beach volleyball tournaments, the resort also encourages its guests to celebrate their tranquil environs with a stroll through landscaped gardens, a sunset walk along the breezy beach, or a massage and facial by the pool.

Situated on a private, crystalline bay between the Baja peninsula and Punta Estero, the resort boasts a gorgeous estuary and beach, perfect for sunbathing, swimming, beachcombing, windsurfing, bicycling, and bird-watching. From here, you'll spy a variety of aquatic birds, including loons, pelicans, cormorants, herons, and egrets. For a more riveting experience, you can rent a horse, a kayak, or a Jet Ski, or bring your own boat down to the resort's private ramp, from which it's a quick journey across the shallow 1-mile (1.6-km) gap between the shoreline and Punta Estero, into Bahía de Todos Santos (best if traveled during high tide, so as to avoid the sandbar). Not to be outdone, Estero Beach also offers guided scuba-diving trips, kayaking instruction, narrated whale-watching tours in winter, and deep-sea fishing excursions to the Islas de Todos Santos, Punta Banda, and the San Miguel reef.

If you have a proclivity for history, the resort can satisfy that urge, too. On the premises is a museum that presents a pictorial account of Ensenada's past, fossil displays of regional marine flora and fauna, and artifacts from Mexico's ancient indigenous tribes, such as the Olmecs, Aztecs, and Mayans. Also nearby, in downtown Ensenada, stands the Riviera del Pacífico Civic and Cultural Center, an imposing, white-washed Spanish mission–style building amid sculpted gardens. Opened by boxer Jack Dempsey in 1929, this former hotel and casino is rumored to have been financed by legendary gangster Al Capone. Once frequented by movie stars and

American icons, from Lucille Ball to William Randolph Hearst, the capacious structure and grounds presently house a pleasant café, a cozy bar, an outdoor souvenir market, a small natural history museum, as well as fountains and monuments that honor Baja's history.

To the east of Estero Beach lies yet another attraction, the Baja Country Club, which offers Baja's most challenging 18-hole golf course amid a quiet, breezy canyon. Boasting over 250 lush acres (100 hectares), this prestigious golf resort is as lovely as it is stimulating. Surrounding mountains and inland lakes provide an idyllic backdrop to the well-landscaped greens, and, better still, guests at the Estero Beach Hotel/Resort are eligible for money-saving coupons for each round of golf played at the Baja Country Club.

RV sites, facilities: Adjacent to the luxurious hotel (with rooms, suites, and cottages), the lovely RV park provides a shady tent-camping area in addition to 38 large RV sites, with full hookups (including 30-amp electricity), concrete patios, gravel drives, beautiful bay views, grassy and shady areas, and enough space to accommodate 45-foot (13.7-meter) motor homes and travel trailers. Long-term leases are also available for mobile home owners or renters in the nearby trailer park. Amenities include colorful flower gardens, clean (though aging) restrooms with flush toilets and occasionally hot showers, a coin laundry, a swimming pool with a swim-up bar, two whirlpool tubs, public pay phones, basketball and volleyball courts, a fenced children's playground, a recreation center, and 24-hour security.

The nearby hotel, accessible via a paved walkway along the estuary, also offers four tennis courts, a boat ramp, several upscale shops, a Mexican cultural museum, and an indoor/outdoor bar and restaurant. Las Terrazas, the on-site restaurant, presents fresh seafood, sushi, traditional Mexican cuisine, and, of course, margaritas. English-speaking employees are present. Children and leashed pets are allowed. There is no dump station. Although you'll probably find most of what you need in the hotel complex, grocery stores, gas stations, and bottled water are close at hand, in nearby Ensenada and along Highway 1.

Reservations, fees: Reservations are recommended, especially given the park's popularity among RV caravans. Daily rates for each RV site, based on double occupancy, are $35 September–June, $40 in July and August, and $45 during holiday periods. Monthly rates are $840–1,120, depending on the season and length of stay. Towed vehicles cost $5 per night, additional guests are $5 per night, and there is a one-time fee ($30) for use of the boat ramp. In addition to hotel rooms and suites, there are also scuba diving, kayaking, deep-sea fishing, whale-watching, horseback riding, Jet Skiing, and spa packages available for a fee. Cash (Mexican pesos or U.S. dollars) and major credit cards (Visa and MasterCard) are accepted. The hotel and RV park are open all year.

Directions: From the intersection of Avenida Reforma and Calle Augustin Sanginés in Ensenada, head south on Highway 1 for 5.2 miles (8.4 km). Turn right (west) onto the Estero Beach road, drive for 1 mile (1.6 km), and turn left at the sign for the Estero Beach Hotel. When you reach the gate, continue down a long entrance drive and stop at the reception office, where you'll be assigned a campsite.

Contact: Estero Beach Hotel/Resort, P.M.B. #1186, 482 West San Ysidro Boulevard, San Ysidro, CA 92173, tel. 619/335-1145 (U.S.), 646/176-6225 (Mexico), 646/176-6230 (Mexico), or 646/176-6235 (Mexico), fax 646/176-6925 (Mexico), www.hotelesterobeach.com.

20 EL FARO BEACH MOTEL AND TRAILER PARK

Scenic Rating: 7

south of Ensenada

See map page 50

To its advantage, this simple campground sits directly next to the beach, on a sandy, curbed lot alongside the lovely Bahía de Todos Santos. Fresh air, breathtaking vistas, and soft, clean sand make El Faro an ideal locale for families, couples, and solitary travelers alike. Of course, this also means that, oftentimes, the small, normally quiet beach can become crowded with busloads of noisy beachgoers from Ensenada.

Despite such crowds (especially on sunny days), the beach is a wonderful place for swimming; the water is warm, and the surf is mild. It's also not a bad spot to use as a home base for Ensenada, where you'll find myriad restaurants, cantinas, sportfishing fleets, and boutiques, selling Mexican pottery, kaleidoscopic kites, hand-woven Oaxacan rugs, hand-carved Guadalajaran furniture, and Cuban cigars, among other delights.

RV sites, facilities: On the beach that lies below the motel and restaurant, there are 23 back-in RV sites, some with water hookups and 15-amp electric service. There's also ample space between the lot and the beach for over 100 tent campers. The maximum length for RVs is 30 feet (9.1 meters). Facilities include a dump station, a summer-only camp store, and aging restrooms with flush toilets and cold showers. There are no laundry facilities. Because of the poorly maintained restrooms, this campground is most ideal for self-contained RVs. The park is secured with on-duty guards and a perimeter fence, and some staff members speak limited English. Children and leashed pets are welcome. Given the relatively remote location, it's advisable to purchase groceries, gasoline, propane fuel, purified water, and other necessities from stores in Ensenada or along Highway 1. Water is especially important, as the campground water is provided by an untreated cistern.

Reservations, fees: Reservations are accepted. The fees for RV spaces are moderate: $15 per night without electricity and $25 per night with electricity. Tent camping costs $10 per night (for one vehicle and up to four people). Weekly and monthly rates are available, as are motel rooms (with or without kitchens). Credit cards are not accepted; cash (Mexican pesos or U.S. dollars) is the only acceptable form of payment. The motel and park are open all year.

Directions: From the intersection of Avenida Reforma and Calle Augustin Sanginés in Ensenada, head south on Highway 1 for 5.2 miles (8.4 km), to the Km 15 marker. Turn right (west) onto the Estero Beach turnoff, drive for 1.6 miles (2.6 km), veer left at the fork, and continue for another 0.3 mile (0.5 km). You'll find the El Faro Beach Motel at the end of the road.

Contact: El Faro Beach Motel and Trailer Park, Apartado Postal #108, Ensenada, Baja California, C.P. 22785, Mexico, tel. 646/177-4630, fax 646/177-4620, elfarobc@yahoo.com.

21 MONALISA BEACH RESORT

Scenic Rating: 7

south of Ensenada

See map page 50

As with most campgrounds on the Baja peninsula, this down-to-earth resort is most popular in summertime, though winters are pleasant here, and the fishing in nearby Bahía de Todos Santos is terrific during the colder months. Situated behind a rocky ridge above the beach, the park itself resembles a small compound, with RV sites, a tent-camping area, and numerous structures amid quaint, cobblestone streets. Its location is ideal for outdoor enthusiasts, being close to the charms of the Estero Beach Resort and not too far from the fishing charters and boating excursions of Ensenada.

Since its rough beginning in 1960, when the property was little more than a series of enormous sand dunes, this family-operated resort has welcomed countless travelers to its breezy coastal setting. Favorite pastimes here include watching glorious sunsets over the Pacific Ocean, snagging fish along the shore, and traipsing down to the beach with little more than a bathing suit and a book. As a whimsical bonus, the park contains several artistic touches, from the stony-faced, Aztecan-style totems at the entrance, to numerous colorful murals depicting scenes from Mexican history.

RV sites, facilities: Besides six hotel rooms, the park offers 20 tent campsites, with thatched *palapas,* tables, shade trees, and central water for washing dishes and the like. In addition, there are 15 back-in RV spaces, with full hookups (including 50-amp electricity, water service, sewer access, and satellite television), concrete pads, shady *palapas,* fire rings, picnic tables, trees, and room for large RVs (up to 40 feet/12.2 meters long). Unfortunately, the RV spots do not overlook the water. Other facilities include a restaurant; a snack stand; a playground; old, dark restrooms with flush toilets and hot showers; and a souvenir shop that sells everything from metallic animal figurines to Mexican sombreros. There are public pay phones, and the staff speaks English. There is, however, no laundry or dump station. A gated fence surrounds the park, and the owner lives on the property. Children and leashed pets are welcome. Although purified bottled water is available on the premises, it's a good idea to stop in Ensenada, en route to the campground, for food, fuel, water, and other supplies. Because of the poorly maintained restrooms, this campground is most suitable for self-contained RVs.

Reservations, fees: Reservations are accepted. RV spaces (each of which can accommodate a motor home and one towed vehicle, or a 5th-wheel/travel trailer with one towing vehicle) cost $17.50 per night in winter and $22.50 per night in summer (a $22.50 deposit is required to reserve a spot); weekly rates are $105 in winter, $135 in summer. The daily rates for tent sites (which allow one vehicle and one tent per space) are $15 in winter and $20 in summer (a $20 deposit is required to reserve a spot); weekly rates are $90 in winter, $120 in summer. Monthly rates are also possible. Daily rates for the hotel rooms are $35 in winter and $40 in summer; weekly rates are available. Oceanfront condominiums and *casas* are also provided. Credit cards are acceptable only for online deposits; otherwise, cash (Mexican pesos or U.S. dollars) is the customary form of payment. The resort is open all year.

Directions: From the intersection of Avenida Reforma and Calle Augustin Sanginés in Ensenada, head south on Highway 1 for 5.2 miles (8.4 km), to the Km 15 marker. Turn right (west) onto the Estero Beach turnoff, drive for 1.6 miles (2.6 km) on the paved road, veer right at the fork, and continue for another 0.2 mile (0.3 km). Turn left onto the dirt road, and you'll spot the Monalisa entrance arch ahead.

Contact: Monalisa Beach Resort, Apartado Postal #607, Ensenada, Baja California, C.P. 22800, Mexico, tel. 646/177-5100, or c/o Elisa Farrell, P.O. Box 182008, Coronado, CA 92178-2008, www.monalisabeach.com.

22 CORONA BEACH RV PARK

Scenic Rating: 4

south of Ensenada

See map page 50

Space, not scenery, is the highlight of this basic campground. Punctuated by small palm trees and a vivid water tower, the park is essentially an expanse of hard-packed sand, with plenty of room for large rigs, though no view of the nearby beach. Although it's one of the least picturesque campgrounds in the northwest part of Baja, the location isn't bad. After all, it's just a quick stroll to the tranquil shores of Bahía de Todos Santos, where sunbathing, swimming, kayaking, fishing, and horseback riding are all popular activities.

RV sites, facilities: In addition to a tent-camping area, there are 28 pull-through RV sites here, all of which have water hookups, 15-amp electric service, and enough space for lengthy motor homes and travel trailers (up to 45 feet/13.7 meters long). Clean restrooms, cold showers, and a dump station are also available. Other amenities include English-speaking employees, easy access to the beach, and limited security, courtesy of a fence and the on-site owner.

There are no laundry facilities. Children and leashed pets are allowed. A small convenience store offers only beer, soda, snacks, and other limited supplies during the summer months, so be sure to stop in Ensenada or along Highway 1 for additional food, fuel, and drinking water.

Reservations, fees: Reservations are accepted. RV and tent spaces, with water and electricity, are $15 per night (for up to four occupants). Full-hookup sites (including sewage) cost $25 per night. Credit cards are not accepted; cash (Mexican pesos or U.S. dollars) is the customary form of payment. The campground is open all year.

Directions: From the intersection of Avenida Reforma and Calle Augustin Sanginés in Ensenada, head south on Highway 1 for 5.2 miles (8.4 km), to the Km 15 marker. Turn right (west) onto the Estero Beach turnoff, drive for 1.6 miles (2.6 km) on the paved road, veer right at the fork, and continue for another 0.3 mile (0.5 km). Follow the road to the right, make a quick left, and continue straight for 0.2 mile (0.3 km). The campground lies at the end of the road, beside a yellow water tower with "Corona Beach" painted on all sides. You'll have to stop at the office first, to the left of which is a stop sign and crossing arm.

Contact: Corona Beach RV Park, Apartado Postal #1149, Ensenada, Baja California, C.P. 22800, Mexico, tel. 646/173-7326.

23 CENTRO RECRETIVO MI REFUGIO

Scenic Rating: 9

east of Punta Banda

See map page 50

En route to La Bufadora, near the southern end of Punta Estero, you'll spy a strange castle, complete with towers and parapets. Oddly enough, the owners of this unusual private dwelling decided to open a pleasant RV park in their own backyard, with terrific views of the boats below.

Situated above the same small bay upon which sits the Estero Beach Resort, this park also offers the same easy access to these mild waters, perfect for swimming, kayaking, boating, fishing, and other marine-related activities. From here, you're also not far from the rest of the Punta Banda peninsula, including the rugged mountains, rocky coves, and incredible waterspout at La Bufadora. Despite such an ideal location, this is not the best place for lengthy motor homes and travel trailers. The entrance road is steep, and the sites are snug. It's advisable to park along the highway, walk down the road, and check out the available spaces before coming down with any rig longer than 30 feet (9.1 meters), as turning around promises to be a challenge.

RV sites, facilities: The campground offers 15 full-hookup sites, with water service, sewer access, and 15-amp electricity; all are pull-in or back-in spaces, and with careful maneuvering, some are suitable for midsized RVs (up to 30 feet/9.1 meters long). A tent-camping area sits on the muddy beach below. Facilities include a nearby restaurant, a small store, a playground, and a modern restroom building with hot showers. Public pay phones and wireless Internet access are also available. There is no laundry or dump station. Children and leashed pets are allowed. Given the scarcity of major stores on the Punta Banda peninsula, you should stop in Ensenada or Maneadero, or along Highway 1, for groceries, fuel, purified water, and other supplies, before heading down to the campground.

Reservations, fees: Reservations are accepted. RV spaces cost $15 per night, while overnight tent camping costs $10 daily. Weekly and monthly rates are available. Credit cards are not accepted; cash (Mexican pesos or U.S. dollars) is the only acceptable form of payment. The campground is open all year.

Directions: From the Gigante supermarket in Ensenada, on the corner of Avenida Reforma and Calle Augustin Sanginés, head south on Highway 1. Drive about 9 miles (14.5 km) to

Maneadero and turn right onto Highway 23, toward La Bufadora. The campground lies on the right side of the road, roughly 5.5 miles (8.9 km) from the Highway 1/Highway 23 junction.

Contact: Centro Recretivo Mi Refugio, Km 8.5 de la Carretera Maneadero–La Bufadora, Ensenada, Baja California, Mexico, tel. 646/154-2756.

24 CAMPO MENESES

Scenic Rating: 8

in Punta Banda

See map page 50

A steady work-in-progress, this relatively new campground has been evolving for the past few years. Essentially, it's a lengthy lot extending from the highway to the beach, which partially forms the southern shore of Bahía de Todos Santos. Hiking, mountain biking, swimming, fishing, boating, birding, and sunset viewing are all popular pastimes here. If you have a tow vehicle, feel free to take a scenic drive along the high cliffs of the Punta Banda peninsula, where you'll be treated to breathtaking views of the Islas de Todos Santos, Pacific Ocean, and La Bufadora waterspout.

RV sites, facilities: The campground offers enough space for 50 RVs and tents, along a central divider; the space can accommodate lengthy rigs (up to 40 feet/12.2 meters long). Presently, the on-site facilities include water service, a dump station, and restrooms with flush toilets and warm showers. In addition, RVers can run electrical cords to obtain limited power. Future plans entail full-hookup sites with cement patios. Only self-contained RVs and rugged tent campers should park here, preferably in pairs or groups, as there's no drinking water, laundry, or security. Children and leashed pets are welcome. Stop in Ensenada or Maneadero, or along Highway 1, for food, purified water, fuel, and other supplies, as there are few stores near the campground. Be sure to pack out all trash when you leave.

Reservations, fees: Reservations are accepted. RV spaces cost $15 per night, while overnight tent camping costs $10 daily. Credit cards are not accepted; cash (Mexican pesos or U.S. dollars) is the only acceptable form of payment. The campground is open all year.

Directions: From the Gigante supermarket in Ensenada, on the corner of Avenida Reforma and Calle Augustin Sanginés, head south on Highway 1. Drive about 9 miles (14.5 km) to Maneadero and turn right onto Highway 23, toward La Bufadora. The campground lies on the right side of the road, roughly 7.5 miles (12.1 km) from the Highway 1/Highway 23 junction.

Contact: Campo Meneses, Km 12 de la Carretera Maneadero–La Bufadora, Punta Banda, Ensenada, Baja California, C.P. 22791, Mexico, tel. 646/176-1363.

25 LA JOLLA BEACH CAMP

Scenic Rating: 7

in Punta Banda

See map page 50

The word "enormous" doesn't do this active campground justice. Although a lot of trailers are permanently located here, there are also several empty dirt lots, situated near the water and along the south side of the highway, which provide enough room for over 300 RVs and tents. Of course, such wide-open space makes this a rather popular place during summer and on holiday weekends, when it's teeming with tourists. Fortunately for the flexible traveler, however, the campground is virtually empty during the winter months, giving you plenty of primitive elbowroom with which to explore this intriguing outdoor paradise.

The Punta Banda peninsula, after all, offers a plethora of impressive sights and activities, from the 100-foot-high (30-meter-high) spray of La Bufadora (The Blowhole) on the Pacific side to the deep-sea fishing excursions available in Bahía de Todos Santos, where sea bass, yellowtail, and halibut are just some of the tasty specimens in abundance here. Scuba diving, swimming, and kayaking are favorite diversions, too. In addition, the park offers a boat ramp, from which you can launch small, seafaring vessels for private fishing and snorkeling trips into the bay.

RV sites, facilities: The campground offers large, spacious lots for primitive camping. During the off-season, when the lots are less crowded, there's plenty of room for lengthy rigs (up to 45 feet/13.7 meters long). None of the spaces have utility hookups, though the waterfront sites allow you to run an electrical cord from a few low-amp outlets near the restroom building. Other facilities include water access, a dump station, a restaurant, a small grocery store, a boat launch, public pay phones, and basic restrooms with hot showers and flush toilets. Security is provided by a guarded gate, and the staff speaks limited English. There is no laundry. Tent campers, children, and leashed pets are allowed. Supplies should be purchased in Ensenada, in Maneadero, or along Highway 1.

Reservations, fees: Reservations are accepted, though most travelers simply opt for the first-come, first-served method. Fees are moderate here: RV and tent sites cost $15 per night, $350 per month. Rates are based on a two-adult occupancy; there is a charge of $3 for each extra person. Credit cards are not accepted; cash (Mexican pesos or U.S. dollars) is the only acceptable form of payment. The campground is open all year.

Directions: From Maneadero, head west on the paved road (Highway 23) to La Bufadora. Drive 7.8 miles (12.6 km) to the Km 12.5 marker, and you'll spot the La Jolla Beach Camp on the right side, beside the Bahía de Todos Santos.

Contact: La Jolla Beach Camp, Km 12.5 de la Carretera Maneadero–La Bufadora, Apartado Postal #102, Punta Banda, Ensenada, Baja California, C.P. 22791, Mexico, tel. 646/154-2004 or 646/154-2005, fax 646/154-2380.

26 VILLARINO RV PARK & CAMPING

Scenic Rating: 7

in Punta Banda

See map page 50 **BEST**

Just a stone's throw away from the shimmering Bahía de Todos Santos, this well-tended, long-standing park (named after the manager, Adolfo Villarino) is a far cry from its neighbor, the La Jolla Beach Camp. Not only does each delineated campsite have its very own utility hookups and shade tree, but also the park itself is more intimate, often more tranquil, and typically less crowded than the larger campground to the east.

Situated beside a lovely, clean beach, this area is safe for swimmers, teeming with tidepools, and ideal for strolling along the sand. Anglers, boaters, and water-skiers can launch their boats right in front of the campground, and horseback riders can rent horses close by. In addition, there are natural thermal springs under the sand here; you can unearth your very own hot tub at low tide. The only obvious drawback to the park is the beachfront fence that thwarts a clear view of the ocean.

Although some of the spaces are occupied by permanent residents, the campground welcomes temporary travelers, especially large groups. Perhaps you can use this lovely spot to stow your RV while you explore the attractions of bustling Ensenada to the north and the sights of rugged Punta Banda to the west. Just be sure to return by late afternoon: This is a wonderful place to sit on the beach and watch the sun go down.

RV sites, facilities: The park offers a large packed dirt area, shaded by trees, ideal for tents and self-contained RVs, and suitable for midsized rigs (up to 35 feet/10.7 meters long). There are 100 spaces in total, 30 percent of which are usually occupied by monthly retirees and 70 percent of which are open to temporary guests. Some of the campsites have full hookups (15-amp electricity, water, and sewer access), and some have only electricity and water. Most of the spaces are back-ins; only a few provide pull-through access. Many sites will accommodate large RVs, though the entrance and access road can be challenging to navigate. Picnic tables and fire rings are available, and other amenities include a communal barbecue/picnic area near the beach, a restaurant, a well-stocked country store, a post office, a boat launch, boat rentals, a volleyball court, a horseshoe pit, biking and hiking trails, a swimming beach, barbecue grills, a public pay phone, cable television, telephone and Internet access, and clean restrooms with hot showers and flush toilets. A guarded gate provides security, and the staff speaks limited English. There is no laundry or dump station on the premises. Children and leashed pets are welcome, and food, water, fuel, and other supplies can be purchased in Ensenada or Maneadero, or along Highway 1.

Reservations, fees: Reservations are accepted (with a deposit of $30 during summer and holidays). Each full-hookup site (with electricity, water, and sewer) costs $27.50 per night; sites with only electricity are $22.50 per night. The rates are based on double occupancy (with one vehicle). For each additional adult, there is a charge of $7.50 per day. For each additional child (under 14 years old), there is a charge of $5 per day. Weekly and monthly rates are also available. Credit cards are not accepted. Cash (Mexican pesos or U.S. dollars) and money orders (made out to Adolfo Villarino) are the only acceptable forms of payment on-site; personal checks are accepted via mail one month prior to the camping date. The campground is open all year.

Directions: From Maneadero, head west on the paved road (Highway 23) to La Bufadora. Drive 8.1 miles (13 km) to the Km 13 marker, and you'll spot the Villarino RV Park on the right side, just beyond the La Jolla Beach Camp.

Contact: Villarino RV Park & Camping, Km 13 de la Carretera Maneadero–La Bufadora, Punta Banda, Ensenada, Baja California, C.P. 22791, Mexico, tel. 646/154-2045, fax 646/154-2044, or c/o Adolfo Villarino, P.O. Box #2746, Chula Vista, CA 91912, tel. 619/819-8358 (U.S.), villarvpark@prodigy.net.mx.

27 CAMPO NO. 8

Scenic Rating: 9

west of Punta Banda

See map page 50

One of three inexpensive, *ejido*-run campgrounds on the road to La Bufadora, this small operation sits along a mountain ridge on the north side of the Punta Banda peninsula, high above the glistening Bahía de Todos Santos. From here, the panoramic views are incredible; you can see the Pacific Ocean, the Islas de Todos Santos, the bustling bay, the port of Ensenada, and the settlements along the eastern shore. Amenities are lacking here, and the steep access road to the campground can be difficult for lengthy rigs (more suitable for smaller vehicles), but the breathtaking scenery—not to mention the proximity to swimming beaches, fishing charters, and whale-watching vessels—certainly makes up for such challenges.

RV sites, facilities: There are no designated RV sites here—you can park wherever you like. The open space will accommodate lengthy motor homes (up to 40 feet/12.2 meters long) as well as tents, though larger vehicles will have trouble maneuvering the precipitous entrance road. Besides the incredible views and hiking possibilities, there are few amenities—just pit toilets, in fact. Only rugged tent campers and self-contained RVs should park here, preferably in pairs or groups, as there's no drinking water, dump station, electricity, or security. Showers, laundry facilities, and English-speaking staff members are also unavailable. Children and pets are welcome, but the terrain is not suitable for wheelchairs. Stop in Ensenada or Maneadero for food, water, fuel, and other supplies, as there are no stores nearby, and be sure to pack out all trash when you leave.

Reservations, fees: Reservations are not

accepted; spaces are available on a first-come, first-served basis. Given its primitive status, the campground is moderately priced at $5 per night, for RVs or tents. There are no extra fees or long-term rates. Credit cards are not accepted; cash (Mexican pesos or U.S. dollars) is the only acceptable form of payment. The campground is open all year.

Directions: From Maneadero, head west on the paved road (Highway 23) to La Bufadora and drive roughly 9 miles (14.5 km) from the Highway 1/Highway 23 junction. The campground lies on the right side of the road, past the Villarino RV Park.

Contact: Since there's no official contact person, mailing address, or phone number for Campo No. 8, it's best just to drive into the camping area and see which spots are available. For details about the Ensenada area, visit www.ensenada.com.

28 CAMPO NO. 7

Scenic Rating: 9

west of Punta Banda

See map page 50

The mountainous Punta Banda peninsula, which shelters the southern edge of Bahía de Todos Santos, south of Ensenada, is home to a wide array of modern RV parks and primitive campgrounds. Beyond the Villarino RV Park, en route to the spectacular marine geyser at La Bufadora, you'll find four of the low-key variety. Just past Campo No. 8 lies this simple campground, situated on the Pacific side of the peninsula, offering stupendous views of the ocean.

Reaching this oceanside campground can be quite a challenge, especially for large RVs. The paved highway from Maneadero to Punta Banda climbs steadily along the ridge, so to make up the difference in altitude, the dirt road that descends to this lower elevation is exceedingly steep. In fact, only tent campers, van owners, and drivers of four-wheel-drive pickup trucks should attempt this precipitous access road, which could prove to be a real hazard for all others.

Despite its tricky access and few amenities, it's a wonderfully rich place to enjoy the natural world. Here, you can hike amid the rugged landscape, watch for birds and other marine life (including migrating gray whales in the winter months), and head down the mountain for boating, fishing, swimming, and beach-related activities along the stretch between Punta Banda and Ensenada.

RV sites, facilities: There are no designated RV sites here—you can park wherever you like. The open space will accommodate lengthy motor homes (up to 40 feet/12.2 meters long) as well as tents, though larger vehicles will have trouble maneuvering along the precipitous entrance road. Besides the incredible views and hiking possibilities, the only other amenities consist of simple pit toilets. As a result, only rugged tent campers and self-contained RVs should park here, preferably in pairs or groups, as there's no drinking water, dump station, electricity, or security. Showers, laundry facilities, and English-speaking staff members are also unavailable. Children and pets are welcome, but the terrain is not suitable for wheelchairs. Stop in Ensenada or Maneadero for food, water, fuel, and other supplies, as there are no stores nearby, and be sure to pack out all trash when you leave.

Reservations, fees: Reservations are not accepted; spaces are available on a first-come, first-served basis. Given its primitive status, the campground is moderately priced at $5 per night, for RVs or tents. There are no extra fees or long-term rates. Credit cards are not accepted; cash (Mexican pesos or U.S. dollars) is the only acceptable form of payment. The campground is open all year.

Directions: From Maneadero, head west on the paved road (Highway 23) to La Bufadora and drive roughly 10.5 miles (16.9 km) from the Highway 1/Highway 23 junction. The campground lies on the right side of the road, past Campo No. 8.

Contact: Since there's no official contact person, mailing address, or phone number for Campo No. 7, it's best just to drive into the camping area and see which spots are available. For details about the Ensenada area, visit www.ensenada.com.

29 CAMPO NO. 5

Scenic Rating: 10

west of Punta Banda

See map page 50 BEST

Perched high above the Pacific Ocean, this rustic campground is, by far, the most popular of the primitive selections situated along the Punta Banda peninsula, south of Ensenada. From this high locale, you can watch the foamy waves crash against the rocky shore below. Despite its limited facilities and challenging access road—which is perhaps too steep for lengthy motor homes and unwieldy 5th-wheel trailers—it's a spectacular place to hike amid the rugged peaks, watch passing birds and whales, explore native flora and fauna via horse or mountain bike, take a dip in the ocean, or fish for sea bass, halibut, rockcod, and yellowtail.

The two-lane road from Maneadero is an experience in itself. You'll pass through fertile farmland, encounter produce stands (selling everything from olives to coconuts to homemade tamales), and absorb breathtaking views from the highway as you ascend the mountainside. Beyond the campground, you can take the road to La Bufadora (The Blowhole), an impressive geyser that can sometimes reach 100 feet (30 meters) high. Paved walkways, some with wheelchair-accessible ramps, lead to observation decks around this mighty sight. Also nearby is a dive shop, arts-and-crafts stands, kayak rentals, and whale-watching cruises in winter.

As an interesting historical note, Campo No. 5 has also been called Ejido Coronel Esteban Cantú, named after the first territorial governor of Baja California Norte. Most locals consider him to have been an extraordinary military officer, with an unusual capacity to empathize with others. Descended from conquistadors, Cantú (1880–1966) was sent to Mexicali in 1911 to colonize and protect the area. As governor, he improved the regional economy, implemented educational reform, and oversaw the construction of a road that joined the desert to the mountains to the sea. So, it's appropriate that a mountainous, oceanside campground—in addition to other locales in Baja—be named after him.

RV sites, facilities: There are no designated RV sites here—you can park wherever you like. The open space will accommodate lengthy motor homes (up to 40 feet/12.2 meters long) as well as tents, but larger vehicles might have trouble maneuvering along the precipitous entrance road. Facilities include flush toilets and cold showers in a simple restroom building. Only rugged tent campers and small, self-contained RVs should park here, preferably in pairs or groups, as there's no drinking water, dump station, electricity, or security. Showers, laundry facilities, and English-speaking staff members are also unavailable. Children and pets are welcome, but the terrain is not suitable for wheelchairs. Stop in Ensenada for food, water, fuel, and other supplies, as there are no major stores, gas stations, or public pay phones nearby, and be sure to pack out all trash when you leave.

Reservations, fees: Reservations are not accepted; spaces are available on a first-come, first-served basis. Given its primitive status, the campground is moderately priced at $5 per night, for RVs or tents. There are no extra fees or long-term rates. Credit cards are not accepted; cash (Mexican pesos or U.S. dollars) is the only acceptable form of payment. The campground is open all year.

Directions: From Maneadero, head west on Highway 23, toward La Bufadora, and drive roughly 12 miles (19.3 km) from the Highway 1/Highway 23 junction. The campground lies on the right side of the road, between Campo No. 7 and Rancho La Bufadora.

Contact: Since there's no official contact person, mailing address, or phone number for Campo No. 5, it's best just to drive into the camping area and see which spots are available. For details about the Ensenada area, visit www.ensenada.com.

30 RANCHO LA BUFADORA

Scenic Rating: 8

in La Bufadora

See map page 50 BEST

La Bufadora, one of the world's most remarkable marine geysers, is greatly responsible for the tourism that's developed along the Punta Banda peninsula. Some believe that this "blowhole" is finer than those found in Hawaii, Australia, and Tahiti. Within a rocky inlet on the Pacific side of the rugged peninsula, ocean swells surge through a deep underwater canyon, into a narrow cave alongside the cliff, and retreat the same way, creating a tremendously loud, 100-foot-high (30-meter-high) spout of compressed air and water, which sounds as if an enormous, enraged animal is roaring amid the salty spray.

According to a century-old local legend, a mother whale was returning to the Arctic with her new calf, who'd recently been born in a lagoon near Guerrero Negro to the south, when the baby whale drifted away to explore a mysterious cave in the cliffs of Punta Banda. During the night, the whale calf grew so quickly that, by morning, he was too large to squeeze through the slender entrance tunnel of the cave. Soon, some nearby whalers heard the petrified sobs of the trapped baby whale and witnessed a small spout rising from the cave. As the years passed, the lamentations loudened and the spouts increased in size, eventually becoming the roaring geyser that it is today—supposedly, the blowhole of a trapped, full-grown leviathan.

Whatever you might believe, however, the fact is that La Bufadora lures crowds of visitors on a regular basis. If you'd like an up-close view of the waterspout, you'll enjoy staying in the simple campground at Rancho La Bufadora, essentially a parking lot for tent campers and dry-docking recreational vehicles. Situated along a craggy shore, beside an equally rocky beach, this no-frills campground is also close to a boat ramp, a dive shop, and a small cove perfect for scuba diving. In fact, this is considered to be one of the best diving spots along the northern coast of Baja, recommended for experienced divers only. Luckily, Dale's Dive Shop assists beginners by leading guided scuba-diving and snorkeling tours; the shop also rents diving gear, charters fishing *pangas,* and leads whale-watching excursions in the winter months.

RV sites, facilities: There are no designated RV sites here—you can park wherever you like. The open lot will accommodate lengthy motor homes (up to 40 feet/12.2 meters long). Tents are welcome in the unpaved area between the lot and the ocean. Facilities include a few fire rings, a dive shop, a boat ramp, and a simple restroom building with flush toilets and cold, run-down showers. Only rugged tent campers and self-contained RVs should park here, preferably in pairs or groups, as there's no drinking water, dump station, electricity, or security. There is also no laundry on-site. Children and pets are allowed, but the terrain may not be suitable for wheelchairs. The campground manager and dive shop staff speak English. Although you will encounter several produce stands as well as a flea market in this area, you probably should stop in Ensenada or Maneadero for food, water, fuel, and other supplies, as there are no major stores, gas stations, or pay phones nearby. Be sure to pack out all trash when you leave.

Reservations, fees: Reservations are not accepted; spaces are available on a first-come, first-served basis. Given its primitive status, the campground is moderately priced at $15 per night for motor homes and $10 per night for cars and tents. The fees are based on a two-adult occupancy; extra guests cost $2 per night, though children can stay for free. There are no long-term rates. Credit cards are not accepted; cash (Mexican pesos or U.S. dollars) is the only acceptable form of payment. The campground is open all year.

Directions: From Ensenada, head south on Highway 1. In the town of Maneadero, turn right onto Highway 23, toward La Bufadora. When you reach La Bufadora (near the end of the line), avoid the crowded parking lots around the blowhole and, instead, watch for the sign for "Rancho La Bufadora" down a left-hand side road. Turn left onto the access road and follow it down toward the coast, around to the left, and into the camping lot.

Contact: For more information about Rancho La Bufadora, email the campground administrator at bufadora@prodigy.net.mx. Given that replies are rare, however, it's probably best just to drive into the camping area and see which spots are available. For more information about Dale's Dive Shop, call 646/154-2092 or visit www.labufadoradive.com.

31 DIAMOND JACK'S RV RANCH

Scenic Rating: 4

east of Jamul, California

See map page 50

The modest town of Jamul has an elevation of 1,000 feet (305 meters), so the winter season can be chilly here. In addition, controversy has brewed in recent years over a proposed Kumeyaay Indian casino. Even still, if you long to stay in a rustic setting while making day-long trips to bustling San Diego, nearby lakes and reservoirs, and Tecate, Mexico, it's certainly a decent place to park your RV.

Golfing enthusiasts will especially enjoy the area. Jamul is home to one of Southern California's finest golf clubs, the Steele Canyon Golf Club, where visitors will find three nine-hole courses in environments as varied as rugged hills and canyons, a picturesque working ranch, and a valley floor with stunning forests, streams, and native wildlife.

Of course, the real reason for settling here is the park's proximity to the U.S.-Mexico border. Tecate is only a 30-mile (48-km) drive southeast. More laid-back than Tijuana, Tecate and its environs offer a variety of relaxing diversions, from brewery tours to mountainside hikes to destination spas.

RV sites, facilities: There are 55 RV sites, with water hookups, 20/30-amp outlets, and enough room for lengthy RVs (up to 40 feet/12.2 meters long). Roughly 20 of the sites are available for nightly visitors, and the rest are occupied by semipermanent tenants. The spaces are a mix of pull-through and back-in types. There is also a tent-camping area, which will accommodate at least 10 tents. Amenities include clean restrooms, hot showers, a dump station, propane service, laundry facilities, and a swimming pool. Children and pets are welcome. Food, water, and other supplies can be purchased in San Diego, Tecate, and, to a limited degree, Jamul itself.

Reservations, fees: Reservations are accepted. The nightly rate is $20 for RVs and $15 for tents. Credit cards are not accepted; cash (U.S. dollars) and checks are the customary forms of payment. The campground is open all year.

Directions: From San Diego, take Highway 94 East (which begins at I-5 south of Balboa Park). Turn left onto Lyons Valley Road, which becomes Skyline Truck Trail at the stop sign. Drive 2 miles (3.2 km) and take a sharp right onto Lawson Valley Road. Take a sharp left onto Lyons Valley Road and continue for 1 mile (1.6 km). On the left side, you'll see the sign for Diamond Jack's RV Ranch. Turn left here to reach the campground.

Contact: Diamond Jack's RV Ranch, 15724 Lyons Valley Road, Jamul, CA 91935, tel./fax 619/669-0099 (U.S.). For more information about the Steele Canyon Golf Club, call 619/441-6900 (U.S.) or visit www.steelecanyon.com.

32 SKYLINE RANCH RV PARK

Scenic Rating: 7

east of Jamul, California

See map page 50

Spread across 42 hilltop acres (17 hectares), this spacious campground has a tranquil ambience, enhanced by shady oak trees and scenic hiking and biking trails. Picnicking beneath the trees, sitting around the campfire, and taking scenic drives are popular pastimes. Small caravans are especially fond of this pastoral setting. Even better, this family-friendly park isn't at all far from the U.S.-Mexico border, just 30 miles (48 km) from Tecate and its shops, parks, cantinas, and brewery.

West of this relaxing Mexican town—a far cry from bustling Tijuana—you'll find the world's first destination spa, Rancho La Puerta. Founded within a sheltered valley in 1940, this 3,000-acre (1,210-hectare) property presents an incredible environment for physical and spiritual rejuvenation. Offered here are an assortment of fitness activities, revitalizing spa treatments, luxurious accommodations, and nightly entertainment—not to mention world-class gardens, an organic farm, and mountainside trails and meadows, perfect for a long nature hike.

RV sites, facilities: There are 35 campsites for RVs and tents, 14 of which have full hookups (water, sewage, and 50-amp electricity). Some are pull-through spaces, but most are back-in, and all can accommodate midsized RVs (up to 30 feet/9.1 meters long). Besides shady oak trees, stately pines, and picnic areas, amenities include hiking trails, campfire rings, and a dump station. No restrooms or laundry facilities are available, making the campground mostly suitable for self-contained RVs. Several lakes, popular with boaters and anglers, surround Jamul, and groceries and supplies are available in nearby San Diego and across the border in Tecate. Tent campers and children are welcome, but pets are not allowed.

Reservations, fees: Reservations are accepted. Campground rates are $30 per night and $150 per week. Monthly rates are also available. Cash (U.S. dollars) and credit cards are accepted. The park is open all year.

Directions: From San Diego, take Highway 94 East, which begins at I-5 south of Balboa Park. After 13.3 miles (21.4 km), turn right onto Campo Road/Highway 94 and continue for 4.4 miles (7.1 km). In Jamul, turn left onto Lyons Valley Road and drive for 1.6 miles (2.6 km). Stay straight to remain on Skyline Truck Trail. Continue for 4.8 miles (7.7 km), until you see the Skyline Ranch RV Park on the north (left) side of the road.

Contact: Skyline Ranch RV Park, 17120 Skyline Truck Trail, Jamul, CA 91935, tel. 619/468-0097 (U.S.), fax 619/468-9197 (U.S.). For more information about Rancho La Puerta, call 800/443-7565 (U.S.) or visit www.rancholapuerta.com.

33 POTRERO COUNTY PARK

Scenic Rating: 10

in Potrero, California

See map page 50

If your Baja trip will begin in Tecate, you might want to consider staying your first night in a California park—if only to make last-minute plans for your journey south. This pleasant county park, located 45 miles (72 km) east of San Diego, is by far the closest U.S. campground to Tecate's port of entry into Mexico. Named for the Spanish word *potrero,* which means "pasturing place," the campground is nestled within a broad valley, enhanced by rocky hillsides, grassy meadows, and century-old coastal live oaks. Hiking, mountain biking, camping, and picnicking are popular activities year-round, despite hot summers and possible snowfall in winter. Wildlife enthusiasts will also relish this area, where bobcats, mule deer, coyotes, raccoons, rabbits, snakes, golden eagles, and acorn woodpeckers are frequently spotted (and heard). Keep an eye out for mountain lions, which have also been known to prowl the mountainous terrain.

Of course, such outdoor pleasures aren't the

only reason to choose this pastoral spot. The nearby town of Potrero houses a general store, a café, and a post office. Campo, California, has an interesting attraction, the Pacific Southwest Railway Museum, which offers train rides into Mexico; and Tecate is just a few minutes away by car.

RV sites, facilities: The 115-acre (46.5-hectare) park offers 39 partial-hookup RV sites (with water and electricity) as well as a primitive area for tent camping. The spaces can accommodate midsized RVs (up to 30 feet/9.1 meters long). Other amenities include hot showers, a dump station, picnic areas, ball fields, a dance pavilion, playgrounds, and hiking trails. Laundry facilities are unavailable. Children and pets are welcome. Limited supplies can be purchased in small towns like Potrero and Campo, though San Diego's supermarkets and shopping malls are only 45 miles (72 km) to the west.

Reservations, fees: Reservations can be made via phone (8 A.M.–5 P.M. Mon.–Fri.) or online (24 hours daily). There is a $5 fee for reserving a space, and there are also fees for canceling or transferring a reservation. Each partial-hookup RV site costs $20 per night, while tent camping costs $15 nightly. Each site accommodates up to eight people, though there is a $2 fee for each extra vehicle and a $1 charge for each pet. Payment can be made by cash (U.S. dollars), check, money order, Visa, or MasterCard. The campground is open all year.

Directions: From San Diego, take Highway 94 East toward Tecate. Pass the Highway 188 junction and drive 2.3 miles (3.7 km) to the Potrero exit and turn left onto Potrero Valley Road. After 0.3 mile (0.5 km), turn right onto Potrero Park Road. The campground lies at the end of the entrance road.

Contact: Potrero County Park, 24800 Potrero Park Drive, Potrero, CA 91963, tel. 858/565-3600 (U.S.), 858/694-3049 (U.S.), or 877/565-3600 (U.S.), www.sdcounty.ca.gov/parks. For more information about the Pacific Southwest Railway Museum, call 619/478-9937 (U.S.) or visit www.sdrm.org.

34 LAKE MORENA RV PARK

Scenic Rating: 7

north of Campo, California

See map page 50

Encircled by the Cleveland National Forest, within the Santa Rosa Mountains of San Diego County, Lake Morena provides a beautiful, high-altitude setting for fishing, boating, canoeing, kayaking, hiking, cycling, picnicking, and bird-watching. Chaparral-covered hills, enormous oak trees, and large rock formations surround this remote reservoir. In summer, temperatures can range from 90°F (32°C) in the daytime to 50°F (10°C) at night. Wintertime is far cooler, perhaps 60°F (16°C) during the day and 40°F (4°C) after sunset. The adjacent RV park might be small, but its friendly vibe, well-maintained facilities, and shaded environs certainly make up for its size.

Besides a wide array of trails and lake-related activities, RV travelers can also enjoy a nearby nine-hole golf course. If you're using this park as a home base for sightseeing trips, you'll be delighted to know that, from here, you're roughly 50 miles (80 km) east of San Diego's attractions and only 20 miles (32 km) from the Tecate port of entry into Mexico.

RV sites, facilities: The park has 41 RV sites, 14 of which have full hookups (including water, electricity, sewage access, television, and telephone service) and 27 of which just have sewage access. The spaces can accommodate a maximum length of 40 feet (12.2 meters). There are no restrooms, laundry facilities, or dump stations. Children and pets are welcome; tent camping, however, is not allowed. Limited supplies can be purchased in nearby Campo.

Reservations, fees: Reservations are accepted. Sites cost $28 nightly, $175 weekly, and $400 monthly. Cash (U.S. dollars), check, and credit cards are all acceptable forms of payment. The park is open all year.

Directions: From San Diego, take Highway 94 East, which begins at I-5 south of Balboa Park, and drive 8.2 miles (13.2 km). Stay to the left, take Highway 125 North, continue for 2.2 miles (3.5 km), and merge onto I-8 East. Drive 36.6 miles (58.9 km), take Exit #51 (Buckman Springs Road), turn right onto Buckman Springs Road/County Route S1, and continue for 5.3 miles (8.5 km). Turn right onto Oak Drive, continue for 1.2 miles (1.9 km), turn left onto Molchan Road, then right onto Lake Morena Drive.

Contact: Lake Morena RV Park, 2330 Lake Morena Drive, Campo, CA 91906, tel. 619/478-5677 (U.S.), lkmorenarv@earthlink.net.

35 OUTDOOR WORLD RV PARK

Scenic Rating: 9

in Boulevard, California

See map page 50

Travelers in search of quietude and relaxation will certainly appreciate this pastoral locale, situated within the hilly countryside east of San Diego. Serenity-seekers will relish the hiking trails that wind amid acres of mature oak trees, manzanita shrubs, rugged canyons, and rocky outcroppings. RV caravans especially like this roomy park, which serves as a solid base of operations for sightseeing and other leisure activities in the vicinity. Via car, you're roughly a 25-minute drive from rock climbing in the Laguna Mountains, fishing in Lake Morena, and exploring the brewery, restaurants, spas, *alfarerías* (pottery and tile works), and *vidrierías* (glassworks) of Tecate, Mexico.

RV sites, facilities: The park offers a tent campground and 151 RV spaces, all of which have water, 50-amp electricity, and room for lengthy motor homes and travel trailers (up to 40 feet/12.2 meters long). Some also have sewer access. There is a mix of back-in and pull-through sites. Other amenities include wireless Internet access, renovated restrooms, hot showers, a dump station, and a general store. Also on the premises is an adobe-style clubhouse, rumored to have been a stagecoach stop and now serving as a meeting facility, with a complete kitchen, a big-screen television, satellite hookups, and group seating. There is no laundry on-site. Children and pets are welcome. Limited supplies can be purchased in the surrounding towns.

Reservations, fees: Reservations are accepted, though cancellation fees do apply. Based on two adults and two children (under 12), rates for RV sites are $37 per night. Tent camping is $27 per night. Additional guests are $3 per day, and there is a maximum of eight people per site. Weekly and monthly rates are possible, and bunkhouses are also available for rent. Cash (U.S. dollars) and credit cards are accepted. The park is open all year.

Directions: From San Diego, take I-8 East, drive 46.7 miles (75.1 km), and exit at Crestwood Road (Exit #61). Turn right onto Crestwood Road, which becomes Old Highway 80, and continue for another 2.3 miles (3.7 km). Turn right onto Live Oak Springs Road, drive for 1.3 miles (2.1 km), and turn right onto Campo Road/Highway 94. In 0.8 mile (1.3 km), you will see the park on your left.

Contact: Outdoor World RV Park, 37133 Highway 94, Boulevard, CA 91905, tel. 619/766-4480 (U.S.), www.outdoorworldrvpark.com.

36 RANCHO OJAI

Scenic Rating: 8

east of Tecate

See map page 50 **BEST**

Once an award-winning KOA park, this working ranch and campground is nestled amid a rolling countryside, peppered with old oak trees. Travelers will find a multitude of activities here, especially in the warm summer months, though even the chilly, often snowy winters bring out this area's beauty. Several scenic hiking and cycling trails wind across the property. The park also comprises a playground, horseshoe pits, and ranch animals that can be viewed and petted, and the staff offers hayrides as well as bicycle rentals. Other popular pastimes include swimming, volleyball, basketball, and miniature golf.

If you honestly can't find enough to do here, there are plenty of other diversions in this part of Baja. The wineries of the Valle de Guadalupe are roughly 60 miles (97 km) to the south. Tijuana's shops, art galleries, and bull rings are 42 miles (68 km) to the west. Even closer, of course, is Tecate, a charming border town surrounded by lush, breathtaking mountains and filled with a wide spectrum of activities, from brewery tours to abundant bird-watching opportunities. In addition, there are two revitalizing spas, Rancho La Puerta and Rancho Tecate Resort, the second of which also offers a spectacular nine-hole golf course amid the mountains south of town.

RV sites, facilities: Altogether, there are 75 RV sites; 41 of them are flat, pull-through spaces with full hookups (including water service, sewer access, and 30/50-amp power outlets) and enough room for lengthy RVs (up to 40 feet/12.2 meters long). The rest are back-ins. Small trees and large oaks provide cool shade throughout the property, and the park also includes 15 tent campsites and a spacious overflow area for dry docking. In addition, there are 14 cabins and cottages available for rent.

Amenities include picnic tables, central barbecues, a coin laundry, a heated pool and spa, a ranch-style clubhouse, a grocery store, a children's playground, a petting zoo, a volleyball court, a horseshoe pit, a mini-golf course, bicycle rentals, a dump station, and new tiled restrooms with flush toilets and hot showers. Normally, the campground also offers horse rentals, but horseback riding has been suspended indefinitely. The fence-enclosed property is secured by a resident caretaker and an entrance gate, which is locked at night. Children and leashed pets are welcome. The staff speaks English. There's a restaurant outside the grounds, only a short walk across the pasture. Although the drinking water is safe here and there's an on-site store, you might want to obtain food, fuel, and other supplies in Tecate, where you'll find a greater selection.

Reservations, fees: Reservations are recommended; although they can be made via the website, it's better to make them by phone. Full-hookup RV sites cost $32 per night, $180 per week, and $540 per month, while tent spaces cost $11 per night, $60 per week, and $180 per month. Cabins are also available. Cash (Mexican pesos or U.S. dollars), credit cards, and personal checks are all acceptable forms of payment. The park is open all year.

© RANCHO OJAI

a snowy day at Rancho Ojai

Directions: From Tecate, drive east on Highway 2 for 13 miles (20.9 km) until you reach the Km 112 marker and see the Rancho Ojai sign and gate on the north (left) side of the road. Turn left onto the dirt access road, pass through the stone arch entrance, and then turn right into the ranch. If you take the toll road from Tecate, you'll have to turn around at the El Hongo tollbooth, travel west on Highway 2 for 7.4 miles (11.9 km), and turn right onto the dirt road beside the Rancho Ojai sign. From Mexicali, head west on Highway 2 to the El Hongo stop, take the free road to Tecate West, drive 7.4 miles (11.9 km), and turn right onto the dirt access road.

Contact: Rancho Ojai, Km 112 de la Carretera Libre Mexicali–Tecate, Tecate, Baja California, Mexico, tel. 665/655-3014, fax 665/655-3015, or P.O. Box 280, Tecate, CA 91980, www.rancho-ojai.com.

37 HACIENDA SANTA VERÓNICA RV RESORT

Scenic Rating: 7

southeast of Tecate

See map page 50 **BEST**

The rural areas around Tecate, Mexico, constitute Baja's horse country. In fact, this campground, located 28 miles (45 km) east of Tecate, is an exceptional place to explore the natural world via horseback. You can also view your pastoral surroundings from the top of a strangely carved watchtower on the premises.

The property isn't easy to reach via its rough, partially paved access road, especially for larger, more unwieldy RVs, but it's well worth the effort. This rustic, Spanish Colonial–style, 5,000-acre (2,020-hectare) *rancho* offers primitive camping among grassy slopes and cool oak trees, a setting that lures off-road motorcyclists and eager equestrians, especially in summer and on winter weekends. Since travelers frequently stay longer in this remote, primitive locale than expected, it's wise to purchase enough groceries, purified water, gasoline, and propane to last you and your guests at least a solid week. Of course, if any needs arise, Tecate is only a short drive away.

RV sites, facilities: The primitive camping area is essentially a grassy meadow, shaded by large oak trees. Spaces are unmarked, so you can park your RV or pitch your tent wherever you prefer. There are no hookups, but the area can accommodate any RV, from small camper vans to 45-foot (13.7-meter) motor homes. Clean restrooms and cold showers are available, and there is a decent restaurant and bar on-site. Other amenities include a roomy hotel, a swimming pool, a coin laundry, tennis and basketball courts, horse and bicycle rentals, picnic areas, off-road trails, and occasional bullfights. There is no dump station, and the staff speaks only limited English. Children and leashed pets are welcome. Despite the presence of a small store, supplies should be purchased in Tecate.

Reservations, fees: Reservations are accepted. RV and tent sites cost $20 per night. Hotel rooms are also available. Credit cards are not accepted; cash (Mexican pesos or U.S. dollars) is the only acceptable form of payment. The park is open all year.

Directions: From Tecate, drive east on Highway 2 for 13 miles (20.9 km), pass Rancho Ojai on the north (left) side of the road, and continue east for another 8.7 miles (14 km) to the small town of El Hongo. Near the center of town, turn right (south) onto a road marked by a "Hacienda Santa Verónica" sign. Drive for 1.1 miles (1.8 km) and follow the curve to the right. After 4.7 miles (7.6 km), you'll reach a fork in the road. Veer to the right. You'll see the entrance gate to the Hacienda Santa Verónica in 1.5 miles (2.4 km).

Contact: Hacienda Santa Verónica RV Resort, Km 35 de la Carretera Tecate, Tecate, Mexico, or #4558 Boulevard Agua Caliente, Piso #1, Oficina #105, Torres de Agua Caliente, Tijuana, Baja California, C.P. 22420, Mexico, tel. 664/681-7428 (Tijuana).

38 RANCHO SORDO MUDO RV PARK

Scenic Rating: 6

northeast of El Sauzal

See map page 50 BEST

Since the late 1960s, this ministry has served as a free Christian home and school for deaf children. Founded by Ed and Margaret Everett, the school offers an accepting environment, where students can learn, despite their handicap, how to read and write, communicate through sign language, adopt a trade, and worship God. Visitors are welcome; there's even a campground for those with RVs or tents, the proceeds of which benefit the school. Although the original purpose of these overnight spaces was to accommodate volunteers for the ministry, travelers are embraced (as long as they dress modestly, respect the children and animals, and follow the park rules), and you'll certainly find other diversions in the area.

The rugged countryside is perfect for a long hike, though rattlesnakes and other critters can be a danger. In addition, the campground is located within the heart of Valle de Guadalupe, once a Russian settlement and now one of Mexico's finest wine-producing regions. Tours of nearby wineries, including Domecq and L.A. Cetto, are available by advance arrangement. Ask the campground owners about planning such tours during your visit.

RV sites, facilities: The campground, located in a grassy field near the school, has 20 pull-through RV sites and 10 back-in sites, some of which have full hookups (including water service, sewer access, and 50-amp power) and the rest of which only have electricity and water. All of the RV spaces can accommodate midsized motor homes and travel trailers (up to 30 feet/9.1 meters long). For tent campers, there are 10 sites, all of which have water, electricity, and sewer access. Amenities include a small store, a dump station, flush toilets, hot showers, and small orange trees, the fruit of which is free to pick. The property also houses a gym, a playground, a full-sized basketball court, a playing field, a Frisbee golf course, and a swimming pool. Security is provided by a resident manager and a few large dogs. The staff members speak English and Spanish. There is no laundry on-site. Children and leashed pets are allowed. Since the water here is not completely safe for nonresidents to drink, and there are no major stores in the vicinity, it's best to purchase groceries, purified water, extra fuel, and other supplies in Tecate or Ensenada, prior to your trip here.

Reservations, fees: Reservations are accepted via phone or email. The suggested donation for RV and tent camping is $15 per night. Credit cards are not accepted; cash (Mexican pesos or U.S. dollars) is the customary form of payment. The campground is open all year.

Directions: After crossing the U.S.-Mexico border in Tecate, turn left at the first light, onto Highway 2. Travel one block and turn right at the *alto* (stop) sign, onto what will become Highway 3. Take this road through town and continue for about 44 miles (70.8 km) to the Domecq Winery on your right. Continue for another mile (1.6 km). The entrance to Rancho Sordo Mudo is on the right-hand side. Drive through the yellow walled gate and up the dirt driveway. From Ensenada, drive 6 miles (9.7 km) northwest on Highway 1, veer right onto Highway 3, and drive 19 miles (30.6 km) to the Km 75 marker. The campground entrance is on your left.

Contact: Rancho Sordo Mudo RV Park, Km 75 de la Carretera Ensenada–Tecate, Valle de Guadalupe, Baja California, Mexico, tel. 646/155-2201, or P.O. Box 1376 (or P.O. Box 7441), Chula Vista, CA 91912, www.ranchosordomudo.org.

39 RANCHO MARÍA TERESA

Scenic Rating: 9

in Valle de Guadalupe

See map page 50

Accentuated with breezy palm trees and winding swimming pools, this relaxing, family-

the mountains near Tecate

oriented oasis sits within the rugged terrain of the Valle de Guadalupe, along the Ruta del Vino (Wine Route). Besides offering proximity to all of the wineries and vineyards that lie along Highway 3, this recreation complex also presents scenic hiking and cycling trails through their private vineyards, olive trees, and citrus orchards.

Depending on the season, you might find a few other welcome campgrounds along Highway 3. During the warmer months, for instance, Rancho Cuesta Mar has been known to welcome RV and tent campers. Located near Km 101, close to El Sauzal, this recreation area offers swimming pools, barbecue grills, playgrounds, and other such family-oriented diversions.

RV sites, facilities: Although the official campground caters to tent campers, RVers are welcome to stay overnight in the secure parking lot. Amenities include hot showers, clean bathrooms, lovely gardens, two large swimming pools, one children's pool, shady trees, picnic tables, charcoal grills, volleyball and basketball courts, swings, a pool table, a restaurant called Campestre Los Naranjos, and a basic hotel called Posada Inn Misión de Guadalupe. There is no dump station or laundry, but the staff speaks limited English. Children and pets are welcome, though littering, obscene language, loud music, and improper swimwear are forbidden. Limited supplies, as well as gasoline, are available along Highway 3, though more extensive purchases can be made in Tecate to the north or Ensenada to the south.

Reservations, fees: Reservations are accepted for hotel rooms and tent sites. Primitive RV spots in the overnight parking lot are first-come, first-served. The recreation area, which includes the pools and game zones, costs $10 per day per person. Overnight camping costs an additional $2 daily (for each camper). For $20, a person may use the recreation area for two days and stay the night in between. Children (under three years old) may enter the premises for free. Single and duplex motel rooms are also available. Credit cards are not accepted; cash (Mexican pesos or U.S. dollars) is the only acceptable form of payment. The recreation complex and campground are open all year.

Directions: From Ensenada, drive 6 miles (9.7 km) northwest on Highway 1, veer right onto Highway 3, and drive 14.4 miles (23.2 km) to the Km 82.5 marker. The campground entrance is on your left.

Contact: Rancho María Teresa, Km 82.5 de la Carretera Ensenada–Tecate, Valle de Guadalupe, Ensenada, Baja California, Mexico, tel./fax

646/155-2450, www.ranchomariateresa.com. For more information about Rancho Cuesta Mar, call 646/176-2739; be prepared, however, to know a little Spanish before calling.

40 PARQUE NACIONAL CONSTITUCIÓN DE 1857

Scenic Rating: 10

east of Ensenada

See map page 50 BEST

If you've tired of the crowded beachside campgrounds for which Baja California is known, there are a few places that offer an untamed, more serene camping experience. The 12,350-acre (5,000-hectare) Parque Nacional Constitución de 1857 is one such locale. Here, you'll sleep amid the cool atmosphere of a wooded, mountainous region, only a few hours east of Ensenada. Most tranquility-seekers come in the spring, summer, and autumn, though travelers are welcome in winter, too.

Within this breathtaking park, you'll find two shallow, inland lakes, the Laguna Hanson and the Laguna Chica, both of which evaporate in summer and fill up again every winter. Also prevalent are the pine forests of the Sierra de Juárez, providing an important refuge for a wide range of wildlife, including Cimarron lambs, gray foxes, coyotes, raccoons, squirrels, eagles, hawks, owls, ducks, and herons. Popular pastimes include hiking and mountain biking through the forests, watching the skies for majestic birds of prey, and, when there's enough water in the lakes, swimming, kayaking, and fishing for catfish and large-mouth bass. Just watch out for ticks, rattlesnakes, and other potentially dangerous wildlife, and remember that hunting is prohibited. On the road back to Ensenada, you might want to veer south of Highway 3 and check out the thermal springs at Agua Caliente.

RV sites, facilities: There are no designated RV sites here—you can park wherever you like. Besides the forests, mountains, and lakes, however, there are few amenities, just pit toilets, barbecue pits, and picnic tables. Only small, self-contained RVs and rugged tent campers should stay here, preferably in pairs or groups, as there's no drinking water, dump station, electricity, or security. Showers and laundry facilities are also unavailable. Children and leashed pets are welcome, but the terrain is not suitable for wheelchairs. Stop in Ensenada for food, water, fuel, and other supplies, as there are no stores nearby, and be sure to pack out all trash when you leave.

Reservations, fees: Given the ultra-primitive, remote status of this campground, reservations are not accepted; spaces are available on a first-come, first-served basis. There is a nominal charge for RV and tent camping ($5 daily). Credit cards are not accepted; cash (Mexican pesos or U.S. dollars) is the only acceptable form of payment. The campground is open all year.

Directions: Although you can access this national park from the north or south, the southern route is infinitely easier. From Ensenada, take Highway 3 east to Ojos Negros, a distance of roughly 24.5 miles (39.4 km). Turn left (north) onto a short 1.3-mile (2.1-km) paved road, into the village, and follow the route to its end, where you'll turn right onto a graded dirt road. Continue for 7.6 miles (12.2 km), then turn right at the junction. Drive another 3.1 miles (5 km), turn left, then continue for another 16.3 miles (26.2 km) to the ranger station. Once inside the park, traverse the pine forests to Laguna Hanson, which might be dry in summer, and select a campsite. After a spring rain, this road could be impassable, so take care when driving. You should probably survey the area in a four-wheel-drive vehicle before bringing a motor home or travel trailer along this potentially hazardous route.

Contact: Since there's no official contact person, mailing address, or phone number for the Parque Nacional Constitución de 1857, it's best just to drive into the park and see which spots are available.

MEXICALI TO SAN FELIPE

© CANYONMANROB

BEST RV PARKS AND CAMPGROUNDS

If you're accustomed to the Pacific side of Baja Norte, you might wonder where all the water has gone. The northeastern portion of Baja California, easily accessible via two border crossings in Calexico, California, is far drier than the opposite side. Apparently, there was a time when the salty, usually arid Laguna Salada basin was kept flooded by the Río Colorado and the Sea of Cortez. Today, however, the *desierto* stretches as far as your eyes can see.

On the eastern side of Baja Norte, near the U.S.-Mexico border, lies Mexicali, the state capital and a sprawling city, known for the manufacturing of trucks and electronics and surrounded by thousands of acres of fertile, thriving *tierras de labranza* (farmland). With several supermarkets, modern shopping centers, and numerous gas stations, Mexicali is considered by most RV travelers to be just a pit stop on the road to San Felipe, but there are plenty of reasons to stay for a while. In recent years, this border town has blossomed into an energetic, multifaceted metropolis, where visitors can watch bullfights and baseball games; explore museums and art galleries; unwind in various bars and nightclubs; and attend annual events like the Fiestas del Sol, an exposition of agriculture and industry and a celebration of music, dance, art, and regional cuisine.

Unfortunately, however, the closest RV parks to Mexicali lie on the U.S. side of the international border. So, unless you plan to make a quick day trip from California, you'll have to stay in one of the campgrounds near the Río Hardy, about 33 miles (53 km) southeast on Highway 5, or the Cañón de Guadalupe, where a campground lies amid palm trees, waterfalls, and soothing *baños de agua caliente* (hot springs), 52 miles (84 km) to the southwest.

After exploring Mexicali and its bustling environs, you'll surely be ready to relax on the beach. Luckily, the coast is only 84 miles (135 km) south of the Río Hardy area – where Highway 5 veers toward San Felipe, a friendly waterfront town beside the Sea of Cortez. Famed for its sandy beaches, ever-present sunshine, and laid-back ambience, San Felipe welcomes foreign tourists, who come as much for the rejuvenating landscape as they do for the town's exuberant annual celebrations, including the ever-popular Feria del Camarón (Shrimp Festival) in early November.

Around San Felipe, RVers can stroll along the lovely *malecón* (waterfront promenade), watch the *pangueros* retrieve their beached boats at low tide, hunt for sand dollars at Laguna Percebú south of town, and boondock in several picturesque spots along the coast. At one time, there was a lengthy string of *playas* and *campos* (with names like Playa Los Amigos and Campo Numero Uno) that stretched north and south of San Felipe and provided plenty of inexpensive spots to park for the night. As in other areas of Baja, however, recent real-estate development has resulted in the closure of several RV parks and campgrounds, so consult local residents before camping on a seemingly welcoming beach. Most of the area's remaining options have limited hookups (if any) and cannot accommodate large rigs, but a few, such as Campo San Felipe, offer basic amenities, including electricity, hot showers, laundry facilities, beachfront views, and a short walk to shops and restaurants.

Roughly 54 miles (87 km) south of San Felipe, you'll come upon another little gem alongside the Sea of Cortez. The remote town of Puertecitos is known for its thermal springs, and for better fishing spots than its northern neighbor. It's also not far from central Baja – a scenic landscape of deserts, mountains, lagoons, and offshore islands.

But expect a truly primitive camping experience in Puertecitos, where most beachside campgrounds cannot accommodate lengthy RVs. Still, this rugged region is worth a visit, especially if you're a fan of fishing and boating in the Sea of Cortez, off-road driving in the desert, exploring the steep canyons and hidden oases of nearby mountains, and simply enjoying the tranquility of this sleepy seaside village.

If you and your vehicle are willing to risk the infamously jarring, four-hour drive from Puertecitos to Bahía San Luis Gonzaga, you'll be treated to breathtaking vistas that few foreign travelers get the chance to see. After passing Punta Bufeo, a rocky area with views of offshore islands, you'll reach the bay itself, a stretch of sandy beaches, tidepools, and primitive campgrounds between Punta Willard and Punta Final. Beachcombers, kayakers, swimmers, anglers, and motorcyclists especially love this isolated area. Although getting here is worth the slow-going journey, those with unwieldy motor homes and travel trailers should probably not attempt the uneven route; it's definitely a road made for four-wheel-drive jeeps and shock-absorbent pickup trucks.

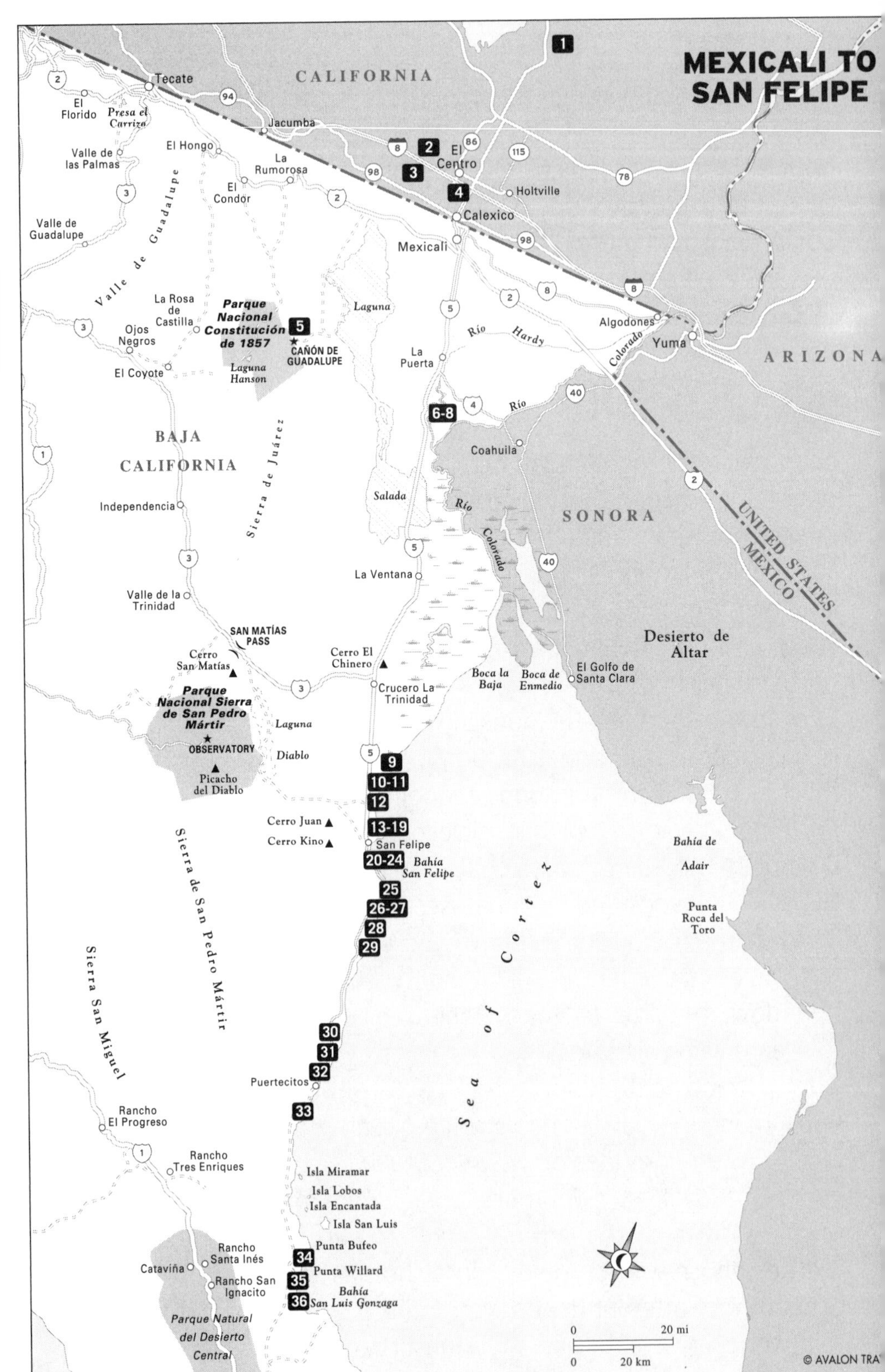

MEXICALI TO SAN FELIPE
CALIFORNIA
BAJA CALIFORNIA
SONORA
ARIZONA
UNITED STATES
MEXICO
Tecate
El Florido
Presa el Carrizo
Jacumba
Valle de las Palmas
El Hongo
La Rumorosa
El Condor
El Centro
Holtville
Calexico
Mexicali
Valle de Guadalupe
Valle de Guadalupe
La Rosa de Castilla
Parque Nacional Constitución de 1857
CAÑÓN DE GUADALUPE
Laguna Hanson
Ojos Negros
El Coyote
Laguna Salada
Algodones
Yuma
Río Hardy
Colorado
La Puerta
Río
Coahuila
Sierra de Juárez
Independencia
Río Colorado
La Ventana
Valle de la Trinidad
SAN MATÍAS PASS
Cerro San Matías
Cerro El Chinero
Crucero La Trinidad
Boca la Baja
Boca de Enmedio
El Golfo de Santa Clara
Desierto de Altar
Parque Nacional Sierra de San Pedro Mártir
OBSERVATORY
Picacho del Diablo
Laguna Diablo
Cerro Juan
Cerro Kino
San Felipe
Bahía San Felipe
Bahía de Adair
Punta Roca del Toro
Sea of Cortez
Sierra de San Pedro Mártir
Sierra San Miguel
Puertecitos
Rancho El Progreso
Rancho Tres Enriques
Isla Miramar
Isla Lobos
Isla Encantada
Isla San Luis
Punta Bufeo
Punta Willard
Bahía San Luis Gonzaga
Rancho Santa Inés
Cataviña
Rancho San Ignacito
Parque Natural del Desierto Central
1
2
3
4
5
6-8
9
10-11
12
13-19
20-24
25
26-27
28
29
30
31
32
33
34
35
36
0 20 mi
0 20 km
© AVALON TRA

1 DEL YERMO RV PARK

Scenic Rating: 5

in Calipatria, California

See map page 90

Southeast of the enormous, man-made Salton Sea, in the lovely desert town of Calipatria, lies this simple RV park. Small but friendly, the campground offers overnight guests proximity to sand dunes, bird refuges, hunting areas, and the Salton Sea State Recreation Area, popular among boaters, kayakers, anglers, and water-skiers. Hikers, mountain bikers, rockhounds, off-road enthusiasts, and bird-watchers also relish the Imperial Valley—which can be unbearably hot from July to September. From here, visitors are only a few hours from San Diego, Palm Springs, and Joshua Tree National Park, but even closer is the complex Mexican border town of Mexicali, Baja California Norte's state capital. So, besides being surrounded by a plethora of desert-related activities, the park is an ideal locale to stay before or after a trip across the U.S.-Mexico border.

RV sites, facilities: The park has 45 full-hookup spaces, with 30/50-amp electricity, water service, and cable television. Six of the sites are pull-throughs, but all can accommodate lengthy motor homes and travel trailers (up to 40 feet/12.2 meters long). Other amenities include hot showers, a coin laundry, wheelchair-accessible restrooms, and a dump station. Tents, children, and well-behaved pets are welcome. Water, gasoline, and other supplies are available in Calipatria; several restaurants, stores, and medical offices are within walking distance of the park.

Reservations, fees: Reservations are accepted. Campsites cost $16 daily and $90 weekly. There is an extra fee for the use of more than one air-conditioning unit. Cash (U.S. dollars) and credit cards are accepted. The campground is open all year.

Directions: From I-8 East, just past El Centro, merge onto Highway 111 North via Exit #118B and head toward Brawley for 14.5 miles (23.3 km). Turn left onto Highway 111/Highway 78. After 1.6 miles (2.6 km), turn right onto Highway 111/North 8th Street and drive 10.3 miles (16.6 km). Take a right onto East Alamo Street and drive 0.2 mile (0.3 km). The campground is on the right (south) side of the street.

Contact: Del Yermo RV Park, 263 East Alamo Street, Calipatria, CA 92233, tel./fax 760/348-7633 (U.S.), delyermorvpark@sbcglobal.net.

2 SUNBEAM LAKE RV RESORT

Scenic Rating: 9

in El Centro, California

See map page 90

If you're a first-time visitor to Baja, you might feel more comfortable staying overnight in a California park before heading across the border. If so, this resort is a wonderful option. With rugged mountains in the distance, a well-stocked lake at its core, and rustling palm trees everywhere, this handsome, 35-acre (14-hectare) desert oasis offers a comfortable, secure home base for day trips to Mexicali or preparations for the long drive down the Baja peninsula. It doesn't hurt that, on any given day, you can visit San Diego's museums and other attractions, play golf in Palm Springs, fish for bass and trout in Sunbeam Lake, take a bike ride through the park, and watch a spectacular desert sunset.

Other area attractions include the Imperial Sand Dunes, Anza-Borrego Desert State Park, and Salton Sea, all favored among hikers and nature lovers. Popular with snowbirds, the park also offers a number of communal activities, including pancake breakfasts, bingo games, water volleyball, poker tournaments, trips to nearby casinos and golf courses, and tours to Mexicali, where a myriad of restaurants, cultural centers, and other unique diversions await.

RV sites, facilities: This well-maintained park offers 310 spacious, full-hookup, gravel sites, with 20/30/50-amp electricity, free wireless

Internet access, cable television, telephone service, and enough room for lengthy motor homes (up to 45 feet/13.7 meters long) with multiple slide-outs. Both back-ins and pull-throughs are available, and many sites have concrete patios. The wide, paved streets allow for easy maneuvering. Facilities consist of a heated, saltwater swimming pool; a soothing whirlpool spa; a roomy Spanish-style clubhouse; a stocked lake and boat ramp; a carpeted billiard room; several shuffleboard and pickleball courts; ping-pong tables; horseshoe pits; an Internet lab; a game room; a lounge; a library; a fitness room; a fenced pet-walk area; and kitchen facilities. Other amenities include clean restrooms, hot showers, barbecue grills, individual mailboxes, a secure storage facility, and trails for walking and biking. Two modern laundry facilities offer a total of 16 washers and 16 dryers, plus several folding tables, irons and ironing boards, wash tubs, and rolling laundry carts. Park models and empty mobile home spaces are also available for lease. There is no dump station. Children and pets are welcome, but tents are not allowed. Groceries, water, gasoline, and other supplies are available in El Centro.

Reservations, fees: Reservations are recommended, especially during the busy winter season. General sites cost $35 daily and $197 weekly; lagoon sites cost $37 daily and $208 weekly; and lake sites cost $39 daily and $218 weekly. All rates are based on double occupancy, so each additional guest will be charged $3 per day and $15 per week. Long-term leases (plus metered electricity) are also available. Cash (U.S. dollars), personal checks, Visa, and MasterCard are all acceptable forms of payment. The park is open all year.

Directions: From San Diego, take I-8 East to Exit #107 (Drew Road) and turn left (north) onto County Highway S29. Drive 0.5 mile (0.8 km) and turn right onto Sunbeam Lake Drive. You'll spy the park entrance in 0.25 mile (0.4 km).

Contact: Sunbeam Lake RV Resort, 1716 West Sunbeam Lake Drive, El Centro, CA 92243, tel. 760/352-7154 (U.S.) or 800/900-7154 (U.S.), fax 760/352-8992 (U.S.), www.sunbeamlake.com.

3 RIO BEND RV & GOLF RESORT

Scenic Rating: 10

in El Centro, California

See map page 90

For those who need a place to stay prior to their RV trip down to Baja, this Imperial Valley park might not be the best choice—after all, it's so luxurious that you might forget to leave for Mexico. Besides offering a PGA-rated golf course, this 120-acre (49-hectare) resort is adjacent to some wetlands, a bird sanctuary, and an 80-acre (32-hectare) lagoon, all of which provide ample opportunities for bird-watchers and wildlife enthusiasts. With mild winters, a dry climate, and 360 days of sunshine, this friendly, award-winning park is popular among snowbirds and RV caravans, especially given its vast array of communal activities, from aerobics to craft classes to holiday events. Feel free to stay a few days and chase your cares away, before heading south to Mexicali, an intriguing border town with two ports of entry and a host of absorbing attractions.

RV sites, facilities: The resort offers 500 well-landscaped RV sites, including pull-throughs and group areas—perfect for caravans and lengthy motor homes (up to 40 feet/12.2 meters long). Every site has complete utilities, cable television, and telephone hookups. Facilities comprise a state-of-the-art fitness center, a café and country store, a heated pool and spa, a clubhouse, a library/puzzle area, an activity center, a billiards room, a golf course and pro shop, and horseshoe pits, as well as shuffleboard, volleyball, and croquet courts. Other on-site amenities include modern restrooms, hot showers, new laundry facilities, wireless Internet access, fishing lakes, a picnic area, and a pet park. There is, however, no dump station on-site. Children and pets are welcome, but tent camping is prohibited. Groceries, water, fuel, and other supplies can be purchased in El Centro.

Reservations, fees: Reservations are recommended, especially during the busy winter season. Depending on the time of year, RV sites cost $38–50 daily, $250–300 weekly, and $450–550 monthly. All rates are based on double occupancy; each additional guest will be charged $3 per day. Group, seasonal, and year-round rates are also available. All discount cards, such as AARP, Good Sam, Escapees, AAA, etc., are accepted. Cash (U.S. dollars) and credit cards are both acceptable forms of payment. The park is open all year.

Directions: From San Diego, take I-8 East to Exit #107 (Drew Road) and turn right (south) onto Drew Road/County Highway S29. Drive 0.4 mile (0.6 km) until you reach the park entrance, which will be on your right.

Contact: Rio Bend RV & Golf Resort, 1589 Drew Road, El Centro, CA 92243, tel. 800/545-6481 (U.S.), fax 800/250-8223 (U.S.), www.riobendrvgolfresort.com.

4 DESERT TRAILS RV PARK AND GOLF COURSE

Scenic Rating: 10

in El Centro, California

See map page 90

In a California town that's known for more sunny days than almost any other place in the United States, visitors are hard-pressed to feel ill at ease, especially in a park as lovely and as active as this one. It's especially popular with snowbirds. Boasting panoramic views of duck ponds and palm trees, this well-tended RV park offers a myriad of diversions, including hiking, bicycling, fishing, hunting, off-road driving, bird-watching, and, of course, golf. In addition, wintertime guests are often treated to awe-inspiring (if ear-splitting) practice runs by the U.S. Navy's elite Blue Angel Flight Demonstration Team.

While the park is close to destinations like San Diego, Palm Springs, the Salton Sea, the Imperial Sand Dunes, and Yuma, Arizona, those headed to Baja will be even more delighted to be so close to Mexico. After all, Mexicali's two international ports of entry lie less than 10 miles (16.1 km) south of the park, so whether you just want to hop across the border for a day trip to Baja Norte's state capital or make last-minute preparations for your long journey down the Baja peninsula, it's an ideal place to stay for the night—if not longer.

RV sites, facilities: There are 387 full-hookup sites, with 30/50-amp electricity, water service, sewer access, cable television, and room for one RV (up to 40 feet/12.2 meters long) and two vehicles. Many sites are pull-throughs, and most have concrete pads and phone hookups. The wide paved access streets make it easy to navigate lengthy motor homes and trailers through the park and into the spaces. On-site facilities consist of banquet and meeting rooms, a library, a billiards room, a nine-hole executive golf course, shuffleboard courts, horseshoe pits, a whirlpool spa, and a swimming pool that can be heated in the winter and cooled in the summer. Other amenities include Internet access, propane delivery, clean restrooms, hot showers, a coin laundry, public pay phones, and a dump station. The staff is courteous, and children and pets are welcome, though tents are not allowed. Groceries, water, fuel, and other supplies are available in nearby El Centro.

Reservations, fees: Reservations are recommended, especially during the busy winter season. Full-hookup spaces cost $39 daily, $238 weekly, and $467 monthly. Sites with just water and electric service cost $31 daily, $186 weekly, and $418 monthly. Dry-camping sites cost $22 daily, $126 weekly, and $322 monthly. All rates are based on double occupancy, so extra guests cost $3 daily, $15 weekly, and $40 monthly. The fees are higher from January to March. Daily and weekly rates include all utilities and cable television, while monthly rates only include the cable. RV storage and group discounts are possible, and fully-furnished park models are available for rent. Beyond two vehicles per space, there is a charge for each additional one ($3 per day or $40 per month). Although credit/debit cards are accepted, there is a 2.5 percent discount for all rental payments (daily, weekly, and monthly) made by cash (U.S. dollars) or money order. The park is open all year.

Directions: From I-8 East, near El Centro, take Exit #115 (4th Street/Highway 86) and turn right onto Corfman Road/Highway 86. Drive 0.1 mile (0.2 km) south and take a left onto Wake Avenue. The campground entrance will be on your right.

Contact: Desert Trails RV Park and Golf Course, 225 Wake Avenue, El Centro, CA 92243, tel. 760/352-7275 (U.S.), fax 760/352-7474 (U.S.), www.deserttrailsrv.com.

5 GUADALUPE CANYON HOT SPRINGS & CAMPGROUND

Scenic Rating: 9

southwest of Mexicali

See map page 90 **BEST**

Ensconced by craggy mountains, sculpted boulders, and lush palm tree groves, the Cañón de Guadalupe provides a wonderfully relaxing alternative to the bustling towns of northern Baja. If you're looking to escape civilization, embrace nature, and rejuvenate your weary soul, this desert oasis is the perfect place to do all that and more. Amid the remote Sierra de Juárez, you can hike to cold canyon pools and cascading waterfalls, try your hand at rock climbing, explore unique flora and fauna, tour prehistoric Indian cave paintings, contemplate stunning sunrises and rainbows, or simply relax in a natural, rock-rimmed tub, filled with crystal-clear geothermal mineral water. The best time to visit is from early November to late May, before the brutal temperatures of summer descend upon the desert.

Founded in 1940 by cattle rancher Don José Loya Murillo, this campground is one of the oldest in Baja. Murillo first entered the Cañón de Guadalupe via horseback, while in search of some stray cows. After discovering the therapeutic benefits of the steaming mineral water and rejuvenating palm oases, he quit ranching and created a few small hot tubs, which gradually multiplied into the nearly two dozen that exist today. Following his death at the age of 99, his sons Arturo and Angel took over operation of the campground.

Since each of the campground's nine secluded sites offers private hot tubs and amenities like stone fireplaces, thatched-roof shelters, and incredible cliffside views, they're suitable for large groups, families on vacation, and couples seeking a little romance. Each site offers its own unique features, and each has its own unique name, including Castillo, El Mirador, El Sol, La Cueva, La Paloma, La Jolla (A and B), San Marcos, and El Dorado.

Just be advised that, while the spectacular vistas and guaranteed solitude are well worth the drive, the lengthy trek to the Cañón de Guadalupe, across a desolate desert landscape, can be difficult for some vehicles. High ground clearance is a must, and tools such as shovels, boards, and rope might be helpful if your vehicle gets stuck in a sandy or muddy spot, especially after a heavy rain in winter. Be aware, too, that motor homes and trailers cannot travel the last mile (1.6 km) into Guadalupe Canyon; it's simply too rocky and uneven for anything but four-wheel-drive vehicles such as jeeps and pickup campers.

Luckily, however, the managers (Rob and Isabel Williams) are creating an RV park not too far away. The Two Seasons RV Park at Guadalupe Canyon, which will be finished by 2010, will offer pull-through sites and amenities for RVs of all types. In addition, visitors will be able to access the nearby hot springs, and they'll have ample opportunities for hiking, rock climbing, dirt biking, and bird-watching.

RV sites, facilities: The campground offers nine primitive sites, all of which have private

a shady *palapa* in the El Sol campground at Guadalupe Canyon

hot tubs (with temperature controls), picnic tables, shady *palapas,* and room for tents and small RVs (such as pickup trucks with cab-over campers). Most of the spaces have fireplaces, sinks, barbecue pits, and water hoses, though none have hookups of any kind. All of them are within walking distance of flush toilets, a restaurant, and a small store that sells beer and soda. Amenities also include a large swimming pool and several hiking trails. In addition, Rigo, the son of co-owner Arturo Loya, runs two-hour jeep tours to ancient Indian rock-art sites in the nearby canyons. There is no laundry, dump station, or shower house on the premises, but some staff members speak English. Children and pets are welcome, though much of the terrain might not be suitable for wheelchairs. Despite the presence of a small store, it's necessary to bring supplies with you, so be sure to pick up groceries, water, fuel, and other necessities in Mexicali (or Tecate) before the trip.

For motor homes and travel trailers, which cannot traverse the sandy, uneven entrance road and fit into the tight canyon, there is an alternative RV park currently in progress. The Two Seasons RV Park at Guadalupe Canyon, which lies 2 miles (3.2 km) from this part of the Cañón de Guadalupe, will allow access to hiking trails, hot springs, and the swimming pool. When completed in 2010, the RV park will offer 30 large pull-through spaces, a dump station, a small swimming pool, a camp store, restrooms, picnic tables, shady *palapas,* long-term storage areas, and full-time managers.

Reservations, fees: Reservations are recommended, especially on holiday weekends. Each campsite costs $50–75 per weekday night. Rates are much more expensive on weekends (up to $275 for two nights) and holidays (up to $500 for three nights). Spaces in the future RV park will cost $25 per night, $150 per month, and $1,000 per year (use of the hot springs will cost extra). Firewood is on sale for a nominal fee. Credit cards are not accepted; cash (Mexican pesos or U.S. dollars) is the only acceptable form of payment. The campground is open all year.

Directions: Although the Parque Nacional Constitución de 1857 lies just west of the Cañón de

© CANYONMANROB

a hot tub in the Castillo campground at Guadalupe Canyon

Guadalupe, it's much easier to reach the campground from the east (and not via the national park). From Mexicali, take Highway 2 toward Tecate. Roughly 9.8 miles (15.8 km) west of Colonia Progreso, you will pass an ordinary dirt road (which crosses the Laguna Salada). Drive another 2.7 miles (4.3 km) to a graded dirt road. Turn left at the sign and head south for 27.4 miles (44.1 km), turn right, and drive 7.4 miles (11.9 km) to the campground.

Contact: Guadalupe Canyon Hot Springs & Campground, P.O. Box 4003, Newport Beach, CA 92661, tel. 949/673-2670 (U.S.), www.guadalupe-canyon.com.

6 CAMPO SONORA

Scenic Rating: 4

southeast of Mexicali

See map page 90

Situated roughly 33 miles (53 km) southeast of Mexicali, the Río Hardy area is less remarkable than others parts of Baja, especially with the majestic Sea of Cortez only a couple hours away, but it's still popular among local hunters, anglers, and bird-watchers. Hiking, cycling, and water-related activities in a nearby lake are also popular diversions. Though not in the best of condition and rarely visited by RVers, this primitive (often deserted) campground is one of three along this route. Besides outdoor activities, such as fishing for perch and hunting for waterfowl, the location also offers relatively quick access to Mexicali, a multifaceted city that, in recent years, has shed its dingy, border-town image and offers a plethora of diversions, from bullfights to cultural centers.

In addition to the poorly maintained facilities, the other major drawback of this run-down campground is the noise factor. Its proximity to the highway might be convenient for exploring northeast Baja Norte, but the traffic can be distracting day and night.

RV sites, facilities: There are no designated RV sites here—you can park wherever you like. Besides the nearby Río Hardy, however, there are few official amenities, save for a small store, a nearby restaurant, some shady *ramadas,* and poorly maintained restrooms with flush toilets. Only small, self-contained RVs and rugged tent campers should park here, preferably in pairs or groups, as there's no drinking water, dump station, electricity, or security available. There are also no showers or laundry facilities on the premises. Children and pets are welcome, though the facilities are not wheelchair-accessible. Stop in Mexicali (or San Felipe, if you're headed north) for food, water, fuel, and other supplies, as there are no major stores nearby. Be sure to pack out all trash when you leave.

Reservations, fees: Reservations are not accepted; spaces are available on a first-come, first-served basis. Overnight camping costs less than $10 per night. Credit cards are not accepted; cash (Mexican pesos or U.S. dollars) is the only acceptable form of payment. The campground is open all year.

Directions: From Mexicali, drive southeast on Highway 5 for 32.3 miles (52 km) to Km 52. The campground is on the left (east) side of the road. From San Felipe, head north on Highway 5 for 85.8 miles (138.1 km) and turn right at Km 52.

Contact: Since there's no official contact person, mailing address, or phone number for Campo Sonora, it's best just to drive toward the campground and see which spots are available.

7 CAMPO MOSQUEDA

Scenic Rating: 5

southeast of Mexicali

See map page 90

Closer to Mexicali than San Felipe, this is the second of three fairly primitive campgrounds in the Río Hardy area, which has, for a long time, been favored by anglers, boaters, hunters, and bird-watchers. Serving as a pseudo-resort for Mexicali residents and especially preferred during the winter months, this campground is considerably larger and nicer than Campo Sonora. Located near the river and peppered with trees, it even has its own freshwater lake, which is fully stocked with catfish and bass and is ideal for canoeists, kayakers, and water-skiers. The sandy beach is popular with children, and young-at-heart adults frequently use the wide dirt lot (between the beach and the campsites) for flying kites, testing model rockets, and practicing their golf swings.

Regular visitors try to keep its location closely guarded, but more and more people have been discovering this low-key spot during the last few years. The biggest drawback to this "secret" place is the water quality, which has recently been threatened by sewage runoff in Mexicali, raising serious concerns about favorite pastimes like swimming and fishing. Consult local residents before testing the waters.

RV sites, facilities: The campground provides an indeterminate number of spaces for tents and midsized RVs (up to 35 feet/10.7 meters long). Low-amp electricity is provided at some of the sites. Besides the nearby Río Hardy, the only other amenities include a small store, a restaurant, a children's playground, volleyball and basketball courts, a soccer field, pedal boats, shady *palapas,* barbecue pits, and restrooms with flush toilets and cold showers. Only self-contained RVs and rugged tent campers should park here, preferably in pairs or groups, as there's no drinking water or dump station, and only limited security is provided. There is no laundry on the premises. The staff speaks limited English. Children and pets are welcome, though the facilities are not wheelchair-accessible. Stop in Mexicali (or San Felipe, if you're headed north) for food, water, fuel, and other supplies, as there are no major stores nearby. Be sure to pack out all trash when you leave.

Reservations, fees: Reservations are not accepted; spaces are available on a first-come, first-served basis. Overnight camping costs less than $10 per night. Credit cards are not accepted; cash (Mexican pesos or U.S. dollars) is the only acceptable form of payment. The campground is open all year.

Directions: From Mexicali, drive southeast on Highway 5 for 33.5 miles (53.9 km) to Km 54.

Turn left (east) onto a rough gravel road and head 1.3 miles (2.1 km) to the campground, which is on the right side of the road. From San Felipe, head north on Highway 5 for 84.6 miles (136.1 km) and turn right at Km 54.

Contact: For more information about Campo Mosqueda, call 686/566-1520. If no one answers, simply stop by the campground and see which spots are available.

8 EL MAYOR TRAILER PARK

Scenic Rating: 4

southeast of Mexicali

See map page 90

As the third of three primitive campgrounds in the Río Hardy area, this is the closest one to San Felipe—for most RVers, the ultimate destination in the northeastern region of Baja Norte. Since the trailer park itself doesn't have much to offer, its location is probably its best feature. Besides bustling Mexicali, the campground is close to the desolate expanse of Laguna Salada, small mountain ranges such as the Sierra Cucapa and Sierra Mayor, and the Colorado River Delta—terrific locales for hiking, mountain biking, watching wildlife, and exploring nature. En route to San Felipe, you'll pass between the rugged Sierra San Felipe and the sparkling Sea of Cortez, a dramatic juxtaposition of contrasting landscapes that impresses most travelers with its desolate atmosphere. Before heading south, just make sure that you have the supplies you'll need—you'll have a much better selection in the supermarkets and shopping centers of Mexicali than in the *mercados* and *panaderías* (bakeries) of San Felipe.

RV sites, facilities: The campground provides 15 sites, with no hookups but room for lengthy motor homes and travel trailers (up to 40 feet/12.2 meters long). Besides the nearby Río Hardy, the only other amenities include a nearby restaurant and basic restrooms with cold showers. Only self-contained RVs and rugged tent campers should park here, preferably in pairs or groups, as there's no drinking water, dump station, electricity, or security available. In addition, there is no laundry, and the staff speaks only limited English. Children and pets are welcome, though the facilities are not wheelchair-accessible. Stop in Mexicali (or San Felipe, if you're headed north) for food, water, fuel, and other supplies, as there are no major stores nearby. Be sure to pack out all trash when you leave.

Reservations, fees: Reservations are not accepted; spaces are available on a first-come, first-served basis. Overnight camping costs $10–15 per night. Credit cards are not accepted; cash (Mexican pesos or U.S. dollars) is the only acceptable form of payment. The campground is open all year.

Directions: From Mexicali, drive southeast on Highway 5 for 34.2 miles (55 km) to Km 55. The campground is on the left (east) side of the road. From San Felipe, head north on Highway 5 for 83.9 miles (135 km) and turn right at Km 55.

Contact: Since there's no official contact person, mailing address, or phone number for the El Mayor Trailer Park, simply drive to the campground and see which spots are available.

9 BIG RV'S CAMP

Scenic Rating: 7

north of San Felipe

See map page 90 **BEST**

Located just north of the El Dorado Ranch—a posh, private resort that was once open to vacationing RVers—this campground is one of the only spots in San Felipe that can still accommodate full-sized motor homes with slide-outs. Unfortunately, it only caters to monthly and annual renters, but if you plan to stay in the San Felipe area for a little while, it's not a bad place to call home. After all, you're only 100 yards (91 meters) from the beach, a mile (1.6 km) north of the 18-hole championship golf course at the La Ventana del Mar resort (Las Caras de México, part of El Dorado Ranch), and less than 10 miles (16.1 km) from the town of San Felipe, with its authentic *panaderías*, knowledgeable fishing guides, and spirited cantinas. Because the campground mainly houses permanent residents, it promises a more serene locale than Pete's Camp to the south. If you've come to Mexico for natural beauty and spiritual rejuvenation, you're in the right place: The Sea of Cortez and its sandy coastline are perfect for hiking, swimming, kayaking, watching birds and marine life, meditating on gorgeous sunrises, and chasing away your cares.

RV sites, facilities: The gated RV park provides numerous spaces, all of which can accommodate multiple slide-outs and lengthy RVs (up to 45 feet/13.7 meters long). Each space has full hookups, including water service, sewer access, and 50-amp electricity. Amenities include beach access, an upper deck overlooking the ocean and mountains, and plenty of car parking. There is no dump station, laundry, or bath house. Well-behaved children and pets are welcome, but tent camping is not allowed. The facilities are not wheelchair-accessible. A security guard is on duty 24 hours daily, and the staff speaks English. Groceries and other supplies can be obtained in nearby San Felipe.

Reservations, fees: Reservations are accepted. The park only allows monthly and yearly rentals; contact the owner for details. Credit cards are not accepted; cash (Mexican pesos or U.S. dollars) is the only acceptable form of payment. The beach and park are open all year.

Directions: From downtown San Felipe, take Highway 5 north for 8.5 miles (13.7 km) to the El Dorado Ranch near Km 176. Continue for another 1.2 miles (1.9 km). Between Km 175 and Km 174, you will notice a blue sign on your right that reads "Centro Vacacional Burócrata." Turn right (east) and follow the campground access road to the entrance gate.

Contact: For more information about Big RV's Camp, contact Tommy: tel. 760/427-6469 (U.S.) or fax 760/352-1317 (U.S.). For more information about the Las Caras de México golf course, visit www.lascarasdemexico.com.

10 PETE'S CAMP

Scenic Rating: 8

north of San Felipe

See map page 90 **BEST**

Mainly a community of permanent trailers north of San Felipe, this long-standing park also provides a spacious camping area overlooking the beach. Although it can be tranquil at times, it's often a boisterous place, filled with regular visitors—usually the partying kind. In addition to hiking, swimming, fishing, kayaking, snorkeling, and other water-related activities amid the semidesert landscape, RVers can participate in karaoke, daily happy hours, and live music every Friday at the nearby cantina and restaurant.

The coast stretches for miles north and south of this campground, along the stunning Sea of Cortez. Over the years, many beachside spots, from Campo San Marino to Playa Encantada to El Jacalito Camp, have welcomed tent campers and owners of small, maneuverable RVs. In many cases, these inexpensive, primitive campgrounds have offered little more than pit toilets, shady *ramadas,* cold showers (if any), and clean beaches. Given the development craze that's recently hit San Felipe—turning some old favorites, such as the El Dorado Ranch and the El Cachanilla RV Park, into private communities for home owners and seasonal residents—temporary RV guests should not be surprised to find formerly welcoming *campos* and *playas* closed to overnight camping. As in other parts of Baja, when in doubt about an area's status, consult local residents before pulling in for the night. For now, at least, Pete's remains a viable option.

Besides offering easy access to the Sea of Cortez and its myriad wonders, Pete's is only

0.8 mile (1.3 km) south of the La Ventana del Mar Golf and Beach Resort, a private community that allows nonowners access to its 18-hole championship golf course, the only one in the San Felipe area. Called Las Caras de México (The Faces of Mexico), this gorgeous, seaside golf course offers well-maintained fairways, a driving range, several practice areas, and a full-service clubhouse. Currently, nonresidents can play a round of golf for $70–85, depending on the day.

RV sites, facilities: While the 79 sites have no hookups, some have enough room to accommodate lengthy motor homes and travel trailers (up to 40 feet/12.2 meters long). Small RVs can fit beneath the thatched-roof *ramadas,* and larger RVs can park beside them. Expect many of the sites to be occupied by permanent or semipermanent RVs. In addition to the beach, guests will find a dump station, drinking water, flush toilets, hot showers, a restaurant, and a festive cantina. With plenty of neighbors and a night watchman on duty, the campground is fairly secure (though it's always advisable in Baja to keep belongings stored when you're not around). There is no laundry on the premises, but the staff speaks English. Children, pets, and tent campers are allowed, though fireworks, generators, and excessively noisy motorcycles are prohibited in the campground. Supplies can be purchased in San Felipe to the south.

Reservations, fees: Reservations are recommended and must be cancelled at least two weeks ahead of time. Sites are $15 per night, though RVs and trailers over 15 feet (4.6 meters) long must pay for two sites. Each water tank costs $3 to fill up, and hot showers are available for $2 each. Credit cards are not accepted; cash (Mexican pesos or U.S. dollars) is the customary form of payment. The campground is open all year.

Directions: From the entrance monument in San Felipe, take Highway 5 north for 7.5 miles (12.1 km), exit at Km 177.5, and follow the campground access road east for 1.2 miles (1.9 km).

Contact: Pete's Camp, P.O. Box 516, Temecula, CA 92593, tel. 951/694-6704 (U.S.), www.petescamp.com. For more information about tent camping and RV boondocking at El Jacalito Camp, call 686/577-1465. For more information about the Las Caras de México golf course, visit www.lascarasdemexico.com.

11 RANCHO JACARANDAS CLUB

Scenic Rating: 7

north of San Felipe

See map page 90

Not far from the area once known as Campo Los Compadres, this wide-open space offers primitive camping on a roomy beach beside the incredible Sea of Cortez. Although there are few official amenities, it's a pleasant spot to stay for a while, especially if you like the water. The campground slopes gently toward the sea, and the beach stretches for miles in both directions. You can spend countless days swimming in the mild waters, exploring tidepools along the coast, hiking in the Sierra San Felipe to the west, and watching a myriad of shorebirds. Kayaking, fishing, and windsurfing are also popular diversions here. Families especially like this campground, as do off-road enthusiasts, so be prepared for crowds and noise at times.

As with other *campos* and *playas* along the coastline north and south of San Felipe, however, it's possible that privatization or real-estate development will soon make this campground unavailable to vacationing RVers. If in doubt about its status, simply consult local residents.

RV sites, facilities: Although there are several designated tent and RV sites in this beachfront campground—each of which has a shady *palapa*—there's a lot of extra space for additional tent camping and dry-docking RVs, even midsized ones (up to 35 feet/10.7 meters long). Other amenities include pit toilets, cold showers, picnic areas with barbecue grills, children's playing areas, a lighting system, and an on-site manager. Only self-contained RVs and rugged tent campers should stay here, preferably in pairs or groups, as there's no drinking water, dump station, electricity, or laundry. There is, however, a 24-hour security and maintenance staff. Make sure that you're equipped with shovels, boards, rope, and other tools in case your wheels get stuck in the sand. Children and pets are welcome, though the facilities are not wheelchair-accessible. Stop in San Felipe for food, water, fuel, and other supplies, as there are no major stores nearby. Remember to pack out all trash when you leave.

Reservations, fees: Reservations are not accepted; spaces are available on a first-come, first-served basis. Sites cost $10–15 per night, for RVs or tents. Credit cards are not accepted; cash (Mexican pesos or U.S. dollars) is the only acceptable form of payment. The campground is open all year.

Directions: From San Felipe, drive 7.2 miles (11.6 km) north on Highway 5, just past the El Cachanilla RV Park. Turn right (east) onto the signed entrance road and drive 1.1 miles (1.8 km) to the Rancho Jacarandas Club. From the border in Mexicali, drive south for 4.4 miles (7.1 km) to Highway 2 and head east on the highway for 4.8 miles (7.7 km). Turn right (south) onto Highway 5 and drive 110.9 miles (178.5 km) to the turnoff for the campground.

Contact: Since there's no official contact person, mailing address, or phone number for the Rancho Jacarandas Club, it's probably best just to drive toward the campground and see which spots are available.

12 PLAYAS DEL SOL

Scenic Rating: 7

north of San Felipe

See map page 90 **BEST**

The heart and soul of this modest beachside campground is the popular neighborhood restaurant and bar known as El Sol. Besides authentic Mexican cuisine, the joint offers happy-hour drink specials almost every afternoon and karaoke on Saturday nights. It's a festive place to relax, with a margarita in your hand and your eyes fixed on the sky above the Sea of Cortez, where rosy sunsets give way to serene moonrises.

This well-maintained campground is situated on several terraces, overlooking a lovely, spacious beach that's ideal for kite-flying, swimming, sunbathing, surf fishing, bird-watching, and other beach-related activities. Stay here long enough and you might just feel the urge to take a stroll through the soft, somewhat white sand, perhaps to the southern end of San Felipe and beyond.

RV sites, facilities: This large campground offers numerous RV and tent sites, each of which is sheltered by a shady *palapa*. Small RVs can park beside the *palapas,* while midsized motor homes and trailers (up to 30 feet/9.1 meters long) can park behind them. Besides the primitive beachfront camping, the only other amenities include flush toilets, hot showers, a resident manager, and, of course, El Sol Restaurant & Bar, which serves authentic Mexican cuisine, from taquitos to enchiladas. Just remember that the restaurant is closed on Monday and Tuesday.

Only self-contained RVs and rugged tent campers should stay here, preferably in pairs or groups, as there's no drinking water, dump station, electricity, or official security. There is also no laundry on-site. Make sure that you're equipped with shovels, boards, rope, and other tools in case your wheels get stuck in the sand. Children and pets are welcome, though the facilities are not wheelchair-accessible. Stop in San Felipe for food, water, fuel, and other supplies, as there are no major stores nearby. Remember to pack out all trash when you leave.

Reservations, fees: Reservations are not accepted; spaces are available on a first-come, first-served basis. Sites cost $10–15 per night, for RVs or tents. There is a nominal fee for use of the showers. Credit cards are not accepted; cash (Mexican pesos or U.S. dollars) is the only acceptable form of payment. The restaurant, beach, and campground are open all year.

Directions: From San Felipe, drive 4.5 miles (7.2 km) north on Highway 5 to Km 183. Turn right (east) onto the signed entrance road and drive 1.2 miles (1.9 km) to Playas del Sol. From Mexicali, drive about 113.6 miles (182.8 km) on Highway 5, to the turnoff for Playas del Sol.

Contact: Playas del Sol, Apartado Postal #128, San Felipe, Baja California, Mexico, tel. 686/576-0282 or 686/576-0292, playasol@telnor.net.

13 MARCO'S RV PARK

Scenic Rating: 6

in San Felipe

See map page 90

San Felipe, Baja California's "shrimp capital" and home of the annual Feria del Camarón (Shrimp Festival) each November, is a laid-back town beside the majestic Sea of Cortez. Despite the fact that it lies along the northeastern coast of the Baja peninsula—and, therefore, away from the heavily visited tourist corridor between Tijuana and Ensenada—San Felipe is still a popular spot among American vacationers and other foreign visitors. Unfortunately, such popularity has resulted in a development boom in recent years, turning parks once friendly to RVers into private resort communities. Luckily, some RV parks remain, including Marco's near the town's northern border.

Although the campground doesn't sit directly on the beach, it's just across the street from the sand and sea. So, not only are you close to heart-pumping activities like swimming, hiking, sportfishing, kayaking, and windsurfing, you're also close to downtown San Felipe, where you can stroll along the scenic *malecón,* procure supplies in various *mercados* and *panaderías,* and browse through a few small shops, including The People's Gallery on Avenida Mar de Cortez, which displays handcrafted furniture, masks, paintings, and jewelry.

Because of its convenient, semiprivate location, many visitors favor this park. So, even though most RV and tent campers prefer staying right next to the beach, in plain view of the gulf, you should be prepared for a fairly full campground most of the time.

RV sites, facilities: The park has 20 full-hookup, back-in RV sites around its perimeter. All the spaces have 15-amp power, water service, sewer access, leveled concrete pads, picnic tables, shady *palapas,* and a little shrubbery, which allows for limited privacy. Although there's plenty of room in the middle of the park, the sloping terrain and somewhat short spaces make it difficult for lengthy rigs (over 30 feet/9.1 meters long) to maneuver here. On-site amenities include a small meeting room with a library and a sundeck; clean, well-maintained restrooms with flush toilets and hot showers; and easy access to the beach. There is no dump station or laundry, and the staff does not speak English. Children and pets are allowed in the park, though tent campers are prohibited. Stores, restaurants, banks, gas stations, laundry facilities, and medical offices are within walking distance.

Reservations, fees: Reservations are accepted. Sites typically cost $10–15 per night, though rates are higher for waterfront sites and during holiday weekends. Weekly and monthly rates are available. Credit cards are not accepted; cash (Mexican pesos or U.S. dollars) is the only acceptable form of payment. The park is open all year.

Directions: From Mexicali, head south on Highway 5. When you reach the *glorieta* (traffic circle) at the entrance to San Felipe, head left (northeast) on Avenida Mar Caribe. After about 0.8 mile (1.3 km), the road will curve to the right, toward Bahía San Felipe. Drive another 0.2 mile (0.3 km) to a T junction, turn left onto Avenida Golfo de California, and look for the park entrance on the left. From Puertecitos, drive north on Highway 5 to the *glorieta* in San Felipe and follow the above directions.

Contact: Marco's RV Park, Avenida Golfo de California #788, San Felipe, Baja California, Mexico, tel. 686/577-1875. For more information about The People's Gallery, call 686/577-2898.

14 PLAYA BONITA RV PARK

Scenic Rating: 8

in San Felipe

See map page 90

Located across the street from Marco's, this beachfront campground sits amid a condominium development, beside a pleasant beach and a secluded cove. Although the condos are the management's primary focus, the small campground is neat, clean, and ideal for beach lovers. After all, swimming, sunbathing, snorkeling, waterskiing, surf fishing, windsurfing, volleyball, and other sunny diversions are only a few steps away. Hiking, horseback riding, birdwatching, and kite-flying are also possible along this extensive beach, and the sunrises here are exquisite. The only thing to bear in mind is the weather—although you can expect sunshine all year long, you can also anticipate up to 110°F (43.3°C) in July and August. So, bring along lots of water.

RV sites, facilities: The park has 32 campsites, equipped with concrete pads, shady *palapas,* and picnic tables. Most of the sites have full hookups, including 15-amp electricity, water service, and sewer access. The spaces can accommodate tents, vans, and small motor homes and trailers (up to 30 feet/9.1 meters long). On-site amenities include furnished condominiums; secured parking; a coin laundry; older restrooms with flush toilets and lukewarm showers; cool palm trees and inviting benches on a waterfront patio; and easy access to the beach. The park is secured by gates, a resident manager, and a 24-hour, English-speaking staff. There is no dump station on the premises. Children and pets are allowed in the park, though pets are prohibited in the condos. Stores, restaurants, banks, gas stations, and medical offices are within walking distance.

Reservations, fees: Reservations are accepted. Tent and RV sites typically cost $10–25 per night during the winter, $35–40 per night in summer, and $40–45 per night during holidays and special events. Certain spaces cost $5 more per night for motor homes. Long-term rates, condo rentals, and boat/trailer storage are also available. Credit cards are not accepted; cash (Mexican pesos or U.S. dollars) is the only acceptable form of payment. The park is open all year.

Directions: From Mexicali, head south on Highway 5. When you reach the *glorieta* (traffic circle) at the entrance to San Felipe, head left (northeast) on Avenida Mar Caribe. After about 0.8 mile (1.3 km), the road will curve to the right, toward Bahía San Felipe. Drive another 0.2 mile (0.3 km) to a T junction, turn left onto Avenida Golfo de California, and look for the park entrance on the right, directly across from Marco's RV Park. From Puertecitos, drive north on Highway 5 to the *glorieta* in San Felipe and follow the above directions.

Contact: Playa Bonita RV Park, 475 East Badillo Street, Covina, CA 91723, tel. 686/577-1215 (Mexico) or 626/967-8977 (U.S.), www.sanfelipebeachcondos.com.

15 KIKI'S RV CAMPING & MOTEL

Scenic Rating: 7

in San Felipe

See map page 90

As the relatively new sign indicates, this campground is actually part of the old Ruben's RV Park, a popular beachfront spot for years. In fact, a fence now divides the property into two halves. Apparently, Kiki, Ruben's cousin, owns and operates the northern half. On crowded weekends, especially during Mexican holidays, the double-decker *palapas* and numerous vehicles give this campground the air of a parking garage, the kind you might see alongside an apartment complex. If you're not a fan of noise and activity, you might want to try alternative campsites along the coast of Bahía San Felipe. But, for many repeat visitors, this festive home-away-from-home has no peer, especially with an expansive beach and warm waters so close, perfect for swimming, snorkeling, kayaking, windsurfing, boating, and other sunny diversions.

RV sites, facilities: The beachside campground has 30 full-hookup sites, a mix of back-ins and pull-throughs, with 15-amp electricity, water service, and sewer access. Each site has a two-story *palapa,* which provides shade for tents and nice ocean views from the covered upper deck. Small RVs (under 30 feet/9.1 meters long) can park between the *palapas.* It would be difficult for longer RVs to negotiate this cramped park. Tent camping is also allowed on the adjacent beach. On-site amenities include a small store; an ice machine and public pay phone; clean motel rooms (with full bathrooms and air-conditioning); restrooms with hot showers; and easy access to the beach. Although the property also houses a restaurant, it's usually closed these days, due to a family feud. The park staff offers limited security. There is no dump station or laundry on the premises, and the motel bathrooms and two-story *palapas* were not designed with wheelchairs in mind. Children and pets are allowed in the park. Stores, restaurants, banks, gas stations, laundry facilities, and medical offices are within walking distance.

Reservations, fees: Reservations are accepted. Tent and RV sites typically cost $20 per night, with rates higher during holidays. Clean, air-conditioned motel rooms are also available. Credit cards are not accepted; cash (Mexican pesos or U.S. dollars) is the only acceptable form of payment. The park is open all year.

Directions: From Mexicali, head south on Highway 5. When you reach the *glorieta* (traffic circle) at the entrance to San Felipe, head left (northeast) on Avenida Mar Caribe. After about 0.8 mile (1.3 km), the road will curve to the right, toward Bahía San Felipe. Drive another 0.2 mile (0.3 km) to a T junction, turn left onto Avenida Golfo de California, and look for the park entrance on the right, just south of Playa Bonita RV Park. From Puertecitos, drive north on Highway 5 to the *glorieta* in San Felipe and follow the above directions.

Contact: Kiki's RV Camping & Motel, Apartado Postal #59, Avenida Golfo de California #703, San Felipe, Baja California, Mexico, tel./fax 686/577-2021, www.kiki.com.mx.

16 RUBEN'S RV PARK

Scenic Rating: 6

in San Felipe

See map page 90

A longtime favorite, Ruben's RV Park once comprised a motel, restaurant, and campground, all of which have been extremely popular with American tourists and Mexicans on vacation. A few years ago, however, the property was divided by a fence, leaving only the southern half in Ruben's hands. The northern half, meanwhile, which includes the motel and part of the campground, is now owned and operated by Ruben's cousin, Kiki. Sadly, there has been so much disagreement between family members that the once-festive restaurant is usually closed nowadays.

Nonetheless, Ruben's RV Park offers a convenient spot for tent and RV campers alike. Situated beside a wide beach and not far from the Sea of Cortez, the campground is ideally positioned for outdoor enthusiasts, from hikers and bird-watchers to swimmers and sea kayakers. Fishing, windsurfing, and sunbathing are popular options, too. Like adjacent Kiki's, the campground is often crowded and boisterous, especially during Mexican holidays. The sight of numerous RVs and other vehicles parked amid the two-story *palapas* displeases some travelers. After all, despite the obvious beauty of the nearby ocean, the campground often has the air of an overcrowded parking garage.

RV sites, facilities: The beachside campground has 20 full-hookup sites, with 15-amp electricity, water service, and sewer access. Each site has a two-story *palapa,* which provides shade for tents and nice ocean views from the covered upper deck. Small RVs (under 30 feet/9.1 meters long) can park between the *palapas.* It would be difficult for longer RVs to negotiate this cramped park. Tent camping is also allowed on the adjacent beach. Besides easy access to the shore, other amenities consist of a public pay phone; restrooms with hot showers; and the facilities at adjacent Kiki's, including a small store, an ice machine, clean motel rooms (with full bathrooms and air-conditioning), and a restaurant that is often closed. The park staff offers limited security, though little English is spoken here. There is no dump station or laundry on the premises, and the two-story *palapas* were not designed with wheelchairs in mind. Children and pets are allowed in the park. Stores, restaurants, banks, gas stations, laundry facilities, and medical offices are within walking distance.

Reservations, fees: Reservations are not accepted; spaces are available on a first-come, first-served basis. Tent and RV sites typically cost $20 per night, with rates higher during holidays. Credit cards are not accepted; cash (Mexican pesos or U.S. dollars) is the only acceptable form of payment. The park is open all year.

Directions: From Mexicali, head south on Highway 5. When you reach the *glorieta* (traffic circle) at the entrance to San Felipe, head left (northeast) on Avenida Mar Caribe. After about 0.8 mile (1.3 km), the road will curve to the right, toward Bahía San Felipe. Drive another 0.2 mile (0.3 km) to a T junction, turn left onto Avenida Golfo de California, and look for the park entrance on the right, just south of Kiki's. From Puertecitos, drive north on Highway 5 to the *glorieta* in San Felipe and follow the above directions.

Contact: Ruben's RV Park, Apartado Postal #59, Avenida Golfo de California #703, San Felipe, Baja California, Mexico. Since there's no phone number, you should probably just stop by and see if any spots are available.

17 CAMPO LA PALAPA

Scenic Rating: 7

in San Felipe

See map page 90

If you like hot weather, then you will relish this modest beachfront campground during the height of summer. For milder temperatures, visit in spring, autumn, and winter. No matter when you come, however, you'll be treated to a pleasant hideaway beside the magnificent Sea of Cortez. Also called Josefina's RV Park and La Palapa RV Camp at one time or another, this park shares much in common with Kiki's and Ruben's next door, including the presence of double-decker *palapas* and quick access to an expansive, sandy beach. Of course, it tends to be somewhat quieter than its boisterous neighbors. Visitors pursue a wide array of diversions along this coast, from mountain biking and horseback riding to swimming and windsurfing.

RV sites, facilities: This beachfront campground offers 22 full-hookup sites, with 15/30-amp electricity, water service, sewer access, concrete pads, picnic tables, and two-story *palapas* (with helpful ladders) that provide shade and ocean views. Tents can be set up beneath the *palapas.* Vans and small RVs (under 30 feet/9.1 meters long) can park between them. It would be difficult for longer RVs to negotiate this cramped park, and the spots are simply too short to accommodate such big rigs. Besides easy access to the beach, on-site amenities include a small store, a public pay phone, and poorly maintained restrooms with flush toilets and hot showers. A resident manager and an entrance gate provide limited security. The staff speaks little English, and there is no dump station or laundry on the premises. Unfortunately, the two-story *palapas* were not designed with wheelchairs in mind. Children and pets are allowed in the park. Stores, restaurants, banks, gas stations, laundry facilities, and medical offices are within walking distance.

Reservations, fees: Reservations are not accepted; spaces are available on a first-come, first-served basis. RV and tent sites cost $10–15 per night. Rates are higher for waterfront sites and holiday weekends. Credit cards are not accepted; cash (Mexican pesos or U.S. dollars) is the only acceptable form of payment. The campground is open all year.

Directions: From Mexicali, head south on Highway 5. When you reach the *glorieta* (traffic circle) at the entrance to San Felipe, head left (northeast) on Avenida Mar Caribe. After about 0.8 mile (1.3 km), the road will curve to the right, toward Bahía San Felipe. Drive another 0.2 mile (0.3 km) to a T junction, turn left onto Avenida Golfo de California, and look for the small sign immediately on your right. From Puertecitos, drive north on Highway 5 to the *glorieta* in San Felipe and follow the above directions.

Contact: Since there's no official contact person, mailing address, or phone number for Campo La Palapa, it's best just to drive toward the campground and see which spots are available.

18 VISTA DEL MAR RV PARK

Scenic Rating: 7

in San Felipe

See map page 90

Situated beside a baseball field, this sloping park might not be located directly on the beach, but it still offers pleasant views of the gulf to the east and the hills to the north. It's also within easy walking distance of the coast as well as downtown San Felipe. Although staying beside the Sea of Cortez is the desire of most visitors who come to this area, the park is preferred by those who appreciate its manicured grounds, clean facilities, handsome red brick roadways, and peaceful ambience, a result of being a short distance from the beachside campgrounds that are favored by party-goers. It's an ideal location, in fact—quiet when quiet matters, while still being just a short stroll from the bars, restaurants, and shops that line Avenida Mar Caribe, Avenida Mar de Cortez, and the *malecón*. Sadly, however, it often suffers from a lack of patronage. In fact, it occasionally closes during particularly slow periods.

RV sites, facilities: This well-maintained park offers 21 back-in sites on both sides of an inclined lot. The spaces have full hookups (water, sewer, and 15/30-amp power), concrete pads, barbecue pits, picnic tables, and tile-roofed patios. It would be difficult for longer RVs (over 30 feet/9.1 meters long) to negotiate the short, though level, spaces. On-site amenities include shady palm trees, a communal barbecue area, and clean restrooms with flush toilets and hot showers. A resident manager and an entrance gate provide limited security. There is no laundry or dump station on the premises. Children, pets, and tent campers are allowed in the park. Stores, restaurants, banks, gas stations, medical offices, laundry facilities, and the beach are within walking distance.

Reservations, fees: Reservations are accepted. RV and tent sites cost $10–15 per night. Rates are higher during holiday weekends. Credit cards are not accepted; cash (Mexican pesos or U.S. dollars) is the only acceptable form of payment. The park is open all year, although it occasionally closes when visitation is low.

Directions: From Mexicali, head south on Highway 5. When you reach the *glorieta* (traffic circle) at the entrance to San Felipe, head left (northeast) on Avenida Mar Caribe. After about 0.8 mile (1.3 km), the road will curve to the right, toward Bahía San Felipe. Drive another 0.1 mile (0.2 km) to Avenida Mar de Cortez and turn right. The Vista del Mar RV Park is on the left side of the road, between the baseball field and Avenida Puerto Vallarta. From Puertecitos, drive north on Highway 5 to the *glorieta* in San Felipe and follow the above directions.

Contact: Vista del Mar RV Park, Avenida Mar de Cortez #601, San Felipe, Baja California, Mexico, tel. 686/577-1252.

19 CAMPO POSADA DEL MAR

Scenic Rating: 6

in San Felipe

See map page 90

Despite the fact that this long-standing campground is larger than many others in this area, few tourists seem to favor it above the rest. Nestled between two city streets north of downtown San Felipe, this park isn't perched directly on the beach, which is what most visitors prefer. Still, it has the same cool double-decker *palapas* that Kiki's, Ruben's, and Campo La Palapa have, and it's within walking or biking distance of all that San Felipe has to offer—the beach, the lighthouse, the *malecón,* and a number of cantinas, restaurants, markets, and shops.

RV sites, facilities: This campground offers 65 full-hookup sites with low-amp power, water service, sewer access, two-story *palapas,* concrete pads, picnic tables, barbecue pits, and shady trees. The small spaces are suitable for vans, tent campers, and short motor homes and trailers (under 30 feet/9.1 meters long). Amenities include a few motel rooms as well as some poorly maintained restrooms with flush toilets and hot showers. A resident manager and an entrance gate provide limited security. There is no laundry or dump station on the premises, and the two-story *palapas* were not designed with wheelchairs in mind. Children and pets are allowed in the park. Stores, restaurants, banks, gas stations, medical offices, laundry facilities, and the beach are within walking distance.

Reservations, fees: Reservations are accepted. RV and tent sites cost $10–20 per night. Rates are higher during holiday weekends. Credit cards are not accepted; cash (Mexican pesos or U.S. dollars) is the only acceptable form of payment. The campground is open all year.

Directions: From Mexicali, head south on Highway 5. When you reach the *glorieta* (traffic circle) at the entrance to San Felipe, head left (northeast) on Avenida Mar Caribe. After about 0.8 mile (1.3 km), the road will curve to the right, toward Bahía San Felipe. Drive another 0.2 mile (0.3 km) to a T junction, turn right onto Avenida Golfo de California, and look for the park entrance on your right, 0.3 mile (0.5 km) from the turn. From Puertecitos, drive north on Highway 5 to the *glorieta* in San Felipe and follow the above directions.

Contact: Campo Posada del Mar, Avenida Golfo de California #555, San Felipe, Baja California, Mexico, tel. 686/577-1543.

20 CAMPO SAN FELIPE

Scenic Rating: 7

in San Felipe

See map page 90

Located beside the Costa Azul Hotel, which offers six rooms with complete bathrooms, this modest, seaside campground promises views of the gorgeous Sea of Cortez, easy access to the beach, and a short walk to San Felipe's quaint shops and restaurants—and it delivers on all counts. Arranged in several neat rows, parallel to the spacious beach, the RV sites are relatively comfortable, though the small park makes it difficult to maneuver lengthy motor homes and travel trailers.

Be aware, too, that the campground is fairly popular, having served as a tourist haven for many years. Its friendly vibe and proximity to everything guarantee repeat visitors, so reservations might be necessary, especially during holiday weekends and the milder winter months.

RV sites, facilities: There are 34 full-hookup sites, all with 30-amp outlets, sewer access, water service, concrete patios, picnic tables, and shady *palapas*. Most are pull-through sites, but the tight streets make it difficult to accommodate RVs longer than 35 feet (10.7 meters). Additionally, there are five smaller spaces, equipped with sewage drains and water faucets only. Other on-site amenities include clean restrooms with flush toilets and hot showers; a public pay phone; a dump station; a coin laundry; a recreation room; Internet access; and English-speaking staff members. A resident manager provides limited security. Children, pets, and tent campers are welcome. Markets, restaurants, fish taco stands, gasoline stations, and medical offices are available in downtown San Felipe.

Reservations, fees: Given the park's moderate size, reservations are recommended. RV sites typically cost $20–25 per night. Tent camping costs $10–15 per night. Note that waterfront sites and holiday weekends will usually warrant higher rates than inland spots and off-seasons. The rates are set for double occupancy, so each extra guest will be charged $2 per day. Weekly and monthly rates are also available. Credit cards are not accepted; cash (Mexican pesos or U.S. dollars) is the customary form of payment. The park is open all year.

Directions: From Mexicali, head south on Highway 5. When you reach the *glorieta* (traffic circle) at the entrance to San Felipe, turn right onto Avenida Mar Caribe (toward the airport), drive three blocks, and turn left onto Avenida Manzanillo. Descend toward the beach and turn right at the T junction, onto Avenida Mar de Cortez. The campground is on the left (east) side of the street, just past the Costa Azul Hotel. From Puertecitos, drive north on Highway 5 to Avenida Manzanillo, turn right, and follow the above directions.

Contact: Campo San Felipe, Avenida Mar de Cortez #301, San Felipe, Baja California, Mexico, tel. 686/577-1012, www.camposanfelipe.com.

21 PLAYA DE LAURA RV PARK

Scenic Rating: 7

in San Felipe

See map page 90

Nestled between Campo San Felipe and Campo Turístico Bajamar, this is one of the closest parks to downtown San Felipe. Although this old park is not as well maintained as its neighbors, it's literally just a stroll away from restaurants, stores, the often-photographed lighthouse, and the pleasant *malecón*. Of course, being next to the popular beach that lines Bahía San Felipe, it can also be too crowded and rowdy for some visitors, especially during American and Mexican holidays. Luckily, despite massive changes to San Felipe's RV situation in recent years, the seaside town still offers several camping options. So, if this park is too festive for you, you're sure to find a more serene choice farther north or south along the coast. Popular diversions include hiking, swimming, windsurfing, kayaking, kite-flying, bird-watching, and fishing, whether from the shore or a small boat, which can be launched across the sand.

RV sites, facilities: The park has 43 sites, arranged in parallel rows that face the beach. All the spaces have 15-amp outlets, water hookups, concrete pads, picnic tables, barbecue pits, and two-story *palapas* that provide shade down below and ocean views up above. Some of the sites have sewer access. Some are pull-through sites, with room for motor homes and travel trailers up to 35 feet (10.7 meters) long, though the cramped park allows limited space for maneuvering vehicles of any size. Other amenities include older restrooms with flush toilets and hot showers; a dump station; an ice machine; a public pay phone; and quick access to the beach. There is, however, no laundry on-site, and the two-story *palapas* were not designed

the lighthouse in San Felipe

with wheelchairs in mind. The fact that the park is often full promises limited security, but as always, you should keep watch over your belongings. Children, pets, and tent campers are welcome. Laundry facilities, small markets, restaurants, fish taco stands, medical services, and gasoline stations are available in downtown San Felipe.

Reservations, fees: Given the park's moderate size, reservations are recommended. Sites on the beach typically cost $26 per night, while sites away from the beach cost $20 per night. Note that holiday weekends will usually warrant higher rates than off-seasons. The rates are set for double occupancy, so each extra guest will be charged $4 per day. Weekly and monthly rates are also available. Credit cards are not accepted; cash (Mexican pesos or U.S. dollars) is the only acceptable form of payment. The park is open all year.

Directions: From Mexicali, head south on Highway 5. When you reach the *glorieta* (traffic circle) at the entrance to San Felipe, turn right onto Avenida Mar Caribe (toward the airport), drive three blocks, and turn left onto Avenida Manzanillo. Descend toward the beach and turn right at the T junction, onto Avenida Mar de Cortez. The campground is on the left (east) side of the street, just past Campo San Felipe. From Puertecitos, drive north on Highway 5 to Avenida Manzanillo, turn right, and follow the above directions.

Contact: Playa de Laura RV Park, Avenida Mar de Cortez #333, San Felipe, Baja California, Mexico, tel. 686/577-1128, tel./fax 686/554-4712 (Mexicali), or P.O. Box 686, Calexico, CA 92232, hernanh@telnor.net.

22 CAMPO TURÍSTICO BAJAMAR

Scenic Rating: 8

in San Felipe

See map page 90

Far from the bustling tourist corridor that lies along Baja's Pacific coast, San Felipe still lures its share of American visitors and other foreign tourists. While this quintessentially laid-back coastal town offers convenient access to wide, sandy beaches—ideal for swimmers, kayakers, windsurfers, anglers, hikers, and other outdoor enthusiasts—it's also a quaint, festive place to experience a dose of Mexican culture. Every season, with festivals and holiday events, the town celebrates some aspect of the country's spirit, from tequila to shrimp to Catholicism. And this particular campground, situated beside the beach and close to downtown San Felipe, is one of the newest and least crowded in town—and a pleasant place to stay for a night, a week, or infinitely longer.

RV sites, facilities: This beachfront campground has 60 large back-in sites with full hookups, including water service, sewer access, and 15-amp outlets with 30-amp breakers. In addition, all of the gravel sites have patios, picnic tables, and barbecue pits. Some even sport shady *palapas.* Accessible via paved roads with curbs, the spaces can accommodate tents, vans, and large RVs (up to 40 feet/12.2 meters long). Other amenities include poorly maintained restrooms with flush toilets and hot showers; a coin laundry; a dump station; an ice machine; a children's playground; a large waterfront patio; some small tables shaded by umbrellas; and quick access to the beach as well as downtown San Felipe. A resident manager provides limited security. Children and pets are welcome. Markets, restaurants, fish taco stands, gasoline stations, and medical offices are available in downtown San Felipe.

Reservations, fees: Reservations are not accepted; spaces are available on a first-come, first-served basis. RV and tent sites cost $15–20 per night. Rates are higher for beachfront sites and holiday weekends. Weekly and monthly rates are also available. Credit cards are not accepted; cash (Mexican pesos or U.S. dollars) is the only acceptable form of payment. The campground is open all year.

Directions: From Mexicali, head south on Highway 5. When you reach the *glorieta* (traffic circle) at the entrance to San Felipe, turn right onto Avenida Mar Caribe (toward the airport), drive three blocks, and turn left onto Avenida Manzanillo. Descend toward the beach and turn right at the T junction, onto Avenida Mar de Cortez. The campground is on the left (east) side of the street, just south of Playa de Laura RV Park. From Puertecitos, drive north on Highway 5 to Avenida Manzanillo, turn right, and follow the above directions.

Contact: Campo Turístico Bajamar, Avenida Mar de Cortez, San Felipe, Baja California, Mexico, or Avenida Madero #702, Zona Centro, Mexicali, Baja California, C.P. 21100, Mexico. Since there's no phone number for this campground, it's probably best to drive down and see which spots are available.

23 VICTOR'S RV PARK

Scenic Rating: 6

in San Felipe

See map page 90

Operated by the nearby Hotel El Cortez, this popular, long-standing park sits amid a row of beachfront campgrounds in the southern part of San Felipe. As with most of the town's RV accommodations, Victor's provides convenient access, whether by foot or by bicycle, to numerous downtown businesses, landmarks like the Virgin of Guadalupe Shrine, and, of course, all manner of wide, sandy beaches. So, whether you're a fan of traditional *panaderías,* Mexican fiestas, or outdoor pleasures, from riding dune buggies and all-terrain vehicles on the beach to deep-sea fishing in the gulf, this isn't a bad place to stay for a while. Besides the severely hot summers (from which all San Felipe–area parks suffer), the only potential downsides to this well-maintained park are its inability to accommodate lengthy RVs and its popularity. Not only does it fill up quickly during holidays, it also attracts permanent tenants and long-term RVs, lending it a more residential air than other seaside spots.

RV sites, facilities: This beachfront park offers 50 pull-through sites, about 40 percent of which are usually available for temporary vacationers. All the spaces have full hookups, including 30-amp electricity, and covered patios. The spaces can accommodate tents, vans, and, in some cases, lengthy RVs (up to 35 feet/10.7 meters long). Other amenities include clean restrooms with flush toilets and hot showers; a meeting room; a coin laundry; and quick access to the beach. The adjacent motel has a swimming pool and a restaurant, both of which the RV and tent campers can use. A perimeter fence and resident manager provide limited security. There is no dump station, and the motel staff speaks limited English. Children and pets are welcome. Markets, restaurants, fish taco stands, gasoline stations, and medical offices are available in downtown San Felipe.

Reservations, fees: Reservations are not accepted; spaces are available on a first-come, first-served basis. RV and tent sites cost $15–20 per night. Rates are higher for beachfront sites and holiday weekends. Weekly, monthly, and annual rates are also available. Credit cards are not accepted; cash (Mexican pesos or U.S. dollars) is the only acceptable form of payment. The campground is open all year.

Directions: From Mexicali, head south on Highway 5. When you reach the *glorieta* (traffic circle) at the entrance to San Felipe, turn right onto Avenida Mar Caribe (toward the airport), drive three blocks, and turn left onto Avenida Manzanillo. Descend toward the beach and turn right at the T junction, onto Avenida Mar de Cortez. The campground is on the left (east) side of the street, just south of Campo Turístico Bajamar. From Puertecitos, drive north on Highway 5 to Avenida Manzanillo, turn right, and follow the above directions.

Contact: Victor's RV Park, c/o Hotel El Cortez, P.O. Box 1227, Calexico, CA 92232, tel. 686/577-1055 (Mexico) or 686/577-1056 (Mexico), fax 686/577-1752 (Mexico), cortezho@telnor.net.

24 CLUB DE PESCA RV PARK

Scenic Rating: 7

in San Felipe

See map page 90 **BEST**

An old favorite among foreign travelers, this RV park is located on the southern end of town, within walking distance of San Felipe's markets, bars, and restaurants as well as the beach. As with many of the area's other campgrounds, its drawbacks include unbearably hot summers, an inability to accommodate lengthy RVs, and the potential to fill up quickly, especially during holiday weekends. In addition, the park seems to cater more to permanent mobile home residents and less to vacationing RVers.

Situated at the end of Avenida Mar de Cortez, this is the last San Felipe–area campground you'll encounter prior to heading south toward Puertecitos and Bahía San Luis Gonzaga. It's also the closest campground to San Felipe's harbor, where visitors can launch their own boats for free. From here, you can embark upon deep-sea fishing excursions through Tony Reyes Fishing Tours, a knowledgeable charter-boat operation that's been leading fruitful weeklong fishing tours along the coastline and to the islands of the Sea of Cortez since 1987. There's even a flesh-toned statue of Tony Reyes, the company's founder and a Baja fishing legend, along San Felipe's *malecón.*

RV sites, facilities: This beachfront park offers 54 sites in all. Along the beach, there are 32 spots with 30-amp electricity, water service, concrete pads, shady *palapas,* and room for tents, vans, and smaller RVs. The other 22 sites, situated at the rear of the park, have 15-amp outlets, water service, sewer hookups, and more room for larger motor homes and travel trailers (perhaps up to 45 feet/13.7 meters long). Some of these sites are occupied by permanent residents. Amenities include tidy, clean restrooms with flush toilets and hot showers; a dump station; a recreation room (with a ping-pong table); a mini-market, a public pay phone; an inexpensive boat launch; limited security; and easy access to the beach as well as downtown San Felipe. There is no laundry on the premises. Children and pets are welcome. Laundry facilities, markets, restaurants, fish taco stands, gasoline stations, and medical offices lie within walking or cycling distance.

Reservations, fees: Reservations are accepted. RV and tent sites cost $15–20 per night. Rates are higher for beachfront sites and holiday weekends. Weekly, monthly, and annual rates are also available. Credit cards are not accepted; cash (Mexican pesos or U.S. dollars) is the customary form of payment. The campground is open all year.

Directions: From Mexicali, head south on Highway 5. When you reach the *glorieta* (traffic circle) at the entrance to San Felipe, turn right onto Avenida Mar Caribe (toward the airport), drive three blocks, and turn left onto Avenida Manzanillo. Descend toward the beach and turn right at the T junction, onto Avenida Mar de Cortez. The campground lies at the end of the road, on the left (east) side, just south of Victor's RV Park. From Puertecitos, drive north on Highway 5 to Avenida Manzanillo, turn right, and follow the above directions.

Contact: Club de Pesca RV Park, P.O. Box 3090, Calexico, CA 92232, tel. 686/577-1180 (Mexico), fax 686/577-1888 (Mexico), clubdepescasf@yahoo.com. For more information about Tony Reyes Fishing Tours, visit www.tonyreyes.com or contact The Longfin, 2730 East Chapman Avenue, Orange, CA 92869, tel. 714/538-9300 (U.S.) or 714/538-8010 (U.S.), longfin123@aol.com.

25 CAMPO SAN FERNANDO

Scenic Rating: 6

southeast of San Felipe

See map page 90

Perched upon a bluff above the Sea of Cortez, this formerly bustling campground offers a spectacular view of the gulf. Beyond the vista, however, there's little else to recommend this humble spot, which is poorly maintained nowadays and frequently unattended. Located a few miles south of the San Felipe Marina Resort & Spa and a few miles north of the Las Conchas del Mar development—two more places that have discontinued overnight RV parking to clear the way for beachside villas and condominiums—this spot is little more than a place to stop for the night. In fact, given its diminishing status in recent years and the prevalence of real-estate developments in the region, it's highly probable that, by the time you reach this part of Baja, it will no longer be open to visitors. Of course, it could just as easily be purchased and redeveloped into a sparkling RV resort again. Simply consult local residents before deciding to stay here.

RV sites, facilities: This beachfront campground offers 20 primitive sites, some of which are occupied by permanent trailers. Although the sites have full hookups, only the sewage has been accessible lately. The spaces can accommodate tents, vans, and small RVs (under 30 feet/9.1 meters long). Save for flush toilets, cold showers, and easy access to the beach, this campground no longer offers much in the way of amenities. Only self-contained RVs and rugged tent campers should park here, preferably in pairs or groups, as there's no drinking water, dump station, electricity, or security available. There is also no laundry on the premises, and the terrain is not suitable for wheelchairs. Children and pets are welcome. Since there are no stores within walking distance, it's best to pick up groceries, purified water, gasoline, and other necessities in San Felipe to the north. Remember to pack out all trash when you leave.

Reservations, fees: Reservations are accepted. RV and tent sites cost $10–15 per night. Weekly, monthly, and annual rates have been available in the past. Credit cards are not accepted; cash (Mexican pesos or U.S. dollars) is the customary form of payment. For now, the campground appears to be open all year.

Directions: From Mexicali, drive south on Highway 5. At the *glorieta* (traffic circle) near the entrance to San Felipe, turn right onto Avenida Mar Caribe/Highway 5 (toward the airport) and head south for 6.3 miles (10.1 km) to the airport road. Veer to the left, continue on Highway 5 for another 3.5 miles (5.6 km), and watch for the sign for Campo San Fernando. Turn left (east) onto the dirt road that leads toward the campground. From Puertecitos, drive north on Highway 5 for about 44 miles (70.8 km) and turn right onto the entrance road.

Contact: Campo San Fernando, P.O. Box 23, Calexico, CA 92232. Since there's no official contact person or phone number, it's best just to drive toward the campground and see which spots are available. For more information about the San Felipe Marina Resort & Spa, visit www.sanfelipemarina.net.

26 VILLA MARINA CAMPO TURÍSTICO

Scenic Rating: 9

southeast of San Felipe

See map page 90

Roughly a mile (1.6 km) south of the former El Faro RV Park (renamed the Residence Betel II a while back and scheduled for real-estate development) lies this simple RV park, one of the most modern south of San Felipe. Although it's an easy drive to restaurants, shops, and festivals to the north, most visitors come here for the great outdoors. With the beach so close, popular diversions include swimming, kayaking, windsurfing, fishing, and other water-related diversions. Hiking, mountain biking, and exploring desert flora and fauna are also possible in the Sierra San Felipe to the west.

RV sites, facilities: This beachfront RV park offers 26 campsites on a low bluff above a pleasant beach. All sites have full hookups (including 15-amp electricity), concrete patios, picnic tables, and barbecue pits. Although you must take care in maneuvering your vehicle, many of these sites are long enough and wide enough to accommodate lengthy motor homes and travel trailers (up to 40 feet/12.2 meters long). Facilities include a community pavilion; a dump station; a laundry facility; modern restrooms with flush toilets and hot showers; a few trees; and relatively easy access to the beach. In addition, some *palapas* offer cool shade and stairways that lead to upper terraces with lovely ocean views. Only self-contained RVs and rugged tent campers should park here, preferably in pairs or groups, as there's no drinking water, dump station, or electricity available, and the security is limited to a gate and a resident guard. There is no laundry on the premises. Children and pets are welcome. Since there are no stores within walking distance, it's best to pick up groceries, purified water, gasoline, and other necessities in San Felipe to the north.

Reservations, fees: Reservations are accepted. RV and tent sites cost $15–20 per night. Weekly, monthly, and annual rates are also available. Credit cards are not accepted; cash (Mexican pesos or U.S. dollars) is the customary form of payment. The campground is open all year.

Directions: From Mexicali, drive south on Highway 5. At the *glorieta* (traffic circle) near the entrance to San Felipe, turn right onto Avenida Mar Caribe/Highway 5 (toward the airport) and head south for 6.3 miles (10.1 km) to the airport road. Veer to the left, continue on Highway 5 for another 5.4 miles (8.7 km), then turn left (east) onto the gravel road that leads for 0.3 mile (0.5 km) toward the campground. From Puertecitos, drive north on Highway 5 for about 42.1 miles (67.7 km) and turn right onto the gravel entrance road.

Contact: Villa Marina Campo Turístico, Km 8.5 de la Carretera San Felipe–Puertecitos, San Felipe, Baja California, Mexico, tel. 686/577-1342.

27 RANCHO VISTA HERMOSA

Scenic Rating: 7

southeast of San Felipe

See map page 90

Baja is a land rife with primitive, no-frills campgrounds, and as with most of those spots along this rugged peninsula, this one's natural environment is its biggest selling point. One of several inexpensive, poorly maintained *campos* and *playas* that span the coastline from north of San Felipe all the way south to Bahía San Luis Gonzaga, Rancho Vista Hermosa sits on a low bluff above a wonderful beach, which offers proximity to the diverse Sea of Cortez, a watery playground for kayakers, swimmers, scuba divers, deep-sea anglers, windsurfers, and everything in between. If you decide to come here, be prepared for extremely hot summers, alternate names for the same place (such as Quinta Playa Hermosa), maneuvering challenges in soft sand, and the possibility that an established campground like this one can be closed and redeveloped for condominiums and/or a golf course at any time.

RV sites, facilities: This small beachfront campground offers roughly 15 shady *palapas* for tent campers and small RVs (up to 25 feet/7.6 meters long). It should be noted, however, that those with four-wheel-drive pickup campers will find it easiest to park here. Given the soft sand and eroded sites, it's advisable to bring along some boards, shovels, chains, and rope in case your wheels get stuck and need to be liberated. Besides pit toilets, cold showers, and easy access to the beach, there are no official amenities on the premises. Only self-contained RVs and rugged tent campers should park here, preferably in pairs or groups, as there's no drinking water, dump station, electricity, or security available. There is also no laundry on the premises, and the facilities are not suitable for wheelchairs. Children and pets are welcome. Since there are no major stores nearby, it's best to pick up groceries, purified water, gasoline, and other necessities in San Felipe to the north. Remember to pack out all trash when you leave.

Reservations, fees: Reservations are not accepted; spaces are available on a first-come, first-served basis. The nightly rate is $10–20. Credit cards are not accepted; cash (Mexican pesos or U.S. dollars) is the customary form of payment. The campground is open all year.

Directions: From Mexicali, drive south on Highway 5. At the *glorieta* (traffic circle) near the entrance to San Felipe, turn right onto Avenida Mar Caribe/Highway 5 (toward the airport) and head south for 6.3 miles (10.1 km) to the airport road. Veer to the left, continue on Highway 5 for another 5.5 miles (8.9 km), and watch for the sign on the left, just past the Villa Marina Campo Turístico. Turn left (east) onto the gravel road and drive 0.2 mile (0.3 km) toward the campground. From Puertecitos, drive north on Highway 5 for about 42 miles (67.6 km) and turn right onto the entrance road.

Contact: Since there's no official contact person, mailing address, or phone number for Rancho Vista Hermosa, it's best just to drive toward the campground and see which spots are available.

28 PLAYA PUNTA ESTRELLA

Scenic Rating: 7

southeast of San Felipe

See map page 90 **BEST**

Along the route from San Felipe to Puertecitos, you'll encounter enormous specimens of the *cardón,* the world's largest cactus, in the aptly named Valle de los Gigantes. Not far from this intriguing sight is Playa Punta Estrella, a wide expanse of soft sand, spanning far to the north and to the south. The modest campground here offers easy access to this engaging coast, with its glorious sunrises, warm waters, and constant sea breezes—an ideal spot for any beach-related activity. The intriguing desert—attractive to hikers, naturalists, off-road enthusiasts, and wildlife lovers—isn't far to the west.

RV sites, facilities: This large beachfront campground offers 70 sites along the sand. All have shady *palapas* and light bulbs, but no hookups for RVs. Because of the soft sand between shelters, the campground is really only suitable for tent campers. RVs (perhaps up to 35 feet/10.7 meters long), however, can boondock behind the *palapas,* where the sand is harder. Amenities include ample parking; basic restrooms with flush toilets and hot showers; and access to miles of beautiful beaches and off-road courses. Only self-contained RVs and rugged tent campers should park here, preferably in pairs or groups, as there's no drinking water or dump station, and only limited security is provided by a resident manager. There is no laundry on the premises, and the terrain is not suitable for wheelchairs. Children and pets are welcome. Since there are no major stores nearby, it's best to pick up groceries, purified water, gasoline, and other necessities in San Felipe to the north.

Reservations, fees: Reservations are not accepted; spaces are available on a first-come, first-served basis. The nightly rate is $10–15. Weekly rates are also available. Credit cards are not accepted; cash (Mexican pesos or U.S. dollars) is the customary form of payment. The campground is open all year.

Directions: From Mexicali, drive south on Highway 5. At the *glorieta* (traffic circle) near the entrance to San Felipe, turn right onto Avenida Mar Caribe/Highway 5 (toward the airport) and head south for 6.3 miles (10.1 km) to the airport road. Veer to the left, continue on Highway 5 for another 7.7 miles (12.4 km), and watch for the sign on the left for Playa Punta Estrella. Turn left (east) onto the dirt road and drive 1 mile (1.6 km) toward the campground. From Puertecitos, drive north on Highway 5 for about 39.8 miles (64 km) and turn right onto the entrance road.

Contact: Playa Punta Estrella, Km 13 de la Carretera San Felipe–Puertecitos, San Felipe, Baja California, Mexico, tel. 686/565-2784 (Mexico) or 760/357-6933 (U.S.).

29 CAMPO TURÍSTICO RANCHO PERCEBÚ

Scenic Rating: 8

southeast of San Felipe

See map page 90

Despite the real-estate development trend that has, in recent years, overtaken many inexpensive *campos* along the coast, several primitive campgrounds remain between San Felipe and Bahía San Luis Gonzaga. Campo Turístico Rancho Percebú, situated beside the sheltered 3.1-mile (5-km) Estero Percebú, is one such welcoming spot. More than just a pit stop on the road from San Felipe to Puertecitos, this beachside locale offers a friendly watering hole and proximity to a relaxing white-sand beach, perfect for swimmers, kayakers, anglers, and other water lovers.

RV sites, facilities: This large beachfront campground offers plenty of room for tent and RV camping along the sand. Although there are no hookups, amenities include shady *palapas;* basic restrooms with flush toilets and hot showers; a family-owned restaurant and bar; and access to a beautiful white-sand beach beside a sheltered tidal estuary. Because of the soft sand, the campground is really only suitable for tents and four-wheel-drive vehicles. In fact, it's advisable to bring along shovels, boards, rope, and other useful tools for dislodging half-buried wheels. Only small, self-contained RVs and rugged tent campers should park here, preferably in pairs or groups, as there's no electricity, drinking water, dump station, or official security available. There is also no laundry on-site. Children and pets are welcome, but the terrain might not be suitable for wheelchairs. Since there are no major stores nearby, it's best to pick up groceries, purified water, gasoline, and other necessities in San Felipe to the north.

Reservations, fees: Reservations are not accepted; spaces are available on a first-come, first-served basis. The nightly rate is $10–15 for tent and RV camping. Credit cards are not accepted; cash (Mexican pesos or U.S. dollars) is the customary form of payment. The campground is open all year.

Directions: From Mexicali, drive south on Highway 5. At the *glorieta* (traffic circle) near the entrance to San Felipe, turn right onto Avenida Mar Caribe/Highway 5 (toward the airport) and head south for 6.3 miles (10.1 km) to the airport road. Veer to the left, continue on Highway 5 for another 12.9 miles (20.8 km), and watch for the sign on the left for Campo Turístico Rancho Percebú. Turn left (east) onto the graded dirt road and drive 2.5 miles (4 km) toward the campground. From Puertecitos, drive north on Highway 5 for about 34.6 miles (55.7 km) and turn right onto the entrance road.

Contact: Campo Turístico Rancho Percebú, Km 21 de la Carretera San Felipe–Puertecitos, San Felipe, Baja California, Mexico, tel. 686/577-1259, www.ranchopercebu.com.

30 PLAYA DESTINY

Scenic Rating: 7

north of Puertecitos

See map page 90

Now that the paving of Highway 5 has been completed, Puertecitos—the last bit of civilization that you'll encounter before the jarring road to Bahía San Luis Gonzaga—will probably experience its own wave of development soon, just as San Felipe, its neighbor to the north, has in recent years. For now, however, Puertecitos remains a fairly isolated place, defined by its brownish rough-hewn earth, its typically clear blue skies, and the aquamarine waters of the adjacent Sea of Cortez. The town is little more than a collection of rocks, trailers, decrepit houses, small shops, kayaks, and fishing boats, and it's often quiet in the spring, summer, and fall. Those who favor such desolation usually descend in the winter months, when temperatures are milder.

If you're coming from San Felipe—and, unless you have a serious four-wheel-drive vehicle, you probably will be headed from the north—you'll pass several scenic spots along the coast, such as Punta Estrella, Laguna Percebú, and Bahía Santa María, where several homes have been erected. Along the way, you might also spy a string of *campos* and *playas,* which sport names like Campo García, Punta Baja, Rancho El Zimarron, and Campo La Violeta. Over the years, these primitive spots have offered inexpensive camping, though little else. Consult local residents about the possibility of staying in such places, as private development has begun to overtake these formerly welcoming campgrounds.

Presently, Playa Destiny has resisted the pull toward development. Although there are few official amenities, you can expect year-round sunshine, starry night skies, and excellent water for wading and swimming. Hiking, mountain biking, surf fishing, kayaking, and bird-watching are also popular pastimes here. In addition, hikes into the nearby Sierra Santa Isabel can be arranged. Just be prepared for lots of neighbors and off-road vehicles during the winter months.

RV sites, facilities: There are no designated RV sites here—you can park wherever you like. Besides the nearby Sea of Cortez, however, there are few official amenities, save for basic restrooms, cold showers, sporadic palm trees, picnic tables, barbecue pits, and shady *ramadas,* beside which RVs can park. Only small, self-contained RVs and rugged tent campers should stay here, preferably in pairs or groups, as there's no drinking water, dump station, electricity, or security available. There is also no laundry on-site. Make sure that you're equipped with shovels, boards, rope, and other tools in case your wheels get stuck in the sand. Children and pets are welcome, though the facilities are not wheelchair-accessible. Stop in San Felipe for food, water, fuel, and other supplies, as there are no major stores in nearby Puertecitos. Sometimes, you can purchase soda and beer on nearby beaches. Be sure to pack out all trash when you leave.

Reservations, fees: Reservations are not accepted; spaces are available on a first-come, first-served basis. The overnight camping fee (for RVs and tents) is $15 per vehicle. Credit cards are not accepted; cash (Mexican pesos or U.S. dollars) is the only acceptable form of payment. The beach and campground are open all year.

Directions: From Puertecitos, drive north on Highway 5 for 2.4 miles (3.9 km). Turn right onto the entrance road (which lies halfway between Km 71 and Km 72) and drive 0.1 mile (0.2 km) toward the gulf. The campground is located directly on the beach. From downtown San Felipe, drive 51.4 miles (82.7 km) south on Highway 5 to the turnoff.

Contact: For limited information about Playa Destiny, visit www.puertecitos.net. Since there are few specifics at this website, it's probably best just to drive toward the campground and see which spots are available.

31 PLAYA ESCONDIDA

Scenic Rating: 8

north of Puertecitos

See map page 90

Also known as Campo Octavio, Playa Escondida (which means "Hidden Beach" in Spanish) is primitive camping at its finest. Situated on a small cove, this modest campground offers easy access to the beach, where hiking, swimming, surf fishing, kayaking, and bird-watching are popular diversions. Some pleasant hot springs lie about a mile (1.6 km) south, along the point that partially forms the bay of Puertecitos; just be advised that you can only enjoy the springs during high tide, when the cool seawater makes the super-hot pools bearable. North of Playa Escondida, you'll spy Speedy's Campo, a long-time convenience store, the owner of which has often allowed inexpensive camping on his property.

Deep-sea fishing, though, is probably the most preferred activity in this bailiwick. From Playa Escondida, anglers can often rent *pangas* for fishing excursions in the offshore waters of the bountiful Sea of Cortez. Prices are usually negotiable. Simply consult local residents to learn about any commercial fishermen and *pangueros* that might be willing to take you out for the morning or afternoon.

RV sites, facilities: There are no designated RV sites in the camping area—you can park wherever you like. Besides the nearby Sea of Cortez, however, there are few official amenities, save for pit toilets, cold showers, and *panga* charters for sportfishing. Only small, self-contained RVs and rugged tent campers should stay here, preferably in pairs or groups, as there's no drinking water, dump station, electricity, or security available. There is also no laundry on-site. Make sure that you're equipped with shovels, boards, rope, and other tools in case your wheels get stuck in the sand. Children and pets are welcome, though the facilities are not wheelchair-accessible. Stop in San Felipe for food, water, fuel, and other supplies, as there are no major stores in nearby Puertecitos. Sometimes, you can purchase soda and beer on nearby beaches. Remember to pack out all trash when you leave.

Reservations, fees: Reservations are not accepted; spaces are available on a first-come, first-served basis. The overnight camping fee (for RVs and tents) is $10–15 per vehicle. Credit cards are not accepted; cash (Mexican pesos or U.S. dollars) is the only acceptable form of payment. The beach and campground are open all year.

Directions: From Puertecitos, drive north on Highway 5 for 0.6 mile (1 km). Turn right onto the entrance road and drive 0.4 mile (0.6 km) toward the gulf. The campground lies directly on the beach. From downtown San Felipe, drive 53.2 miles (85.6 km) south on Highway 5 to the turnoff.

Contact: Since there's no official contact person, mailing address, or phone number for Playa Escondida, it's best just to drive toward the campground and see which spots are available.

32 CAMPO PUERTECITOS

Scenic Rating: 8

in Puertecitos

See map page 90

As with many places in Baja, this modest spot on the beach goes by various names, including Campo Turístico Puertecitos and the Puertecitos Campground. But whatever you call it, this primitive place offers winning views across a minute bay, to the Sea of Cortez. On the other side of the point, within walking distance of the campground, lie several natural thermal baths, bubbling up below the high-tide mark. Beyond the peak season (winter), you might be able to snag a tub for yourself. Built into the rocks, they are only pleasant at high tide, when the seawater mixes with the scalding, sulfurous springs, cooling the water to a tolerable temperature. Do not attempt to use these tubs at low tide, as you will likely burn yourself badly in the steaming water, which can reach upwards of 150°F (65.6°C).

Besides the springs, the sandy shore offers ample opportunities for beachcombing and surf fishing. Swimmers, kayakers, off-road drivers, and wildlife enthusiasts also favor this desolate region. In addition, it's possible to hike or bike through the rugged Sierra Santa Isabel to the west. Of course, most visitors come for the deep-sea fishing. Local anglers will charter their *pangas* for reasonable rates and guide you to various fishing grounds in the Sea of Cortez, including the five islands that lie 20 miles (32 km) south of town. Depending on the season, you're sure to find yellowtail, dorado, sierra, white sea bass, and other tasty varieties.

RV sites, facilities: The campground offers 14 primitive sites, each equipped with a shady *palapa,* a concrete pad, a low-amp electrical outlet, running water, a picnic table, and a barbecue pit. Other amenities include a tiny rustic hotel, a steep boat launch (suitable for large crafts), a seasonal restaurant, restrooms with cold showers, and space for boats and trailers. Only small, self-contained RVs and rugged tent campers should stay here, preferably in pairs or groups, as there's no drinking water, dump station, or security available. There is also no laundry onsite. Make sure that you're equipped with shovels, boards, rope, and other tools in case your wheels get stuck in the sand. Children and pets are welcome, though the facilities are not wheelchair-accessible. Stop in San Felipe for food, water, fuel, and other supplies, as there are no major stores in nearby Puertecitos. Sometimes, you can purchase soda and beer on nearby beaches, and occasionally gasoline is on sale here. Be sure to pack out all trash when you leave.

Reservations, fees: Reservations are not accepted; spaces are available on a first-come, first-served basis. Sites cost $20 per night, for RVs or tents. Hotel rooms are also available. To bathe in the hot springs, there is a charge of $5 per person. Credit cards are not accepted; cash (Mexican pesos or U.S. dollars) is the only acceptable form of payment. The beach and campground are open all year, though the restaurant is only open from October to April.

Directions: From downtown San Felipe, drive 53.8 miles (86.6 km) south on Highway 5 to the turnoff for Puertecitos. The campground is situated directly on the beach, in the center of this tiny village.

Contact: Since there's no official contact person, mailing address, or phone number for Campo Puertecitos, it's probably best just to drive toward the campground and see which spots are available.

33 CAMPO BAHÍA CRISTINA

Scenic Rating: 7

south of Puertecitos

See map page 90

Besides the magnificent Sea of Cortez (also known as the Golfo de California and the Mar de Cortés), this primitive spot offers little in the way of nearby attractions. Even its beach is less than stellar—a brown sandy stretch that almost matches the barren mountains in hue. Still, though it's certainly less developed than Puertecitos to the north, it isn't a bad spot to stop for the night. After all, there's a seasonal restaurant on the premises, and you'll find little else between here and Punta Bufeo, over 35 miles (56.3 km) south on a slow-going route to Bahía San Luis Gonzaga.

RV sites, facilities: This primitive campground offers several shady *palapas* and barbecue grills for both tent and RV campers. Amenities are limited to a well-favored restaurant, clean bathrooms, a small sandy beach, and lovely ocean views. Only small, self-contained RVs and rugged tent campers should stay here, preferably in pairs or groups, as there's no drinking water, dump station, electricity, or security available. There is also no laundry or shower on the premises. Make sure that you're equipped with shovels, boards, rope, and other tools in case your wheels get stuck in the sand. Children and pets are welcome, though the facilities are not wheelchair-accessible. Given the lack of stores in the area, it's advisable to pick up extra groceries, purified water, fuel, and other necessities from the stores in San Felipe to the north. Remember to pack out all trash when you leave.

Reservations, fees: Reservations are not accepted; spaces are available on a first-come, first-served basis. RV and tent sites cost around $15 per vehicle per night. Credit cards are not accepted; cash (Mexican pesos or U.S. dollars) is the customary form of payment. Although the campground is open all year, the restaurant is only open from November to June.

Directions: From Puertecitos, drive 4 miles (6.4 km) south on Highway 5 to the turnoff for Campo Bahía Cristina. The restaurant and campground lie to the left, along the coast.

Contact: Since there's no official contact person, mailing address, or phone number for Campo Bahía Cristina, it's best just to drive toward the campground and see which spots are available.

34 PAPA FERNÁNDEZ RESTAURANT AND CAMPING

Scenic Rating: 9

northwest of Bahía San Luis Gonzaga

See map page 90 **BEST**

The road from Puertecitos to Bahía San Luis Gonzaga is definitely not meant for the faint of heart. In fact, it's not intended for anything less than a four-wheel-drive vehicle. Notoriously rough and necessarily slow-going, this dirt highway will lead you past 44.9 miles (72.2 km) of desolate coastline, with views of occasional primitive campgrounds, such as Campo Bahía Cristina, and several offshore islands, like Isla Lobos and Isla San Luis.

From Playa Costilla to Punta Bufeo—a rocky resort that offers rental cabins, primitive campsites, a restaurant, and a boat anchorage—the road is in particularly poor condition. Drive with extreme caution, and expect the journey to take at least four hours. While Bahía San Luis Gonzaga boasts some spectacular views, this route should not be attempted by those with large motor homes and unwieldy travel trailers. It's better suited for RVers in pickup campers and tent enthusiasts with rugged jeeps—vehicles with sturdy, well-inflated tires and high clearance above the uneven road.

Those who do reach Bahía San Luis Gonzaga will be rewarded with a sense of accomplishment and a belief that magical hideaways still exist, even in an overdeveloped place like Baja. The bay extends from Punta Willard in the north to Punta Final in the south. Between these two points, you'll find vacation homes, tidepools, sandy beaches, primitive campgrounds, and a few establishments that cater to visitors. The Papa Fernández Restaurant is one such place.

Situated on the north side of Punta Willard

(and not on Bahía San Luis Gonzaga), this popular fish camp was founded by Gorgonio "Papa" Fernández in the 1950s, after which his family relocated here from Loreto. Since then, the family has welcomed numerous weary adventurers, including American actor John Wayne. The campground—which is popular among anglers, kayakers, sailboarders, swimmers, snorkelers, hikers, and off-road enthusiasts—faces the open sea, offering less shelter than campgrounds to the south. You'll also find strong currents here, where the sea meets the bay, between Punta Willard and Isla San Luis Gonzaga. A lovely place to watch a glorious Baja sunrise or sunset, it's also ideal for stargazers. With less than two inches of rainfall a year, this area usually has clear nighttime skies, perfect for contemplating the cosmos.

RV sites, facilities: There are several designated tent and RV sites in this beachfront campground, each of which has a shady *palapa*. Besides the nearby Sea of Cortez and the possibility of half-day sportfishing excursions, however, there are few official amenities, save for pit toilets, a hard-surface boat launch, secured parking, and a restaurant that serves beer, soda, and inexpensive, authentic Mexican fare for breakfast, lunch, and dinner. Only small, self-contained RVs and rugged tent campers should stay here, preferably in pairs or groups, as there's no drinking water, dump station, or electricity available. There is also no laundry or shower on-site. Security is good, however, as the Fernández family members that run the joint also live on the premises. Make sure that you're equipped with shovels, boards, rope, and other tools in case your wheels get stuck in the sand. Children and pets are welcome, though the facilities are not wheelchair-accessible. Stop in San Felipe for food, water, fuel, and other supplies, as there are no major stores in Puertecitos or around Bahía San Luis Gonzaga. Remember to pack out all trash when you leave.

Reservations, fees: Reservations are not accepted; spaces are available on a first-come, first-served basis. Sites cost $5 per night, for RVs or tents. Credit cards are not accepted; cash (Mexican pesos or U.S. dollars) is the only acceptable form of payment. The family-run restaurant and campground are open all year.

Directions: From Puertecitos, drive 44.9 miles (72.2 km) south on Highway 5 to the turnoff for Punta Willard. Turn left (east), drive 1.2 miles (1.9 km) to the shore, and look for the restaurant sign.

Contact: For more information about Papa Fernández Restaurant and Camping, visit www.papafernandez.com. To reach someone at Papa Fernández, it's necessary to phone Rancho Grande at 555/151-4065; the staff there will then contact Papa Fernández via marine radio.

35 CAMPO RANCHO GRANDE

Scenic Rating: 8

on Bahía San Luis Gonzaga

See map page 90

The village that sits beside the lovely Bahía San Luis Gonzaga is anchored by the roadside Rancho Grande complex, which offers the area's only grocery store. Given the lack of museums, missions, and other such cultural entities in the immediate vicinity, outdoor diversions are the name of the game here. Besides hiking in the nearby mountains and exploring the adjacent beaches, the two most popular activities are sea kayaking and sportfishing. Unfortunately, kayakers must bring their own sea-faring vessels, but it's well worth the inconvenience—the seven-day kayaking trip to Bahía de los Ángeles is one of the most difficult (and most rewarding) stretches in the entire Sea of Cortez. Although most anglers bring their own boats, it's possible to hire a *panga* at Alfonsina's motel or the Papa Fernández Restaurant for a deep-sea fishing excursion, during which you're likely, depending on the season, to catch bass, cabrilla, yellowtail, grouper, corvina, and sierra.

As a note of caution, you shouldn't attempt the road south to Bahía San Luis Gonzaga in any vehicle with low clearance. In fact, although two-wheel-drive vehicles have been known to accomplish the jarring journey, it's really a route suitable for four-wheel-drive jeeps and heavy-duty pickup trucks (with or without cab-over campers). High clearance and sturdy tires are a must.

RV sites, facilities: There are no designated RV sites in this beachfront campground—you can park wherever you like. Besides the nearby Sea of Cortez, however, there are few official amenities, save for shady *palapas* and a store. Only small, self-contained RVs and rugged tent campers should stay here, preferably in pairs or groups, as there's no running water, dump station, electricity, security, shower house, or laundry available. Make sure that you're equipped with shovels, boards, rope, and other tools in case your wheels get stuck in the sand. Children and pets are welcome, though the facilities are not wheelchair-accessible. Limited supplies, such as beer, tequila, soda, snacks, fresh tamales, gasoline, and diesel, can be purchased at the Rancho Grande store, though it's advisable to pick up most groceries, including purified water, from the stores in San Felipe to the north. Remember to pack out all trash when you leave.

Reservations, fees: Reservations are not accepted; spaces are available on a first-come, first-served basis. Sites cost $5 per night, for RVs or tents. Credit cards are not accepted; cash (Mexican pesos or U.S. dollars) is the only acceptable form of payment. The store and campground are open all year.

Directions: From Puertecitos, drive 47.5 miles (76.4 km) south on Highway 5 to the turnoff for Campo Rancho Grande. Turn left (east), drive about a mile (1.6 km) to the shore, and look for the sign.

Contact: For more information about Campo Rancho Grande, call 555/151-4065. For more information about fishing charters at Alfonsina's, call 555/150-2825.

36 CAMPO BELUGA

Scenic Rating: 8

on Bahía San Luis Gonzaga

See map page 90

If you're looking for even more quietude and isolation on Bahía San Luis Gonzaga than the two northern campgrounds have to offer, then head a little farther south to this primitive place beside the bay. Here, you'll enjoy glorious sunrises, miles of sandy shore, mild waters for swimming, a sheltered bay perfect for kayaking, and ample opportunities for hiking, watching birds and marine life, and contemplating incredibly starry night skies—more clear than you'll ever experience in the light-filled cities and suburbs to which you're probably accustomed.

As a note of caution, you shouldn't attempt the road south to Bahía San Luis Gonzaga in any vehicle with low clearance. In fact, although two-wheel-drive vehicles have been known to accomplish the jarring journey, it's really a route suitable for four-wheel-drive jeeps and heavy-duty pickup trucks (with or without cab-over campers). High clearance and sturdy tires are a must.

RV sites, facilities: There are no designated RV sites in this beachfront campground—you can park wherever you like. Besides the bay and the nearby Sea of Cortez, however, there are few official amenities, save for shady *palapas,* flush toilets, cold showers, and a small store. Only small, self-contained RVs and rugged tent campers should stay here, preferably in pairs or groups, as there's no running water, dump station, electricity, security, or laundry available. Make sure that you're equipped with shovels, boards, rope, and other tools in case your wheels get stuck in the sand. Children and pets are welcome, though the facilities are not wheelchair-accessible. Only limited supplies, such as snacks and beverages, can be purchased at the store, so it's advisable to pick up most groceries, including purified water, from the stores in San Felipe to the north. Remember to pack out all trash when you leave.

Reservations, fees: Reservations are not accepted; spaces are available on a first-come, first-served basis. Sites cost $15 per night, for RVs or tents. Credit cards are not accepted; cash (Mexican pesos or U.S. dollars) is the customary form of payment. The campground is open all year.

Directions: From Puertecitos, drive 48.8 miles (78.5 km) south on Highway 5 to the signed turnoff for Campo Beluga. Turn left (east) onto the sandy road and drive about 1.2 miles (1.9 km) to the shore.

Contact: Since there's no official contact person, mailing address, or phone number for Campo Beluga, it's best just to drive toward the campground and see which spots are available.

CENTRAL PACIFIC AND THE SEA OF CORTEZ

BEST RV PARKS AND CAMPGROUNDS

As you head south from Ensenada, through the wine-rich Valle de Santo Tomás, past the ruins of the Misión de Santo Tomás de Aquino, you'll notice a distinct difference in the vibe of your environs. Here, there's more greenery and far fewer people and vehicles – a welcome respite from the frenzy of border towns like Tijuana and Mexicali.

Down this stretch of Highway 1, en route to the state line (the boundary between Baja California and Baja California Sur), RV travelers will encounter several beachside campgrounds, excellent surf breaks at coastal locales like Punta Santo Tomás, and terrific boating and fishing opportunities at idyllic places like the sheltered Bahía San Quintín, part of a large saltwater lagoon system. Long sandy beaches and several small volcanoes surround this bountiful area, and hunters will enjoy the easy access to ducks and geese in the winter season.

History buffs will appreciate touring the ruins of several Dominican missions, including what was once the largest, the Misión de San Vicente Ferrer, just west of San Vicente, and the oldest, the Misión de Nuestra Señora del Santísimo Rosario de Viñadaco, between the Pacific Ocean and El Rosario. But not all of Baja's history revolves around its Catholic roots. In addition to missions, you'll find the remains of a 19th-century English grist mill, pier, and cemetery in San Quintín.

South of the agricultural town of Colonet, a 65-mile (105-km) dirt road leads nature lovers to the Parque Nacional Sierra de San Pedro Mártir. Larger than Baja California's other national park, this remote, unspoiled wilderness contains pine forests, an *observatorio astronómico nacional* (which contains Mexico's largest telescope and offers infrequent tours), and Baja's highest mountain, Picacho del Diablo (Devil's Peak) – a dangerous ascent, even for experienced mountaineers. Ideal for hiking, backpacking, wildlife-watching, and primitive camping, the park is most popular from April to September.

Farther south, past the famous seafood burritos of El Rosario, the ruins of the Misión de San Fernando Rey de España de Velicatá (the peninsula's only Franciscan mission), and the abandoned onyx mine of El Mármol (The Marble), RV enthusiasts can explore the desert country surrounding Cataviña. A starkly beautiful landscape, Baja's central desert is filled with enormous granite boulders, a unique carrot-like specimen – the *cirio* (candle), or boojum tree – and hundreds of varied desert plants, including yuccas, agaves, ocotillo, organ pipe cactus, prickly pear cactus, and gigantic *cardón*, the world's largest cactus. Despite the high temperatures in summer, travelers love to hike within this arid, fascinating region and snap photographs of these immovable giants.

Besides scanning the terrain for lizards, rattlesnakes, and elephant trees, you might also appreciate Cataviña's solitary motel, which occasionally offers gasoline and other supplies – especially welcome given that there's little else along the 173-mile (278-km) stretch between El Rosario and Rosarito, closer to the state line. Be advised that you'll encounter a Mexican Army checkpoint along this remote part of Baja; the armed soldiers are allowed to search any and all motorists for guns, drugs, and other forbidden items. Although instructed to be courteous to tourists, they have the authority to conduct thorough searches, so it behooves RV travelers to be polite, cooperative, and presentable.

Roughly 64 miles (103 km) south of Cataviña, you'll come upon a junction seemingly in the middle of nowhere. If you veer from Highway 1 and head in a southeasterly direction, toward the Sea of Cortez, you'll soon reach Bahía de los Ángeles – celebrated not so much for the town as for its sparkling blue bay, dramatic backdrop of rocky mountains, and string of offshore islands, from small, nearby ones like Isla Coronado to large, far-off destinations like Isla Tiburón (Shark Island). Here, popular pastimes include fishing, boating, scuba diving, and sea kayaking. Some nature lovers also enjoy viewing endangered sea turtles at a nearby rescue and research facility.

As in other areas of Baja, the RV accommodations here constitute a wide spectrum. You can dry-camp in the mountainous national park, where you'll find fiberglass outhouses, hiking trails, white granite massifs, mountain lions, eagles, and, on occasion, snow. As an alternative, you'll find full hookups, practical amenities, and nearby attractions at campgrounds in Colonia Vicente Guerrero and Bahía de los Ángeles, though many of the year-round campgrounds in the latter town have either limited hookups (meaning intermittent water service and electricity usage) or none at all.

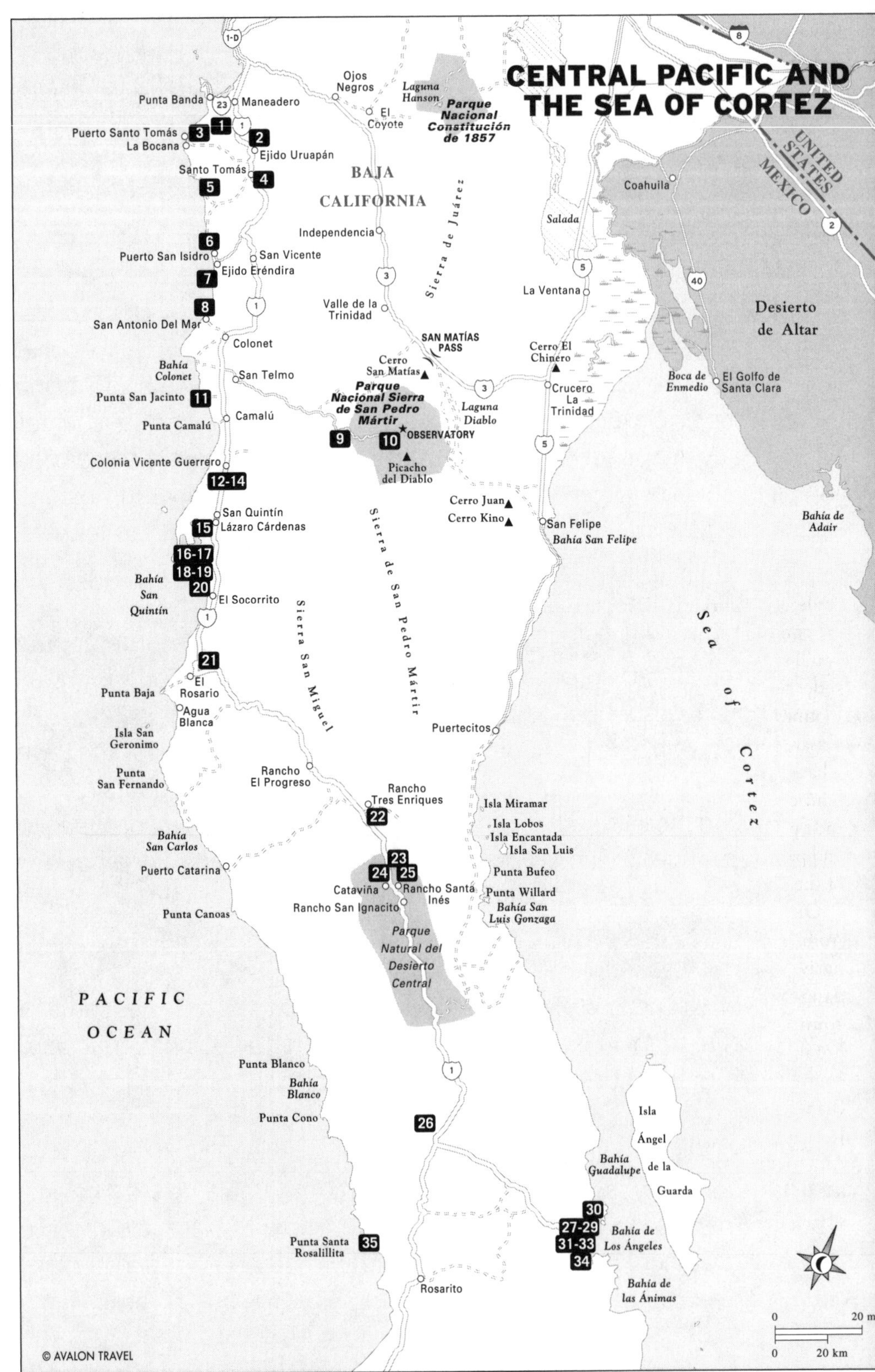
CENTRAL PACIFIC AND THE SEA OF CORTEZ
UNITED STATES
MEXICO
Punta Banda
Maneadero
Ojos Negros
Laguna Hanson
Parque Nacional Constitución de 1857
El Coyote
Puerto Santo Tomás
La Bocana
Ejido Uruapán
Santo Tomás
BAJA CALIFORNIA
Sierra de Juárez
Coahuila
Salada
Independencia
Puerto San Isidro
San Vicente
Ejido Eréndira
La Ventana
Desierto de Altar
Valle de la Trinidad
San Antonio Del Mar
Colonet
SAN MATÍAS PASS
Cerro San Matías
Cerro El Chinero
Bahía Colonet
San Telmo
Parque Nacional Sierra de San Pedro Mártir
Crucero La Trinidad
Boca de Enmedio
El Golfo de Santa Clara
Punta San Jacinto
Laguna Diablo
Camalú
Punta Camalú
OBSERVATORY
Picacho del Diablo
Colonia Vicente Guerrero
Cerro Juan
Cerro Kino
San Quintín
Lázaro Cárdenas
San Felipe
Bahía San Felipe
Bahía de Adair
Sierra de San Pedro Mártir
Bahía San Quintín
El Socorrito
Sierra San Miguel
Sea of Cortez
El Rosario
Punta Baja
Agua Blanca
Isla San Geronimo
Puertecitos
Punta San Fernando
Rancho El Progreso
Rancho Tres Enriques
Isla Miramar
Isla Lobos
Isla Encantada
Isla San Luis
Bahía San Carlos
Puerto Catarina
Punta Bufeo
Cataviña
Rancho Santa Inés
Punta Willard
Bahía San Luis Gonzaga
Rancho San Ignacito
Punta Canoas
Parque Natural del Desierto Central
PACIFIC OCEAN
Punta Blanco
Bahía Blanco
Punta Cono
Isla Ángel de la Guarda
Bahía Guadalupe
Bahía de Los Ángeles
Punta Santa Rosalillita
Bahía de las Ánimas
Rosarito
0 20 mi
0 20 km
© AVALON TRAVEL

1 LAS CAÑADAS CAMPAMENTO

Scenic Rating: 10

south of Maneadero

See map page 126 **BEST**

More than just a safe place to pull off the highway at night, this large, relatively new recreation complex and *balneario* (swimming resort) offers plenty of outdoor diversions, especially for families. Although originally conceived as a day-use facility for local residents of Ensenada, Tijuana, and their suburbs, this park is certainly a pleasant spot for travelers, too.

Surrounded by rugged foothills and shady trees, the property boasts a relaxing and, at times, boisterous setting for hikers, swimmers, tent campers, and volleyball players alike. A strolling path encircles the attractive lake, where anglers can search for catfish, tilapia, and red carp, kayak enthusiasts can test their paddling skills, and others can drift across the surface on complimentary pedal boats. In addition, you'll find a swimming pool with a giant water slide, as well as hiking trails and a track for mountain bikes and all-terrain vehicles. With grassy soccer fields, sandy volleyball courts, and a basketball hoop, children and teenagers can amuse themselves for hours, if not days, giving their parents time to enjoy the pleasant environs and perhaps even take a guided ecological tour of the area.

On these intimate excursions, presented from April to September, you'll learn about native flora and fauna, including those in danger of extinction. In addition, you'll encounter Baja's ecology and geology, most notably the Arroyo de las Ánimas, which contains the 155-mile (249-km) fault of Agua Blanca and was once used in 1769 by Father Junípero Serra's expedition along Baja and Alta California.

RV sites, facilities: The modest campground is situated on a bare hill, away from the crowded water park. There are six pull-through RV sites, with full hookups (including 20-amp power), large concrete patios, barbecue pits, picnic tables, and space for lengthy rigs (up to 45 feet/13.7 meters long). Primitive campers can pitch their tents in any of the grassy areas near the trees, lake, or swimming pools. Facilities consist of a grocery store, 10 ecofriendly rental cabins (for up to six people each), public pay phones, and tiled restrooms with flush toilets and warm showers. Athletic offerings include several swimming pools, a water slide, a children's splash area with water games, a playground, hiking and biking trails, three volleyball courts, three small soccer fields, a basketball court, a lake for anglers, free pedal boats, and off-road vehicle rentals. There is, however, no laundry or dump station on the premises. A guarded gate and chained entrance provide limited security. Children and pets are welcome. Given the rural location of this campground, you might want to stock up on extra groceries, fuel, and purified water in Ensenada or Maneadero before arriving. Also, those interested in renting a cabin should bring their own towels and blankets.

Reservations, fees: Reservations are accepted. The fee is $16 per person for overnight RV and tent camping (including daytime use of the water park). In summer, if you stay the night and leave the following day before 9 A.M., you are entitled to a refund of $9 per person. The cabins, for which reservations are required and cancellations are not possible, cost $65 per night (plus $16 per person). There is no charge for children less than 3 feet (0.9 meters) tall. Credit cards are not accepted; cash (Mexican pesos or U.S. dollars) is the only acceptable form of payment. You can expect deals on admission costs and cabin rentals during the off-season (mid-October–mid-March). The water park closes during the winter months, but the athletic facilities and campground are open all year.

Directions: From the corner of Avenida Reforma and Calle Augustin Sanginés in Ensenada, head south on Highway 1 for about 9 miles (14.5 km) to Maneadero. Pass the turnoff to La Bufadora and continue south for another 6.5 miles (10.5

Las Cañadas Campamento, a *balneario* south of Maneadero

km) to the military checkpoint at the Km 31.5 marker. You'll see the recreation complex on your right, west of the highway. From Santo Tomás, drive northwest on Highway 1 to Km 31.5; the complex will be on your left.

Contact: Las Cañadas Campamento, Km 31.5 de la Carretera Ensenada–San Quintín, Baja California, Mexico, tel. 646/153-1055 or 800/027-3828, www.lascanadas.com. Note: From the United States, you'll have to dial "1" before the "800" number.

2 CAMPO URUAPÁN

Scenic Rating: 5

southeast of Maneadero

See map page 126

Operated by the *ejido* (government-supported farming cooperative) of Uruapán, this modest campground offers travelers a peaceful, rustic setting within the fertile Valle de Uruapán. The closest town is, in fact, the *ejido* from which it derives its name—a tiny, authentic Mexican village, so tiny that it's rarely included on road maps. Unlike the scenic camping areas beside the Pacific Ocean or Sea of Cortez, this primitive locale presents little reason to stay here, especially if you're traveling alone. But, if other campgrounds in the vicinity are full during the summer months and holiday weekends, then this well-shaded parking lot beside the highway will be adequate for one night.

Besides hiking, mountain biking, picnicking, and, if you're lucky, bird-watching, there's little to do near the campground. Although the nearby town of Uruapán isn't much of a destination either, this agricultural region is known for its *tomates, olivas, fresas* (strawberries), and *pimientos* (peppers). In addition, a processing plant prepares and exports *erizos de mar* (sea urchins) to Japan, where they're used in sushi dishes. From November to February, the area is also popular for the hunting of *codorniz* (quail). Inside the village, you'll see signs for some hot springs, located roughly 1.25 miles (2 km) outside of town, via a dirt road. The local *ejido* residents typically do their laundry and bathing there, but visitors are welcome, too. There is a small fee for the hot springs.

RV sites, facilities: There are no designated RV sites in this campground—you can park wherever you like. With careful maneuvering, even big rigs (up to 45 feet/13.7 meters in length) will find room here. Besides the great outdoors, however, there are few amenities—just 15-amp electrical outlets, shady trees, brick barbecue pits, and flush toilets. Only self-contained RVs and rugged tent campers should park here, preferably in pairs or groups, as there's no drinking water, dump station, security, or (for much of the time) staff on duty. There is also no laundry or shower on the premises. Children and pets are welcome, but the terrain is not suitable for wheelchairs. With only the tiny village of Uruapán nearby, it's best to stop in Ensenada for extra food, purified water, fuel, and other supplies before traveling south of Maneadero. Be sure to pack out all trash when you leave.

Reservations, fees: Reservations are not accepted; spaces are available on a first-come, first-served basis. Given its primitive status, the campground is moderately priced at $5 per night. Although it's possible that no one will be present to collect the fee, you should have it ready, just in case. Credit cards are not accepted; cash (Mexican pesos or U.S. dollars) is the only acceptable form of payment. The campground is open all year.

Directions: From the heart of Maneadero, located at Km 21 on Highway 1 (Carretera Ensenada–San Quintín), drive south for 12.4 miles (20 km) to the Km 41 marker. The campground will be on your left, along the eastern side of the highway. From Santo Tomás, drive northwest on Highway 1 to Km 41; the complex will be on your right.

Contact: Since there's no official contact person, mailing address, or phone number for Campo Uruapán, it's best just to drive into the campground and see which spots are available. For details about the Ensenada area, visit www.ensenada.com.

3 PUERTO SANTO TOMÁS RESORT

Scenic Rating: 10

west of Santo Tomás

See map page 126 BEST

As long as you're hugging the northwestern coast of Baja, along the Transpeninsular Highway (Highway 1), most die-hard Baja aficionados believe that the "real Baja" will remain a mystery to you. For the most part, the towns and villages between Tijuana and El Rosario cater to foreign tourists, especially English-speaking vacationers from America. The belief is that anyone willing to venture into the harsh *desierto* east of El Rosario will be able to explore the authentic heart of the peninsula. But travelers to Puerto Santo Tomás on the Pacific side might beg to differ.

This sheltered, picturesque cove, boasting the isolated fishing villages of La Bocana and Puerto Santo Tomás, will make you feel as though you've time-warped to a 19th-century fishing community, disconnected from the modern world. With patience and a sense of adventure, you can reach the villages via a graded dirt road about 16 miles (25.7 km) west of the main drag. La Bocana, which is situated beside a stunning beach, is the first village you'll reach. Here, you'll find a dozen well-equipped *cabañas* atop a hill overlooking the ocean, plus a small store and a footbridge that leads to the beach.

Farther along this challenging road toward the coast, however, you'll encounter Puerto Santo Tomás, a scenic fish camp comprising several colorful shacks perched above the cliffs that ring this smoky-hued, kelp-filled bay. Down below, you'll spy a collection of bobbing *pangas,* and at the road's end, you'll stumble upon a convenient tourist complex, a delightful and seemingly undiscovered place, where you can board fishing charters, watch passing whales and frolicking sea lions, dive or snorkel amid the kelp forests, kayak among dolphins in the bay, enjoy brilliant sunsets and star-studded nights, or simply unwind from the world. Offshore anglers can expect to find black perch, calico bass, halibut, lingcod, rockcod, and sheephead all year long; seasonal species include white sea bass, bonita, barracuda, and yellowtail. Swimming and hiking are popular here, too. How long you stay in this breathtaking port is entirely up to you.

RV sites, facilities: In addition to rental *casas,* cabins, and trailers, the resort presents a primitive cliffside area open to RV campers. A cantina offers seafood and authentic Mexican cuisine. Although the campground offers no hookups, other amenities include fire pits, toilet facilities, hot showers, and fishing charters. The entrance gate, remote locale, and 24-hour staff presence guarantee limited security. Only small, self-contained RVs and rugged tent campers should park here, preferably in pairs or groups, as there's no drinking water, dump station, laundry, or public phone. Solar-powered electricity provides enough energy for lights only, and due to the surrounding mountains, cell phones do not typically work. The staff, however, speaks limited English. Children and pets are welcome, though the terrain is not suitable for wheelchairs. Given the isolated location, you should stop in Ensenada, Maneadero, or Santo Tomás for extra food, purified water, gasoline, firewood, towels, and other supplies before traveling to the coast. Be sure to pack out all trash when you leave.

Reservations, fees: Reservations are accepted. RV and tent campsites cost $5 per person per night (a $10 minimum). Three *casas* offer space for groups; they cost $20–35 per person per night. Cabins costs $15–20 per person per night (note: double occupancy is required). Trailers are also for rent ($10–18 nightly). *Panga* rentals and kayak/boat launches are also available for a fee. Credit cards and personal checks are not accepted; cash (Mexican pesos or U.S. dollars) is the only acceptable form of payment. The campground is open all year.

Directions: From Maneadero, head south for about 16.6 miles (26.7 km) on Highway 1, passing through a military checkpoint along the way (if you reach the village of Santo Tomás, you've gone too far). Between markers for Km 46 and Km 47, you'll see a sign for Puerto Santo Tomás. Approximately 150 feet (45.7 meters) past the road sign, turn right (west) onto a gravel road and continue for 5 miles (8 km). At the cattle crossing, take the left fork onto the bottom road, which is used during the dry season. If it appears to be flooded, use the upper road to the right. Continue for another 10 miles (16.1 km) to La Bocana. Be aware that there will be several forks in the road to the coast; just always keep to the right. At La Bocana, veer to the right and climb the small hill, heading north along the coast for 3 miles (4.8 km). The Puerto Santo Tomás Resort lies at the end of the road. Just stop at the gate and blow your horn to alert the staff. Note that from Santo Tomás to the south, the turnoff on Highway 1 is 2.4 miles (3.9 km) north, on the left-hand side.

Contact: Puerto Santo Tomás Resort, Puerto Santo Tomás, Baja California, Mexico, tel. 646/154-9415, www.puertosantotomas.com.

4 BALNEARIO EL PALOMAR

Scenic Rating: 5

in Santo Tomás

See map page 126 **BEST**

Roughly 19 miles (30.6 km) south of Maneadero lies the small Dominican village of Santo Tomás, named after the surrounding Valle de Santo Tomás, one of Baja's main wine-producing regions. The town owes its origin to the Misión de Santo Tomás de Aquino, founded in a different location in 1791 by missionary José Loriente and moved twice, before settling upon its current upstream spot (now, just some adobe ruins near town) in 1799. The area's wineries also have their roots in the mission system; the Dominicans were responsible for planting thousands of grapevines as well as olive trees.

Via a challenging dirt road, the town is situated less than 20 miles (32.2 km) from Puerto Santo Tomás, a simple coastal fishing settlement where recreational anglers can fish from the shore or charter a *panga,* in search of calico bass, halibut, sheephead, perch, rockcod, lingcod, and other bottom species. In warmer months, it's possible to seek out white sea bass, yellowtail, barracuda, dorado, albacore, and other offshore varieties.

With various fish to catch along the coast, the ruins of an old mission to see, and nearby wineries (including the world-class Bodegas de Santo Tomás, Mexico's oldest winery, founded in 1888) to visit, it's advantageous that the town of Santo Tomás has an RV park of its own. Part of a Mexican-style *balneario* (swimming resort), the campground welcomes tent campers as well as RV enthusiasts. Although the *balneario* is very popular with folks from Ensenada and Tijuana during holidays and summer weekends, it's less crowded than it once was, owing to the presence of the Las Cañadas Campamento water park to the north. If you're not a fan of crowds, you might want to avoid the place in the summertime. During the cooler months, it can be extremely quiet here.

RV sites, facilities: The park offers six pull-through sites and 20 small back-in spaces, all 26 of which have full hookups (including 15-amp electricity), concrete patios, barbecue grills, shady trees, and trash cans. Some of the sites have picnic tables, but no space can accommodate a rig longer than 30 feet (9.1 meters). Facilities include a public pay phone, a dump station, two poorly maintained restroom buildings with flush toilets and occasionally hot showers, two heated swimming pools near the campground, a small lake with a water slide and pedal boats, several picnicking areas, a children's playground, a small zoo, and courts for tennis, basketball, and volleyball.

In the main building on the other side of the highway, you'll find a small grocery and handicraft store, a restaurant, a modest motel, and a tiny Pemex gas station. From time to time, hunting and fishing guides are also available. A chain across the entrance road provides limited security. There is, however, no laundry on the premises. Children, pets, and tent campers are welcome in the park. Despite the presence of gasoline and other supplies, you might still want to pick up extra groceries and purified water in nearby Santo Tomás, if not in a larger town like Ensenada.

Reservations, fees: Reservations are accepted. RV sites cost $17 per night (for two people). Each extra person will be charged $5 per night. Tent sites cost $10 per night. Credit cards are not accepted; cash (Mexican pesos or U.S. dollars) is the customary form of payment. Although the swimming areas close during the winter months, the campground is open all year.

Directions: From Maneadero, drive south on Highway 1 for about 19 miles (30.6 km). Near the north entrance to the town of Santo Tomás, at Km 51.5, you'll see the campground to your left, on the east side of the highway. The office, however, is on the right (west) side. Be advised that the entrance road is very steep, so take care when driving into the park. Also be careful when leaving, as it is difficult to creep back up the incline while simultaneously keeping an eye out for trucks and other vehicles zipping along Highway 1.

Contact: Balneario El Palomar, Km 51.5 de la Carretera Ensenada–San Quintín, Santo Tomás, Ensenada, Baja California, Mexico, tel. 646/153-8002 or 646/153-8071.

5 TWO SEASONS RV PARK AT RANCHO SAN MIGUEL

Scenic Rating: 7

southwest of Santo Tomás

See map page 126

If you're willing to risk some bumpy, slow-going routes, you're likely to find a number of primitive campsites and friendly fish camps along both coasts of the Baja peninsula. Although utility hookups and bathroom facilities are rare in such isolated places, you're usually guaranteed the chance to experience less-crowded beaches and other serene landscapes, even more so depending on the difficulty of the access road.

At the end of one particularly lengthy route, southwest of Santo Tomás, lies this welcome boondocking site not far from the Pacific Ocean. The managers of the Guadalupe Canyon Hot Springs & Campground, located southwest of Mexicali, own this year-round primitive spot near Punta San José. Offering 25 acres (10 hectares) of rolling hills and access to some incredible ocean views, the campground welcomes RV and tent campers alike. Despite the lack of amenities, it's a terrific home base for numerous diversions, including surfing, swimming, fishing, scuba diving, boating, off-road biking, horseback riding, and hiking amid the brushy hills and along the rocky coast. The area is especially pleasant during the breezy summer months.

Although the campground is currently quite primitive, improvements are in the works. Features like restrooms and hot tubs should be in place by the summer of 2009. For now, however, the area is best appreciated by those willing to "rough it" or those equipped with self-contained vehicles.

RV sites, facilities: This beachside campground offers space for an indeterminate number of RVs and tents. Although there are no designated campsites or hookups at the present time, visitors do have access to a small boat launch about a half mile (0.8 km) away, and security is provided by a resident American family. Scheduled for completion by mid-2009, the campground will eventually provide 20 pull-through sites for motor homes and travel trailers of any length (up to 45 feet/13.7 meters long) as well as flush toilets, cold showers, underground septic tanks, picnic tables, hot tubs, and shady *palapas*.

Only self-contained RVs or rugged tent campers should park here, preferably in pairs or groups, as there's no drinking water, electricity, dump station, laundry, or cell phone service available. Satellite dishes, however, are able to pick up television signals here. Children, pets, dirt bikes, and quads are welcome, but the terrain is not suitable for wheelchairs. The management will not tolerate barking dogs, and there is a 5-mph (8-kph), no-dust policy for off-road vehicles. Given the difficulty of reaching this campground, you should purchase enough groceries, water, fuel, and other supplies in Ensenada, Maneadero, Santo Tomás, or San Vicente before attempting the long route here. Be sure to pack out all trash when you leave.

Reservations, fees: Reservations are accepted but not required. The fee is reasonable: $10 per night (whether camping via RV or tent) or $50 per month. Long-term storage and yearly leases are also available. In the future, there will be extra fees for amenities like showers, hot tubs, and firewood. Credit cards are not accepted; cash (Mexican pesos or U.S. dollars) is the only acceptable form of payment. The campground is open all year, though summer is the best time to visit.

Directions: If you're heading south on Highway 1, through the town of Santo Tomás, drive 0.2 mile (0.3 km) past the El Palomar motel and gas station and turn right onto a steep, graded dirt road beside a small store. From south of Santo Tomás, head north on Highway 1 and turn left onto the dirt road, 0.2 mile (0.3 km) south of the El Palomar complex. Continue southwest on this winding 20-mile (32.2-km) route, which snakes past several *ranchos,* toward the coast. The entrance to the trailer park lies to your right, within the expansive Rancho San Miguel. From Highway 1, the entire trip will require at least two hours for the average motor home or travel trailer with tow vehicle.

Contact: Two Seasons RV Park at Rancho San Miguel, c/o Rob & Isabel Williams, P.O. Box 4003, Newport Beach, CA 92661, tel. 949/673-2670 (U.S.), www.guadalupe-canyon.com.

6 COYOTE CAL'S

   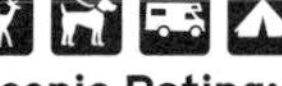

Scenic Rating: 10

in Puerto San Isidro

See map page 126 **BEST**

Young-at-heart surfers, backpackers, anglers, and off-road enthusiasts flock to this international hostel, situated in a breathtaking spot alongside the Pacific Ocean, not too far south from Ensenada. Even RV travelers will find plenty of reasons to stay a few days, if not longer. You can learn how to surf, enjoy numerous hiking trails, embark upon an off-road biking adventure, watch passing dolphins and gray whales, snorkel amid the aquamarine waters, fish in offshore hot spots, relax on a prime beach only a quarter mile (0.4 km) north, and, yes, party all night in the hostel's new Barefoot Bar & Cantina. The friendly, knowledgeable staff will help you plan nature hikes, point you toward the area's best surf breaks, or wake you up early for a deep-sea fishing excursion. The place is so popular that people have been known to hitchhike to reach it, though that's definitely not recommended.

Just a mile (1.6 km) south of Coyote Cal's sits Castro's Fishing Place, where you can arrange for a charter into offshore waters. As in other spots along the Pacific side, you can expect to find saltwater varieties like black sea bass, yellowtail, red snapper, halibut, sheephead, barracuda, even thresher shark.

In addition, there is ample opportunity for free boondocking all along the coast here. Punta Cabras, north of Coyote Cal's, is a particularly popular spot. In this area, you'll find lovely coves, good surf fishing, and excellent hikes. Just be aware that occasional thefts do occur on the beach, so keep an eye on your belongings.

RV sites, facilities: Besides dorms and private rooms inside the white, mural-covered building, the hostel offers space for tents and midsized RVs (up to 30 feet/9.1 meters long), though you should expect primitive camping here. Self-contained RVs are, in fact, a must. Amenities include a coin laundry, barbecue pits, pool and ping-pong tables, dartboards, videos, a communal kitchen, and a barefoot bar. In addition, bicycles, boogie boards, surfboards, and snorkeling equipment are available for rent. You can also enjoy pancake breakfasts and rice-and-bean lunches. On-site staff members speak English and provide limited security. Children and pets are welcome, but the terrain may not be suitable for wheelchairs. There is no dump station or shower for RVers, and it's best to bring your own purified water with you. Given the remote location, you should purchase enough groceries, water, fuel, and other supplies in Ensenada, Maneadero, Santo Tomás, or San Vicente before attempting the route here. Be sure to pack out all trash when you leave.

Reservations, fees: Reservations are accepted. Tent and RV sites cost $10 per person per night (plus $3 each for breakfast). Dorm rooms cost $15–18 per person per night. Private rooms and suites are also available for $40–60 per couple per night. Cash (Mexican pesos or U.S. dollars) and major credit cards (Visa and MasterCard) are accepted here. The hostel and campground are open all year.

Directions: From Highway 1, between Santo Tomás and San Vicente, look for a turnoff toward the coast, just south of the Km 78 marker. If you're coming from Santo Tomás to the north, turn right onto the turnoff. If you're headed from San Vicente, turn left. You'll then drive south on a paved road for 10.5 miles (16.9 km), heading west toward the *ejido* Eréndira. At the fork in the road, veer right toward the village. Continue for another 2 miles (3.2 km), past Castro's Fishing Place, to Puerto San Isidro. Despite the decent signage, it is definitely not advisable for RVs longer than 25 feet (7.6 meters) to attempt the access road without first consulting local residents; with storms, development, and other variables, road conditions can change at any time.

Contact: Coyote Cal's, 339 Citrus Avenue, Imperial Beach, CA 91932, tel. 646/154-4080

(Mexico), www.coyotecals.com. For more information about Castro's Fishing Place, call 646/176-2897.

7 MALIBU BEACH SUR RV PARK

Scenic Rating: 5

south of Puerto San Isidro

See map page 126

Although this beachfront campground is difficult to reach and has few official amenities, the view is well worth the arduous journey. After all, the Pacific Ocean lies just below the modest bluff on which the isolated, somewhat dirty parking lot sits. There might be more scenic beaches along the western coast of Baja, but few will be as peaceful as this one. Of course, much of that is due to the challenging entrance road, which many larger motor homes and travel trailers will be unable to traverse.

Only a couple miles north lies the small *ejido* of Eréndira. If you're up for an adventure, head about 4 miles (6.4 km) beyond this little village to Puerto San Isidro. From here, you can charter a *panga* and fish among the kelp-filled waters. Hiking, mountain biking, swimming, surf fishing, and sea kayaking are also popular activities along this remote coastline.

RV sites, facilities: This beachfront campground offers 14 pull-through sites, with full hookups (including 15-amp electricity), concrete patios, enough room for midsized RVs (up to 35 feet/10.7 meters long), and, for the seven front spaces, ocean views. There are 16 additional sites farther from the shore, but none of these have utilities. Facilities include a coin-operated washer and dryer, tiled restrooms with flush toilets and hot showers, and stairs that descend the 15-foot (4.6-meter) bluff to the beach. On-site owners provide limited security. Children, pets, and tent campers are welcome, and the RV spaces can accommodate wheelchairs. There is, however, no dump station on the premises, and it's best to bring your own purified water with you. Given the difficulty of reaching this campground, you should purchase enough groceries, water, fuel, and other supplies in Ensenada, Maneadero, Santo Tomás, or San Vicente before attempting the route here. Be sure to pack out all trash when you leave.

Reservations, fees: Reservations are not accepted; spaces are available on a first-come, first-served basis. The fee is reasonable: $10 per night for two people (whether camping via RV or tent). Credit cards are not accepted; cash (Mexican pesos or U.S. dollars) is the only acceptable form of payment. The campground is open all year.

Directions: From Highway 1, between Santo Tomás and San Vicente, look for a turnoff toward the coast, just south of the Km 78 marker. If you're coming from Santo Tomás to the north, turn right onto the turnoff. If you're headed from San Vicente, turn left. You'll then drive south on a paved road for 10.2 miles (16.4 km), veering west toward the *ejido* Eréndira. On the edge of town, turn left (south) at a faded sign for Malibu Beach Sur RV Park and continue along an ungraded road for 3.2 miles (5.2 km), across a riverbed (that will hopefully be dry), past a cluster of houses, and through some tomato fields. Along this unpaved route, you'll encounter several other roads. Although there are many well-marked signs for the campground, it can be a confusing path. If you ever see a fork that is not marked, follow the branch that leads south along the coast. Despite the open countryside and decent signage, it is definitely not advisable for RVs longer than 25 feet (7.6 meters) to attempt the access road without first consulting local residents; with storms, development, and other variables, road conditions can change at any time.

Contact: Malibu Beach Sur RV Park, Ejido Eréndira, Baja California, Mexico, tel. 646/154-4028. Since there's no official mailing address for the Malibu Beach Sur RV Park, it's best just to drive into the campground and see which spots are available.

8 SAN ANTONIO DEL MAR BEACH

Scenic Rating: 8

west of Colonet

See map page 126 BEST

If you can safely reach this remote destination along the Pacific Ocean, you'll be treated to a vast, fantastic beach, bordered by scrubby hills and filled with acres of soft sand dunes, perfect for hikers and off-road vehicles. Outdoor enthusiasts will relish other pastimes here as well, from swimming and surf fishing to bird-watching and sea kayaking. Travelers and local residents, which include fishing families and American expatriates, also enjoy clamming along this beach. (Just remember that you need a Mexican fishing license to go clamming, and the limit is a dozen clams per person. Also, because fishing regulations and importation laws can change at any time, you should always consult local authorities or operators before clamming on your own.)

But the route to this lovely spot is definitely not for the faint of heart. In fact, those with lengthy motor homes and unwieldy travel trailers shouldn't even attempt the journey, especially after a rainstorm. It's a suitable place only for tents and four-wheel-drive vehicles, such as pickup trucks with cab-over campers.

In addition, be advised that, while this beach is often quite desolate and peaceful, it's usually teeming with Mexican families from elsewhere on the weekends. If the occasional crowds and frequent windy conditions impede your serenity, head north to one of a few sheltered coves. Just be careful while driving on the sand; it's easy to get stuck here, even with a four-wheel-drive vehicle.

RV sites, facilities: There are no designated campsites—you can park wherever you like. Besides the sand and sea, however, there are no amenities. Only small, self-contained RVs or rugged tent campers should park here, preferably in pairs or groups, as there's no drinking water, electricity, dump station, or security available. In addition, there is no laundry or shower house on the premises. Children and pets are welcome, but the terrain is definitely not suitable for wheelchairs. Be sure to bring tools like shovels, boards, and rope in case your wheels get stuck in the sand. Given the remote location, it's best to stop in Colonet for extra food, purified water, fuel, and other supplies before traveling toward the coast. Remember to pack out all trash when you leave.

Reservations, fees: Reservations are not accepted; spaces are available on a first-come, first-served basis. Given the campground's primitive status, RV and tent camping is moderately priced at $5 per night. Although it's possible that no one will be present to collect the fee, you should have it ready, just in case. Credit cards are not accepted; cash (Mexican pesos or U.S. dollars) is the only acceptable form of payment. The beach is open all year.

Directions: From the north side of Colonet, near the bridge that crosses the town's small river, you'll spot a sign for San Antonio del Mar. Turn west onto the dirt road and drive 7 miles (11.3 km) toward the coast. You'll see several beach houses, among which you can access the beach.

Contact: Since there's no official contact person, mailing address, or phone number for San Antonio del Mar Beach, it's best just to drive into the campground and see which spots are available. For details about the Ensenada area (which, to a certain degree, includes towns like Santo Tomás, San Vicente, and Colonet), visit www.ensenada.com.

9 RANCHO LOS MANZANOS

Scenic Rating: 8

east of Colonet

See map page 126 BEST

Just a few miles west of the Parque Nacional Sierra de San Pedro Mártir, this small, nondescript campground is supposed to be open during the summer months. Be forewarned, however, that it's not always open, even in summer. If you find it closed, don't fret; you can always find a spot in the national park.

Surrounded by shady oak trees, *piñon* pine trees, Jeffrey pines, and cool springs, the campground provides a gorgeous backdrop for those seeking solace in the natural world. It also serves as a decent base camp for those interested in hiking, climbing, backpacking, and bird-watching excursions in the nearby park. There, you'll encounter sugar pine, cedar, aspen, and juniper trees, as well as the endemic San Pedro Mártir cypress—not to mention mountain meadows, trout-filled streams, and birds of every ilk, from red crossbills and pygmy nuthatches in the lower regions to western bluebirds and mountain chickadees in the upper reaches.

Also nearby is Rancho Meling, which you pass en route to the Manzanos campground. Operated by four generations of the Meling family since the early 1900s, the 10,000-acre (4,050-hectare) cattle ranch offers guests comfortable accommodations, all-you-can-eat family-style meals, access to a swimming pool and a graded airstrip, hiking trails, horseback riding, and guided backpacking trips into the Parque Nacional Sierra de San Pedro Mártir.

RV sites, facilities: This small primitive camping area offers room for up to 25 tents and small RVs (up to 25 feet/7.6 meters long). There is running spring water at each of the dirt sites. Since the access road can be so inconsistent, the park is probably best suited for those with four-wheel-drive vehicles, especially pickup trucks with cab-over campers. Facilities include a dump station as well as poorly maintained bathrooms with flush toilets and cold showers. Only self-contained RVs or rugged tent campers should park here, preferably in pairs or groups, as there's no electricity, laundry, or security available. Children and pets are allowed, but the terrain may not be suitable for wheelchairs. Given the remoteness of this campground, you should definitely stop in Colonet or Camalú for extra food, purified water, fuel, and other supplies before traveling toward the park. Be sure to pack out all trash when you leave.

Reservations, fees: Reservations are not accepted; spaces are available on a first-come, first-served basis. The overnight fee for RV and tent camping is nominal—only $5. Credit cards are not accepted; cash (Mexican pesos or U.S. dollars) is the only acceptable form of payment. The park is open during the summer months only.

Directions: From the San Antonio del Mar turnoff in Colonet, head south on Highway 1 for roughly 8.7 miles (14 km) to Km 141 and turn left (east) onto the paved route, near the small town of San Telmo de Abajo. If you're coming from San Quintín, head north on Highway 1 for about 30 miles (48.3 km) to Km 141 and turn right (east). Once you've turned, follow the winding paved road, which runs past the town of San Telmo and beside the Río San Telmo, for 14.5 miles (23.3 km), and then continue along an unpaved portion for another 16.7 miles (26.9 km) to the Rancho Meling turnoff. From the guest ranch, the road becomes tougher to traverse, but with a four-wheel-drive vehicle, you can travel another 14.2 miles (22.8 km) to the Rancho Los Manzanos campground, on the right side of the road and just a few miles west of the Parque Nacional Sierra de San Pedro Mártir.

Contact: Since there's no official contact person, mailing address, or phone number for Rancho Los Manzanos, it's best just to drive into the campground and see which spots are available. For more information about Rancho Meling, visit www.melingguestranch.com.

10 PARQUE NACIONAL SIERRA DE SAN PEDRO MÁRTIR

Scenic Rating: 10

east of Colonet

See map page 126 **BEST**

Although it might seem difficult to believe, the Baja peninsula is composed of more than just oceanside *playas* and cactus-filled *desiertos.* High-altitude coniferous forests exist here, too. You'll find them within the mountainous, 160,000-acre (64,750-hectare) Parque Nacional Sierra de San Pedro Mártir, noticeably larger than Baja Norte's other national park. In some areas, this rather undeveloped place reaches heights of over 9,000 feet (2,740 meters), making it cool year-round and potentially snowy in winter. Most visitors come during the spring and summer months, when vibrant wildflowers are blooming.

Those with four-wheel-drive vehicles will be able to explore more of the rugged terrain, since most of the tracks throughout the park are terribly uneven. A triple-domed *observatorio astronómico nacional,* established in 1971 and situated atop the 9,290-foot (2,830-meter) Cerro de la Cúpula (Hill of the Dome), offers pre-arranged tours for stargazers. Anglers can fish for endemic rainbow trout in various mountain streams. Sharp granite peaks, including the 10,150-foot (3,090-meter) Picacho del Diablo, Baja's highest mountain, lure adventurous rock climbers. Those who reach the top of dangerous Devil's Peak are treated to breathtaking views of the Sea of Cortez and the *desierto* landscape surrounding San Felipe to the east.

But probably the most popular pastimes here include hiking amid the wooded mountains and viewing native wildlife, such as desert bighorn sheep, mule deer, cougars, foxes, coyotes, owls, eagles, and falcons. Though a truly untapped wilderness for hikers, the park's plentiful hiking trails are poorly maintained, and signs are few and far between. To be safe, bring along a compass and GPS, topographical maps, canteens, water purification tablets, proper clothing for cold and/or rainy weather, and a first-aid kit in case of injuries, rattlesnake bites, and other backcountry dangers.

Visiting this park and staying overnight promises to be a truly fantastic way to enjoy Baja's remote beauty. The daytime sky is usually a brilliant shade of blue, and nights typically radiate with unimpeded stars. Rarely will you see other campers, and distractions such as noisy children, obnoxious music, and loud generators are even rarer still.

Along the northwestern border of the park, off-road enthusiasts flock to Mike's Sky Rancho, a backcountry lodge and motorcyclists' haven nestled within a scenic valley and fringed by the pine-covered foothills of the Sierra de San Pedro Mártir. Accessible via a graded, if tricky, dirt road south of Highway 3, this isolated destination lures hundreds of solace-seeking visitors every year, though bikers and jeep drivers more commonly navigate the steep route. Besides offering modest accommodations and hearty meals, the down-to-earth resort presents a large swimming pool, a lively bar, and acres of untamed wilderness for hikers, mountain bikers, and nature lovers.

RV sites, facilities: Expect primitive camping areas in several designated areas, including Campo Noche below Picacho del Diablo, a campground at the base of the observatory access road, and another near the entrance gate. Since the dusty entrance road can be so steep and uneven, the park is probably best suited for tent campers and those with small RVs, especially four-wheel-drive pickup trucks with cab-over campers. Facilities include fiberglass outhouses and concrete fireplaces. Only self-contained RVs and rugged tent campers should park here, preferably in pairs or groups, as there's no drinking water, electricity, dump station, laundry, shower house, or security available. Children and pets are allowed, but the terrain may not be suitable for wheelchairs. Given the remoteness of this campground, you should definitely stop in Colonet or Camalú for extra food, purified water, fuel, and other supplies before traveling toward the park. Be sure to pack out all trash when you leave, and remember that firearms, motorcycles, and off-road driving are prohibited in the national park.

Reservations, fees: Reservations are not accepted; spaces are available on a first-come, first-served basis. The overnight fee for RV and tent camping is nominal—only $7 at the entrance gate. Credit cards are not accepted;

cash (Mexican pesos or U.S. dollars) is the only acceptable form of payment. The park is open all year, though it may be hard to reach during the winter months, due to hard freezes and snow-covered passages.

Directions: Although the national park can technically be reached via Highway 3 (from the northwest) and Highway 5 (from the east), the easiest route enters the park from the western side. From the San Antonio del Mar turnoff in Colonet, head south on Highway 1 for roughly 8.7 miles (14 km) to Km 141 and turn left (east) onto the paved route, near the small town of San Telmo de Abajo. If you're coming from San Quintín, head north on Highway 1 for about 30 miles (48.3 km) to Km 141 and turn right (east). Once you've turned, follow the winding paved road, which runs past the town of San Telmo and beside the Río San Telmo, for 14.5 miles (23.3 km), and then continue along an unpaved portion for another 16.7 miles (26.9 km) to the Meling Ranch. From the ranch to the entrance gate of the Parque Nacional Sierra de San Pedro Mártir, the quality of the 17.7-mile (28.5-km) passage fluctuates so much that only four-wheel-drive vehicles may be able to pass. Be advised that the entrance road, as well as the 12.3-mile (19.8-km) route that ascends to the astronomical observatory, may be closed in winter because of excessive snow.

Contact: Since there's no official contact person, mailing address, or phone number for the Parque Nacional Sierra de San Pedro Mártir, it's best just to drive into the campground and see which spots are available. For more information about Mike's Sky Rancho, call 664/681-5514.

11 PUNTA SAN JACINTO CAMPGROUND

Scenic Rating: 6

west of Camalú

See map page 126 **BEST**

Fairly popular with surfers, this primitive campground sits directly beside the Pacific Ocean, amid some permanent trailers and cottages, near a small fish camp. Since the early 1980s, the shipwrecked *Isla del Carmen* has sat partially submerged just offshore, attracting seagulls and inspiring surfers to dub the location, appropriately enough, "Shipwreck." Swimmers, anglers, hikers, wildlife enthusiasts, adventurous kayakers, and mountain bikers will relish this peaceful spot by the sea, where screeching birds and crashing waves might be the only sounds you'll hear.

If you're in need of a little luxury, then you're in luck. Along this same stretch lies the Northern Baja Surf Resort, a full-service, year-round, oceanfront complex operated by Baja Surf Adventures. The resort offers surfing instruction and guided tours to several uncrowded reef breaks along the shore. In addition, all-day boat tours can take surfers to remote offshore waves. Besides basic overnight accommodations, the property includes a festive cantina (with satellite television), authentic Mexican cuisine, wireless Internet service, kayak and *panga* rentals, pool and ping-pong tables, and, during the high season, in-house massage therapy.

RV sites, facilities: In addition to space for RV and tent camping along the beach, there is a fenced compound that contains some residential trailers, surfer-owned cottages, and 12 partially developed RV sites north of the permanent area. RVs of any size can fit here, though the most prevalent clientele are surfers with small rigs. Fire rings, pit toilets, and cold showers are the only amenities provided. Only self-contained RVs or rugged tent campers should park here, preferably in pairs or groups, as there's no drinking water, electricity, dump station, laundry, or security available. Children and pets are welcome, but the terrain is not suitable for wheelchairs. Given the remote location, it's best to stop in Camalú for extra food, purified water, fuel, and other supplies before traveling toward the coast. Be sure to pack out all trash when you leave.

Reservations, fees: Reservations are not accepted; spaces are available on a first-come, first-served basis. Given the campground's primitive status, camping is moderately priced at $5 per night (for tents or RVs). Although it's possible that no one will be present to collect the fee, you should have it ready, just in case. Credit cards are not accepted; cash (Mexican pesos or U.S. dollars) is the only acceptable form of payment. The campground is open all year.

Directions: From the San Antonio del Mar turnoff in Colonet, head south on Highway 1 for 14.6 miles (23.5 km) to Km 150. From Camalú, the turnoff is 4.8 miles (7.7 km) north along Highway 1. Turn southwest onto a graded dirt road, drive 1.2 miles (1.9 km) to a small village, and follow a "Playa" (Beach) sign that points to the left. After another 0.2 mile (0.3 km), follow a second "Playa" sign to the right and drive 3.1 miles (5 km) to the beach, where you'll spot the campground gate.

Contact: Since there's no official contact person, mailing address, or phone number for Punta San Jacinto Campground, it's best just to drive toward the ocean and see which spots are available. For details about the Ensenada area (which, to a certain degree, includes towns like Santo Tomás, San Vicente, and Colonet), visit www.ensenada.com. For more information about Baja Surf Adventures, call 800/428-7873 (U.S.) or visit www.bajasurfadventures.com.

12 RESTAURANT BAJA FIESTA

Scenic Rating: 4

in Colonia Vicente Guerrero

See map page 126

The only three places in Colonia Vicente Guerrero that advertise RV camping are, strangely enough, all popular restaurants. In the case of the Restaurant Baja Fiesta, a relatively new eatery, RV camping is definitely secondary to the friendly atmosphere and authentic cuisine of the restaurant. With the purchase of a meal, RV travelers are allowed to stay in the parking lot overnight. Despite the presence of public restrooms, however, this choice is only suitable for those willing to dry-dock.

Still, the location is ideal. There's a quaint cactus garden in front of the restaurant, and the town itself isn't far from two area attractions: the 12-mile (19-km) Playa San Ramón and the Misión de Santo Domingo de la Frontera. Playa San Ramón, popular with anglers and surfers, is accessible via a sandy, 2.5-mile (4-km) road toward the Pacific Ocean. You can hike along the entire length of the beach, from the narrow Río Santo Domingo to a set of cliffs, and dig for large Pismo clams along the way. (Just remember that you need a Mexican fishing license to go clamming, and the limit is a dozen clams per person. You should also consult local authorities to make sure regulations haven't changed.) The adobe remains of the Misión de Santo Domingo de la Frontera, relocated here in 1793, lie to the east of Colonia Vicente Guerrero, via a 2.5-mile (4-km) road that leads from the Km 169 marker on Highway 1 to the village of Santo Domingo. Although the mission has eroded into a complex of random walls and structures, there is a palpable sense of history here; travelers curious about Mexico's past will relish the serene setting.

RV sites, facilities: The large parking lot behind the restaurant has plenty of room for self-contained RVs, even lengthy ones (up to 45 feet/13.7 meters). Besides the restaurant itself, the on-site facilities include bathrooms with hot showers. There are no hookups, laundry facilities, or dump stations, but the bilingual owners live behind the restaurant, so security is adequate. Children and pets are welcome, though tents are not allowed. Groceries, purified water, gasoline, and other supplies are available in town.

Reservations, fees: Reservations are not accepted; spaces are available on a first-come, first-served basis. The cost of staying overnight is free with the price of dinner. A shower, however, costs a measly 20 pesos. Credit cards are not accepted; cash (Mexican pesos or U.S. dollars) is the only acceptable form of payment. The restaurant and RV parking lot are open all year.

Directions: The restaurant is located at the southern end of Colonia Vicente Guerrero. From north of town, head south on Highway 1 to Km 172. Keep an eye out for the restaurant—it's just north of Km 173, on the right (west) side of the highway. From the northern edge of San Quintín, drive north for about 9 miles (14.5 km) to Km 173 and turn left just past the marker, into the Restaurant Baja Fiesta parking lot.

Contact: Restaurant Baja Fiesta, Avenida Benito Juárez Sur, Colonia Vicente Guerrero, Baja California, Mexico, tel. 616/166-4011.

13 MESÓN DON PEPE RV PARK AND RESTAURANT

Scenic Rating: 6

in Colonia Vicente Guerrero

See map page 126

There are two restaurant-and-RV-park complexes near the southern edge of Colonia Vicente Guerrero, both of which have long been popular with travelers headed to and from the United States. Both are located on the same entrance road, though you'll encounter this one, the smaller of the two, first. It's a favorite among travelers and locals alike, and it's only 3 miles (4.8 km) north of a small tourist information center, situated at Km 178 on Highway 1.

Visitors should be aware, however, that the campground's proximity to the main highway can make the experience noisy at times. Still, the delicious seafood and authentic Mexican cuisine, all available for reasonable prices at the adjacent restaurant, make this locale more than worth your while. In addition, the Pacific Ocean lies only a few miles to the west, so swimming, surf fishing, sea kayaking, bird-watching, hiking, and other outdoor diversions aren't far away.

RV sites, facilities: Below the restaurant, there is a grassy area for tent camping; water service and 15-amp electrical outlets are available there. A dirt-covered parking lot can accommodate eight small RVs. Given the short sites and challenging access, the space is only suitable for RVs less than 30 feet (9.1 meters) long. Besides the restaurant, other facilities include a dump station, barbecue pits, and an old restroom building with hot showers. Shady trees and trash cans pepper the property. Children and pets are welcome, but there is no laundry or official security on the premises. Groceries, purified water, gasoline, and other supplies are available in nearby Colonia Vicente Guerrero.

Reservations, fees: Reservations are not accepted; spaces are available on a first-come, first-served basis. RV sites cost $10 per night (for a two-person occupancy), while tent sites are $7 nightly. Credit cards are not accepted; cash (Mexican pesos or U.S. dollars) is the only acceptable form of payment. The restaurant and RV park are open all year.

Directions: From the stoplight in Colonia Vicente Guerrero, take Highway 1 south for 1 mile (1.6 km) to a small hill at Km 173. Near the top of the hill, just north of the propane plant and about 100 yards (91.4 meters) south of the sign for the Mesón Don Pepe RV Park and Restaurant, turn right (west) onto the gravel road and take an immediate right into the parking lot for the small restaurant and office. After you check in, you can drive around the back of the campground to find a spot.

Contact: Mesón Don Pepe RV Park and Restaurant, Calle del Turismo #102, Colonia Vicente Guerrero, Baja California, C.P. 22920, Mexico, tel. 616/166-2216 or 616/166-4414, fax 616/166-2268.

14 POSADA DON DIEGO RV PARK & RESTAURANT

Scenic Rating: 7

in Colonia Vicente Guerrero

See map page 126 BEST

Since 1970, this friendly, family-operated park has welcomed RVs of all sizes. As the area's roomiest campground, this tree-studded locale is a favorite among RV caravans. Not far from the Pacific Ocean, the historic, agricultural town of San Quintín, numerous fields of *tomates* and *fresas* (strawberries), and a remote, mountainous national park, this is a comfortable base camp for a plethora of activities, including sipping margaritas and dancing to live music at the adjacent restaurant.

In addition, anglers and surfers can easily reach the ocean from here. A sandy, 2.5-mile (4-km) road heads west to Playa San Ramón, south of the Río Santo Domingo, where surfers will find excellent point and surf breaks, though the water is often cold enough for a wetsuit. Anglers, meanwhile, can search for corvina and perch within the deep waters of Bahía San Ramón. Surf fishing is especially popular; it's even possible to dig up Pismo clams along the shore to use as bait. Just remember that a Mexican fishing license is required, that the limit is 12 clams per person, and that each clam must be at least 4 inches (10.2 cm) in diameter. It's also important to consult local residents to ensure that clamming regulations haven't changed.

History buffs will also find welcome diversions in this region. The adobe remains of the Misión de Santo Domingo de la Frontera, which was relocated here in 1793, lie to the east of Colonia Vicente Guerrero, via a 2.5-mile (4-km) road that leads from the Km 169 marker on Highway 1 to the village of Santo Domingo. Although the mission has eroded into a complex of random walls and structures, the site emanates a palpable sense of history; travelers curious about Mexico's past will relish the serene setting.

RV sites, facilities: The campground contains 100 sites, all of which have water service, 15-amp electricity, concrete patios, picnic tables, and fire rings. Although about 20 of the sites are pull-throughs, most are back-ins, and half of them have sewer access. Many of the spaces are roomy enough to accommodate lengthy rigs (up to 45 feet/13.7 meters long) with slide-outs, and about a third of them are usually occupied by permanent residents. The property also houses a dump station, aging (though clean) restrooms with flush toilets and hot showers, a coin laundry, a restaurant and bar, a meeting room, a gift shop, a volleyball court, a horseshoe pit, and a playground. Closer to the restaurant, some of the sites have wireless Internet access. Motel units, trailer and house rentals, and tent sites are available, too. Children and pets are welcome here, and the staff speaks both English and Spanish. Given the presence of on-site owners, a night guard, and police officers (on occasion), the security is excellent here. The water, however, is a different matter: It's drawn from a well, making it too brackish to drink or use for cooking. Before arriving, you should gather groceries, purified water, and other supplies in nearby Colonia Vicente Guerrero or San Quintín.

Reservations, fees: Since sites can fill up with permanent campers and large caravans, reservations are definitely recommended. RV sites cost $11 nightly; weekly, monthly, and yearly rates are also available. Tent sites are $10 each night. Motel rooms cost $35, and the trailers are $25 each. For a nominal fee, wireless Internet service is available in the sites closest to the restaurant. Note that space and room rates are based on a two-person occupancy; extra guests will be charged additional fees. Cash (Mexican pesos or U.S. dollars) and credit cards are accepted. The park is open all year.

Directions: From the stoplight in Colonia Vicente Guerrero, take Highway 1 south for 1 mile (1.6 km), turn right (west) onto the gravel road just north of the propane plant and about 100 yards (91.4 meters) south of the sign for the Mesón Don Pepe RV Park and Restaurant, and drive 0.5 mile (0.8 km) to the campground. Be advised that, if you're coming from the north, you'll find no sign for Posada Don Diego; from the south, however, you'll see a sign on the roof of a shed.

Contact: Posada Don Diego RV Park & Restaurant, Km 174 de la Carretera Transpeninsular, Colonia Vicente Guerrero, Baja California, C.P. 22920, Mexico, tel. 616/166-2181, fax 616/166-2248, www.posadadondiego.com.

15 OLD MILL MOTEL AND RV PARK

Scenic Rating: 6

south of San Quintín

See map page 126 **BEST**

A favorite among anglers, this simple campground offers stunning views of Bahía San Quintín and terrific access to some bountiful fishing spots in the open water. The lengthy entrance road, often resembling a washboard, deters some travelers, but it's still an advantageous spot if fishing, boating, kayaking, and bird-watching are your preferred activities. Travelers who bring their own boats will especially like this locale. There's a boat launch and bait shop beside the campground, though it's also possible to rent a boat and hire a fishing guide.

If you need a break from water-related diversions and are curious about the area's history, there are some interesting structures nearby. In the late 1800s, American and English settlers attempted to initiate a wheat-farming enterprise in San Quintín, a scheme that was soon abandoned due to lack of rainfall. Although those days are long past, remnants of the ill-fated industry remain. Near the RV park lies the restored *molino viejo* (old mill), and to the southeast a *muelle viejo* (old pier) stretches into the bay, not far from an old English cemetery.

RV sites, facilities: The campground has 20 RV sites, with full hookups (including 15-amp electricity, water service, and sewer access), paved parking pads, fire rings, barbecue grills, and patios. Fifteen of the sites are situated beside the bay, with a nice view of the bird-filled estuary, but little room for longer RVs. The other sites sit farther from the shore, with pull-through access and more space for big rigs (up to 45 feet/13.7 meters long). There is an overflow area, with no hookups, for dry-docking RVers and tent campers. Amenities include a public pay phone, a restaurant and bar, a bait shop, a boat launch, and clean restrooms with flush toilets and hot showers. There is also a motel on the premises, though there's no laundry or dump station. Children and leashed pets are welcome here. Before arriving, you should gather groceries, purified water, gasoline, and other supplies in San Quintín.

Reservations, fees: Reservations are accepted. The RV sites cost $15 per night; tent sites cost $10 per night. Motel rooms are also available. Credit cards are not accepted; cash (Mexican pesos or U.S. dollars) is the customary form of payment. The RV park is open all year.

Directions: From San Quintín, drive south along Highway 1 to the adjacent town of Lázaro Cárdenas. Drive another 0.6 mile (1 km) to the Km 1 marker, where you'll see a sign for the Old Mill Motel and RV Park. Turn right (west) onto a wide, bumpy dirt road and continue for 3.3 miles (5.3 km). Ignore the signs for the Old Pier; that RV park has been closed for a while now. Instead, follow the Old Mill sign to the left. You'll see the restaurant, motel, and RV park at the end of the road. Check in at the bait shop opposite the restaurant or, if it's closed, at the bar.

Contact: Old Mill Motel and RV Park, Apartado Postal #90, San Quintín, Baja California, Mexico, tel. 616/165-6030, or P.O. Box 2448, Chula Vista, CA 91912.

16 CIELITO LINDO MOTEL AND RV PARK

Scenic Rating: 6

south of San Quintín

See map page 126

Along the shores of Bahía Santa María extends one of the finest, if windiest, beaches in northern Baja, a wide expanse of sand that stretches from the mouth of Bahía San Quintín to the Arroyo Socorro, 10 miles (16.1 km) to the south. This long-standing motel and its adjacent RV park are situated just a quarter mile (0.4 km) from the northernmost part of the beach, Playa Santa María. Travelers pursue a wide array of pastimes here, including hiking, mountain biking, watching birds and marine mammals, combing the beach for sand dollars, and surf fishing for perch and corvina. With an on-site sportfishing charter operation, anglers will especially enjoy this spot, from which you're promised a wealth of deep-sea fishing opportunities. Many enjoy searching the rich ocean waters that surround the Isla San Martín for offshore varieties such as bonita, tuna, rockcod, lingcod, and yellowtail.

Visitors especially love to dig for Pismo clams here. Named for Pismo Beach, California, north of the border, these large, meaty shellfish, one of the largest clam species along the Pacific coast, can be fried, boiled, steamed, sautéed, or used in chowder. Playa Santa María happens to be one of the best clam-digging spots on the entire Baja peninsula. All you need is a pitchfork or a pair of hands, a bucket of saltwater, and a Mexican fishing license. Then, at low tide, you can simply walk barefoot to the waterline, feel the sand for a buried clam, unearth the mollusk, and toss it into your bucket, where it should stay until cooking time. Just remember that each clam you keep must be at least 4 inches (10.2 cm) in diameter and that you can keep no more than a dozen per day. (Always check with locals to see if clamming regulations have changed.)

Given the warm waters of Bahía Santa María, the coast also entices swimmers, kayakers, surfers, kite-fliers, and pleasure boaters. The bar/restaurant is also a big attraction, especially during happy hour; cracked crab is the joint's specialty. As a bonus, you'll be treated to live music on occasional nights.

RV sites, facilities: The park offers 15 easy-to-access campsites, eight of which are back-ins with full hookups (including 15-amp, generator-produced electricity) and plenty of room for big rigs (up to 40 feet/12.2 meters in length). The other seven sites are pull-throughs with *palapas* to shade tent and van campers. Besides sheltering pine trees and an inexpensive motel, amenities include a popular restaurant and bar, a playground, a barbecue area, a TV lounge, horse stables, a mini-zoo, a charter boat operation and tackle shop, and clean, recently refurbished restrooms with flush toilets and hot showers (located on the north end of the complex). Children and pets are welcome. Resident managers and nighttime guards provide moderate security. There is no dump station or laundry on the premises. The water is brackish here, so it's best to pick up purified water and other supplies from nearby San Quintín before arriving.

Reservations, fees: Reservations are accepted. The nightly fees are low: $12 for RVs and $10 for tents. Clean motel rooms are also available. Credit cards are not accepted; cash (Mexican pesos or U.S. dollars) is the customary form of payment. The park is open all year.

Directions: From the southern edge of San Quintín, drive south along Highway 1 for 10.2 miles (16.4 km) to Km 11, where you'll spy signs for the La Pinta Hotel and Cielito Lindo Motel. Turn right (west) onto the paved (yet bumpy and pothole-strewn) road and drive for 2.8 miles (4.5 km). Pass the La Pinta entrance, continue along the road (now covered with gravel), and drive an additional 0.8 mile (1.3 km) to the Cielito Lindo Motel. Just watch for the signs; you'll see the RV park near the motel and restaurant.

Contact: Cielito Lindo Motel and RV Park, Apartado Postal #7, San Quintín, Baja California, Mexico. Since there's no phone number, it's best just to drive toward the campground and see which spots are available.

17 GYPSY'S BEACH CAMP

Scenic Rating: 8

south of San Quintín

See map page 126

Not far from the Cielito Lindo Motel lies another fairly ancient campground that travelers seem to adore. Positioned near the northern side of a peninsula, which separates Bahía Falsa and Bahía San Quintín from Bahía Santa María, this casual, beachside locale lures the fun-loving sort. The two-story restaurant and bar, Laura's

Zopilote Mojado (Wet Buzzard), is an especially big attraction, commanding a magnificent view of the Pacific Ocean. It's the perfect place to sit back and watch a glorious Baja sunset while sipping margaritas and Tecate beer.

Situated behind the sand dunes alongside Bahía San Quintín, the campground provides easy access to a superb beach, ideal for swimmers, kayakers, and boaters alike. At the western end of the peninsula, the point offers a terrific position to watch dolphins, sharks, and migrating whales. Anglers can use their own boats or hire others to guide them through the bountiful bays, where halibut, perch, corvina, white sea bass, and blue crabs dwell. Amateur boaters should be careful, however; it's common for mud flats in the channel between the bays to impede a perfectly promising fishing excursion, and the offshore waters can be downright perilous.

In the winter months, Bahía San Quintín becomes one of Baja's prime estuaries for migratory waterfowl. Birding enthusiasts will enjoy watching this active ecosystem, while hunters will find bountiful populations of geese and ducks in the marshes along the northern end of the bay. Another interesting aspect of this region is the San Quintín volcanic field, an array of prominent cones peppering the peninsula that divides Bahía Falsa from the Pacific Ocean. Off-road enthusiasts and primitive tent campers especially love this rugged terrain, though visitors should be prepared for flat tires and should never camp alone. This is, after all, an isolated landscape, farther from help than you might imagine. In recent years, the large influx of migrant workers, helping on surrounding farms, has resulted in an increase in criminal activity, so it's not advisable to camp outside the established campgrounds.

RV sites, facilities: The campground consists of a large lot made of packed dirt, where there's plenty of room for tents and RVs, including lengthy motor homes and travel trailers (up to 45 feet/13.7 meters long). Cement curbs separate some of the sites, but most of them are not delineated. There is a mixture of back-in and pull-through areas. Facilities include a covered area for tent campers, a clubhouse, a restroom building with hot showers and flush toilets, and a spacious bar and restaurant. There is no laundry or dump station on the premises. Children and pets are welcome, and the staff speaks English. A resident guard provides limited security. Stock up on groceries, purified water, gasoline, and other supplies in the nearby town of San Quintín.

Reservations, fees: Reservations are accepted. RV and tent sites cost $10 per night. Credit cards are not accepted; cash (Mexican pesos or U.S. dollars) is the customary form of payment. The park is open all year.

Directions: From the southern edge of San Quintín, drive south along Highway 1 for 10.2 miles (16.4 km) to Km 11, where you'll spy signs for the La Pinta Hotel and Cielito Lindo Motel. Turn right (west) onto the paved (yet bumpy and pothole-strewn) road and drive for 2.8 miles (4.5 km). Pass the La Pinta entrance, continue along the road (now covered with gravel), and drive past the left-hand turnoff for the Cielito Lindo Motel. Instead, veer right onto the dirt road and drive another quarter mile (0.4 km) to Gypsy's Beach Camp, which is visible beside the coast.

Contact: Gypsy's Beach Camp, Apartado Postal #7, San Quintín, Baja California, Mexico. Since there's no phone number, it's best just to drive toward the campground and see which spots are available.

18 EL PABELLÓN TRAILER PARK

Scenic Rating: 8

south of San Quintín

See map page 126 **BEST**

Nowadays, the lovely Playa El Pabellón, a widespread beach with miles of sand dunes and ocean views, boasts two RV campgrounds, separated by a chain-link fence. This one is the oldest. For years, it's attracted countless primitive campers, including RV caravans, to one of Baja's most unimpeded vistas. Although there are few amenities here, travelers appreciate this wide-open landscape, where sportfishing, swimming, kite-flying, surfing, and hiking are the most sought-after diversions. Children, especially, appreciate the whimsical whale skeleton that sits upon these immaculate grounds.

However, this is an extremely windy beach. Most campers try to select a sheltered spot beside a row of trees and shrubs along the edge of the dunes, several yards from the briny tide. Such areas offer not only protection from the frequent winds, but also a modicum of privacy from your neighbors.

Although surf fishing is popular here, more adventurous anglers can charter a *panga* for a deep-sea fishing excursion around the Isla San Martín, an offshore volcanic island that's also ideal for multiday kayaking excursions. For those who want a taste of the sea without the work, never fear. From the *pangas* that operate within the surf beside the campground, Mexican fishermen sell lobster, Pismo clams, stone crab claws, and varied fishes.

RV sites, facilities: The large graded parking area could probably accommodate up to 90 RVs, but only 14 spots have sewer access and water spigots (note that the water is too salty to use in sensitive RV tanks and lines). The campground provides easy access for big rigs (up to 45 feet/13.7 meters in length), and tent campers can set up their sites wherever they like, though usually they choose the beach in front of the "official" campground or the wind-protected area behind the trees. As for amenities, expect little more than concrete sinks, fish-cleaning tables, barbecue pits, and clean restrooms with flush toilets and hot showers.

Only self-contained RVs and rugged tent campers should park here, preferably in pairs or groups, as there's no drinking water, electricity, laundry, or dump station on the premises, and the only security provided comes from a gated entrance. It's also advisable to bring shovels, boards, rope, and other such tools with you, just in case your wheels get stuck in the sand. Children and pets are welcome, but the terrain is not suitable for wheelchairs. Although there's a grocery store within walking distance, you should stop in San Quintín for extra food, purified water, fuel, and other supplies before traveling to the campground. Be sure to pack out all trash when you leave.

Reservations, fees: Reservations are not accepted; spaces are available on a first-come, first-served basis. The overnight camping fee for RVs and tents is $5–10. Credit cards are not accepted; cash (Mexican pesos or U.S. dollars) is the only acceptable form of payment. This beachside campground is open all year.

Directions: From San Quintín, head south on Highway 1 to Km 16. Look for the El Pabellón sign between Km 16 and Km 17. Turn right (southwest) onto the dirt-and-gravel road and drive 1.2 miles (1.9 km) to the entrance gate of the El Pabellón Trailer Park. Note that, if you're driving from El Rosario, you will first encounter a sign for the adjacent El Pabellón Palapas Alvinos. Unless you intend to stay there, ignore it and continue for 0.2 mile (0.3 km) to the turnoff for the original El Pabellón Trailer Park.

Contact: Since there's no official contact person, mailing address, or phone number for the El Pabellón Trailer Park, it's best just to drive toward the ocean and see which spots are available.

19 EL PABELLÓN PALAPAS ALVINOS

Scenic Rating: 8

south of San Quintín

See map page 126

Although a bit farther from the U.S.-Mexico border than, for example, Ensenada, San Quintín is still a popular destination for American travelers hoping for an extended weekend getaway. It's also a convenient overnight stopping point for those headed to and from the southern half of the Baja peninsula. South of San Quintín, the saltwater lagoon system that contains Bahía San Quintín is notable among birding enthusiasts, sea kayakers, deep-sea anglers, swimmers, surfers, hikers, and other nature lovers.

This relatively new campground, situated

even farther south, along the Playa El Pabellón, is a nice place to park your RV or tent—whether you intend to explore San Quintín and its surrounding region or just stay the night before heading south to El Rosario. Although it seems to be just a mere extension of the more northwesterly El Pabellón Trailer Park—only partitioned by a chain-link fence—it is actually a separate campground, run by different individuals. The ocean views, however, are amazing from either park.

RV sites, facilities: The large graded parking area adjoins the beach and offers enough space for a host of tent campers and an entire RV caravan, with easy access for big rigs (up to 45 feet/13.7 meters in length) in addition to a line of water spigots. As for amenities, expect little more than a dump station and clean restrooms with flush toilets and hot showers. Although there is generally someone on duty 24 hours daily, only self-contained RVs and rugged tent campers should park here, preferably in pairs or groups, as there's no drinking water, electricity, laundry, or dump station. Children and pets are welcome, but the terrain is not suitable for wheelchairs. Given the lack of nearby stores, you should stop in San Quintín for extra food, purified water, fuel, and other supplies before traveling to the campground. Be sure to pack out all trash when you leave.

Reservations, fees: Reservations are not accepted; spaces are available on a first-come, first-served basis. The overnight camping fee for RVs and tents is $5–10. Credit cards are not accepted; cash (Mexican pesos or U.S. dollars) is the only acceptable form of payment. This beachside campground is open all year.

Directions: From San Quintín, head south on Highway 1 to Km 16. Look for the El Pabellón Trailer Park sign between Km 16 and Km 17. Pass this entrance and drive 0.2 mile (0.3 km) southeast to Km 16.5, where you'll spot a large sign for El Pabellón Palapas Alvinos. Turn right (southwest) onto the dirt road and continue for 1 mile (1.6 km), passing beside a row of power lines and veering right toward the beachside campground. Note that if you're driving from El Rosario, you will first encounter a sign for El Pabellón Palapas Alvinos, before spotting the original El Pabellón Trailer Park.

Contact: Since there's no official contact person, mailing address, or phone number for El Pabellón Palapas Alvinos, it's best just to drive toward the ocean and see which spots are available.

20 RANCHO EL SOCORRITO

Scenic Rating: 9

north of El Rosario

See map page 126

Although this complex, which includes houses, lots, and an airstrip, is intended for permanent or semipermanent residents, there is a gorgeous beach to the west that offers primitive camping by the sea. Situated just north of Playa El Socorro, the area lures pilots, bicyclists, birdwatchers, rockhounds, hikers, hunters, off-road enthusiasts, and artists. Surf fishing, boating, kayaking, swimming, surfing, sunbathing, and photography are popular pastimes, too. While it might not be the most luxurious spot (given the lack of amenities), it's an ideal midway point between San Quintín and El Rosario.

Be advised, however, that real estate is an ever-evolving entity in Baja. In recent years, beachside areas that have long been welcome to primitive campers are often purchased and redeveloped into exclusive resort communities. So, when in doubt about a campground's status, consult local residents before pulling in for the night.

RV sites, facilities: This beachside campground offers plenty of space for tent and RV campers, though there are no amenities on-site. Only small, self-contained RVs and rugged tent campers should park here, preferably in pairs or groups, as there's no drinking water, electricity, dump station, shower house, laundry, or security available. Children and pets are welcome, but the terrain is not suitable for wheelchairs. In fact, it's advisable to bring tools such as boards, shovels, and rope with you, just in case your wheels get stuck in the sand. Given the lack of nearby stores, you should stop in San Quintín or El Rosario for extra food, purified water, gasoline, and other supplies before traveling to the campground. Be sure to pack out all trash when you leave.

Reservations, fees: Reservations are not accepted; spaces are available on a first-come, first-served basis. Given the primitive setting, the overnight camping fee for RVs and tents is about $5 per vehicle. Credit cards are not accepted; cash (Mexican pesos or U.S. dollars) is the customary form of payment. This beachside campground is open all year.

Directions: From the southern edge of San Quintín, head south on Highway 1 for 18.9 miles (30.4 km) to Km 23. From El Rosario, drive north on Highway 1 for 18 miles (29 km) to Km 23. Turn left (west) onto Camino El Socorrito, pass the residential lots and airstrip, and follow the road to the beach.

Contact: Since there's no official contact person, mailing address, or phone number for the beach beyond Rancho El Socorrito, it's best just to drive toward the ocean and see which spots, if any, are available.

21 MOTEL SINAHI RV PARK

Scenic Rating: 6

in El Rosario

See map page 126

El Rosario, the gateway to Baja's central *desierto* (the "real Baja," according to seasoned travelers), connects the coastal plain beside the Pacific Ocean to the remote arid landscape surrounding Cataviña. The town, which lies only an hour's drive south of San Quintín, is little more than a cluster of structures, including a Pemex gas station, a few hotels, some general stores, the two ruined sites of the former Misión de Nuestra Señora del Santísimo Rosario de Viñadaco, and Mama Espinosa's, a small motel and one of Baja's most famous restaurants. Since the completion of the Transpeninsular Highway (Highway 1) in the early 1970s, Mama's has been a favorite stop for travelers, including James Garner and Steve McQueen. Lobster burritos and huge breakfasts are the joint's specialties. El Rosario's only RV park, part of the Motel Sinahi property, is a terrific spot to park your RV while you explore what little the town and its hinterlands have to offer.

To the southwest of El Rosario lie two areas popular with outdoor enthusiasts, Punta Baja and Punta San Carlos. Both are accessible via a rough, winding road. Surfers and kayakers especially like the area around Punta Baja, which sits 10.2 miles (16.4 km) from town. Windsurfing is a popular pastime around Punta San Carlos, which lies another 49.4 miles (79.5 km) down the coast. If, after exploring El Rosario and its surrounding hotspots, you're ready to experience the central desert region, be sure to stock up on all the groceries, purified water, gasoline, and other supplies you'll need for the journey. If you're headed for the state line, you probably won't find reliable services for over 200 miles (322 km).

RV sites, facilities: Besides a variety of comfortable rooms, the kitschy motel offers 33 RV sites on a plateau behind the motel and down in the yard; the long, flat spaces make it easy to maneuver big rigs (up to 45 feet/13.7 meters long). There are also 25 RV sites above the motel, accessible via a ramp and situated rather close together, making it harder to navigate into and out of this area. All of the sites have 15-amp electricity and cement pads, and most have water service and sewer access. A large lot, adjacent to the motel, provides room for perhaps eight more RVs. On-site you'll find a restaurant, a coin laundry, flush toilets, two hot showers, and a public pay phone. There is, however, no dump station on the premises. Children, pets, and tent campers are welcome. The on-site owner provides limited security, and the staff speaks some English. As with much of Baja, the water isn't safe to drink, so be sure to purchase purified water and other supplies in nearby stores.

Reservations, fees: Reservations are not accepted; spaces are available on a first-come, first-served basis. The overnight fee for RV camping is $16. Tent sites cost $10 per night. Motel rooms are available for $20–25 per night. Credit cards are not accepted; cash (Mexican pesos or U.S. dollars) is the customary form of payment. The park is open all year.

Directions: Heading south from San Quintín via Highway 1, follow the road as it enters El Rosario and turns sharply to the northeast, on the eastern edge of town. After continuing for one mile (1.6 km), you'll see the park on the left (north) side.

Contact: Motel Sinahi RV Park, Km 56.5 de la Carretera Transpeninsular #1056, El Rosario, Baja California, Mexico, tel. 616/165-8818.

22 LONCHERÍA SONORA

Scenic Rating: 4

northwest of Cataviña

See map page 126 **BEST**

On the road from El Rosario, the first RV park you'll encounter isn't much to observe. Encircled by half-buried tires and situated beside a small restaurant, this spacious parking lot might not offer a plethora of amenities, but it's certainly an inexpensive place to rest for the night. Moreover, it's close to several captivating sights, including the former Misión de San Fernando Rey de España de Velicatá (Baja California's only Franciscan mission) as well as some 1,000-year-old petroglyphs along an *arroyo* near the mission. In addition, you're not far from the ruins of the El Mármol onyx quarry, which comprises a cemetery, a former school, and an open pit mine. Perhaps more obvious are the acres of dramatic boulders and unique cactus varieties that surround the *desierto* settlement of Cataviña. Just be prepared for incredibly hot summers—and for a long stretch of bumpy desert road, with little in the way of stores, gas stations, and the like.

RV sites, facilities: The campground is essentially a large parking lot beside a small restaurant. There are no designated RV sites—you can park wherever you like. With careful maneuvering, even big rigs (up to 40 feet/12.2 meters in length) will find room here. Besides the surrounding desert, however, there are few amenities, just the restaurant and an outhouse. Only self-contained RVs and rugged tent campers should park here, preferably in pairs or groups, as there's no drinking water, dump station, electricity, laundry, shower house, or security. Children and pets are welcome, and the lot is accessible to wheelchairs. Given the remote location, it's best to stop in El Rosario for extra food, purified water, fuel, and other supplies before traveling south into the desert. Remember to pack out all trash when you leave.

Reservations, fees: Reservations are not accepted; spaces are available on a first-come, first-served basis. Given its primitive status, the campground is moderately priced at $5 per night. Credit cards are not accepted; cash (Mexican pesos or U.S. dollars) is the customary form of payment. The restaurant and campground are open all year.

Directions: From downtown El Rosario (where Highway 1 veers sharply to the northeast), drive 56.9 miles (91.6 km) into Baja's central desert. Just past the turnoff to El Mármol, you'll spot the Lonchería Sonora restaurant on the left side, near Km 149. From Cataviña, head northwest on Highway 1 for 19.5 miles (31.4 km) and turn right into the restaurant parking lot.

Contact: Since there's no official contact person, mailing address, or phone number for Lonchería Sonora, it's best just to stop by and see if any space is available.

23 PARQUE DEL PALMERITO

Scenic Rating: 6

northwest of Cataviña

See map page 126 **BEST**

If you're headed south from El Rosario, you're bound to spot a pattern in the landscape—desert, desert, and more desert. Despite such repetition, however, this remote region can be quite stunning, especially near sunset, when the dramatic boulders, palm trees, and various cacti seem to be kissed by a halo of gold. Hikers, wildlife enthusiasts, and amateur photographers are all fans of this stark terrain, a definite change from the aquamarine waters that surround much of the Baja peninsula.

Most of this central *desierto* is apparently protected, in one way or another, by the Mexican government. Just west of Cataviña lies this particular park, the 4,940-acre (2,000-hectare) Parque del Palmerito, which is devoted to the conservation of desert flora and fauna, from blossoming cacti to sinister *alacráns* (scorpions). Besides its unique natural features and a series of Cochimí cave paintings, the park offers marked nature trails, ecofriendly restrooms, a free museum, and a primitive campground. So, if you hope to spend some time exploring this alluring habitat, you might want to stop for the night in the fenced area that sits beside the Museo El Palmerito, a light-filled geodesic dome containing a small collection of natural history displays.

RV sites, facilities: The fenced campground beside the museum offers a wide space for any number of tents and RVs. Although there are no designated sites or hookups, you will find a few amenities, including ecofriendly bathroom facilities, picnic areas, several hiking and nature trails, and, of course, the free museum (which accepts donations). Only small, self-contained RVs and rugged tent campers should park here, preferably in pairs or groups, as there's no drinking water, dump station, laundry, or electricity. Children and leashed pets are welcome, though the uneven terrain might not be suitable for wheelchairs. A gate provides limited security.

Visitors must stay on the designated trails, pick up after their pets, bring their own firewood, and only light campfires in the picnic areas. Loud music, off-road driving, littering, and collecting or defacing natural artifacts are strictly forbidden. Given the remote location, it's best to stop in El Rosario for extra food, purified water, fuel, and other supplies before traveling south into the desert; pick up supplies in Guerrero Negro if you're headed north. Remember to pack out all trash when you leave.

Reservations, fees: Reservations are not accepted; spaces are available on a first-come, first-served basis. Entrance into the park (behind the museum) is moderately priced at $10 per vehicle per day (for up to four passengers); the fee includes use of the hiking trails, bathroom facilities, and campground. Children under 12 years old are admitted without charge. Credit cards are not accepted; cash (Mexican pesos or U.S. dollars) is the customary form of payment. The museum and campground are open all year.

Directions: From downtown El Rosario (where Highway 1 veers sharply to the northeast), drive 70.8 miles (113.9 km) into Baja's central desert, toward Cataviña. Near Km 170, you'll see the entrance to the Parque del Palmerito on your left, on the north side of the road. From Cataviña, drive northwest for 5.6 miles (9 km) to Km 170. The park entrance will be on your right. Note that the museum and campground are located between Km 175 and Km 176.

Contact: Parque del Palmerito, Km 170 de la Carretera Transpeninsular, Cataviña, Baja California, Mexico, www.catavina.com.

24 PARQUE NATURAL DEL DESIERTO CENTRAL RV PARK

Scenic Rating: 6

in Cataviña

See map page 126

One confusing, yet endearing, aspect of Baja California is the question of names—and the fact that most places have more than one. Baja's central *desierto* is no exception. The dramatic landscape that surrounds the minuscule town of Cataviña has been called the Parque Natural del Desierto Central, the Valle de los Cirios Area Protegida, and, in parts, the Parque Natural

Palmerito, among other monikers. No matter what you call this remote terrain—a land of strange boulders and a variety of desert plants, including the gigantic, multipronged *cardón* and the tapering, often arching *cirio*—it's an intriguing place to visit, especially for hikers, wildlife enthusiasts, and amateur photographers. Just be aware that, as with any desert, water is a necessity, so bring lots of it. Also, you should stay alert for potentially perilous desert creatures, such as *alacráns* (scorpions), *serpientes de cascabel* (rattlesnakes), and *tarántulas.*

The campground here is one of several fenced compounds built by the Mexican government following the completion of the Transpeninsular Highway (Highway 1). Although there are few official amenities, the park is relatively clean, with similar landscaping (boulders and cacti) as the surrounding *desierto.* The only two obvious drawbacks are its severe heat in summer and its highway noise at night.

RV sites, facilities: The fenced campground offers several large sites, with sewer access and enough space to accommodate lengthy RVs (up to 40 feet/12.2 meters long). Most of the sites are pull-throughs. Besides the intriguing landscape, the only other amenities include bathrooms, with toilets that are flushed using buckets of water (when available). Only self-contained RVs and rugged tent campers should park here, preferably in pairs or groups, as there's no drinking water, dump station, laundry, or electricity available, and a gate provides only limited security. Children and leashed pets are welcome, though the uneven terrain might not be suitable for wheelchairs. Given the remote location, it's best to stop in El Rosario for extra food, purified water, fuel, and other supplies before traveling south into the desert; pick up supplies in Guerrero Negro if you're headed north. Remember to pack out all trash when you leave.

Reservations, fees: Reservations are not accepted; spaces are available on a first-come, first-served basis. RV and tent sites are moderately priced at $10 per night. Credit cards are not accepted; cash (Mexican pesos or U.S. dollars) is the customary form of payment. The campground is open all year.

Directions: From downtown El Rosario (where Highway 1 veers sharply to the northeast), drive 76.4 miles (122.9 km) into Baja's central desert, to Cataviña. Between Km 178 and Km 179, you'll see the campground on your right, on the south side of the road and just west of the La Pinta Motel (and the abandoned Pemex gas station).

Contact: Since there's no official contact person, mailing address, or phone number for the Parque Natural del Desierto Central RV Park, it's best just to drive into the campground and see which spots are available.

25 RANCHO SANTA INÉS

Scenic Rating: 5

east of Cataviña

See map page 126

Because it's not situated beside the main drag—as are the other three campgrounds near Cataviña—this spot is easy to miss. After all, you have to drive over half a mile north of the Transpeninsular Highway (Highway 1) to reach the entrance to Rancho Santa Inés, a fourth-generation, century-old ranch that's long been a popular pit stop for desert-weary travelers and eccentric old-timers. But, of course, besides the small adjacent restaurant and its knowledgeable owners, that's one of this park's best features—its off-the-beaten-path location means you're guaranteed more quietude at night. The only disadvantages of this campground are the hot summers and the occasional stray dogs, which have been known to disturb tent campers. As in other parts of Baja, it's a good idea to safeguard your belongings and avoid traveling alone.

Obviously, there are no bodies of water in these parts, so your activities are limited to hiking, mountain biking, viewing wildlife, taking photographs, and the like. Besides exploring the region's strange granite boulders, Indian rock-art sites, various cactus plants, elephant trees, and elusive creatures, you can also hike east to the adobe ruins of the short-lived Misión de Santa María de los Ángeles Cabujacaamang. Just remember to bring lots of water for your journey, and be prepared to stay overnight in the desert.

RV sites, facilities: The campground is essentially a large flat dirt parking lot. Although there are no utility hookups and only a few shady trees, the space is wide enough to accommodate lengthy RVs (up to 40 feet/12.2 meters long), making it a favorite among caravans. Besides the intriguing landscape, the only other amenities include a small restaurant, a water faucet, some dorm rooms, and a bathroom with one flush toilet and occasionally hot showers. Only self-contained RVs and rugged tent campers should park in the lot, preferably in pairs or groups, as there's no drinking water, dump station, laundry, or electricity. Children and leashed pets are welcome, though the uneven terrain might not be suitable for wheelchairs. The on-site owners provide limited security. Given the remote location, it's best to stop in El Rosario for extra food, purified water, fuel, and other supplies before traveling south into the desert; pick up supplies in Guerrero Negro if you're headed north. Remember to pack out all trash when you leave.

Reservations, fees: Reservations are not accepted; spaces are available on a first-come, first-served basis. RV and tent sites are moderately priced at around $10 per night. Credit cards are not accepted; cash (Mexican pesos or U.S. dollars) is the customary form of payment. The campground is open all year.

Directions: From downtown El Rosario (where Highway 1 veers sharply to the northeast), drive 77.6 miles (124.9 km) into Baja's central desert, to Cataviña. Near Km 181 (less than a mile east of the La Pinta Motel), you'll see a well-marked road on the north side. Turn left here and follow the paved road for about 0.7 mile (1.1 km). The campground will be on your left. From south of the Cataviña area, drive north to Km 181 and turn right onto the paved entrance road.

Contact: Since there's no official contact person, mailing address, or phone number for Rancho Santa Inés, it's best just to drive into the campground and see which spots are available.

26 PUNTA PRIETA RV PARK

Scenic Rating: 5

west of Bahía de los Ángeles

See map page 126

Open at sporadic times, this old government campground offers plenty of space for tent campers and lengthy RVs. Although you might find the gates closed on occasion, it's worth a quick stop, just to be sure. After all, it's the only official campground you'll find between Cataviña, Bahía de los Ángeles, and the state line.

As with the campgrounds near Cataviña, most of the utility hookups aren't functioning and the landscaping consists of mere rocks and desert plants, similar to its stark environs. Hiking, mountain biking, and viewing wildlife are the most popular activities in this remote region. In fact, it's probably safe to say that the area's most interesting sights lie along the two-lane highway north and south of here.

En route from Cataviña, for instance, you'll encounter a few small *ranchos,* the appropriately named Cerro Pedregoso ("Rocky Hill"), a jagged road that leads to Coco's Corner (an infamous middle-of-nowhere convenience store), a dry lake bed known as Laguna Chapala, and the peaks of two mountain ranges, the Sierra Colombia and the Sierra de la Asamblea. If that's not enough to keep you busy, you can head south of the campground, where the highway edges closer to the coast. Roughly 32.8 miles (52.8 km) south of the L.A. Bay Junction, near Rosarito, there is a poorly maintained 20.5-mile (33-km) turnoff that will take you northeast to one of the desert's most alluring landmarks, the well-preserved Misión de San Francisco de Borja Adac, a Jesuit mission founded in 1762 and surrounded today by acres of lush elephant trees, *cardón* cacti, and boojum trees. Of course, the most popular attraction around here is Bahía de los Ángeles, a kayaker and angler's paradise that lies approximately 41 miles (66 km) southeast of the L.A. Bay Junction. As a side note about the road to Bahía de los Ángeles, there is an alternative 20.3-mile (32.7-km) route that leads to the turnoff for the Misión de San Francisco de Borja Adac; the route lies 27.7 miles (44.6 km) from the L.A. Bay Junction.

RV sites, facilities: The campground is essentially a large flat dirt parking lot, with plenty of room for RVs as well as tents. Although there are no utility hookups, the space is wide enough to accommodate lengthy RVs (up to 40 feet/12.2 meters long), making it convenient for caravans. Besides the intriguing landscape, the only other amenities include toilets that are flushed using a bucket of water, if there's any on hand. Only self-contained RVs and rugged tent campers should park here, preferably in pairs or groups, as there's no drinking water, dump station, electricity, laundry, shower house, or security available. Children and leashed pets are welcome, though the uneven terrain might not be suitable for wheelchairs. Given the remote location, it's best to stop in El Rosario for extra food, purified water, fuel, and other supplies before traveling south into the desert; pick up supplies in Guerrero Negro if you're headed north. Remember to pack out all trash when you leave.

Reservations, fees: Reservations are not accepted; spaces are available on a first-come, first-served basis. RV and tent sites are moderately priced at $5 per night. Credit cards are not accepted; cash (Mexican pesos or U.S. dollars) is the customary form of payment. The campground should be open all year, but do not be surprised to find it closed at times.

Directions: From El Rosario, drive south along Highway 1 for roughly 140.7 miles (226.4 km). The campground will be on your right, near Km 281 and just northwest of the road that leads to Bahía de los Ángeles. From Guerrero Negro, drive north for about 83.7 miles (134.7 km) to the L.A. Bay Junction and pass the turnoff. The campground will be on your left.

Contact: Since there's no official contact person, mailing address, or phone number for Punta Prieta RV Park, it's best just to drive into the campground and see which spots are available.

27 BRISA MARINA RV PARK

Scenic Rating: 7

in Bahía de los Ángeles

See map page 126

The name is a remnant of its former glory, when the Brisa Marina really was a full-fledged, government-run RV park, complete with utility hookups. These days, it's simply a primitive campground beside the bay, not far from the beach and a sea turtle station (operated by the neighboring campground, Campo Archelón). Although it's not as popular as Daggett's Campground, for instance, this humble locale certainly attracts its share of campers, especially those who appreciate its low fee, its lovely ocean and island views, and its proximity to Bahía de los Ángeles, one of Mexico's most gorgeous bays and a wonderland for anglers, kayakers, boaters, and all other water lovers.

RV sites, facilities: Formerly a complete RV park (with full hookups), this beachside campground is now simply a large lot, with plenty of room for tent campers and boondocking RVs (up to 45 feet/13.7 meters long). Amenities include sewer hookups and an adjacent sea turtle station, where visitors can view the endangered turtles that dwell in several open water tanks. There are no restrooms, laundry facilities, camp stores, or other such conveniences. Only self-contained RVs and rugged tent campers should park here, preferably in pairs or groups, as there's no drinking water, dump station, electricity, or security available. Children and leashed pets are welcome, though the uneven terrain might not be suitable for wheelchairs. Given the remote location of Bahía de los Ángeles—a place where all supplies, including water, are expensively imported by truck—it's best to bring a lot of groceries, purified water, fuel, and other necessities with you. Despite the presence of a few markets in Bahía de los Ángeles, you'll have a greater selection in towns like El Rosario (to the north) and Guerrero Negro (to the south). Remember to pack out all trash when you leave.

Reservations, fees: Reservations are not accepted; spaces are available on a first-come, first-served basis. RV and tent sites are moderately priced at $5 per night. There is a $2 admission fee for the sea turtle research facility. Credit cards are not accepted; cash (Mexican pesos or U.S. dollars) is the customary form of payment. The campground is open all year.

Directions: From the L.A. Bay Junction on Highway 1, drive east on a well-signed 41-mile (66-km) paved road. As you enter the town of Bahía de los Ángeles, take a left toward the airport (and the northern beaches beyond). Follow the paved road for 0.8 mile (1.3 km), turn right, and continue straight for 0.8 mile (1.3 km), passing the turnoff to Daggett's and sticking to the unpaved route. The campground lies ahead, beside the beach.

Contact: Since there's no official contact person, mailing address, or phone number for Brisa Marina RV Park, it's best just to drive into the campground and see which spots are available. For more information about Bahía de los Ángeles, visit www.bahiadelosangeles.info.

28 CAMPO ARCHELÓN

Scenic Rating: 7

in Bahía de los Ángeles

See map page 126

While supplies and services are precious in the remote town of Bahía de los Ángeles, there is indeed no shortage of small boat launches and primitive, beachside campgrounds. Operated by the same folks (biologist Antonio Reséndiz and his wife Betty) who run the adjacent sea turtle research project, this campground is just slightly north of neighboring Brisa Marina RV Park. Like its neighbor, Campo Archelón offers magnificent views of several offshore islands as well as the sparkling waters of Bahía de los Ángeles, Canal de Ballenas, and the Sea of Cortez. In addition, the campground provides a few convenient amenities, including easy access to a lovely beach, a perfect spot to begin a challenging kayaking excursion.

The modest sea turtle station, whose owner-operators and volunteers conduct research on the biology, ecology, and conservation of various sea turtle species—which were unfortunately depleted by former turtle fisheries in the area—is definitely worth a look, too. For a small admission fee, you can see endangered sea turtle species like the leatherback and the hawksbill in several large round water tanks. The station is open every day but Wednesday and Sunday.

RV sites, facilities: This beachside campground is simply a large lot, with no utility hookups and limited space for tent campers and boondocking RVs (under 25 feet/7.6 meters long). Amenities include well-maintained toilets, hot showers, rental *cabañas* (with kitchens and private patios), a dump station, a sea turtle research facility, and several thatched-roof *palapas* near the beach. There are no laundry facilities, camp stores, or other such conveniences. Only self-contained RVs and rugged tent campers should park here, preferably in pairs or groups, as there's no drinking water, electricity, or official security available. Children and leashed pets are welcome, though the uneven terrain might not be suitable for wheelchairs. Given the remote location of Bahía de los Ángeles—a place where all supplies, including water, are expensively imported by truck—it's best to bring a lot of groceries, purified water, fuel, and other necessities with you. Despite the presence of a few markets in Bahía de los Ángeles, you'll have a greater selection in towns like El Rosario (to the north) and Guerrero Negro (to the south). Remember to pack out all trash when you leave.

Reservations, fees: Reservations are not accepted; spaces are available on a first-come, first-served basis. RV and tent sites are moderately priced at $10 per night. The *cabañas* cost $40 per night. The sea turtle station charges an admission fee of $2 per person. Credit cards are not accepted; cash (Mexican pesos or U.S. dollars) is the customary form of payment. The campground is open all year.

Directions: From the L.A. Bay Junction on Highway 1, drive east on a well-signed 41-mile (66-km) paved road. As you enter the town of Bahía de los Ángeles, take a left toward the airport (and the northern beaches beyond). Follow the paved road for 0.8 mile (1.3 km), turn right, and continue straight for 0.8 mile (1.3 km), passing the turnoff to Daggett's and sticking to the unpaved route. In front of the Brisa Marina RV Park, turn left onto another unpaved route, which parallels the beach, and head north for 0.1 mile (0.2 km) to Campo Archelón.

Contact: For more information about Campo Archelón, you can try emailing resendizshidalgo@yahoo.com. Since a reply is unlikely, however, and since there's no official mailing address or phone number for Campo Archelón, it's probably best just to drive into the campground and see which spots are available. For more information about Bahía de los Ángeles, visit www.bahiadelosangeles.info.

29 DAGGETT'S CAMPGROUND

Scenic Rating: 9

in Bahía de los Ángeles

See map page 126 **BEST**

Nestled between rugged mountains, sandy beaches, and the diverse Sea of Cortez, Bahía de los Ángeles is celebrated by many travelers as one of the most scenic locales in all of Baja—if not all of Mexico. Though partially protected by a string of barrier islands, including the enormous Isla Ángel de la Guarda, this magnificent bay still experiences its share of strong winds, which can make boating rather perilous for inexperienced captains. Nevertheless, fishing, diving, kayaking, and wildlife-watching are popular diversions in the bay and around the offshore islands.

With lovely Bahía de los Ángeles at its doorstep, this intimate, picturesque campground—owned and managed by Ruben Daggett—is the perfect base of operations for this fun-filled region. After setting up your motor home, trailer, van, or tent, you can board a fishing or diving charter, go snorkeling in the sea, join a whale-watching tour (in winter), or rent canoes, kayaks, and boats for more private adventures. Watching the sunrise here can be relaxing and rewarding. Watching the sunset, however, can be a little less tranquil—the returning fishermen are often a noisy bunch. Expect to hear rambunctious music as they clean their daily catch.

RV sites, facilities: The campground offers 10 beachside *palapas* for tent campers and 20 additional *palapas,* alongside which RVers can park their vehicles. Although none of the sites have hookups, all have barbecue pits, and several have enough space to accommodate lengthy motor homes and travel trailers (up to 40 feet/12.2 meters long). Other amenities include a dump station, a launch ramp (for small boats), a fish-cleaning station, a restaurant, and clean bathrooms with flush toilets and hot propane showers. Cabins are also available for rent. In addition, the campground offers scenic boat rides, canoe and kayak rentals, whale-watching excursions, fishing charters, and diving/snorkeling tours.

Children and pets are welcome, but facilities are not wheelchair-accessible. On-site owners provide limited security, but there is no laundry on the premises. Given the remote location of Bahía de los Ángeles—a place where all supplies, including water, are expensively imported by truck—it's best to bring a lot of groceries, purified water, fuel, and other necessities with you. Despite the presence of a few markets in Bahía de los Ángeles, you'll have a greater selection in towns like El Rosario (to the north) and Guerrero Negro (to the south).

Reservations, fees: Given the campground's small size and its popularity among outdoor enthusiasts, reservations are definitely recommended. RV and tent sites cost $10 per night. Cabins cost about $50 per night. Credit cards are not accepted; cash (Mexican pesos or U.S. dollars) is the customary form of payment. This beachside campground is open all year.

Directions: From the L.A. Bay Junction on Highway 1, drive east on a well-signed 41-mile (66-km) paved road. As you enter Bahía de los Ángeles, take a left toward the airport (and the northern beaches beyond). Follow the paved road for 0.8 mile (1.3 km), turn right, and continue for another 0.5 mile (0.8 km). Turn left, drive another 0.3 mile (0.5 km), and watch for the sign for Daggett's Campground on the right. Turn right onto the entrance road and head toward the beach and campground.

Contact: Daggett's Campground, Apartado Postal #83, Guerrero Negro, Baja California Sur, C.P. 23940, Mexico, tel. 200/124-9101, fax 200/124-9102, www.campdaggetts.com.

30 PLAYA LA GRINGA

Scenic Rating: 8

north of Bahía de los Ángeles

See map page 126 **BEST**

Situated near Punta La Gringa, along the northern edge of Bahía de los Ángeles, this stretch of coastline, consisting of both sandy and gravel beaches, is popular among the primitive camping set. Anglers, too, often stay here, using the shallow shore to launch small boats toward the fruitful fishing grounds around Isla Smith. Despite the lack of facilities and the presence of a fence (due to an ownership dispute), campers always seem to be around, especially on clear, sunny days. While the fence runs parallel to the coast, access to the beach is still possible. So, if you enjoy swimming, kayaking, snorkeling, fishing, and other water-related activities, you'll relish this seaside location, especially given its incredible views of numerous offshore islands.

Its remoteness makes it doubly attractive to many vacationers, but such isolation can also be dangerous at times. Solo camping is, therefore, not recommended. In addition to safety issues, Playa La Gringa's other major drawback is the washboard road from town; in the past, some travelers have opted for the sandy path that meanders along the western side of the main route.

RV sites, facilities: This beachside campground has no designated RV or tent sites—you can park wherever you like. The primitive campsites are situated above the beach and accessible via side roads that branch off the main gravel road. Although there are no utility hookups, some of the spaces away from the beach are wide enough (and firm enough) to accommodate lengthy RVs (up to 40 feet/12.2 meters long). Besides the intriguing landscape, there are no facilities. Only self-contained RVs and rugged tent campers should park here, preferably in pairs or groups, as there's no drinking water, dump station, electricity, laundry, shower house, or security available.

Because the sand is soft, you should bring along shovels, boards, rope, and other tools to help dislodge your vehicle in case your wheels get stuck. Children and pets are welcome, though the uneven terrain might not be suitable for wheelchairs. Given the remote location, it's best to pick up extra food, purified water, fuel, and other supplies in Bahía de los Ángeles, although your selection will be better in towns like El Rosario and Guerrero Negro. Keep an eye on your belongings, and remember to pack out all trash when you leave.

Reservations, fees: Reservations are not accepted; spaces are available on a first-come, first-served basis. RV and tent sites are moderately priced at around $5 per night. Credit cards are not accepted; cash (Mexican pesos or U.S. dollars) is the customary form of payment. This beachside campground is open all year.

Directions: From the L.A. Bay Junction on Highway 1, drive east on a well-signed 41-mile (66-km) paved road. As you enter Bahía de los Ángeles, take a left toward the airport (and the northern beaches beyond). Follow this coastal road for about 7 miles (11.3 km) to Playa La Gringa. Note that the route is paved for the first 2 miles (3.2 km), after which motorists will encounter a military checkpoint and a washboard road. Although lengthy motor homes can make the journey, slow driving is advisable.

Contact: Since there's no official contact person,

mailing address, or phone number for Playa La Gringa, it's best just to drive toward the beach and see which spots are available. For more information about Bahía de los Ángeles, visit www.bahiadelosangeles.info.

31 VILLA VITTA HOTEL RESORT

Scenic Rating: 8

in Bahía de los Ángeles

See map page 126 BEST

Located within the heart of quaint, isolated Bahía de los Ángeles, this roomy campground is ideal for lengthy RVs and perfect for large caravans. With incredible views of the bay and several distant islands, this popular RV park offers proximity to a string of beaches and boat ramps. Consequently, the most prevalent diversions here are water-related ones like swimming, sea kayaking, fishing, waterskiing, and windsurfing. The resort even offers guided fishing trips through the Sea of Cortez.

Of course, with such beautiful surroundings and year-round sunshine, the area is also ideal for hiking, mountain biking, off-roading, digging for clams, diving for lobsters and oysters, hunting for game birds, and taking a boat ride (with a local guide) to the nearby islands, where you'll spot a variety of birds, sea lions, dolphins, and finback whales. It's also not a bad place to stroll along the beach on a balmy night and marvel at the star-studded sky—the advantage of a town with inconsistent electricity.

For a change of scenery, however, you can walk to the only *museo* in Bahía de los Ángeles, the Museo de Naturaleza y Cultura, a small brick building that offers informative displays about the area's history and wildlife. Here, you'll see fossils and whale skeletons, as well as exhibits about silver mines, Cochimí Indian traditions, and Mexican ranch life. The route to the museum is on the west side of the town's main drag, between the Villa Vitta Hotel and Guillermo's.

RV sites, facilities: This beachside campground, essentially a flat, shadeless dirt lot with no landscaping, offers 30 spaces with electrical hookups and 20 spaces without hookups. Most of the spots have plenty of room for lengthy rigs (up to 40 feet/12.2 meters long). Several of the spaces are pull-throughs, while the rest are back-ins along the beach. Amenities include patios, a dump station, a restroom building (which offers flush toilets and hot showers, and for which a key is required), a boat launch ramp, and, of course, an air-conditioned hotel (with a swimming pool, a whirlpool spa, and its own bar and seafood restaurant). Guided fishing trips are also available. There is, however, no laundry on the premises.

Because of the lack of water hookups and the fact that electric service is only offered for a few hours each evening, the park best suits self-contained RVs. Children, pets, and tent campers are welcome. A gate offers limited security. Given the remote location of Bahía de los Ángeles—a place where all supplies, including water, are expensively imported by truck—it's best to bring a lot of groceries, purified water, fuel, and other necessities with you. Despite the presence of a few markets in Bahía de los Ángeles, you'll have a greater selection in towns like El Rosario (to the north) and Guerrero Negro (to the south).

Reservations, fees: Reservations are accepted. RV and tent sites are moderately priced at $10 per night. Motel rooms and fishing packages are also available. For an extra charge, guests can use the boat launch. Credit cards are not accepted; cash (Mexican pesos or U.S. dollars) is the customary form of payment. The hotel and campground are open all year.

Directions: From the L.A. Bay Junction on Highway 1, drive east on a well-signed 41-mile (66-km) paved road. Once you've reached Bahía de los Ángeles, pass the turnoff toward the airport and Daggett's Campground and continue south until you see the Villa Vitta Hotel on the right. The campground is across the street, on the left (east) side.

Contact: Villa Vitta Hotel Resort, 416 West San Ysidro Boulevard, Suite #564, San Ysidro, CA 92173, tel. 200/124-9103 (Mexico) or 619/454-6108 (U.S.), www.villavitta.com.

32 GUILLERMO'S SPORTFISHING, HOTEL, & RESTAURANT

Scenic Rating: 8

in Bahía de los Ángeles

See map page 126 BEST

Positioned south of the Villa Vitta campground, Guillermo's offers visitors a convenient spot from which to explore the lovely waters of Bahía de los Ángeles. With its own launch ramp, this hotel and campground encourages visitors to bring their own boat, canoe, or kayak and embark upon a journey to one of more than two dozen offshore islands, from small ones like Isla El Piojo (Louse Island) to the enormous Isla Ángel de la Guarda (Guardian Angel Island).

While a landscape of rugged natural beauty surrounds this park, it isn't exactly known for the best views. After all, permanent trailers stand between the bay and the sites reserved for travelers. Still, Guillermo's has probably the most popular restaurant in town, and it's definitely one of the best spots for sportfishing. Not only do the on-site guides have terrific advice regarding rods, lures, and other such equipment, but they also lead daily *panga* excursions into the Sea of Cortez, where bountiful schools of yellowtail, sheephead, whitefish, sculpin, cabrilla, and dorado await.

RV sites, facilities: This beachside campground offers 40 sites, 15 of which have full hookups (with water service, sewer access, and 15-amp electricity) and many of which have patios. Most of the sites are pull-throughs and have plenty of room for lengthy rigs (up to 40 feet/12.2 meters long). Unfortunately, permanent trailers lining the beach impede any view of the ocean. If a view matters to you, consider the few no-hookup parking spots south of the restaurant, along the water. On-site amenities include a restroom building (with flush toilets and hot showers), a dump station, a public pay phone, a long-time bar and restaurant, a store (offering ice and groceries), a boat launch ramp, fishing charters, and, of course, a small motel. Children, pets, and tent campers are welcome, and English-speaking employees are present. There is, however, no laundry on the premises.

Given the sporadic electric service (provided by a generator), the inconsistent presence of water (which must be delivered by truck), and the lack of official security, the park is probably best suited for self-contained RVs. Because of the remote location of Bahía de los Ángeles—a place where all supplies, including water, are expensively imported—it's best to bring a lot of groceries, purified water, fuel, and other necessities with you. Despite the presence of a few markets in Bahía de los Ángeles, you'll have a greater selection in towns like El Rosario (to the north) and Guerrero Negro (to the south).

Reservations, fees: Reservations are accepted. RV sites are moderately priced at $16 per night. Primitive tent sites are closer to $5 per night. Hotel rooms cost $45 per night in winter and $65 per night in summer (when air-conditioning is required). Fishing trips usually cost around $300 per day. Credit cards are not accepted; cash (Mexican pesos or U.S. dollars) is the customary form of payment. The hotel and campground are open all year.

Directions: From the L.A. Bay Junction on Highway 1, drive east on a well-signed 41-mile (66-km) paved road. Once you've reached Bahía de los Ángeles, pass the turnoff toward the airport and Daggett's Campground and continue south until you see the Villa Vitta Hotel on the right. Guillermo's hotel and campground is on the left (east) side of the road, just past the Villa Vitta campground.

Contact: Guillermo's Sportfishing, Hotel, & Restaurant, Boulevard Bahía de los Ángeles, Bahía de los Ángeles, Baja California, Mexico, tel. 200/124-9104, fax 200/124-9102, www.guillermos.net.

33 CASA DÍAZ

Scenic Rating: 7

in Bahía de los Ángeles

See map page 126

Discovered in 1746 by Padre Fernando Consag—a Jesuit missionary hoping to find an easier route between the Sea of Cortez and the Misión de San Francisco de Borja Adac in the mountains to the southwest—Bahía de los Ángeles has changed little during the past 260 years. The surrounding mountains still look lovely against the vibrant blue of the sky and sea. The offshore islands still lure birds, dolphins, sea lions, and whales. The bay and adjacent Sea of Cortez (also known as the Golfo de California and the Mar de Cortés) still boast a variety of tasty fish. And the town itself has little more than an airstrip for small planes, one history museum, a limited number of hotels and restaurants, a few markets and paved roads, several boat launches, and two Pemex gas stations (one of which is usually open 6:30 A.M.–11 P.M., unless, of course, the town is experiencing electrical issues).

Casa Díaz is one of several basic campgrounds in this remote area. Its amenities are limited and its maintenance is inconsistent at best, but its location is definitely convenient. In fact, the family-run establishment (one of the oldest in Bahía de los Ángeles) is situated at the end of the town's main drag, only a little farther south of Guillermo's tourist complex. Like Guillermo's, the property houses its own motel, restaurant, store, and boat launch.

RV sites, facilities: This small, poorly maintained campground offers six RV and tent sites, with full hookups (including water service, sewer access, and 15-amp electricity) and enough room for lengthy rigs (up to 40 feet/12.2 meters long). On-site amenities include shady structures, a restaurant, a store, a launch ramp, and a somewhat dirty motel. If the restroom building is unusable, which is often the case, ask about using the toilet and shower at the motel. Children and pets are welcome, but the campground is only suitable for rugged tent campers and self-contained RVs. After all, there's no dump station, laundry, or security available, and both the water service and electricity are very inconsistent. Because of the remote location of Bahía de los Ángeles—a place where all supplies, including water, are expensively imported by truck—it's best to bring a lot of groceries, purified water, fuel, and other necessities with you. Despite the presence of a few markets in Bahía de los Ángeles, you'll have a greater selection in towns like El Rosario (to the north) and Guerrero Negro (to the south).

Reservations, fees: Reservations are accepted. RV and tent sites are moderately priced at $10 per night, which includes use of the launch ramp. Motel rooms are also available. Credit cards are not accepted; cash (Mexican pesos or U.S. dollars) is the customary form of payment. The motel and campground are open all year.

Directions: From the L.A. Bay Junction on Highway 1, drive east on a well-signed 41-mile (66-km) paved road. Once you've reached Bahía de los Ángeles, pass the turnoff toward the airport and Daggett's Campground and continue south, past the Villa Vitta Hotel on the right and Guillermo's complex on the left. When you reach the T junction at the end of the road, turn left. Casa Díaz will be on your right, around the rock wall.

Contact: Casa Díaz, Apartado Postal #579, Ensenada, Baja California, Mexico, tel. 200/124-9112. For more information about Bahía de los Ángeles, visit www.bahiadelosangeles.info.

34 CAMP GECKO

Scenic Rating: 8

south of Bahía de los Ángeles

See map page 126

It's probable that Bahía de los Ángeles has rarely been characterized as a particularly noisy, rowdy town. After all, one has to drive 41 miles (66 km) out of the way to reach this remote place.

In addition, despite the presence of a few festive cantinas, the most popular activities in these parts involve the water. Anglers, sea kayakers, windsurfers, boaters, and scuba divers tend to be early risers, fixated more often on exploring the open water and offshore islands and less focused on carousing along the beach.

Still, if you have a hankering for a more quiet, more private locale along the Bahía de los Ángeles, you can head south of town, toward this breezy, isolated campground. Here, you'll find lovely beaches with incredible views of the mountains, the bay, and the islands beyond. The region is pleasant all year long, with balmy summers and mild winters. Be forewarned, however—the road to Camp Gecko has its share of bumps and dips. Take it slowly, especially in a motor home with low clearance.

Besides being relatively close to the restaurants and markets of Bahía de los Ángeles, Camp Gecko serves as a gateway to other scenic bays to the south. With a high-clearance, four-wheel-drive vehicle, you can follow the graded dirt road beyond the campground and drive roughly 26 miles (41.8 km) toward an uneven turnoff that will lead you to isolated Bahía de las Ánimas, known for gorgeous, white-sand beaches, star-studded night skies, and ample opportunities to spy seals, dolphins, whales, sea turtles, and all manner of birds and fish. Farther south, other poorly maintained roads lead to equally beautiful bays, from Bahía San Rafael to Bahía San Francisquito to Bahía San Juán Bautista just above the state line.

RV sites, facilities: This beachside campground offers an indeterminate number of spaces for RV and tent camping. There are several *palapas* under which you can pitch a tent or beside which you can park a self-contained van, pickup camper, or small motor home or travel trailer. Camp Gecko also provides a large parking area away from the beach, with enough room for lengthy rigs (up to 40 feet/12.2 meters long). Although the sites have no utility hookups, there are a few on-site amenities, including a small boat launch ramp, several stone rental cabins above the beach, and a restroom building with flush toilets and hot showers. Children and pets are welcome, and English-speaking staff members are present.

Only self-contained RVs and rugged tent campers should park here, though, as there is no electricity, drinking water, laundry, or dump station available. Limited security, however, is provided by the resident owners. Because of the remote location of Bahía de los Ángeles—a place where all supplies, including water, are expensively imported by truck—it's best to bring a lot of groceries, purified water, fuel, and other necessities with you. Despite the presence of a few markets in nearby Bahía de los Ángeles, you'll have a greater selection in towns like El Rosario (to the north) and Guerrero Negro (to the south). Be sure to bring along shovels, boards, rope, and other tools intended to dislodge vehicles stuck in the sand, and remember to pack out all trash when you leave.

Reservations, fees: Reservations are not accepted; spaces are available on a first-come, first-served basis. RV and tent sites cost $15 per night. Credit cards are not accepted; cash (Mexican pesos or U.S. dollars) is the customary form of payment. The beach and campground are open all year.

Directions: From the L.A. Bay Junction on Highway 1, drive east on a well-signed 41-mile (66-km) paved road. Once you've reached Bahía de los Ángeles, pass the turnoff toward the airport and Daggett's Campground and continue south, past the Villa Vitta Hotel on the right and Guillermo's complex on the left. When you reach the T junction at the end of the road, you will see a rock wall and the entrance to Casa Díaz. Turn right onto a washboard dirt road and drive south toward the small village of El Porvenir. After 4 miles (6.4 km), turn left (east) on a sandy road, at the end of which lies Camp Gecko.

Contact: Camp Gecko, Bahía de los Ángeles, Baja California, Mexico, http://gecko.mystarband.net. For more information about Bahía de los Ángeles, visit www.bahiadelosangeles.info.

35 PUNTA SANTA ROSALILLITA

Scenic Rating: 8

west of Rosarito

See map page 126 BEST

The Baja peninsula probably boasts as many primitive, boondocking campsites as it does official RV parks. After all, there are numerous fish camps along the Pacific coast and Sea of Cortez shoreline that allow free (or almost-free) overnight camping. The only drawbacks are usually access and security. Entrance routes from the highway are often lengthy, poorly maintained, and, therefore, time-consuming. As a result, fewer tourists frequent these areas, which means that safeguarding one's belongings and traveling in pairs or groups is highly recommended in these remote locales. Of course, such isolation is often the main attraction.

Punta Santa Rosalillita is one such primitive spot. Located west of Rosarito, the gorgeous, sheltered Bahía Santa Rosalillita lures anglers, surfers, and wildlife enthusiasts alike. While the village of Santa Rosalillita appears to be simply a dusty fish camp, it also happens to be the starting point for one of the Mexican government's grandest plans—the Escolera Náutica (Nautical Staircase). Once completed, this enormous tourism-related endeavor will eventually link the Pacific Ocean to the Sea of Cortez via a wide paved road, allowing yachters to bypass the Los Cabos region and travel directly to upscale marinas along the gulf side.

Camping in this area is extremely primitive, and it requires a high-clearance vehicle in most places. Beaches north and south of Santa Rosalillita, including El Tomatal to the south, allow tent campers and boondocking RVs to park for free, though there are obviously no amenities in these remote, if breathtaking, spots. Surfers especially appreciate this area: Punta Santa Rosalillita and Punta Rosarito are particularly good surf breaks.

RV sites, facilities: There are no designated campsites along the beaches north and south of Santa Rosalillita—you can park wherever you like. Although there are no utility hookups or official amenities, some of the spaces may be able to accommodate lengthy RVs (up to 40 feet/12.2 meters long). The problem is navigating such big rigs from Highway 1 to the coast; in fact, this area is probably best suited to those with four-wheel-drive, high-clearance vehicles. Only self-contained RVs and rugged tent campers should park along these beaches, preferably in pairs or groups, as there's no drinking water, dump station, electricity, shower house, laundry, or security available. Because the sand is soft, you should bring along shovels, boards, rope, and other tools to help dislodge your vehicle in case your wheels get stuck. Children and pets are welcome, though the uneven terrain isn't suitable for wheelchairs. Given the remote location, it's best to pick up extra food, purified water, fuel, and other supplies along Highway 1; your selection will be best in towns like El Rosario and Guerrero Negro. Keep an eye on your belongings along this isolated coast, and remember to pack out all trash when you leave.

Reservations, fees: Reservations are not accepted; spaces are available on a first-come, first-served basis. Overnight camping is typically free here. The beaches are open all year.

Directions: Although Punta Santa Rosalillita can be accessed by three different routes—including a gravel road to the northwest and an even worse road to the southeast—the best route is via Highway 1. From the interstate, roughly 8.9 miles (14.3 km) northwest of Rosarito, drive southwest for 11.5 miles (18.5 km) toward the Pacific coast. Be forewarned—the route to Punta Santa Rosalillita ranges from paved to dirt to gravel to awful. It's probably best suited to those with four-wheel-drive, high-clearance vehicles and a lot of patience.

Contact: Since there's no official contact person, mailing address, or phone number for the beaches north and south of Punta Santa Rosalillita, it's best just to drive toward the ocean and see which spots are available.

GUERRERO NEGRO TO BAHÍA CONCEPCIÓN

BEST RV PARKS AND CAMPGROUNDS

A large Mexican flag and an enormous metallic eagle mark the border between the two states of Baja California: Baja Norte and Baja Sur. After passing through the inspection point and crossing the 28th parallel, you'll encounter the small, relatively new town of Guerrero Negro, which offers several claims to fame, including some expansive *salinas* (salt flats) that can only be visited with permission from the company that mines them. History buffs can head east to explore El Arco, a former gold-mining town and now a supply center for surrounding *ranchos*. Just down the road lies the *ciudad fantasma* (ghost town) of Pozo Alemán, which still contains the ruins of a blacksmith's shop, smelter, company store, and windmill. Also nearby is the isolated Misión de Santa Gertrudis La Magna, the remains of which are fairly extensive, compared to many other mission sites in Baja; here, you'll find several chambers, a church, and a belfry.

Nature lovers, however, will likely appreciate this region even more. After all, the swamps and estuaries south of Guerrero Negro boast a variety of bird species, from white pelicans to gray herons to royal eagles. In addition, there are numerous islands in the area, including Isla Cedros and Isla Natividad. Anglers, surfers, and kayakers especially relish the waters surrounding these islands, and the remote shoreline of the enormous Península Vizcaíno, though not easy to reach via road, is also favored among outdoor enthusiasts. The most popular activity here, however, is whale-watching. From January to March, migrating California gray whales give birth to their young in the nearby Laguna Ojo de Liebre (also known as Scammon's Lagoon), a perfect place to snag an up-close view of these majestic creatures.

As you continue across the northern end of Baja California Sur, you'll notice a stark contrast between the ocean views of Guerrero Negro, the vegetated sand dunes and mesquite trees of the Desierto de Vizcaíno (part of the expansive Reserva de la Biósfera El Vizcaíno), and the rugged *montañas* of the Sierra de San Francisco. Heading south, you'll encounter several dry *arroyos* (brooks); acres of large *cardón*, the world's largest cactus; and the date palm oases of San Ignacio.

For those RVers interested in art and anthropology, adventure outfits in San Ignacio offer guided tours to see the ancient *pinturas rupestres* (cave paintings) of human and animal figures, nestled within the surrounding Sierra de San Francisco. In addition, architecture aficionados can visit the impressive Misión de San Ignacio de Kadakaamán, a well-preserved church made of sturdy lava rock and located in the town's main square. San Ignacio also serves as a pleasant base camp for hiking excursions amid the surrounding mesas as well as whale-watching trips to Laguna San Ignacio.

From here, Highway 1 heads toward the Sea of Cortez, turning south along the shore. In the coastal village of Santa Rosalía – a fishing and ferry port that was once a copper-mining town – you'll spy several 19th-century, French Colonial-style buildings as well as a church designed by Gustave Eiffel, the same architect who crafted the Eiffel Tower.

Not far south lie two more treasures along the Sea of Cortez coastline. First, you'll come to Mulegé, a lovely date-palm oasis, situated in a picturesque valley and known for its friendly people, well-preserved mission, historic prison (the only state penitentiary without bars), nearby rock-art sites, and decent fishing, diving, and kayaking opportunities. Farther south, you'll spot the sandy beaches, shallow waters, and primitive bayside campgrounds of Bahía Concepción, the ultimate Baja destination for many RVers, especially those who favor gorgeous views over luxurious amenities.

As in other parts of Baja, there are probably as many official campgrounds between Guerrero Negro and Bahía Concepción as there are primitive boondocking areas. For those willing to risk driving on some of the worst roads in Mexico, several stunning (if rugged and remote) campsites await along the coast, including a string of fish camps southeast of the Península Vizcaíno – namely, in places like Bahía Asunción, La Bocana, Punta Abreojos, and Laguna San Ignacio, all of which are budget-friendly, ideal for viewing whales and dolphins, and safest if visited by pairs or groups of RV travelers.

One fact to remember is that, as you cross from Baja Norte to Baja Sur, you're also leaving *hora oficial del Pacífico* (Pacific standard time) and entering *hora oficial de las montañas* (mountain standard time), so don't forget to adjust your watches and clocks one hour ahead – including the one on the microwave!

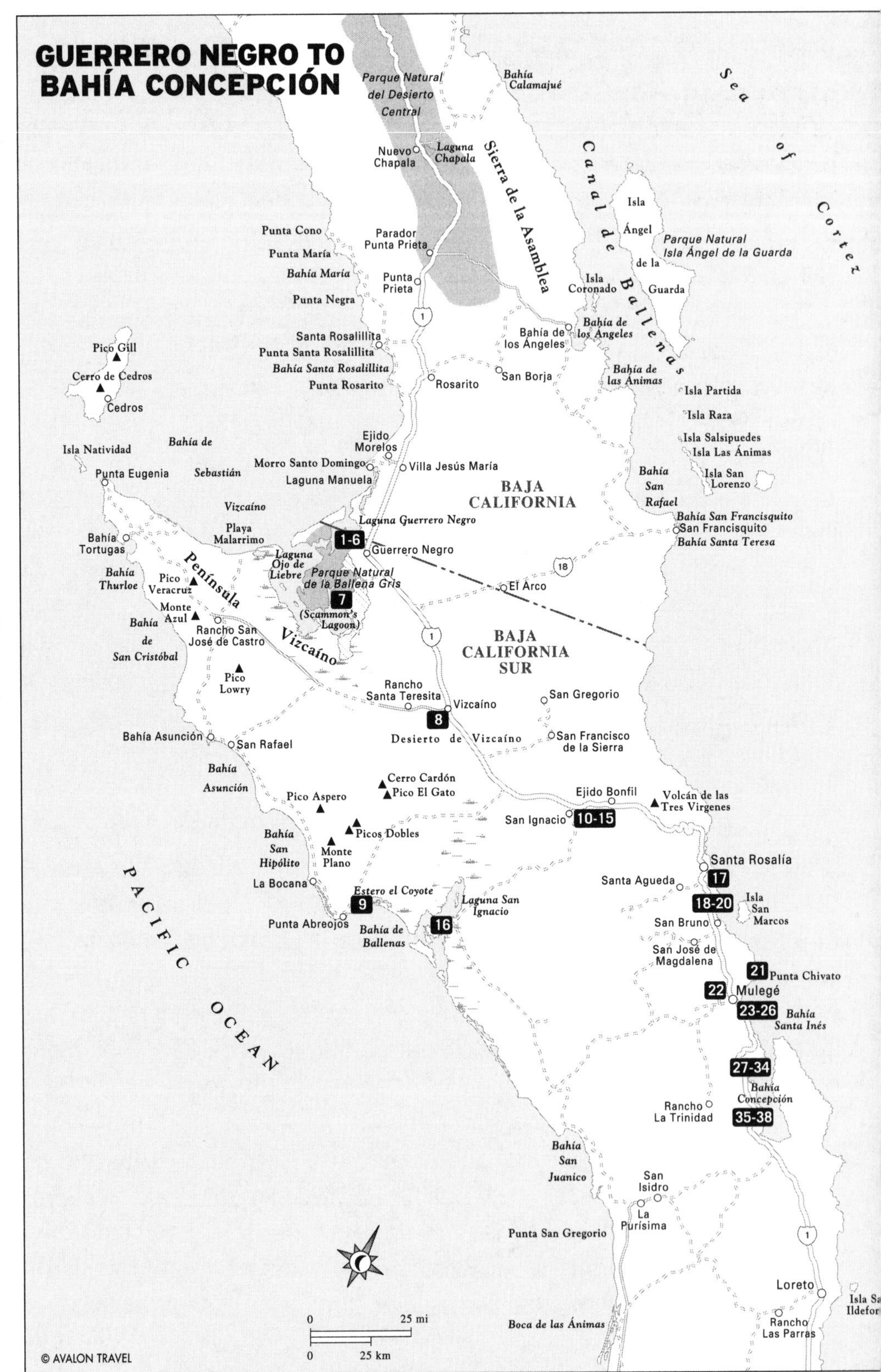
GUERRERO NEGRO TO BAHÍA CONCEPCIÓN
Parque Natural del Desierto Central
Bahía Calamajué
Sea of Cortez
Nuevo Chapala
Laguna Chapala
Sierra de la Asamblea
Canal de Ballenas
Isla Ángel de la Guarda
Parque Natural Isla Ángel de la Guarda
Punta Cono
Punta María
Bahía María
Punta Negra
Parador Punta Prieta
Punta Prieta
Isla Coronado
Bahía de los Ángeles
Santa Rosalillita
Punta Santa Rosalillita
Bahía Santa Rosalillita
Punta Rosarito
Rosarito
San Borja
Bahía de las Ánimas
Isla Partida
Isla Raza
Isla Salsipuedes
Isla Las Ánimas
Pico Gill
Cerro de Cedros
Cedros
Isla Natividad
Bahía de Sebastián Vizcaíno
Punta Eugenia
Ejido Morelos
Morro Santo Domingo
Laguna Manuela
Villa Jesús María
BAJA CALIFORNIA
Bahía San Rafael
Isla San Lorenzo
Bahía San Francisquito
San Francisquito
Bahía Santa Teresa
Playa Malarrimo
Laguna Guerrero Negro
1-6
Guerrero Negro
Bahía Tortugas
Península Vizcaíno
Laguna Ojo de Liebre
Parque Natural de la Ballena Gris
7
(Scammon's Lagoon)
18
El Arco
Bahía Thurloe
Pico Veracruz
Monte Azul
Bahía de San Cristóbal
Rancho San José de Castro
1
BAJA CALIFORNIA SUR
Pico Lowry
Rancho Santa Teresita
Vizcaíno
8
San Gregorio
Bahía Asunción
San Rafael
Desierto de Vizcaíno
San Francisco de la Sierra
Bahía Asunción
Cerro Cardón
Pico El Gato
Pico Aspero
Ejido Bonfil
Volcán de las Tres Vírgenes
San Ignacio
10-15
Picos Dobles
Bahía San Hipólito
Monte Plano
Santa Rosalía
17
Santa Agueda
La Bocana
Estero el Coyote
9
Laguna San Ignacio
18-20
Isla San Marcos
Punta Abreojos
Bahía de Ballenas
16
San Bruno
San José de Magdalena
PACIFIC OCEAN
21
Punta Chivato
22
Mulegé
23-26
Bahía Santa Inés
27-34
Bahía Concepción
Rancho La Trinidad
35-38
Bahía San Juanico
San Isidro
La Purísima
Punta San Gregorio
1
Loreto
Isla San Ildefonso
0 25 mi
0 25 km
Boca de las Ánimas
Rancho Las Parras

1 LA ESPINITA MOTEL, RESTAURANT, AND RV PARK

Scenic Rating: 4

north of Guerrero Negro

See map page 164

For those RVers headed south of Bahía de los Ángeles via the Transpeninsular Highway (Highway 1), there is little in the way of accommodations until nearing the Paralelo 28, the border between Baja California (Baja Norte) and Baja California Sur (Baja Sur). While Guerrero Negro, the town just south of the state line, contains several camping options, there's only one RV park north of the 28th parallel. In recent years, this modest tourist complex has steadily expanded. Today, in addition to the small campground, it includes a motel, a restaurant, and a *tienda* (small store).

Although there are nicer places in town, La Espinita is certainly a welcome sight after miles and miles of Baja's central *desierto.* It's also not a bad pit stop for those headed north, toward Cataviña, and it's a decent home base for exploring Guerrero Negro's surrounding attractions, from the migrating *ballenas gris* (gray whales) in Scammon's Lagoon to the abandoned *ciudad fantasma* (ghost town) of Pozo Alemán off Highway 18.

If you're coming from the north and hope to explore Baja Sur, just remember that you'll have to pass through a military checkpoint at the border between the states. The soldiers are ordered to stop everyone that crosses this state line. For the most part, they are simply searching for drugs, firearms, and other such forbidden items. Typically, they will treat travelers in a professional, courteous manner. If you treat them, in turn, with polite compliance, you should have no problem moving on to Guerrero Negro.

One additional note of warning involves the campground's electricity. As in other parks in Guerrero Negro, the voltage here can fluctuate wildly. To avoid damage to your RV, please monitor the current while connected to the park's hookups.

RV sites, facilities: The complex has eight full-hookup RV sites, with 15-amp electricity, water service, sewer access, and enough room for lengthy rigs (up to 40 feet/12.2 meters long). The parking lot also offers plenty of room for dry-docking RVs—up to 50 of them. On-site amenities include a motel, a restaurant, a small store, a dump station, a public pay phone, and a restroom building with flush toilets and hot showers. There is, however, no laundry on the premises. Children, leashed pets, and tent campers are welcome, though the facilities are not necessarily wheelchair-accessible. English-speaking employees are present, and the staff offers a limited measure of security. Grocery stores, gas stations, and other services are available in nearby Guerrero Negro.

Reservations, fees: Reservations are not accepted; spaces are available on a first-come, first-served basis. RV sites cost $15 per night, while tent camping is roughly $5 per night (or perhaps free with the purchase of a meal). Hot showers cost $2 each, and motel rooms are available for around $20 per night. Credit cards are not accepted; cash (Mexican pesos or U.S. dollars) is the customary form of payment. The motel and RV park are open all year.

Directions: From Rosarito, drive south on Highway 1 for approximately 48.5 miles (78 km), toward Guerrero Negro. La Espinita Motel, Restaurant, and RV Park will be on your right, about 0.2 mile (0.3 km) north of the giant eagle statue that marks the border between Baja California and Baja California Sur. From south of Guerrero Negro, drive northwest on Highway 1 and cross the border. The La Espinita tourist complex will be on your left.

Contact: Since there's no official mailing address or phone number for La Espinita Motel, Restaurant, and RV Park, you should simply drive into the parking lot and see which spots are available.

2 TRAILER PARK BENITO JUÁREZ

Scenic Rating: 4

northeast of Guerrero Negro

See map page 164

By Baja's standards, Guerrero Negro is a relatively young town. Unlike Loreto, for instance, which has been steadily growing for over three centuries—ever since the founding of the lovely Misión de Nuestra Señora de Loreto Conchó in 1697—Guerrero Negro has only existed for a little over five decades. Established in 1957 and named after a Massachusetts-based whaling ship that sank near the coast in the 1850s, Guerrero Negro (which means "Black Warrior" in Spanish) was ostensibly created in an effort to mine the *salinas* (salt marshes) that abound in this region.

Nowadays, tourists are familiar with this town and its surrounding lagoons for one main reason: whale-watching season. From December to April, visitors flock to this part of Baja to watch California *ballenas gris* (gray whales) as they migrate to Laguna Ojo de Liebre for breeding purposes—a practice that was first noticed during the mid-19th century by an American whaler, Captain Charles Melville Scammon. Hence the inlet's other name: Scammon's Lagoon.

The Trailer Park Benito Juárez, which is situated by the newly refurbished Desert Inn (formerly part of the La Pinta Hotel chain), is one of several government-built campgrounds on the Baja peninsula—and it's the last to offer electricity to RVers. Operated by the nearby *ejido* Benito Juárez (named after a former president of Mexico) and popular among RV caravans, this spacious campground offers plenty of room for lengthy motor homes and travel trailers. It's appealing, too, for its desert landscaping; several cactus varieties pepper the property. Besides its less-than-scenic environs, the park's only disadvantages are its occasional closures, its fluctuating voltage (which can potentially harm your equipment), its inconsistent maintenance, and the fact that, thanks to its location, you're forced to pass through the agricultural inspection station every time you head south into town.

RV sites, facilities: This large trailer park offers 60 full-hookup, pull-through RV sites, with 15-amp electricity, water service, sewer access, concrete pads, and enough room for lengthy rigs (up to 40 feet/12.2 meters long). On-site amenities include a small store, a picnic area, and an old restroom building with flush toilets and (usually) hot showers; the adjacent hotel contains a restaurant, a cocktail lounge, a gift shop, and 28 comfortable rooms. There is, however, no laundry or dump station in the trailer park. Children, leashed pets, and tent campers are welcome, though the facilities are not necessarily wheelchair-accessible. The manager speaks limited English, and a gated perimeter fence offers some measure of security. Grocery stores, gas stations, and other services are available in nearby Guerrero Negro.

Reservations, fees: Reservations are not accepted; spaces are available on a first-come, first-served basis. Tent and RV sites cost $10–15 per night. Credit cards are not accepted; cash (Mexican pesos or U.S. dollars) is the customary form of payment. The park is open all year.

Directions: From Rosarito, drive south on Highway 1 for approximately 48.7 miles (78.4 km) to the state line. Just south of the giant eagle statue that marks the border between Baja California and Baja California Sur, you'll see the Desert Inn (formerly the La Pinta Hotel) on the right-hand (west) side. Trailer Park Benito Juárez is just south of the hotel. From south of Guerrero Negro, drive northwest on Highway 1, pass through the agricultural inspection station, and look for the trailer park on your left.

Contact: Trailer Park Benito Juárez, Asunción Morian Canales, Apartado Postal #188, Guerrero Negro, Baja California Sur, Mexico, tel. 615/157-0025. For more information about the adjacent Desert Inn, visit www.desertinns.com.

3 MARIO'S TOURS AND RESTAURANT

Scenic Rating: 4

east of Guerrero Negro

See map page 164 **BEST**

What began, over two decades ago, as a small, desert-based restaurant owned by two young newlyweds (Mario and Sara Amaya) has become quite a multifaceted operation. Located along the Transpeninsular Highway (Highway 1), between the state border and the town of Guerrero Negro, this *palapa*-style eatery not only serves fresh seafood and fish tacos in a rustic atmosphere, it also houses a tourist information office, provides guided whale-watching and cave-painting tours, offers easy access to town, and shelters a spacious RV park.

With its own fleet of vans, the daily ecotourism service leads small groups of visitors on daylong hiking excursions amid historic missions, old mining towns, and spectacular cave murals in the Sierra de San Francisco. In addition, the operation owns several small boats, upon which visitors are taken on intimate, government-authorized observation trips across the Laguna Ojo de Liebre (Eye of the Hare Lagoon), where they can observe dolphins, sea lions, birds, and, of course, California *ballenas gris* (gray whales). Besides providing bilingual guides, life vests, raincoats, box lunches, and post-tour margaritas, the company teaches respect for Baja's native landscapes, flora, and fauna, especially for the majestic, curious cetaceans who breed seasonally in the lagoon.

Besides whale-watching tours, Guerrero Negro presents a variety of intriguing sights, including the world's largest salt mine, a historic pier and lighthouse, incredible sand dunes, migratory bird colonies, and miles of surrounding deserts, part of the Reserva de la Biósfera El Vizcaíno. Just remember to bring an assortment of weather gear with you; Guerrero Negro, which has the climate of a Mediterranean desert, can be cold and humid in the morning, warm and sunny by midday, and cold and windy at night. Remember, too, that Guerrero Negro adheres to *hora oficial de las montañas*

salt dunes near Guerrero Negro

(mountain standard time), so don't forget to adjust your clocks and watches—or the tours will leave without you.

One additional note of warning involves the electricity in Mario's park. As in other campgrounds in Guerrero Negro, the voltage here can be inconsistent, so take precautions when connecting your electric cord to the park's hookups. You wouldn't want to damage your RV so far from home.

RV sites, facilities: In the parking lot behind the restaurant, approximately 75 full-hookup, pull-through sites are equipped with 30-amp outlets, sewer access, and city water. Each space provides enough room for lengthy rigs (up to 70 feet/21.3 meters long). A relatively new restroom building offers clean toilets and hot showers, and the rustic restaurant presents an assortment of fresh seafood, a complete buffet service, a lounge area, a tourist information office, live music on the weekends, and ecotourism tours. The staff speaks English and provides limited security. There is, however, no dump station or laundry available. Children, leashed pets, and tent campers are welcome, though the facilities are not wheelchair-accessible. Groceries, fuel, purified water, and other supplies are available in nearby Guerrero Negro.

Reservations, fees: Reservations are accepted, especially for the whale-watching trips in winter. RV sites cost $12 nightly, while tent camping is available for $5 each night. Guided tours are available, too. Long-term stays, however, are not possible here. Credit cards are not accepted; cash (Mexican pesos or U.S. dollars) is the only acceptable form of payment. The restaurant, tour operation, and campground are open all year.

Directions: From the border between the two Baja states, drive south on Highway 1 for 0.6 mile (1 km). The restaurant is on the right (west) side of the highway, south of the agricultural inspection station and near the Km 218 marker. From south of Guerrero Negro, drive northwest on Highway 1 and look for the restaurant on your left.

Contact: Mario's Tours and Restaurant, Km 217.3 de la Carretera Transpeninsular (Highway 1), Guerrero Negro, Baja California Sur, C.P. 23940, Mexico, tel. 615/157-1940, fax 615/157-0120, www.mariostours.com.

4 LA POSADA DE DON VICENTE

Scenic Rating: 3

in Guerrero Negro

See map page 164

Essentially the courtyard of a basic, two-story motel, this simple campground might not be as spacious or as picturesque as some of Guerrero Negro's other RV parks, but it does provide easy access to town services, including ecotourism operators like Mario's and Malarrimo's. In addition to whale-watching excursions to the Laguna Ojo de Liebre and guided hikes to historic missions and ancient cave paintings in the Sierra de San Francisco, you'll find a number of other interesting sights in the Reserva de la Biósfera El Vizcaíno, which surrounds Guerrero Negro, from impressively massive white-sand dunes to acres of salt-marsh bird refuges west of town. This part of Baja is truly a wildlife lover's paradise. Just remember to bring a variety of clothing with you: Although you might be wearing summery duds in the *desiertos* north and south of town, it might be necessary to don long pants and jackets once you reach Guerrero Negro, especially during the winter months.

In all honesty, the campground that lies within the courtyard of La Posada de Don Vicente seems rarely used, particularly in an area that contains a number of other options. Although it's unlikely that every other RV spot in the Guerrero Negro area will be taken (even during the busy whale-watching season), you might want to keep this place in mind if all others fail. As in other campgrounds in Guerrero Negro, the electric hookups here provide inconsistent voltage, so monitor your equipment to avoid unnecessary damage.

RV sites, facilities: Adjacent to a modest motel,

this no-frills campground offers 10 back-in RV sites, equipped with water service and 15-amp electricity. Lined against a concrete wall, the spaces are rather tight for lengthy motor homes and travel trailers; in fact, the lot is probably best suited for small RVs (up to 30 feet/9.1 meters long), though longer RVs can certainly give it a try. Besides motel rooms, the only other amenities include a nearby restaurant, a dump station, a public pay phone, and some poorly maintained restrooms with flush toilets and warm showers. The managers here are friendly and helpful. There is, however, no laundry room on the premises. Children, leashed pets, and tent campers are welcome, though the facilities are not wheelchair-accessible. Groceries, purified water, fuel, and other supplies are available in nearby Guerrero Negro.

Reservations, fees: Reservations are accepted. Campsites (for RVs or tents) cost $10 per night. Motel rooms are available for $8–35 per night. Credit cards are not accepted; cash (Mexican pesos or U.S. dollars) is the only acceptable form of payment. The park is open all year.

Directions: From the border, drive south on Highway 1 and enter Guerrero Negro from the east. The motel is on the right (north) side, 0.7 mile (1.1 km) from the turnoff. From south of Guerrero Negro, drive northwest on Highway 1, turn left (west) into town, and look for the motel on your right.

Contact: La Posada de Don Vicente, Boulevard Emiliano Zapata S/N, Guerrero Negro, Baja California Sur, C.P. 23940, Mexico, tel. 615/157-0288.

5 MALARRIMO RESTAURANT, MOTEL Y RV PARK

Scenic Rating: 7

in Guerrero Negro

See map page 164 **BEST**

On the Baja peninsula, it's not unusual for RV enthusiasts to choose a park simply because of the nearby cuisine. For over 20 years, RVers have flocked to the popular Malarrimo Restaurant, open daily and offering a menu of seafood and international dishes, from broiled Pacific lobster to filet mignon with mushroom sauce. Today, however, they don't just stay overnight for the food (and the decent facilities). The Malarrimo Eco-Tours outfit provides guided excursions to see migrating whales, the world's biggest *salinas* (salt works), and giant, ancient *pinturas rupestres* (cave paintings). In addition to the restaurant, RV park, and ecotourism service, this popular tourist complex houses the Motel Malarrimo (also called the Cabañas Don Miguelito), Guerrero Negro's nicest motel, containing clean, colorful rooms and landscaped with vibrant flower gardens.

Like Mario's Tours, Malarrimo's offers daily guided trips to nearby lagoons and historic sites. During the winter months, small boats (which fit no more than 10 passengers and are led by bilingual guides) leave twice each morning for half-day voyages into the Laguna Ojo de Liebre, where migrating California gray whales dwell during the breeding season. For history buffs, Malarrimo's also offers full-day or three-day cultural excursions along old Cochimí trails, taking in sights like cactus-filled valleys, the old mining towns of El Arco and Pozo Alemán, and giant, indigenous, 4,000-year-old *pinturas rupestres* within the Sierra de San Francisco, known as Baja's Great Mural Region and cited as a protected archaeological zone on UNESCO's World Heritage list. Just remember to pack all-weather gear (for heat, cold, and rain) and adjust your watches to *hora oficial de las montañas* (mountain standard time), so you don't miss the tour.

As an additional note of warning, the electricity at Malarrimo's must be monitored at all times. Unfortunately, Guerrero Negro suffers from fluctuations in voltage, which can severely damage your RV and other equipment if left unchecked. So, stay alert whenever you're hooked up. In addition, you might want to unplug your vehicle's electrical cord while on a whale-watching trip down south.

RV sites, facilities: All 45 back-in sites have concrete pads and full hookups, including water, sewage, and 30-amp electricity, and lengthy coaches (up to 40 feet/12.2 meters long) can be accommodated in most spots (with careful maneuvering). Besides the restaurant, the property has a tent-camping area, a gift shop, a convenience store, a pool table, and clean restrooms with flush toilets and hot showers. Adjacent to the RV park stands an attractive 18-room motel with clean, well-painted chambers, private baths, hot showers, color television, free wireless Internet access, and colorful flower gardens. The outfit also offers whale-watching excursions and cultural tours (the cost of which includes round-trip transportation, a knowledgeable guide, and a light lunch). Staff members are friendly and bilingual, and a guard provides limited security. There is, however, no dump station or laundry room on-site. While leashed pets are permitted in the RV park, they are not allowed in the motel rooms. Children are welcome anywhere (except perhaps the bar), though the facilities are not wheelchair-accessible. Groceries, purified water, and other supplies are available in the on-site store and in nearby Guerrero Negro.

Reservations, fees: Due to the park's popularity, reservations are recommended. The daily camping fees are $14 for tents, $16 for vans and pickup campers, and $20 for motor homes, travel trailers, and 5th-wheel trailers. Motel rooms cost $38–49 per night. Rates are based on double occupancy; each extra guest is charged $10 per night. Whale-watching tours are offered for a one-time fee: $49 per adult or $39 per child (under 11 years old). Guided cultural excursions are also available for $450–900 per person per trip. Credit cards and cash (Mexican pesos or U.S. dollars) are acceptable forms of payment. The restaurant, motel, and RV park are open all year.

Directions: From the border, drive south on Highway 1, enter Guerrero Negro from the east, and travel 1 mile (1.6 km) west from the turnoff. The park is on the right (north) side of the road, one block past La Posada de Don Vicente. From south of Guerrero Negro, drive northwest on Highway 1, turn left into town, and look for the complex on your right.

Contact: Malarrimo Restaurant, Motel y RV Park, Boulevard Emiliano Zapata S/N, Guerrero Negro, Baja California Sur, C.P. 23940, Mexico, tel. 615/157-0250, fax 615/157-0100, www.malarrimo.com.

6 MOTEL BRISA SALINA

Scenic Rating: 4

in Guerrero Negro

See map page 164

Guerrero Negro—a relatively young town that's especially popular during whale-watching season (officially, mid-December through mid-April)—offers several affordable options for RV travelers, all of which are adjacent to motels and/or restaurants. While not the best choice, the Motel Brisa Salina offers its own version of an RV park. Perhaps a tad simpler than outfits like Mario's and Malarrimo's, this campground still provides a convenient home base for natural and cultural excursions around Guerrero Negro.

Although destinations like Ensenada, La Paz, and Cabo San Lucas tend to be higher priorities for foreign tourists, Guerrero Negro—a company town that owes its existence to the world's largest evaporative *salinas* (salt marshes)—presents a myriad of diversions. Here, visitors can tour the salt mines, hike amid the enormous sand dunes known as the Dunas de Soledad (Dunes of Solitude), watch migratory birds and whales in the Laguna Ojo de Liebre (Eye of the Hare Lagoon), attend the annual Festival Cultural de la Ballena Gris (Gray Whale Cultural Festival), and venture into the Desierto de Vizcaíno and Sierra de San Francisco, where desert fauna, historic missions and towns, and 4,000-year-old cave paintings await.

RV sites, facilities: The campground is behind the motel, in an enclosed courtyard that has 22 sites with full hookups (including water service, sewer access, and 15-amp outlets with 30-amp breakers). If this potentially cramped park is only partially filled, then lengthy rigs (up to 45 feet/13.7 meters long) will have no trouble parking here. Small, musty motel rooms, a restaurant, restrooms with hot showers, a public pay phone, and friendly staff members are also available. There is, however, no laundry room or dump station on-site. Children, leashed pets, and tent campers are welcome; however, the facilities were not designed with wheelchairs in mind. Groceries, purified water, fuel, and other supplies are available in Guerrero Negro.

Reservations, fees: Reservations are not accepted; spaces are available on a first-come, first-served basis. RV spaces cost $12 per night. Budget-friendly motel rooms are available for $20–25 per night. Credit cards are not accepted; cash (Mexican pesos or U.S. dollars) is the customary form of payment. The motel and campground are open all year.

Directions: From the border, drive south on Highway 1, enter Guerrero Negro from the east, and drive 1.6 miles (2.6 km). The park is on the right (north) side of the road, well past the Malarrimo Restaurant, Motel y RV Park. From south of Guerrero Negro, drive northwest on Highway 1, turn left (west) into town, and look for the motel on your right.

Contact: Motel Brisa Salina, Boulevard Emiliano Zapata S/N, Guerrero Negro, Baja California Sur, C.P. 23940, Mexico. Since there's no official phone number for the Motel Brisa Salina, you should simply drive into the parking lot and see which spots are available.

7 LAGUNA OJO DE LIEBRE CAMPGROUND

Scenic Rating: 8

south of Guerrero Negro

See map page 164 **BEST**

If your main purpose in visiting Guerrero Negro is to view wildlife at play, then you might consider heading directly to the Laguna Ojo de Liebre (Eye of the Hare Lagoon), where you'll even find a primitive, winter-only campground near the tidal flats. Also called the Parque Natural de la Ballena Gris, this capacious bay seems to lure the greatest number of *ballenas gris* of any of Baja's whale-watching sites, including Bahía Magdalena to the south. Camping here during the winter months can be a pure delight; although there are few official amenities, this coastal locale definitely affords decent views of the breeding cetaceans, and listening to the whales' own brand of music isn't a bad way to wake up in the morning. Luckily, lengthy motor homes and travel trailers can fit here; just be aware of the shifting tides and sandier spots, so as to avoid getting your vehicle stuck.

Part of the enormous 6.29-million-acre (2.55-million-hectare), UNESCO-designated Reserva de la Biósfera El Vizcaíno—which includes a rich diversity of landscapes, from deserts to mountains to beaches to coastal lagoons—the Laguna Ojo de Liebre is popular among anglers, kayakers, birding enthusiasts, and, during the winter months, whale-watchers. While local, licensed *pangueros* are willing to guide visitors (for a reasonable fee) on short whale-watching excursions during the season (mid-December to mid-April), many tourists choose to arrange official tours through hotels or ecotourism operators in Guerrero Negro. Remember that, during whale-watching season, activities like kayaking are forbidden in the shallow lagoon, to protect the cetaceans during their breeding months.

As an ironic historical note, Laguna Ojo de Liebre is also called Scammon's Lagoon, in reference to Captain Charles Melville Scammon, an American whaler who frequented the region in the 1850s. In 1857, he headed south to the Laguna Ojo de Liebre, after learning that the *estero* (marsh) was a breeding ground for *ballenas gris*. Following a few disastrous attempts to hunt the whales, Scammon and his colleagues succeeded in killing so many that, by 1859, the majestic cetaceans were nearly eliminated from the lagoons. Sadly, whaling didn't cease in the region until the mid-1930s. Since then, however, the population has slowly recovered, protected nowadays by U.S. and Mexican laws as well as international agreements.

RV sites, facilities: Situated between a dirt road and the beach beside the lagoon, beyond the visitor parking lot, this primitive campground offers an indeterminate number of RV and tent sites. Although there are no utility hookups, some of the sites provide plenty of space for large RVs (up to 40 feet/12.2 meters long). On-site amenities include a restaurant and tour office, some outhouses with pit toilets, a souvenir store, and whale-watching trips in season. Only self-contained RVs and rugged tent campers should park here, preferably in pairs or groups, as there's no electricity, drinking water, dump station, shower house, or laundry room on the premises. The campground's remote location ensures some measure of security, but you should still be vigilant and protect your belongings at all times. Children and leashed pets are welcome, though the terrain might not be suitable for wheelchairs. Given the lack of markets and other facilities in the area, and considering the slow journey required to reach the coast, it's necessary to pick up groceries, purified water, gasoline, and other supplies in places like Guerrero Negro or Vizcaíno before heading down to the campground.

Reservations, fees: Reservations are not accepted; spaces are available on a first-come, first-served basis. Overnight camping costs $5 per vehicle. Credit cards are not accepted; cash (Mexican pesos or U.S. dollars) is the customary form of payment. The campground is open during whale-watching season, from mid-December to mid-April.

Directions: From Guerrero Negro, head east to Highway 1 and drive southeast for 5.4 miles (8.7 km). Between Km 208 and Km 207, you'll see a sign that says "Parque Natural de la Ballena Gris/Laguna Ojo de Liebre." Turn right onto the wide, graded dirt road (which can alternate between smooth and corrugated conditions) and drive 4 miles (6.4 km) to an entrance gate, where you must register with the guard who controls this access road through the salt flats. Continue for 9.8 miles (15.8 km), past the salt marshes, to a fork in the road. Veer to the right, drive another 1.1 miles (1.8 km), and stop at the entrance gate to the lagoon, where you will pay the requisite fee. From Vizcaíno, head northwest on Highway 1 for 41.1 miles (66.1 km), turn left onto the access road between Km 208 and Km 207, and follow the above directions.

Contact: Since there's no official contact person, mailing address, or phone number for the Laguna Ojo de Liebre Campground, it's best just to drive down and see which spots are available.

8 HOTEL KADEKAMAN

Scenic Rating: 8

in Vizcaíno

See map page 164

Situated at a crossroads of the Carretera Transpeninsular (Highway 1) and the route that leads west to the Península Vizcaíno, the town of Vizcaíno serves as the gateway to several of Baja's most biologically diverse ecosystems. From here, you can reach the multiple bays and deserted beaches of the Península Vizcaíno, plan a bass-fishing trip to the small Isla Natividad west of the Bahía de Sebastián Vizcaíno, hike amid the unique cactus varieties and desert fauna of the Desierto de Vizcaíno, and visit the ancient painted caves within the Sierra de San Francisco to the east—most of which are part of UNESCO's Reserva de la Biósfera El Vizcaíno.

Vizcaíno is also a convenient home base for daylong trips to the historic sites just north of the state line—namely, the former gold-mining town of El Arco; the *ciudad fantasma* (ghost town) of Pozo Alemán, which still contains the ruins of a blacksmith's shop, smelter, company store, and windmill; and the isolated Misión de Santa Gertrudis La Magna, the extensive remains of which include several chambers,

flora of the Desierto de Vizcaíno

a church, a belfry, and Indian artifacts. From Pozo Alemán, you can also reach (albeit via a slow-going, 47-mile/75.6-km dirt road) Punta San Francisquito, where an isolated resort and a primitive campground attract the hardiest tourists.

Despite the wonderful diversity of its surrounding landscapes, Vizcaíno unfortunately contains only one place for overnight RVers. The family-operated Hotel Kadekaman, a pleasant, brick complex ensconced by vibrant flowers and cactus gardens, provides limited space for traveling RVers and tent campers. Even if you have no intention of exploring the town's environs, it's comforting to know that there's somewhere to go if you're caught on the road at night (which, incidentally, isn't advisable on the Baja peninsula).

RV sites, facilities: The rear parking lot offers six campsites for RVs and tents. Each site has electric and water hookups and enough space for lengthy rigs (up to 40 feet/12.2 meters long). Other on-site facilities include a hotel (with clean, colorful rooms, well-appointed suites, and bottled water), a festive café/restaurant/grill called Afrodita, a restroom (in the hotel) with a flush toilet and hot shower, and a public pay phone. Wireless Internet access is also available, and the staff speaks limited English. Only self-contained RVs and rugged tent campers should park here, as there is no drinking water, dump station, or laundry room on the premises. Security, however, is offered by the hotel staff. Children and tent campers are welcome, and the facilities are wheelchair-accessible. While leashed pets are allowed in the camping area, they are not permitted in the hotel or restaurant. Vizcaíno, the main supply point for those headed into the desert or onto the isolated peninsula, has markets, restaurants, hardware stores, and a gas station, so you won't have to go far for groceries, purified water, and other necessities.

Reservations, fees: Reservations are accepted. RV spaces cost around $10 per night (for two adults), while tent campsites cost $5 per person. Each extra guest is charged $5 per night. Air-conditioned hotel rooms and suites are available

for around $42–75 per night. Cash (Mexican pesos or U.S. dollars) and major credit cards are both acceptable forms of payment. The hotel, restaurant, and campground are open all year.
Directions: From Guerrero Negro, drive southeast on Highway 1 for 46.5 miles (74.8 km) to Vizcaíno. The Hotel Kadekaman is near Km 143, on the right (west) side of the highway. From San Ignacio, drive west (then northwest) on Highway 1 for 44.4 miles (71.4 km) and look for the hotel on your left, near Km 143 in Vizcaíno.
Contact: Hotel Kadekaman, Boulevard Lázaro Cárdenas S/N (Km 143 de la Carretera Transpeninsular), Vizcaíno, Baja California Sur, Mexico, tel. 615/156-4112, www.hotelkadekaman.com.

9 CAMPO RENE

Scenic Rating: 9

southwest of San Ignacio

See map page 164 **BEST**

For outdoor enthusiasts, the Pacific coast between the Bahía de Sebastián Vizcaíno and Laguna San Ignacio contains a wealth of remote, picturesque spots—ideal for hikers, swimmers, surfers, sea kayakers, boaters, anglers, birders, and whale-watchers. Primitive boondocking sites abound along this rugged shoreline, though many are not easy to reach with ordinary vehicles. Campo Rene, on the stunning, shallow Estero El Coyote, which is adjacent to the Bahía de Ballenas, is one of the best official campgrounds in this remote part of Baja, and while the 48.6-mile (78.2-km) access road between Highway 1 and the estuary is only partially paved, it's possible for most RVs to navigate the lengthy route. Still, sturdy tires, high clearance, and four-wheel drive would undoubtedly make the trip a bit easier.

Although Campo Rene provides furnished *cabañas* for rent, the campground presents little in the way of amenities. Nonetheless, it's a wonderful place to experience the great outdoors. The Estero El Coyote, a shimmering mangrove-lined marsh and a wintertime refuge for a multitude of bird species, can be a delight for kayakers, canoeists, clam diggers, and wildlife lovers. Campo Rene even rents kayaks for those who have forgotten to bring their own. In addition, staff members offer sportfishing trips and, in winter, whale-watching excursions. Just remember: Whether you plan to fish in the Bahía de Ballenas or hunt for clams, scallops, and oysters in the Estero El Coyote, you'll need a Mexican fishing license. Be aware, too, of any catch limits, size restrictions, or regulation changes.

With a rugged vehicle (such as a four-wheel-drive jeep or a heavy-duty pickup camper) and your own water and supplies, you can even reach other *puntas, esteros,* and *bahías* along the coast. Punta Abreojos, for instance, is a sandy fishing town and terrific surfing locale just 11.3 miles (18.2 km) to the west. Farther along this rough (often corrugated) coastal road, you'll encounter a few fish camps, such as La Bocana on Bahía San Hipólito, Punta Prieta and Bahía Asunción on opposite ends of a crescent-shaped bay, and, depending on your fortitude, Bahía Tortugas on the Pacific side of the Península Vizcaíno. Most of these isolated communities allow free, no-frills camping on the beach. Just be careful: Although the villagers are very friendly, none of these destinations offer much in the way of security, so it's probably best to travel with others and camp together.
RV sites, facilities: The campground—essentially a parking lot beside an estuary—provides space for an indeterminate number of tents and small RVs (up to 30 feet/9.1 meters long). Also available are *cabañas* (with hot water) and shady *palapas* (with water, electric light, propane, a refrigerator, a heater, and security). Other amenities include barbecue grills, restrooms with hot showers, a bar, a restaurant (with an extensive menu), a landing strip, a boat launch ramp, an event room, and kayak and motorbike rentals. Campo Rene also offers guided sportfishing and whale-watching trips, and the staff speaks limited English. Only self-contained

RVs and rugged tent campers should park here, as there's no drinking water, electricity, dump station, or laundry available. Children and leashed pets are welcome, but the facilities are not wheelchair-accessible. Due to the remote location, it's advisable to buy enough groceries, purified water, fuel, and other supplies in Vizcaíno or San Ignacio before heading down to the campground.

Reservations, fees: Reservations are accepted (via cell phone). Primitive RV and tent sites cost $10 per night (which includes hot showers and barbecue grills). For $20 per night, you can rent a *cabaña* or a *palapa*. Kayaks can be rented for $15 per hour. Credit cards are not accepted; cash (Mexican pesos or U.S. dollars) is the customary form of payment. The campground is open all year.

Directions: From Vizcaíno, drive southeast on Highway 1 for 29 miles (46.7 km), turn right (southwest) onto the access road, and continue for 48.6 miles (78.2 km) to the turnoff for Campo Rene. Turn left (east) and drive 3.1 miles (5 km) to the campground. From San Ignacio, drive west (then northwest) on Highway 1 for 15.4 miles (24.8 km) to the turnoff toward Estero El Coyote, turn left, and follow the above directions.

Contact: Campo Rene, Estero El Coyote, Baja California Sur, Mexico, tel. 615/103-0008 or 615/161-7360, www.camporene.com. Note that the above numbers are for cell phones, so you must dial "1" between the country code and area code to complete the call.

10 RICARDO'S RICE AND BEANS RV PARK

Scenic Rating: 7

west of San Ignacio

See map page 164 **BEST**

Perhaps the most popular (and definitely the nicest) tourist complex in the San Ignacio area, Ricardo Manuel Romo Cota's place offers weary travelers a true oasis in the desert (despite the noise from highway traffic, especially at night). Located on the outskirts of town, on the road to San Lino, and situated on a hill overlooking the Río San Ignacio, this well-tended property contains a modest hotel, a well-regarded Mexican restaurant, and an RV park with full hookups and enough space for large RVs. In addition, it offers a terrific home base for exploring the natural and cultural delights that abound within and around San Ignacio, an oasis in its own right.

Surrounded by miles and miles of arid desert terrain (within the Desierto de Vizcaíno), this historic, Spanish Colonial–style village is situated within a fertile valley, alongside a picturesque river that winds amid a verdant date palm forest. From here, you can take backpacking and rock-climbing excursions into the Sierra de San Francisco, participate in guided trips to explore amazing, pre-Columbian *pinturas rupestres* (cave paintings), and head south to the Laguna San Ignacio to watch breeding whales during the winter months. Hiking up the mesas that surround San Ignacio can also be a delightful way to explore the region. Up there, you'll encounter well-marked trails, old adobe ruins, and pleasant views of the surrounding desert.

Even lovely San Ignacio is worth investigating. After all, the Misión de San Ignacio de Kadakaamán—founded by Jesuit missionaries in 1728, completed by the Dominicans in 1786, and still dominating the town's tree-lined plaza—is one of Baja's most elaborate, most well-preserved missions. Inside lies an 18th-century altarpiece dedicated to San Ignacio de Loyola, the town's patron saint and the inspiration for San Ignacio's Fiesta Patronal every July.

Just south of the mission is the Museo de Pinturas Rupestres de San Ignacio, a history museum operated by the Instituto Nacional de Antropología e Historia (INAH). Inside, you'll find art and artifacts from early settlers, displays pertaining to the region's ancient rock-art sites, and an INAH office, from which you must secure permission (and a guide) before visiting any of the rock-art sites in the area. In addition, you must agree to a series of restrictions intended to preserve the paintings, such as refraining from the use of alcohol, cigarettes, and flash photography within the vicinity of the caves and formations. Be advised, too, that you'll need your own vehicle as well as proficiency in Spanish to arrange such an adventure; it will be infinitely easier (though more expensive) to take a formal tour through a company like Ecoturismo Kuyimá.

The only obvious disadvantages to Ricardo's Rice and Beans RV Park are its lack of shade and its proximity to the noisy Transpeninsular Highway (Highway 1). Still, the views of San Ignacio's thriving date palm forest might be worth overlooking such drawbacks.

RV sites, facilities: The RV park—essentially an open lot situated on two terraces—has 30 full-hookup, pull-through sites, with 15-amp outlets, 30-amp breakers, water service, sewer access, palm trees, and room for lengthy motor homes and travel trailers (up to 40 feet/12.2 meters long). There are eight additional back-in sites. Other amenities include a modest hotel (with large rooms and balcony views), a Mexican restaurant (with a computer for Internet service), a bar, a coin laundry, a public pay phone, restrooms with flush toilets and hot showers, and limited security. Wireless Internet access is possible in the campsites closest to the restaurant. The friendly, informative owner (and English-speaking staff members) can help guide you around the San Ignacio area, and whale-watching and/or cave-painting trips can be arranged from the park. Children, leashed pets, and tent campers are welcome, though the facilities are not wheelchair-accessible. Groceries, purified water, fuel, and other supplies can be obtained in nearby San Ignacio.

Reservations, fees: Reservations are accepted. RV spaces cost $30 per night, while tent camping costs $10 per night. Hotel rooms are also available. There is a nominal fee for wireless Internet access. Cash (Mexican pesos or U.S. dollars), travelers checks, and major credit cards are all acceptable forms of payment. The hotel, restaurant, and RV park are open all year.

Directions: From Vizcaíno, drive southeast on Highway 1 for 44.1 miles (71 km), toward San Ignacio. Near Km 73.5, west of the San Ignacio turnoff, you'll see a sign for Ricardo's Rice and Beans RV Park. Take a sharp right turn onto the paved road that leads to San Lino; as an alternative to this tricky turn, you can continue toward the Pemex gas station on the left side of the highway, make a U-turn, and turn left (south) onto the access road. Follow this paved route west for about 0.4 mile (0.6 km). The complex is up the driveway on your right. From Santa Rosalía, drive west for 45.3 miles (72.9 km), just past San Ignacio, and turn left onto the well-marked turnoff, then follow the above directions.

Contact: Ricardo's Rice and Beans RV Park, Carretera Transpeninsular S/N, San Ignacio, Baja California Sur, C.P. 23930, Mexico, tel./fax 615/154-0283, http://ricardoriceandbeans.googlepages.com/home. For more information about INAH, visit www.inah.gob.mx (just be aware that most of the site is presented in Spanish). For details about Ecoturismo Kuyimá, visit www.kuyima.com.

11 LAKESIDE RV PARK

Scenic Rating: 8

in San Ignacio

See map page 164

Also known as Don Chon's, this spacious, affordable campground might be little more than a dusty dirt parking lot, but its location is undeniably rewarding. Shaded by a grove of numerous palm trees and situated alongside a verdant freshwater lagoon fed by the Río San Ignacio, the Lakeside RV Park offers a peaceful setting for swimmers, kayakers, bird-watchers, and those who just enjoy relaxing on a grassy bank, watching the current drift past acres of thriving date palm trees. Besides natural beauty, the campground—the first you'll encounter after making the turn from Highway 1 to San Ignacio—also promises easy access to several restaurants, shops, and other attractions in San Ignacio, including the magnificent Misión de San Ignacio de Kadakaamán. From here, you can also arrange guided hiking excursions into the Sierra de San Francisco to the north and whale-watching trips across the Laguna San Ignacio to the southwest.

RV sites, facilities: This large, primitive campground is essentially a dusty dirt lot with 40 no-hookup sites, shaded by numerous palm trees. Those with tents or small rigs (under 30 feet/9.1 meters long) might find it easier to maneuver among the trees, but the spaces will certainly accommodate lengthy RVs (up to 40 feet/12.2 meters long). Besides proximity to the lagoon and downtown San Ignacio, the only other amenities include a run-down outhouse with pit toilets. Only self-contained RVs and rugged tent campers should park here, preferably in pairs or groups, as there's no electricity, drinking water, dump station, shower house, or laundry room available. A perimeter fence and occasional daytime manager provide security. Be aware that the campground is rarely attended by staff. Children and leashed pets are welcome, but the facilities are not wheelchair-accessible. Groceries, purified water, fuel, and other supplies are available in nearby San Ignacio.

Reservations, fees: Reservations are not accepted; spaces are available on a first-come, first-served basis. RV and tent sites cost around $5 per night. Although the campground is rarely attended, someone should stop by to collect the fee, so have it ready. Credit cards are not accepted; cash (Mexican pesos or U.S. dollars) is the customary form of payment. The campground is open all year.

Directions: From Vizcaíno, drive southeast on Highway 1 for 44.4 miles (71.4 km), to San Ignacio. Near Km 73 (opposite the Pemex gas station), turn right and follow the road south for about 0.2 mile (0.3 km), toward town. The Lakeside RV Park will be on your left (you might see signs that indicate Lakeside RV Park as well as Camping Don Chon's, both of which refer to the same RV park). From Santa Rosalía, drive west for 45 miles (72.4 km), turn left toward San Ignacio (onto a turnoff just beyond Km 72), and look for the campground on your left.

Contact: Since there's no official contact person, mailing address, or phone number for the Lakeside RV Park, it's probably best to drive into the campground and see which spots are available.

12 CAMPO MIKASA

Scenic Rating: 7

in San Ignacio

See map page 164

Positioned beside a lovely lagoon fed by the Río San Ignacio and just south of the Lakeside RV Park, the Mikasa Coctelería is a small restaurant, where patrons can relax over seafood and cocktails, with a terrific view of the palm-fringed lagoon. Besides favored vittles, the *coctelería* offers simple overnight camping in its small parking lot. RV travelers and tent campers are all welcome in this inexpensive campground. While there are few amenities, the location is unbeatable. The restaurant's proximity to the river is ideal for swimmers, kayakers, hikers, cyclists, and birding enthusiasts. In addition, you're not terribly far from San Ignacio's historic town plaza, where you can arrange whale-watching trips and cave-painting excursions through cooperatives like Ecoturismo Kuyimá.

RV sites, facilities: Adjacent to the Mikasa restaurant, this small parking lot has room for just a handful of RVs. Although there are no hookups, there's enough space for lengthy motor homes and travel trailers (up to 40 feet/12.2 meters long). Besides proximity to the lagoon and downtown San Ignacio, the only other amenities include shady palm trees, hot showers, and the restaurant itself. Only self-contained RVs and rugged tent campers should park here, preferably in pairs or groups, as there's no electricity, drinking water, dump station, laundry, or security available. In fact, the restaurant owners do not stay on-site overnight. Children and leashed pets are welcome, but the facilities are not wheelchair-accessible. Groceries, purified water, fuel, and other supplies are available in nearby San Ignacio.

Reservations, fees: Reservations are not accepted; spaces are available on a first-come, first-served basis. RV and tent sites cost $5 per night. Credit cards are not accepted; cash (Mexican pesos or U.S. dollars) is the customary form of payment. The restaurant and campground are open all year.

Directions: From Vizcaíno, drive southeast on Highway 1 for 44.4 miles (71.4 km), to San Ignacio. Near Km 73 (opposite the Pemex gas station), turn right and follow the road south for about 0.4 mile (0.6 km), toward town. The Mikasa restaurant will be on your left, just south of the Lakeside RV Park and just north of the lagoon crossing. From Santa Rosalía, drive west for 45 miles (72.4 km), turn left toward San Ignacio (onto a turnoff just beyond Km 72), and look for the campground on your left.

Contact: Since there's no official contact person, mailing address, or phone number for the Campo Mikasa, it's probably best just to drive into the parking lot and see which spots are available. For more information about Ecoturismo Kuyimá, visit www.kuyima.com.

13 CAMPING LA MURALLA

Scenic Rating: 7

in San Ignacio

See map page 164

San Ignacio is one of the most picturesque towns on the entire Baja peninsula. Nestled within a fertile valley and situated beside a verdant lagoon (fed by the Río San Ignacio, which runs southeast toward the Laguna San Ignacio), this historic village is known far and wide for its thriving date palm trees—a literal oasis in the midst of desolate mountains and miles of desert terrain. Although San Ignacio serves as a convenient home base for exploring the mountainous Sierra San Pedro to the southeast, ancient cave paintings in the Sierra de San Francisco (for which a permit is required), and Laguna San Ignacio (a prime whale-watching site) to the south, the town has a few diversions of its own.

Besides the gorgeous Misión de San Ignacio de Kadakaamán and interesting Museo de Pinturas Rupestres de San Ignacio, the town presents lovely antique houses, a quaint central plaza, and several festive Mexican restaurants, many of which sit amid lush palm groves beside the lovely river-fed lagoon. La Muralla Restaurant, which offers space for overnight RVs, is one such outdoor eatery, popular for its seafood dishes, well-prepared steaks, Mexican cuisine, and tasty margaritas.

RV sites, facilities: Adjacent to La Muralla Restaurant, this small parking lot has room for a handful of RVs. Although there are no hookups, these shaded, primitive sites provide enough space for small motor homes and travel trailers (under 30 feet/9.1 meters long). Besides proximity to the lagoon and downtown San Ignacio, the only other amenities include shady palm trees, bathrooms with hot showers, a communal barbecue pit, and the restaurant itself. Only self-contained RVs and rugged tent campers should park here, preferably in pairs or groups, as there's no electricity, drinking water, dump station, laundry room, or security available. Children and leashed pets are welcome, but the facilities are not wheelchair-accessible. Groceries, purified water, fuel, and other supplies are available in nearby San Ignacio.

Reservations, fees: Reservations are not accepted; spaces are available on a first-come, first-served basis. RV and tent sites cost around $5 per night. Credit cards are not accepted; cash (Mexican pesos or U.S. dollars) is the customary form of payment. The campground and restaurant are open all year.

Directions: From Vizcaíno, drive southeast on Highway 1 for 44.4 miles (71.4 km), to San

Ignacio. Near Km 73 (opposite the Pemex gas station), turn right and follow the road south for about 0.4 mile (0.6 km), toward town. Camping La Muralla will be on your right, just across the street from the Campo Mikasa and along the north bank of the lagoon. From Santa Rosalía, drive west for 45 miles (72.4 km), turn left toward San Ignacio (onto a turnoff just beyond Km 72), and look for the campground on your right.

Contact: Since there's no official contact person, mailing address, or phone number for Camping La Muralla, it's probably best to drive into the campground and see which spots are available.

14 CAMPING LOS PETATES

Scenic Rating: 8

in San Ignacio

See map page 164

Yet another in a cluster of primitive campgrounds alongside the palm-fringed lagoon, fed by the Río San Ignacio, the relatively new Camping Los Petates is a pleasant place to stay for a few days—if not longer. After all, it could take at least a week to explore all that San Ignacio and its surrounding wilderness has to offer. With mild weather year-round, this historic oasis is an ideal place to enjoy Baja's great outdoors and cultural landmarks. On any given day, you can visit a historic mission, take a wildlife-watching trip to the Laguna San Ignacio or a cave-painting excursion into the Sierra de San Francisco, and watch the sunset as you sip margaritas on the verdant shore of a pleasant lagoon.

RV sites, facilities: This primitive campground offers space for perhaps 15 RVs and tents. Although there are no hookups, these rustic, shaded sites provide enough space for lengthy motor homes and travel trailers (up to 40 feet/12.2 meters long). Those with large rigs might, however, find it difficult to maneuver amid the palm trees. Besides proximity to the lagoon and downtown San Ignacio, the only other amenities include shady palm trees, barbecue pits, and pit toilets. Only self-contained RVs and rugged tent campers should park here, preferably in pairs or groups, as there's no electricity, drinking water, dump station, shower house, laundry room, or security available. The manager does not live on-site. Children and leashed pets are welcome, but the facilities are not wheelchair-accessible. Groceries, purified water, fuel, and other supplies are available in nearby San Ignacio.

Reservations, fees: Reservations are not accepted; spaces are available on a first-come, first-served basis. RV and tent sites cost $5 per night. Credit cards are not accepted; cash (Mexican pesos or U.S. dollars) is the customary form of payment. The campground is open all year.

Directions: From Vizcaíno, drive southeast on Highway 1 for 44.4 miles (71.4 km), to San Ignacio. Near Km 73 (opposite the Pemex gas station), turn right and follow the road south for about 0.5 mile (0.8 km), toward town. Camping Los Petates will be on your right, along the southern bank of the lagoon. From Santa Rosalía, drive west for 45 miles (72.4 km), turn left toward San Ignacio (onto a turnoff just beyond Km 72), and look for the campground on your right, just south of the lagoon.

Contact: Since there's no official contact person, mailing address, or phone number for Camping Los Petates, it's probably best to drive into the campground and see which spots are available.

15 EL PADRINO RV PARK

Scenic Rating: 6

in San Ignacio

See map page 164

As the closest campground to San Ignacio's tree-lined town plaza, the El Padrino RV Park places travelers within walking distance of the elaborate Misión de San Ignacio de Kadakaamán, established by the Jesuits in 1728 and rebuilt by the Dominicans in 1786. It is this second incarnation—a sturdy, volcanic stone structure with heavy wooden beams, massive carved doors, and an ornate altar—that you see today. One of the most well-preserved churches in Baja, the Misión de San Ignacio de Kadakaamán is also one of the few remaining missions in active use. Local parishioners flock here for masses, weddings, even funerals. Inside lies an 18th-century altarpiece dedicated to San Ignacio de Loyola, the town's patron saint and the inspiration for San Ignacio's Fiesta Patronal every July.

Just south of the mission church, a delightful history museum presents art and artifacts from early settlers as well as intriguing displays of the ancient cave murals found within the Sierra de San Francisco and Desierto de Vizcaíno. Operated by the Instituto Nacional de Antropología e Historia (INAH), the Museo de Pinturas Rupestres de San Ignacio also houses an INAH office, from which you must secure permission (and a guide) before visiting any of the rock-art sites in the area. In addition, you must agree to a series of restrictions intended to preserve the paintings, such as refraining from the use of alcohol, cigarettes, and flash photography in the vicinity of the caves and formations. Be advised, too, that you'll need your own vehicle as well as proficiency in Spanish to arrange such an adventure; it will be infinitely easier (though more expensive) to take a formal tour through a company like Ecoturismo Kuyimá.

Located near the Desert Inn (formerly a La Pinta Hotel), this simple campground offers shady spots amid date palm trees and flowering shrubs. Also part of the tourist complex is a festive bar and restaurant known as Flojo's. But, of course, most travelers park here so that they can be close to town, where they can arrange cave-painting tours within the Sierra de San Francisco and whale-watching excursions across the Laguna San Ignacio (from mid-December to mid-April).

RV sites, facilities: The park offers six back-in RV sites, with water service and 15-amp electricity, in addition to perhaps 30 shaded, no-hookup campsites (on dirt) for self-contained RVs and tents. Each space has enough room for lengthy motor homes and trailers (up to 40 feet/12.2 meters long), with slide-outs. Other amenities include shady palm trees, a bar, an indoor/outdoor restaurant (Flojo's), cable television, a dump station, a public pay phone, and poorly maintained restrooms with flush toilets and hot showers. The on-site restaurant contains the park office and provides Internet access. The park is secured by a gated perimeter fence and a resident caretaker, and the English-speaking staff can arrange cave-painting excursions and whale-watching trips to Laguna San Ignacio. There is, however, no laundry room on-site. Children, leashed pets, and tent campers are welcome, though the facilities are not wheelchair-accessible. Groceries, purified water, fuel, and other supplies are available in downtown San Ignacio, which lies within walking distance of the campground.

Reservations, fees: Reservations are not accepted; spaces are available on a first-come, first-served basis. Full-hookup RV sites cost $15 per night, while dry camping (for RVs and tents) costs $10 per night. Guided whale-watching and cave-painting tours are also available for a fee. Credit cards are not accepted; cash (Mexican pesos or U.S. dollars) is the customary form of payment. The park is open all year.

Directions: From Vizcaíno, drive southeast on Highway 1 for 44.4 miles (71.4 km), to San Ignacio. Near Km 73 (opposite the Pemex gas station), turn right and follow the road south for about 1.3 miles (2.1 km), toward town. El Padrino RV Park will be on your right, on the south side of the main road. From Santa Rosalía, drive west for 45 miles (72.4 km), turn left toward San Ignacio (onto a turnoff just beyond Km 72), and look for the campground on your right, just south of where the road turns toward the town's central plaza.

Contact: For more information about the El Padrino RV Park, call 615/154-0089. If no one answers, you should still drive to the park and see which spots are available. For details about the nearby Desert Inn, visit www.desertinns.com. For more information about INAH, visit www.inah.gob.mx (just be aware that most of the site is presented in Spanish). For details about Ecoturismo Kuyimá, visit www.kuyima.com.

16 ECOTURISMO KUYIMÁ

Scenic Rating: 9

southwest of San Ignacio

See map page 164 BEST

Although Kuyimá's headquarters are now in San Ignacio, the actual campground is beside Laguna San Ignacio, roughly 42.1 miles (67.7 km) southwest of town. While inexpensive boondocking is possible in several fish camps along the perimeter of this marshy lagoon, Kuyimá likely provides the best accommodations. Besides the seasonal campground, this ecofriendly resort offers cozy thatched huts on the beach, comfortable restrooms, a restaurant, hiking and biking excursions, and, of course, intimate whale-watching trips (via local *pangueros,* the only people licensed to lead others into the protected lagoon).

Every winter (from mid-December to mid-April), hundreds of magnificent *ballenas gris* (gray whales) travel thousands of miles, from the frigid waters of Alaska's Bering Sea to the warmer bays and lagoons along Baja California's Pacific coast in order to procreate and raise their offspring. Once hunted nearly to extinction, the whales now thrive in Laguna San Ignacio (part of the Reserva de la Biósfera El Vizcaíno), protected by federal law and relished by ecotourists from all over the world.

Through Ecoturismo Kuyimá—an organization that has actively preserved this critical whale-breeding habitat for over a decade—you can choose from a variety of adventures: a five-day trip from Loreto, a four-day trip from San Ignacio, a day trip from San Ignacio, or a quick trip from the Kuyimá campground. Kuyimá also offers day trips, three-day expeditions, and weeklong excursions to see cultural sites like the Cueva del Ratón, Cañón de San Pablo, Cañón de Santa Teresa, Arroyo del Parral, and other historic spots in the Sierra de San Francisco.

While staying at Campo Kuyimá, you can do more than view whales. Hiking or biking around the estuary is a wonderful way to watch the varied birds, from ospreys to cormorants, that make this wildlife refuge their seasonal home. In addition, you can rent a kayak and drift among the mangroves, in search of your inner calm. Swimming and fishing are also favored pastimes. Just remember to avoid areas where the whales are breeding or raising their young; the Laguna San Ignacio is a protected whale sanctuary first, an ecotourism resort second.

RV sites, facilities: This primitive campground offers space for an indeterminate number of tents and RVs, preferably smaller ones (up to 30 feet/9.1 meters long). Although there are no water, electricity, or sewage hookups, the resort provides 10 rustic, yet furnished, thatched huts—each of which can accommodate two adults and one child. Other amenities include a *palapa*-style restaurant that serves Mexican and seafood cuisine; clean, comfortable restrooms with ecofriendly toilets and solar-heated, freshwater showers; a library of natural-history books and videos; seasonal whale-watching excursions; and guided hiking, biking, and kayaking tours to birding sites and ancient cave paintings.

Ecoturismo Kuyimá also offers multiday packages that include accommodations, meals, guided ecotours, round-trip transportation, and access to kayaks and mountain bikes. English-speaking guides are on staff. Only self-contained RVs and rugged tent campers should park here, preferably in pairs or groups, as there's no dump station, laundry room, or security available. Children and leashed pets are welcome, but the facilities are not wheelchair-accessible. Given the remote location of this campground, you should pick up groceries, purified water, fuel, and other supplies in San Ignacio before heading down to the campground.

Reservations, fees: Reservations are highly recommended for RV spaces (and required for the on-site *cabañas*). Overnight camping costs $10 per RV or tent (for up to four people); the price includes access to clean restrooms, hot showers, and drinking water. The resort also rents camping gear (namely, a tent, two sleeping bags, two cots, cotton sheets, and pillows) for $40 per couple. Whale-watching excursions cost $40 per trip. Round-trip transportation from San Ignacio to the lagoon costs $130 per van (for up to 10 passengers). Whale-watching packages (which include accommodations) cost $165–965, and cultural trips (including mule rides) cost $64–927. Credit cards are accepted for tours; cash (Mexican pesos or U.S. dollars) is the suitable form of payment for camping. The tour service is available from October to May, though the campground is only open during whale-watching season (from December to April).

Directions: From San Ignacio, drive south through town and continue on a graded dirt road for 19.7 miles (31.7 km), passing several *ranchos* along the way. Where a side road veers to the left, toward more *ranchos,* continue straight (southwest) for 16 miles (25.7 km). At the next fork in the road, veer to the right and drive 6.4 miles (10.3 km), past the Laguna San Ignacio fish camp. Turn right (northwest) at the well-marked access road for Campo Kuyimá and drive 1.7 miles (2.7 km) toward the shore.

Contact: Ecoturismo Kuyimá, SPR de RL, Morelos #23, Zona Centro, San Ignacio, Baja California Sur, C.P. 23930, Mexico, tel. 615/154-0070, or P.M.B. #2474, 710 East San Ysidro Boulevard, San Ysidro, CA 92173, www.kuyima.com.

17 RV PARK LAS PALMAS

Scenic Rating: 7

southeast of Santa Rosalía

See map page 164 **BEST**

While Santa Rosalía presents a wealth of sightseeing possibilities, this historic coastal town sadly contains no RV parks or campgrounds within its city limits. The closest place for RV travelers, in fact, lies a few miles south of town. Framed by the Sierra San Pedro and peppered with date palm trees, the clean, well-maintained RV Park Las Palmas allows overnight campers relative proximity to the Sea of Cortez—a playground for swimmers, kayakers, boaters, anglers, scuba divers, and wildlife enthusiasts. However, the park is not directly on the beach or within walking distance of Santa Rosalía.

Despite the campground's location outside of town, it's still a convenient base of operations for history buffs. Filled with taco stands and colorful buildings, Santa Rosalía—a vibrant fishing and ferry port that was once a copper-mining town (and, if the rumors are true, may soon be again)—houses a number of 19th-century, French Colonial–style structures and other historic edifices, including the Iglesia Santa Bárbara de Santa Rosalía, a prefabricated iron church designed by Alexandre Gustave Eiffel, the same architect and engineer who crafted the Eiffel Tower. Exhibited in the 1889 Paris World Exposition, the church was disassembled and stored in Belgium, where it stayed until a director of the French-owned Compañía del Boleo (the copper-mining company that built Santa Rosalía in the 1880s) happened upon it in 1895 and had it shipped to Santa Rosalía, reassembled, and adorned with stained-glass windows.

Other notable buildings include the Palacio Municipal (Town Hall), which was originally based on a design by Eiffel; the Biblioteca Mahatma Gandhi, situated within the Parque Morelos near the harbor; and the Hotel Francés, built on the Mesa Francia for French employees of the Compañía del Boleo and offering terrific views of the former copper foundry along the Carretera Transpeninsular (Highway 1). The Fundición del Pacífico, once the main offices of the Compañía del Boleo, today serves as the Museo Boleo (also known as the Museo Histórico Minero de Santa Rosalía), a repository of accounting artifacts, maritime memorabilia, and other preserved items from Santa Rosalía's copper-mining days.

Santa Rosalía truly is one of Baja's most attractive towns, possessing quaint streets, papaya trees, and well-tended gardens, and it's definitely worth a sojourn here, even if your intended destinations are Mulegé and Bahía Concepción to the south. As a note of warning, RV travelers should be aware that Santa Rosalía's avenues and streets are rather narrow and designated as one-way routes, so when sightseeing, it might be best to park your motor homes and travel trailers along the main highway and walk into town.

RV sites, facilities: The park offers 30 grassy, full-hookup, back-in spaces, separated by concrete curbs and arranged around the perimeter of the campground. Each space has 40-amp electricity (with 15-amp outlets), water service, sewer access, palm trees, and enough room for lengthy motor homes and travel trailers (up to 40 feet/12.2 meters long). Other facilities include a seasonal restaurant, a bar, a coin laundry, a dump station, a public pay phone, a swimming pool, shady *palapas,* and aging restrooms with flush toilets and hot showers. A gated perimeter fence and an occasionally on-site owner ensure some security. The owner, however, does not live on the premises and only stops by to collect camping fees. Children, leashed pets, and tent campers are welcome, but the facilities are not wheelchair-accessible. Grocery stores, gasoline stations, and a post office are only a short drive away, in Santa Rosalía.

Reservations, fees: Reservations are not accepted; spaces are available on a first-come, first-served basis. RV sites cost $14 per night. Tent sites cost $10 per night (for up to two people). There is a daily charge of $2 per person for use of the fenced swimming pool. Long-term camping rates are also available. The owner will probably stop by your campsite to the collect the fee, so have it ready. Credit cards are not accepted; cash (Mexican pesos or U.S. dollars) is the only acceptable form of payment. The RV park is open all year.

Directions: From downtown Santa Rosalía, head south on Highway 1 for 2.5 miles (4 km). Just south of the Km 193 marker, you'll spy a sign for the RV Park Las Palmas. Turn left (east) and drive toward the gulf; the park lies ahead. From Mulegé, head northwest on Highway 1 for 36 miles (57.9 km), toward Santa Rosalía. Turn right at the well-marked sign, near Km 193, and head toward the campground.

Contact: RV Park Las Palmas, Apartado Postal #123, Santa Rosalía, Baja California Sur, Mexico. Since there's no official phone number, you should simply drive toward the campground and see which spots are available.

18 RV CAMACHO

Scenic Rating: 6

south of Santa Rosalía

See map page 164

If staying next to the beach is paramount during your trip to Santa Rosalía, then you might want to bypass RV Park Las Palmas and continue south another 7.5 miles (12.1 km) to RV Camacho. Dotted with palm and mesquite trees, this small, beachside campground might present few amenities, but you're guaranteed incredible views of the Sea of Cortez (or Golfo de California) and proximity to all the fun-filled diversions that this magnificent gulf has to offer, from kayaking to deep-sea fishing. It's also not far from the town of Santa Rosalía, where you'll encounter lovely gardens, several taco stands, several French Colonial–style homes and other historic buildings, and an infrequent ferry service that departs from the town's marina and embarks upon a nine-hour journey across the Sea of Cortez to Guaymas, Sonora, on the Mexican mainland. As a bonus, this campground tends to be a lot quieter than the more popular RV Park San Lucas Cove just south of here.

RV sites, facilities: This fenced, primitive campground offers roughly 12 no-hookup, back-in waterfront sites, with easy maneuverability and space for lengthy RVs (up to 40 feet/12.2 meters long). A large lot behind these campsites provides plenty of room for additional tents and RVs. Amenities include shady *palapas,* a boat launch ramp, a dump station, and clean restrooms with flush toilets and hot showers. A perimeter fence, a gated front entrance, and on-duty guards ensure limited security. Only self-contained RVs and rugged tent campers should park here, as there's no electricity, drinking water, or laundry on the premises. Children and leashed pets are welcome, though the facilities are not wheelchair-accessible. Groceries, purified water, gasoline, and other supplies are available in Santa Rosalía to the north or Mulegé to the south.

Reservations, fees: Reservations are not accepted; spaces are available on a first-come, first-served basis. Overnight camping costs $7 per night (for RVs and tents). Long-term rates are also available. Credit cards are not accepted; cash (Mexican pesos or U.S. dollars) is the customary form of payment. The campground is open all year.

Directions: From downtown Santa Rosalía, head southeast on Highway 1 for 9.9 miles (15.9 km). Just north of the Km 181 marker, you'll spy a sign for RV Camacho. Turn left (east), drive about 0.5 mile (0.8 km) down a twisting, sandy road, and veer to the left. The park office (which is usually staffed) lies 0.1 mile (0.2 km) ahead, beside the front gate. From Mulegé, head northwest on Highway 1 for 28.6 miles (46 km), toward Santa Rosalía. Turn right at the well-marked sign, between Km 182 and Km 181, and veer left toward RV Camacho.

Contact: Since there's no official contact person, mailing address, or phone number for RV Camacho, it's probably best to just drive toward the park and see which spots are available. For more information about the Ferry Santa Rosalía, visit www.ferrysantarosalia.com.

19 RV PARK SAN LUCAS COVE

Scenic Rating: 7

south of Santa Rosalía

See map page 164

Those who enjoy staying in lively campgrounds, with lots of neighbors and constant activity, will definitely appreciate RV Park San Lucas Cove, just south of the more serene RV Camacho and beside the same sheltered cove (the Bahía El Islote de San Lucas) as its neighbor. Palm trees surround the sign that you pass as you enter this no-frills destination. Though this beachside campground might offer few amenities, it certainly provides wonderful views of the Sea of Cortez, the Isla San Marcos just offshore, and, of course, the rising and setting sun.

If the numerous boats stretched along the beach are any indication, it's also a terrific spot for water enthusiasts, whether your hobby is kayaking, swimming, fishing, boating, or birding. Swimmers will relish the calm waters of the cove. Beachcombers will enjoy clamming along the shore (just be aware of Mexico's rules and restrictions regarding this activity, which requires a Mexican fishing license and may be illegal for foreigners). Those with small boats and sea kayaks can launch them directly from the park, either across the firm sand or via the on-site boat launch. Anglers, snorkelers, and scuba divers will especially favor the waters around Isla San Marcos, where barracuda, yellowtail, dorado, bass, grouper, and several other fish species dwell. If you don't have a boat of your own, consult the resident manager about local *pangueros* for hire. Fishing is fantastic here—and the main reason that most travelers stop here for the night (or longer).

RV sites, facilities: This primitive beachside campground offers 60 no-hookup, back-in sites, with easy maneuverability and space for lengthy RVs (up to 40 feet/12.2 meters long). Roughly a third of the sites are lined along the water, while the rest lie on a large hard-packed sandy area. Besides the incredible ocean views and convenient beach access, the only other amenities include a boat launch, a dump station, a few *palapas* and shady trees, municipal water hookups, and clean restrooms with flush toilets and (usually) hot showers. A resident manager provides some security. Only self-contained RVs and rugged tent campers should park here, preferably in pairs or groups, as there's no electricity, drinking water, or laundry on the premises. Children and leashed pets are welcome, though the facilities are not wheelchair-accessible. Groceries, purified water, gasoline, and other supplies are available in Santa Rosalía to the north or Mulegé to the south.

Reservations, fees: Reservations are not accepted; spaces are available on a first-come, first-served basis. Overnight camping costs under $10 per night (for RVs or tents). Long-term rates are also available. Credit cards are not accepted; cash (Mexican pesos or U.S. dollars) is the customary form of payment. The campground is open all year.

Directions: From downtown Santa Rosalía, head southeast on Highway 1 for 9.9 miles (15.9 km). Just north of the Km 181 marker, you'll spy a sign for RV Camacho (north of RV Park San Lucas Cove, on the same bay). Turn left (east), drive about 0.5 mile (0.8 km) down a twisting road (made of hard-packed sand), and veer to the right. The campground lies ahead, about 0.1 mile (0.2 km) farther along. From Mulegé, head northwest on Highway 1 for 28.6 miles (46 km), toward Santa Rosalía. Turn right at the well-marked sign, between Km 182 and Km 181, and veer right toward RV Park San Lucas Cove.

Contact: RV Park San Lucas Cove, Apartado Postal #50, Santa Rosalía, Baja California Sur, Mexico. Since there's no official phone number, you should simply drive toward the campground and see which spots are available. For more information about Isla San Marcos, visit www.islasanmarcos.com.

20 PLAYA DOS AMIGOS

Scenic Rating: 6

south of Santa Rosalía

See map page 164

For a beachside spot that's close to the historic sites and natural delights of Santa Rosalía and Mulegé, you can't go wrong with Playa Dos Amigos, a no-frills campground situated between the Sea of Cortez and the mountainous Sierra San Pedro. From here, along the southern shore of the Bahía El Islote de San Lucas, you have a fairly nice view of the Isla San Marcos, with its active gypsum mine, boat ramp, landing strip, and bountiful fishing grounds. In addition, the water is shallow here, with a gently sloping beach that's ideal for launching sea kayaks and small boats.

Although popular activities here involve the water, such as sportfishing, swimming, and kayaking, history buffs will be pleased to know that they're only 11.8 miles (19 km) southeast of the 19th-century, French Colonial–style structures that abound in Santa Rosalía, and roughly 28.6 miles (46 km) northwest of the Misión de Santa Rosalía de Mulegé, a well-preserved stone church founded in 1706, completed in 1766, and surrounded today by lush date palm groves.

RV sites, facilities: This primitive, beachside campground—essentially an expansive field beside the beach—offers an indeterminate number of sites for RVs and tents. Although there are no hookups, amenities include a restaurant, restrooms with flush toilets and hot showers, and plenty of space for lengthy RVs (up to 40 feet/12.2 meters long). In fact, only self-contained RVs and rugged tent campers should park here, preferably in pairs or groups, as there's no electricity, drinking water, dump station, or laundry room on the premises. A resident manager provides limited security. Children and leashed pets are welcome, though the terrain might not be suitable for wheelchairs. Given the lack of stores and other facilities in the area, it will be necessary to pick up groceries, purified water, gasoline, and other supplies in nearby towns like Santa Rosalía or Mulegé before heading down to the campground.

Reservations, fees: Reservations are not accepted; spaces are available on a first-come, first-served basis. RV and tent sites cost $10 per night. Credit cards are not accepted; cash (Mexican pesos or U.S. dollars) is the customary form of payment. The campground is open all year.

Directions: From downtown Santa Rosalía, head southeast on Highway 1 for 11.8 miles (19 km). Just north of the Km 178 marker, you'll spy a billboard for Playa Dos Amigos. Turn left (east), drive about 0.6 mile (1 km) down the access road, and bear left, toward the beachside campground. From Mulegé, head northwest on Highway 1 for 26.7 miles (43 km), toward Santa Rosalía. Turn right at the well-marked sign, near Km 178, and bear left toward Playa Dos Amigos.

Contact: Since there's no official contact person, mailing address, or phone number for Playa Dos Amigos, it's probably best to simply drive toward the campground and see which spots are available. For more information about Isla San Marcos, visit www.islasanmarcos.com.

21 PUNTA CHIVATO

Scenic Rating: 8

north of Mulegé

See map page 164

The sandy beaches, thriving estuaries, curious tidepools, and rocky underwater reefs around Punta Chivato have been luring hikers, beachcombers, wildlife lovers, and scuba divers for years. Apparently, the secret's been out for a while. En route from Highway 1, you'll pass several private homes on your way to the campground, which is directly beside the gorgeous Sea of Cortez (or Golfo de California). Despite the expanding real-estate boom here (and in other parts of Baja), you're still assured rest and relaxation on this attractive peninsula. In fact, many travelers consider this area to be one of the loveliest in Baja, affording an incredible view of the far-off Península Concepción, which lies to the southeast. (Just bear in mind that there are two spots called Punta Chivato: the point that juts out into the gulf, and the settlement on the southern edge of this small peninsula. The point is where this campground is located.)

Boaters, kayakers, and anglers are especially fond of Punta Chivato, as it's relatively easy to launch small vessels and kayaks across the protected beach, into the Sea of Cortez. From here, a popular destination is Isla Santa Inés in the Bahía Santa Inés, where frequent catches include grouper, yellowtail, sierra, and dorado, among other varieties. In addition, anglers and pleasure cruisers can travel around Punta Chivato and head north to Isla San Marcos, a considerably larger island, with excellent fishing, diving, and wildlife-watching opportunities.

So, despite the scarcity of official amenities and the soft sand that makes a four-wheel-drive vehicle preferable, the Punta Chivato campground remains a popular choice for RV enthusiasts. The complicated access road and limited space make this a better option for tent campers and those with small RVs, though big rigs have been known to stop here, too.

RV sites, facilities: This primitive, beachside campground—essentially a large parking area behind the beach—offers an indeterminate number of sites for RVs and tents. Although there are no hookups, amenities include a nearby hotel, some pit toilets and cold showers, a dump station near the hotel, and plenty of space for midsized RVs (up to 35 feet/10.7 meters long). Only self-contained RVs and rugged tent campers should park here, preferably in pairs or groups, as there's no electricity, drinking water, laundry, or security on the premises. Children and leashed pets are welcome, though the terrain might not be suitable for wheelchairs. Given the presence of only one *tienda* in the area, it will be necessary to pick up groceries, purified water, gasoline, and other supplies in nearby towns like Santa Rosalía or Mulegé before heading down to the campground.

Reservations, fees: Reservations are not accepted; spaces are available on a first-come, first-served basis. RV and tent sites cost around $10 per night. Credit cards are not accepted; cash (Mexican pesos or U.S. dollars) is the customary form of payment. The campground is open all year.

Directions: From downtown Santa Rosalía, head southeast on Highway 1 for 26.1 miles (42 km). Just north of the Km 155 marker, in the village of Palo Verde, turn left (east) onto the dirt access road, which winds for 11.4 miles (18.3 km) toward Punta Chivato. After the initial 2.3 miles (3.7 km), you'll encounter a fork in the road. Take the right fork and continue for 3.6 miles (5.8 km), edging toward the shoreline. Turn left and drive parallel to the shore for 2.8 miles (4.5 km). For the next 2 miles (3.2 km), the road turns inland, bypasses a runway, and returns to the beach, before reaching the hotel. Turn left and drive 0.7 mile (1.1 km) to the campground, past a row of beachside houses.

From Mulegé, head northwest on Highway 1 for 12.4 miles (20 km), toward Santa Rosalía. Turn right onto the access road at Km 155 and follow the above directions to Punta Chivato.

Contact: Since there's no official contact person, mailing address, or phone number for Punta Chivato, it's probably best to simply drive toward the campground and see which spots are available. For more information about Isla San Marcos, visit www.islasanmarcos.com.

22 HACIENDA DE LA HABANA

Scenic Rating: 9

southwest of Mulegé

See map page 164 **BEST**

Like lovely San Ignacio, Mulegé is celebrated for the lush palm groves that thrive within its vicinity and along the river that winds through its midst. Both towns are virtual oases on a peninsula predominated by sand—of the beach and desert varieties. Situated beside the Sea of Cortez, Mulegé is a particularly picturesque destination, with several convenient campgrounds on either shore of the winding Río Mulegé. Hacienda de la Habana (Havana House), in a wide valley beyond Mulegé, is the farthest RV park from the town's center. Luckily, however, this well-irrigated place is only a short drive from one of Baja's most well-preserved missions, the Misión de Santa Rosalía de Mulegé, which apparently required six decades to complete. The park is also not far from the neocolonial-style Museo Mulegé, which, long before displaying artifacts such as cotton gins, firearms, religious relics, and antique diving equipment, served as an experimental federal prison. Here, all but the most heinous felons were allowed to leave the "prison without bars" every morning for jobs, dances, and other activities—as long as they returned every evening.

Owned and operated by Ray Lima, Hacienda de la Habana is perhaps most popular for its on-site Cuban restaurant, Ray's Place, which Ray opened following the closure of his original eatery on Playa Santispac to the south. Also known as Ray's Place, that long-standing joint was prized among locals and travelers alike, until a fire burned it beyond recognition and Ray decided not to rebuild. Although the residents of Playa Santispac were heartbroken by the loss, many are at least happy to know that a "Ray's Place" still exists, especially one that has the same delicious food, expert service, and friendly ambience as the original. Grilled yellowtail and oysters Rockefeller are particular winners.

RV sites, facilities: The campground presents 24 spacious, grassy, pull-through sites, with full hookups (including 20-amp electrical outlets, 30-amp breakers, water service, and sewer access) and enough space for lengthy RVs (up to 40 feet/12.2 meters long). Facilities include flush toilets, hot showers, a swimming pool, a lounge area beside the pool, and a restaurant, commonly called Ray's Place. English-speaking staff members are present, but there is no laundry or dump station on-site. Children, leashed pets, and tent campers are welcome, though the facilities are not wheelchair-accessible. Groceries, purified water, gasoline, and other supplies are available in nearby Mulegé.

Reservations, fees: Reservations are not

accepted; spaces are available on a first-come, first-served basis. Tent and RV spaces cost $15–20 per night. Long-term rates are also possible. Credit cards are not accepted; cash (Mexican pesos or U.S. dollars) is the customary form of payment. The campground is open all year.

Directions: From north of Mulegé, head southeast on Highway 1 and make a hard right turn onto Ice House Road (Calle Manuel Marquez De Leon), immediately north of Km 135. Drive for 0.6 mile (1 km) and turn left at the end of the paved road. Drive for 0.1 mile (0.2 km) on the dirt road, turn right, and continue on the main road (which makes four turns: left, right, left, right) for 1.8 miles (2.9 km). Hacienda de la Habana is on the left.

From south of Mulegé, head northwest on Highway 1, cross the Río Mulegé, turn left onto Ice House Road (Calle Manuel Marquez De Leon) near Km 135, and follow the above directions to the campground. Be aware that the roads might not be very well signed in Mulegé.

Contact: Hacienda de la Habana, Apartado Postal #123, Mulegé, Baja California Sur, Mexico. Since there's no official phone number for the Hacienda de la Habana, it's probably best to simply drive toward the campground and see which spots are available.

23 HUERTA DON CHANO

Scenic Rating: 9

east of Mulegé

See map page 164

If you'd prefer to stay closer to the ocean during your visit to Mulegé, you can opt for the farthest campground from the Hacienda de la Habana. Huerta Don Chano, owned and operated by Manuel and Elisa Romero, is on the northern side of the Río Mulegé, between downtown Mulegé and the Sea of Cortez. Not far from the town's historic sites—including a former state penitentiary (the only one without bars) and the Misión de Santa Rosalía de Mulegé—this pleasant RV park, which offers a family-friendly atmosphere and is rarely crowded, is also conveniently close to a myriad of water-related activities, from surf fishing to scuba diving to sea kayaking.

Scuba diving is especially favored in Mulegé, where the water is warm and underwater sites like those north of Punta Concepción offer up-close views of sea turtles, game fish, dolphins, sharks, and whales. Cortez Explorers, an adventure outfitter certified by the Professional Association of Diving Instructors (PADI), offers a variety of diving courses in the Sea of Cortez—perfect for beginners as well as those seeking to be divemasters.

Huerta Don Chano is also an ideal home base for deep-sea anglers as well as cyclists; mountain bikes can even be rented in town. In addition, Playa El Farito, a popular beach (especially for local teenagers), lies along the shore, 1.2 miles (1.9 km) east of the park. Just remember that, while Huerta Don Chano can accommodate midsized RVs, smaller ones (such as vans and pickup campers) will find it easier to navigate through the tight streets of Mulegé. Also, you should bring insect repellent while camping beside the river, and remember that it can get chilly here, especially on winter nights. As in other parts of Baja, theft has been on the rise in Mulegé (though not necessarily in Huerta Don Chano), so keep your valuables under lock and key.

RV sites, facilities: The park offers numerous grassy spaces under shady fruit trees, ideal for both tents and RVs (up to 35 feet/10.7 meters long). Water and electricity hookups are available for RV travelers, and other amenities include clean restrooms with cold showers. Resident owners provide limited security, but there is no laundry on the premises. Given the lack of sewer hookups or a dump station, self-contained RVs are necessary here. Children, leashed pets, and tent campers are welcome, though the facilities are not wheelchair-accessible. Groceries, purified water, gasoline, and other supplies are available in nearby Mulegé.

Reservations, fees: Reservations are not accepted; spaces are available on a first-come, first-served basis. RV spaces cost $15 per night, while tent sites cost around $10 per night. Credit cards are not accepted; cash (Mexican pesos or U.S. dollars) is the customary form of payment. The campground is open all year.

Directions: From north of Mulegé, head southeast on Highway 1 and, just south of Km 135, veer left onto Calle Moctezuma. Turn right onto Calle Martinez, head toward the Sea of Cortez, and merge onto Calle Francisco I. Madero. Follow the Río Mulegé toward Huerta Don Chano, which lies 0.6 mile (1 km) east of Mulegé. From south of Mulegé, head northwest on Highway 1, cross the Río Mulegé, turn right onto Calle Moctezuma, and follow the above directions.

Contact: For more information about Huerta Don Chano, call 615/153-0720. If no one answers, simply drive to the campground and see which spots are available. For details about Mulegé, visit www.mulege.net. For more information about Cortez Explorers, visit www.cortez-explorers.com.

24 HOTEL CUESTA REAL

Scenic Rating: 7

in Mulegé

See map page 164

One of three overnight options nestled between the Río Mulegé and Highway 1, the Hotel Cuesta Real is a popular choice for RV travelers hoping to explore Mulegé, a date palm oasis by the sea. Unfortunately, this modest hotel doesn't offer many campsites, so don't be surprised to find them occupied by long-term RVers. Still, for those with small or midsized RVs, it's worth stopping by the entrance and walking into the campground to check on the possibility of available spaces. Feel free to call ahead, too.

After all, Mulegé is a fantastic place to stay a spell: The weather is mild year-round; the scenery is lush and lovely; the town has a variety of bars, restaurants, shops, and historic sites; and the Sea of Cortez is conveniently close. So, whether you're inclined to visit an 18th-century Spanish mission or board a deep-sea fishing charter, Mulegé can certainly stimulate you for a while.

RV sites, facilities: The park offers 10 spacious RV sites, with full hookups (including water service, sewer access, and 15/30/50-amp outlets) and enough room for midsized motor homes and travel trailers (up to 35 feet/10.7 meters long). Other amenities include a small hotel (with a dozen air-conditioned rooms), a restaurant and cantina, a swimming pool, a gift shop, a coin laundry, and restrooms with hot showers. Internet access (wireless and via computer) and English-speaking employees are also available on-site. There is, however, no dump station on the premises. Children and leashed pets are welcome, though tent camping is not allowed. The facilities are, unfortunately, not wheelchair-accessible. Groceries, purified water, gasoline, and other supplies are available in nearby Mulegé.

Reservations, fees: Reservations are accepted. RV sites cost $25 per night. Long-term rates are available. Credit cards are not accepted; cash (Mexican pesos or U.S. dollars) is the only acceptable form of payment. The hotel, restaurant, and campground are open all year.

Directions: From north of Mulegé, drive southeast on Highway 1, cross the bridge that spans the Río Mulegé, and continue for 1.1 miles (1.8 km), toward Km 132. At the sign for Hotel Cuesta Real, turn left into the driveway and continue toward the hotel and campground. From south of Mulegé, drive northwest on Highway 1, pass the Km 132 marker, and turn right into the driveway.

Contact: Hotel Cuesta Real, c/o Ken, Christina, and Jenice Wright, Km 132 de la Carretera Transpeninsular, Apartado Postal #74, Mulegé, Baja California Sur, C.P. 23900, Mexico, tel.

615/153-0321, www.bajaquest.com/cuestareal or http://cuestareal.tripod.com.

25 VILLA MARÍA ISABEL RV PARK

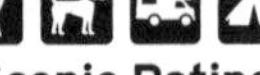

Scenic Rating: 8

in Mulegé

See map page 164

Named after the resident owner, María Isabel, this pleasant campground is one of three convenient spots situated along the southern shore of the Río Mulegé, easily accessible via Highway 1. Accentuated by palm trees of various heights and varieties, this clean, well-maintained property offers numerous dirt campsites, separated by tidy borders of white rocks. Some even have full hookups. Unlike its neighbors—Hotel Cuesta Real and Hotel Serenidad—Villa María Isabel RV Park primarily caters to overnight campers (including semipermanent residents), so it's an ideal place to stay if you plan to explore the historic sites of nearby Mulegé, observe birds in the surrounding palm oases, take a deep-sea fishing cruise into the Sea of Cortez, or launch your own boat and kayak onto the Río Mulegé.

From here, you can also take the challenging drive to Rancho La Trinidad, which lies 15.2 miles (24.5 km) southwest of Mulegé. After checking in with the caretakers at the *rancho* (operated by the Instituto Nacional de Antropología e Historia), you can arrange for a guided hiking (and swimming) excursion to several pre-Columbian rock-art sites within Cañón de la Trinidad. Set amid a marvelous landscape, these multicolored *pinturas rupestres* (cave paintings) illustrate the Cochimí culture, through vivid depictions of humans, fish, sea turtles, and other wildlife. Because the drive to Rancho La Trinidad can be rather difficult for first-timers, you might be better off hiring an expert guide in town; ask local residents for recommendations.

The only obvious drawback for the Villa María Isabel RV Park is its narrow sites, which make slide-outs and awnings impossible whenever the park is full. In addition, RV caravans favor this spacious campground, so without a reservation of your own, you might find yourself out of luck. Despite such challenges, most agree that this pastoral spot is one of your best bets in Mulegé.

RV sites, facilities: There are 40 narrow campsites, some of which have only water and electric service, while 18 of the spaces are pull-throughs with full hookups (including 30-amp electricity, water service, and sewer access). Some of the sites are shady, with grassy areas, and most will accommodate lengthy RVs (up to 40 feet/12.2 meters long), although slide-outs and awnings tend to be impossible luxuries when the campground is full. On-site amenities include a tent-camping area (with a communal *palapa*), a swimming pool, a boat ramp and dock, a coin laundry, a dump station, a public pay phone, clean restrooms with flush toilets and hot showers, a long-term storage area, and a nearby bakery (with terrific bread but irregular hours). The bilingual resident owner (whose house is near the pool) provides limited security. Children and leashed pets are welcome, though the facilities are not wheelchair-accessible. Groceries, purified water, gasoline, and other supplies are available in nearby Mulegé.

Reservations, fees: Reservations are accepted. RV sites cost $20 per night. Overnight tent camping costs $7 per person. Long-term rates are also available. Credit cards are not accepted; cash (Mexican pesos or U.S. dollars) is the customary form of payment. The park is open all year.

Directions: From Mulegé, head southeast on Highway 1, cross the bridge that spans the Río Mulegé, and continue for 1.3 miles (2.1 km). Just past Km 132, you'll see a sign for the Villa María Isabel RV Park on the left side of the road. Turn left into the driveway and continue toward the campground. From Bahía Concepción, head northwest on Highway 1. As you near the bridge that spans the Río Mulegé, you'll see the campground entrance on the right, between Km 131 and Km 132.

Contact: Villa María Isabel RV Park, Apartado Postal #5, Mulegé, Baja California Sur, C.P. 23900, Mexico, tel. 615/153-0246, mulegevilla mariarvpark@yahoo.com.

26 HOTEL SERENIDAD

Scenic Rating: 8

in Mulegé

See map page 164 **BEST**

Like Hotel Cuesta Real, Hotel Serenidad focuses more attention on its rooms and villas than on its campsites. Still, while the campground might be warmer and less impressive than that of the adjacent Villa María Isabel RV Park, this small, popular resort is still a pleasant place to stay, especially if you plan to fish the bountiful waters of the nearby Sea of Cortez. Hotel Serenidad not only charters fishing trips into the gulf (where you'll find amberjack, yellowtail, grouper, sailfish, pargo, sierra, and dorado), it also allows overnight campers to use the boat launch that sits beside the Río Mulegé, not far from the mouth of the river. In fact, prior to the construction of the Transpeninsular Highway (Highway 1), which has certainly eased travel up and down the Baja peninsula, the Hotel Serenidad (which has its own airstrip) was once a favored destination for fly-in anglers.

Surrounded by palm trees, this well-known hotel can be both tranquil and festive—it just depends on the time of day. Although sunbathing on a lounge chair beside the lovely pool is a relaxing way to spend the afternoon, the swim-up bar encourages a party atmosphere in this tropical oasis. Some people, after all, come just for the cocktails and seafood, and on Saturday nights, visitors flock to the hotel's celebrated pig roasts (where for $15 people can sip margaritas, taste all-you-can-eat pork, listen to mariachi music, and watch folkloric dancers).

Offering hotel rooms, cottages, luxurious villas, and a trailer park (with temporary and permanent occupants), Hotel Serenidad welcomes a wide variety of travelers, including anglers, boaters, kayakers, scuba divers, snorkelers, beachcombers, horseback riders, and bicyclists. The staff can also arrange mission and petroglyph tours, hiking treks, and other guided excursions throughout this diverse region.

RV sites, facilities: In a partly shaded, walled campground behind the hotel, the tourist complex offers eight full-hookup, back-in campsites, with 15-amp electricity, water service, sewer access, and only enough room for small RVs (up to 30 feet/9.1 meters long). Other amenities include a bar and restaurant, a nice hotel (with villas, cottages, and 50 rooms), a swimming pool, a tennis court, a recreation room, a boat launch ramp, a dump station, a coin laundry, Internet access, an airstrip called El Gallito, and clean restrooms with flush toilets and hot showers. In addition, the hotel offers fishing trips, bicycle and ATV rentals, and a dive shop. Guards provide limited security, and English-speaking employees are present. Children and leashed pets are welcome, though tent camping is not allowed. The facilities are not wheelchair-accessible. Groceries, purified water, gasoline, and other supplies are available in nearby Mulegé.

Reservations, fees: Reservations are accepted, although a deposit for the first night is required. Cancellations are possible via telephone; a full refund is guaranteed only with a minimum of two weeks' notice. RV sites cost $15 per night and $90 per week (for up to two people); each additional guest will be charged $2.50 per night. Hotel rooms are available for $72–89 per night; two-bedroom cottages cost $128 per night. *Panga* charters cost $120 per trip. Credit cards are not accepted; cash (Mexican pesos or U.S. dollars) is the customary form of payment. Although the restaurant is closed every September, the hotel, bar, and campground are open all year.

Directions: From Mulegé, head southeast on Highway 1, cross the bridge that spans the Río Mulegé, and continue for 2.2 miles (3.5 km).

Near Km 131.5, you'll see the Hotel Serenidad entrance road on the left side of the highway. Turn left (northeast) onto the gravel access road and continue for 0.5 mile (0.8 km). The hotel and tourist complex lie past the El Gallito airstrip. From Bahía Concepción, drive northwest on Highway 1 and turn right at the sign for Hotel Serenidad, near Km 131.5.

Contact: Hotel Serenidad, Apartado Postal #9, Mulegé, Baja California Sur, C.P. 23900, Mexico, tel. 615/153-0530, fax 615/153-0311, www.serenidad.com.

27 PLAYA LOS NARANJOS

Scenic Rating: 9

on Bahía Concepción

See map page 164

Between the Carretera Transpeninsular and the western shore of Bahía Concepción, there are at least a dozen stunning *playas* that welcome overnight campers. For those headed south from Mulegé, Los Naranjos will be the first encountered. With several thatched-roof bungalows spaced along the shore, this beachside campground contains numerous primitive campsites alongside a gravel-sand beach, which it shares with the Playa Punta Arena campground to the south. The gorgeous, aquamarine waters of Bahía Concepción are literally just a stroll away, so it's a popular area for swimmers, snorkelers, anglers, boaters, kayakers, and other water lovers. Sometimes, though, it's nice to simply sit outside your RV, sip a cool beverage, get to know your friendly neighbors, and absorb the remarkable scenery before you. After all, the juxtaposition of the brownish, rugged Península Concepción between the vivid blue bay and the (usually) clear blue sky is quite enthralling.

The Los Naranjos campground occupies the actual *punta*. Campers can stay in the spacious parking area along the northern part of the beach. During windy conditions (especially in the winter months), this area can be less than appealing. As an alternative, campers can stay behind the permanent structures, near the more sheltered beach to the south.

RV sites, facilities: This beachside campground offers an indeterminate number of primitive sites for RVs and tents, with enough room for lengthy RVs (up to 40 feet/12.2 meters long). Although there are no electric or water hookups, the campground contains a few amenities, including thatched-roof bungalows, a restaurant, a dump station, a water supply, a gravel-sand beach, and basic restrooms with flush toilets and hot showers (which you need to request ahead of time). Only self-contained RVs and rugged tent campers should park here, preferably in pairs or groups, as there's no electricity, drinking water, laundry, or official security on the premises. The campground's remote location and frequent guests do, however, offer some measure of security.

Children and leashed pets are welcome, but the sandy terrain is not suitable for wheelchairs. Although it's relatively easy to enter the campground and park your RV, you should bring shovels, boards, rope, and other similar tools, in case your vehicle gets stuck in a soft patch of sand. Given the remote location of Playa Los Naranjos, it's advisable to pick up groceries, purified water, gasoline, and other supplies in Mulegé or Loreto before heading down to the beach.

Reservations, fees: Reservations are not accepted; spaces are available on a first-come, first-served basis. RV and tent sites cost $7 per night. The bungalows are available for rent. Long-term camping rates may also be available, and there is a small fee for use of the showers. Credit cards are not accepted; cash (Mexican pesos or U.S. dollars) is the customary form of payment. This beachside campground is open all year.

Directions: From Mulegé, drive southeast on Highway 1 for 10.4 miles (16.7 km), toward Bahía Concepción. Between Km 119 and Km 118, you'll spy a sign for Punta Arena. Turn left (east) and head toward the gulf for 0.4 mile (0.6 km). At the fork in the road, veer to the left onto a rather bumpy route (which you should negotiate slowly) and continue for 1.7 miles (2.7 km). Playa Los Naranjos lies ahead; take care in the soft sand. From Loreto, head northwest on Highway 1 for 74.8 miles (120.4 km), toward Bahía Concepción. Roughly 0.2 mile (0.3 km) north of Km 118, turn right (east) at Punta Arena and follow the above directions.

Contact: Playa Los Naranjos, c/o Armando y Delia Naranjos, Mulegé, Baja California Sur, Mexico. Since there's no official phone number for Playa Los Naranjos, it's probably best to simply drive toward the campground and see which spots are available.

28 PLAYA PUNTA ARENA

Scenic Rating: 9

on Bahía Concepción

See map page 164

Playa Punta Arena is one of a dozen primitive campgrounds that line the western shore of Bahía Concepción. Sharing the same attractive beach as Playa Los Naranjos, this one offers far fewer amenities than its neighbor. Still, this long, sandy spot is a wonderful place to savor Baja's great outdoors, especially during the summer months, when the wind keeps this open, white-sand beach cooler than the sheltered coves farther south. In addition, you're guaranteed fewer crowds here than on other beaches along Bahía Concepción.

From here, you're only a few steps from the stunning, aquamarine waters of Bahía Concepción, a popular playground for swimmers, boaters, kayakers, snorkelers, and scuba divers. Shaped by the rugged Península Concepción, this remarkable bay is also an ideal launching pad for those hoping to head into the Sea of Cortez for an offshore fishing excursion. Unfortunately, this beachside locale has two obvious drawbacks: It attracts several long-term RVers along the water's edge, and during hurricane season (June–November), mosquitoes can be a nuisance, so don't forget your insect repellent.

RV sites, facilities: This beachside campground offers an indeterminate number of primitive sites for RVs and tents, with enough room for lengthy RVs (up to 40 feet/12.2 meters long).

RVs along Bahía Concepción

Besides the nearby beach, the only other amenities include a few *palapas* and pit toilets. Only self-contained RVs and rugged tent campers should park here, preferably in pairs or groups, as there's no electricity, drinking water, dump station, shower house, laundry room, or official security on the premises. The campground's remote location and frequent guests do, however, offer some measure of security.

Children and leashed pets are welcome, but the sandy terrain is not suitable for wheelchairs. Although it's relatively easy to enter the campground and park your RV, you should bring shovels, boards, rope, and other similar tools, in case your vehicle gets stuck in a soft patch of sand. Given the remote location of Playa Punta Arena, it's advisable to pick up groceries, purified water, gasoline, and other supplies in Mulegé or Loreto before heading down to the beach.

Reservations, fees: Reservations are not accepted; spaces are available on a first-come, first-served basis. RV and tent sites cost $7 per night. Credit cards are not accepted; cash (Mexican pesos or U.S. dollars) is the customary form of payment. This beachside campground is open all year.

Directions: From Mulegé, drive southeast on Highway 1 for 10.4 miles (16.7 km), toward Bahía Concepción. Near Km 118.3, you'll spy a sign for Punta Arena. Turn left (east) and head toward the gulf for 0.4 mile (0.6 km). At the fork in the road, veer to the right on a rather bumpy route (which you should negotiate slowly) and continue for 1.6 miles (2.6 km). Playa Punta Arena lies ahead; take care in the soft sand. From Loreto, head northwest on Highway 1 for 74.8 miles (120.4 km), toward Bahía Concepción. Roughly 0.2 mile (0.3 km) north of Km 118, turn right (east) at Punta Arena and follow the above directions.

Contact: Since there's no official contact person, mailing address, or phone number for Playa Punta Arena, it's probably best to simply drive toward the campground and see which spots are available.

29 PLAYA SANTISPAC

Scenic Rating: 10

on Bahía Concepción

See map page 164 **BEST**

Of the many primitive campgrounds that span the western shore of Bahía Concepción, Playa Santispac has often been one of the most popular, especially among long-term occupants and particularly during the winter months. At one time, numerous motor homes, travel trailers, van campers, and tents extended from one end of the crescent-shaped beach to the other. In recent years, however, this once-crowded destination has undergone several changes. A long-time restaurant, Ray's Place, burned down a while back and was never resurrected (incidentally, Ray Lima now owns another popular eatery, part of his Hacienda de la Habana campground in Mulegé). In addition, while overnight RV camping is still allowed, travelers are no longer permitted to establish semipermanent structures next to their rigs. This fact—plus the loss of Ray's—has caused the exodus of many residents to beaches farther south.

Despite such alterations, Playa Santispac is still a favorite spot for many tourists, especially given the relatively easy access road. Now that the quarters are a bit less cramped, it's easier to appreciate the incredible views on offer. From here, the crystalline waters of Bahía Coyote (part of Bahía Concepción) spread before you, undulating around a few islands in the middle of the bay, with the Península Concepción looming in the background. It's an especially thrilling sight at sunset, when vivid shades of yellow, orange, red, and violet illuminate the skies, shimmer on the water's surface, and turn the islands into dramatic silhouettes. Shaped by barren foothills, the shallow cove is a terrific place to wade into the warm waters, embark upon a scuba-diving trip, or launch kayaks, *pangas,* and small sailboats.

Even though the beach has fewer overnight campers these days, the long-standing restaurant and bar known as Ana's (owned by Russell and Lupe) is still a popular watering hole for locals and travelers alike. Reports sometimes vary about the food's quality, but most find a reason to return—whether it's due to the joint's festive Saturday nights, the plentiful tacos and other Mexican dishes on offer, or the lovely, amusing bartender, Zulema, whom everyone seems to adore. In addition to serving food, the staff at Ana's has been known to rent kayaks, sell fishing tackle, and arrange fishing and scuba-diving excursions.

Although the rumor about a potential real-estate development has been circulating as of late, nothing has yet happened to discourage tourists. The beach at Playa Santispac is, in fact, wide open and available for outdoor enthusiasts. If you're unsure about its status, consult locals before stopping.

RV sites, facilities: This beachside campground offers an indeterminate number of primitive sites for RVs and tents, with enough room for lengthy motor homes and trailers (up to 40 feet/12.2 meters long). Most campers stay near the water. Although there are no electric or water hookups, there are some amenities, including a small restaurant, a tiny store, a dump station, flush toilets, hot and cold showers, and easy access to the beach. English-speaking employees are present. Only self-contained RVs and rugged tent campers should park here, preferably in pairs or groups, as there's no electricity, drinking water, laundry, or official security on the premises.

Children and leashed pets are welcome, but the sandy terrain is not suitable for wheelchairs. Although it's relatively easy to enter the campground and park your RV, you should bring shovels, boards, rope, and other similar tools, in case your vehicle gets stuck in a soft patch of sand. Given the remote location of Playa Santispac, it's advisable to pick up groceries, purified water, gasoline, and other supplies in Mulegé or Loreto before heading down to the beach. Sometimes, however, vendors might pass by to sell you fish, produce, water, and other such goods.

Reservations, fees: Reservations are not accepted; spaces are available on a first-come, first-served basis. RV and tent sites cost $8 per night. There is a small fee to take a hot shower. Credit cards are not accepted; cash (Mexican pesos or U.S. dollars) is the customary form of payment. This beachside campground is open all year.

Directions: From Mulegé, drive southeast on Highway 1 for 13.2 miles (21.2 km), toward Bahía Concepción. Just south of Km 114, you'll spy a sign for Playa Santispac; the beach is visible from the highway. Turn left (east), carefully negotiate the steep grade, and head down the short entrance road; someone will collect the fee at the staffed entrance station. From Loreto, head northwest on Highway 1 for 72 miles (115.9 km), toward Bahía Concepción. Near Km 113.8, turn right (east) at Playa Santispac and follow the above directions.

Contact: Since there's no official contact person, mailing address, or phone number for Playa Santispac, it's probably best to simply drive toward the campground and see which spots are available.

30 POSADA CONCEPCIÓN

Scenic Rating: 7

on Bahía Concepción

See map page 164

While Posada Concepción sits beside the same gorgeous bay as campgrounds Playa Punta Arena, Playa Santispac, and Playa El Coyote, it promises a very different experience. Unlike those wide-open beaches—which, though popular, offer enough room to enjoy the sandy shores, shallow waters, and incredible views—this campground (what some Mexicans disparagingly term a "*gringo* settlement") is far too crowded to ensure such tranquility.

Essentially a jumble of houses and permanently placed RVs, this gated community provides only a handful of sites for travelers. Even worse, none are near the water's edge, so you're guaranteed no clear vista of Bahía Concepción. Needless to say, you might want to try one of the many other campgrounds along the western shore of the bay before settling for this one. If the sun's already set by the time you reach this campground, however, it would be better to stop for the night than to risk driving on narrow Highway 1 in the dark. Before heading out the next morning, you might even want to stroll along the well-sheltered beach or wade in the warm water; at low tide, you'll encounter a few hot springs along the shallow shore.

RV sites, facilities: While this gated beachside community contains mostly permanent RVs, there are six full-hookup sites, with 15-amp electricity, water service, sewer access, and enough space for lengthy RVs (up to 40 feet/12.2 meters long). Other amenities include a tennis court, easy access to the beach, and restrooms with flush toilets and hot showers. There is, however, no dump station, laundry, or official security on the premises, and the water is not safe for consumption. Children and leashed pets are welcome, but the sandy terrain is not suitable for wheelchairs. Tent camping is not allowed. Given the remote location of Posada Concepción, it's advisable to pick up groceries, purified water, gasoline, and other supplies in Mulegé or Loreto before heading down to the beach.

Reservations, fees: Reservations are not accepted; spaces are available on a first-come, first-served basis. RV sites cost $10 per night. Long-term rates are also available. Credit cards are not accepted; cash (Mexican pesos or U.S. dollars) is the customary form of payment. This beachside campground is open all year.

Directions: From Mulegé, drive southeast on Highway 1 for 14.5 miles (23.3 km), toward Bahía Concepción. Just 0.2 mile (0.3 km) south of Km 112, you'll spy a sign for Posada Concepción. Turn left (east) and head toward the campground. From Loreto, head northwest on Highway 1 for 70.7 miles (113.8 km), toward Bahía Concepción. Near Km 111.7, turn right at Posada Concepción and head east toward the campground.

Contact: Posada Concepción, Apartado Postal #14, Mulegé, Baja California Sur, Mexico. Since there's no official phone number for Posada Concepción, it's probably best to simply drive toward the campground and see which spots are available.

31 PLAYA ESCONDIDA

Scenic Rating: 10

on Bahía Concepción

See map page 164

As with Playa Santispac, to the north, this secluded, picturesque beach (whose name means "Hidden Beach" in Spanish) arcs around a shallow, crystalline cove, somewhat sheltered from the wind. A variety of motor homes, travel trailers, pickup campers, and tents curve along the shore. Although on-site EcoMundo (an ecofriendly kayaking outfitter and resort) has been out of business for a while (following management issues, a small hurricane, months of neglect and theft, an auction, and a questionable fire), Playa Escondida is still a wonderful place to pursue a myriad of outdoor pursuits.

Hikers and mountain bikers can explore the brush-covered hills beyond the campground. Beachcombers, bird-watchers, and those in search of clams can stroll along the coast. Of course, swimmers, kayakers, canoeists, boaters, anglers, snorkelers, and scuba divers will probably find the most to do in this part of Baja—Bahía Concepción is a water-lover's playground, and the nearby islands are divine destinations. The only disadvantages to this campground are its popularity, which can make it crowded (though quiet) at times, and the access road, which can be challenging for lengthy motor homes, unwieldy trailers, and any vehicles with low clearance.

RV sites, facilities: This beachside campground offers an indeterminate number of primitive sites for tents and small RVs (up to 30 feet/9.1 meters long). Besides easy access to the beach, the only other amenities include shady *palapas* near the water, cold showers, outhouses with pit toilets, and trash barrels. Only self-contained RVs and rugged tent campers should park here, preferably in pairs or groups, as there's no electricity, drinking water, dump station, or laundry room on the premises. Resident managers and frequent neighbors provide only a limited amount of security. Children, leashed pets, and tent campers are welcome, but the sandy terrain is not suitable for wheelchairs. Given the remote location of Playa Escondida, it's advisable to pick up groceries, purified water, gasoline, and other supplies in Mulegé or Loreto before heading down to the beach.

Reservations, fees: Reservations are not accepted; spaces are available on a first-come, first-served basis. RV and tent sites cost $7 per night. Credit cards are not accepted; cash (Mexican pesos or U.S. dollars) is the customary form of payment. This beachside campground is open all year.

Directions: From Mulegé, head southeast on Highway 1 for 14.7 miles (23.7 km), toward Bahía Concepción. Near Km 111.3, just south of the sign for Posada Concepción, turn left (east) and drive down the rugged access road for 0.5 mile (0.8 km), past the now-defunct EcoMundo buildings, over a hill, and toward the bay. At the fork in the road, veer to the right, toward Playa Escondida. From Loreto, head northwest on Highway 1 for 70.5 miles (113.4 km), toward Bahía Concepción. Roughly 0.2 mile (0.3 km) north of Km 111, turn right onto the access road and follow the above directions.

Contact: Since there's no official contact person, mailing address, or phone number for Playa Escondida, it's probably best to simply drive toward the campground and see which spots are available.

32 PLAYA LOS COCOS

Scenic Rating: 10

on Bahía Concepción

See map page 164

Although Playa Los Cocos is a fairly easy campground for small RVs to enter, it's rather difficult to find, despite the fact that it can be seen from the Transpeninsular Highway. Unlike most of the other places that line the inland shore of Bahía Concepción, this one is not signed at all. For many frequent visitors to this lovely stretch of sand, that's part of its charm. After all, fewer and fewer places are staying a secret on the Baja peninsula, and those that mainstream tourists find challenging to reach (whether because of poor signage or uncomfortable roads) remain treasured hideaways for those in the know.

Playa Los Cocos is an especially fine treat, with its bright white sand, azure-hued crystalline waters, swaying palm trees, thriving nearby mangroves, and stunning view of distant islands in the expansive bay. Swimmers, snorkelers, and kayakers delight in the calm current along this stretch, and anglers can easily launch small boats across the beach and anchor them in the bountiful waters just offshore. Perhaps the only drawback is that, as with many of the sheltered beaches along the western shore of Bahía Concepción, the summers can be extremely hot.

RV sites, facilities: This beachside campground offers an indeterminate number of primitive sites for tents and small RVs (up to 30 feet/9.1 meters long). Besides easy access to the beach, the only other amenities include shady *palapas,* pit toilets, and a dump station. Only self-contained RVs and rugged tent campers should park here, preferably in pairs or groups, as there's no electricity, drinking water, shower house, laundry room, or official security on the premises. Children, leashed pets, and tent campers are welcome, but the sandy terrain is not suitable for wheelchairs. Given the remote location of Playa Los Cocos, it's advisable to pick up groceries, purified water, gasoline, and other supplies in Mulegé or Loreto before heading down to the beach.

Reservations, fees: Reservations are not accepted; spaces are available on a first-come, first-served basis. RV and tent sites cost $7 per night. Long-term rates might also be possible. Credit cards are not accepted; cash (Mexican pesos or U.S. dollars) is the customary form of payment. This beachside campground is open all year.

Directions: From Mulegé, head southeast on Highway 1 for 15.2 miles (24.5 km), toward Bahía Concepción. Near Km 110.5, turn left (east) and drive toward the gulf for 0.3 miles (0.5 km). Playa Los Cocos, which can be difficult to find and challenging to access (due to the poorly maintained entrance road), lies just south of Playa Escondida; consult local residents to make sure of the route. From Loreto, head northwest on Highway 1 for 70 miles (112.6 km), toward Bahía Concepción. Near Km 110.5, turn right onto the access road and follow the above directions.

Contact: Since there's no official contact person, mailing address, or phone number for Playa Los Cocos, it's probably best to simply drive toward the campground and see which spots are available.

33 PLAYA ENSENADA EL BURRO

Scenic Rating: 9

on Bahía Concepción

See map page 164

As with Playa Santispac and Playa Escondida to the north, Playa Ensenada el Burro boasts a sandy beach that curves around a shallow, somewhat sheltered cove (known as Bahía Burro)—ideal for kayakers, especially beginners, and popular among snorkelers. Boaters will be happy to know that it's possible to launch small vessels across the beach. Another terrific aspect of this particular Bahía Concepción–area campground is the friendly people that flock here. The frequent visitors are especially helpful in pointing first-timers in the right direction—whether searching for the perfect margarita along the shore or seeking one of the better fishing spots in the bay itself. Given that the neighbors are watchful and that Bertha, the friendly long-time owner of the clean, inexpensive restaurant at the north end of the cove, is often in residence, the security isn't bad here either. The only obvious drawback, perhaps, is that much of the campground (especially prime spots near the water) is often filled with semipermanent RV tenants, who block access to the nicest stretches of coastline, and RV caravans sometimes opt for most of the remaining spots.

RV sites, facilities: This beachside campground offers an indeterminate number of primitive sites, with enough room for lengthy RVs (up to 40 feet/12.2 meters long). Besides easy access to the beach, the only other amenities include pit toilets, a small restaurant (which sells ice in addition to seafood and Mexican cuisine), some shady *palapas,* a dump station, and limited security. A small store is on the inland side of the highway. The camp office also provides kayak and canoe rentals for exploring the bay and its offshore islands. Only self-contained RVs and rugged tent campers should park here, preferably in pairs or groups, as there's no electricity, drinking water, shower house, or laundry on the premises. Children, leashed pets, and tent campers are welcome, but the sandy terrain is not suitable for wheelchairs. Given the remote location of Playa Ensenada el Burro, it's advisable to pick up groceries, purified water, gasoline, and other supplies in Mulegé or Loreto before heading down to the beach.

Reservations, fees: Reservations are not accepted; spaces are available on a first-come, first-served basis. RV and tent sites cost $8 per night; long-term rates might also be possible. Kayak and canoe rentals are available for $20–25 per day. Credit cards are not accepted; cash (Mexican pesos or U.S. dollars) is the customary form of payment. The beachside campground is open all year.

Directions: From Mulegé, head southeast on Highway 1 for 16.4 miles (26.4 km), toward Bahía Concepción. Halfway between Km 109 and Km 108, turn left (east), veer right at the fork in the road, and drive toward the gulf. Playa Ensenada el Burro, which can be seen from the highway, lies straight ahead. From

Loreto, head northwest on Highway 1 for 68.8 miles (110.7 km), toward Bahía Concepción. Near Km 108.6, turn right onto the access road and head toward the campground.

Contact: Since there's no official contact person, mailing address, or phone number for Playa Ensenada el Burro, it's probably best to simply drive toward the campground and see which spots are available.

34 PLAYA EL COYOTE

Scenic Rating: 10

on Bahía Concepción

See map page 164

In recent years, some of Bahía Concepción's more permanent residents have relocated from Playa Santispac to this particular beach, roughly 4 miles (6.4 km) to the south. With its many trees, sandy shore, and sheltered cove, Playa El Coyote is definitely one of the bay's most alluring and most photographed stretches—and, luckily, it's not as crowded as some of the other choices along Bahía Concepción. The view alone is amazing: a landscape of turquoise waters, rocky islands, and the distant peninsula. The campsites, situated along the shore, are open and spacious, and the on-site, recently remodeled restaurant (known as Estrella del Mar and presently under new management) lures frequent revelers, for dinner, cocktails, live music, pool games, and rounds of darts.

As with most of the beachside campgrounds along the western shore of Bahía Concepción, Playa El Coyote offers a shallow, gentle shore—ideal for launching kayaks and small fishing boats. The shielded cove (which is really a small bay in its own right, known as Bahía Coyote) is also a perfect place for swimming, beachcombing, and snorkeling. Exploring the nearby islands (including Isla Coyote and Isla Guapa) is a favored pastime for bird-watchers, scuba divers, kayakers, and anglers alike. In addition, the rocky outcropping that protects this coastal locale invites hikers to climb upward and survey this remarkable bay from a unique vantage point. Along the rocks, you'll even find a natural thermal spring.

One obvious disadvantage to this campground is its proximity to the highway, which can cause it to be a little noisy, especially at night, when the beach might otherwise be quiet. In addition, the long, narrow entrance road has many soft, sandy spots, suffers from erosion in other places, and provides no room for passing vehicles. So, it's advisable for those with lengthy RVs to survey the area via foot or tow vehicle before attempting the route. Also, tools such as shovels, boards, and rope might be helpful in case your wheels get stuck in the sand.

RV sites, facilities: This beachside campground offers an indeterminate number of primitive sites, ideal for smaller RVs (under 30 feet/9.1 meters long), though longer RVs can fit (as long as they can negotiate the challenging entrance road). Amenities include a small restaurant, shady *palapas,* a dump station, trash cans, cold showers, limited security, an outhouse with pit toilets, and easy access to the beach. Only self-contained RVs and rugged tent campers should park here, preferably in pairs or groups, as there's no electricity, drinking water, or laundry on the premises. Children, leashed pets, and tent campers are welcome, but the sandy terrain is not suitable for wheelchairs. Given the remote location of Playa El Coyote, it's advisable to pick up groceries, purified water, gasoline, and other supplies in Mulegé or Loreto before heading down to the beach.

Reservations, fees: Reservations are not accepted; spaces are available on a first-come, first-served basis. RV and tent sites cost $7 per night. Credit cards are not accepted; cash (Mexican pesos or U.S. dollars) is the customary form of payment. This beachside campground is open all year.

Directions: From Mulegé, head southeast on Highway 1 for 17.2 miles (27.7 km), toward Bahía Concepción. At Km 107.3, turn left (east) at the sign for Playa El Coyote, drive through the open gate, and continue for 0.3 mile (0.5 km) on a sandy road, toward the bay. Turn right and continue for 0.5 mile (0.8 km) along the shore below the cliff. Playa El Coyote lies ahead, beside the bay. From Loreto, head northwest on Highway 1 for 68 miles (109.4 km), toward Bahía Concepción. Near Km 107.3, turn right onto the access road and head toward the campground.

Contact: Since there's no official contact person, mailing address, or phone number for Playa El Coyote, it's probably best to simply drive toward the campground and see which spots are available.

35 BUENAVENTURA RESORT

Scenic Rating: 8

on Bahía Concepción

See map page 164

Nestled between brush-covered slopes and clear, aquamarine waters, Playa Buenaventura presents one of the only resort-style complexes along the western shore of Bahía Concepción. It's also the first official RV-friendly place that you'll spy after leaving Playa El Coyote and heading south on the Transpeninsular Highway (Highway 1), which curves inland for roughly 8.2 miles (13.2 km), before returning to the coast at Playa Buenaventura. Landscaped with cacti and other desert-style plants, the property offers—in addition to a primitive campground—a sports bar and restaurant, several houses and 10 kayaks for rent, and a hotel. RV caravans especially favor this spacious campground; in fact, it's difficult for individual travelers to find a spot here from January to March.

Owned and operated by Mark, an American expatriate, and his Mexican wife, Olivia, the complex has undergone a few changes over the years. Until recently, in fact, the couple had allowed some folks from Tijuana to operate the attractive hotel as a separate entity. Unfortunately, however, the hotel began to decline in condition and popularity, until the new managers were evicted from the property. Happily, the entire resort is back in the hands of its proper owners, who relish welcoming visitors to their festive sports bar and burger joint. Mark is even willing to take guests out on his fishing boat—a terrific way to explore the bountiful waters of Bahía Concepción and the Sea of Cortez. Besides deep-sea fishing, the Buenaventura Resort is also a wonderful place for hiking, mountain biking, swimming, kayaking, bird-watching, and snorkeling. Some visitors even try their hand at surf fishing, though the deeper waters offer a better chance at snagging yellowtail, dorado, or other impressive game fish.

Critics of the Buenaventura Resort usually find this spot more congested than they'd like. While its festive ambience can be appealing for some, others might prefer a more tranquil setting. If so, there are several other *playas* (beaches) along the western shore of Bahía Concepción that will grant you less in the way of amenities and more in the way of solitude. Just pick the campground that best suits your mood and interests.

RV sites, facilities: This beachside campground offers roughly 55 primitive sites, all of which are easy to access and have enough space for lengthy RVs (up to 40 feet/12.2 meters long). Although there are no RV hookups, the resort offers a variety of amenities, including a small hotel (with comfortable rooms and shaded patios), several rental houses, a popular restaurant and bar, a dump station, shady *palapas,* kayak and boat rentals, a concrete boat launch ramp, and restrooms with flush toilets and hot showers. Facilities such as the restaurant and hotel utilize generator-produced electricity and water that must be imported into the resort area. The resident owners (Mark and Olivia) are bilingual and offer some measure of security (along with an entrance gate).

Only self-contained RVs and rugged tent campers should park here, as there's no electricity, drinking water, or laundry on the premises. Children, leashed pets, and tent campers are welcome, but the facilities are not wheelchair-accessible. Given the remote nature of Playa Buenaventura, it's advisable to pick up groceries, purified water, gasoline, and other supplies in Mulegé or Loreto before heading down to the beach.

Reservations, fees: Reservations are accepted (via the cell phone listed below). The nightly fee for overnight camping is $15 per RV or $10 per tent; extra guests (beyond two) will be charged $5 each. Hotel rooms are available for $50–100 per night. Furnished houses on the beach cost $85–150 per night. The resort also offers kayak rentals. Showers are available for a small fee. Credit cards are not accepted; cash (Mexican pesos or U.S. dollars) is the customary form of payment. The resort is open all year.

Directions: From Mulegé, head southeast on Highway 1 for 25.5 miles (41 km), toward Bahía Concepción. Near Km 94, you'll see the entrance for the Buenaventura Resort on the left side of the highway, surrounded by flowering shrubs and trees. Turn left (east) and drive toward the bay. From Loreto, head northwest on Highway 1 for 59.7 miles (96.1 km), toward Bahía Concepción. Near Km 94, turn right onto the access road and head toward the campground.

Contact: For more information about the Buenaventura Resort, call 615/161-1077 (to complete the call, dial "1" between the country and area codes).

36 PLAYA EL REQUESÓN

Scenic Rating: 10

on Bahía Concepción

See map page 164 BEST

While the entire western shore of Bahía Concepción is known for fantastic beaches—with incredible views of the bay, several offshore islands, and the distant peninsula that shapes this breathtaking landscape—most RV travelers agree that Playa El Requesón, a long-time favorite, offers one of the finest, most secluded beaches in this region. Nestled amid grassy slopes, various cacti, and the crystal-clear, aquamarine waters of Bahía Concepción, this sandy, relatively quiet beach curves around a shallow, expansive cove, which is partially formed by a brush-covered, twin-humped island called Isla El Requesón.

Interestingly, a sandy point juts out into the water, bisecting the beach and cove, creating a narrow isthmus at low tide, and consequently joining the campground to the offshore island. Overnight RVers typically park near the point or along the shore that lies on either side of the dividing isthmus. Of course, more daring campers have opted to park on the sandy isthmus itself, where they're surrounded by water and where they risk flooding at high tide. Although you're never alone in this alluring place, it's rarely too crowded to enjoy, and the constant presence of neighbors can ensure a limited measure of security.

The rugged terrain that surrounds this beautiful beach frequently lures hikers and wildlife enthusiasts, while the warm, crystalline waters attract swimmers, snorkelers, and scuba divers. In addition, the shallow shore is an ideal place to launch kayaks and small fishing boats. Digging for clams and scallops is also a popular activity here. Just remember to check Mexico's current fishing regulations before getting started.

RV sites, facilities: This primitive campground offers room for perhaps 30 RVs and tents. Although there are no electric, water, or sewage hookups, there is enough room for lengthy motor homes and travel trailers (up to 40 feet/12.2 meters long) to maneuver and park. Besides easy access to the beach, the only other amenity is an outhouse with pit toilets. Only self-contained RVs and rugged tent campers should park here, preferably in pairs or groups, as there's no electricity, drinking water, dump station, shower house, laundry room, or official security on the premises. Children and leashed pets are welcome, but the sandy terrain is not suitable for wheelchairs. Given the remote location of Playa El Requesón, it's advisable to pick up groceries, purified water, gasoline, and other supplies in Mulegé or Loreto before heading down to the beach.

Reservations, fees: Reservations are not accepted; spaces are available on a first-come, first-served basis. RV and tent sites cost $10 per night. Every evening, someone will stop by to collect the fee. Credit cards are not accepted; cash (Mexican pesos or U.S. dollars) is the customary form of payment. This beachside campground is open all year.

Directions: From Mulegé, head southeast on Highway 1 for 26.7 miles (43 km), toward Bahía Concepción. Just north of Km 92, you'll see a sign for Playa El Requesón. Turn left (east) onto the narrow entrance road and drive 0.3 mile (0.5 km) toward the bay. Take care, as this sandy road often has a lot of potholes, sometimes filled with oyster shells; also, the bushes that line this route have scratched some RVs in the past, so use caution.

From Loreto, head northwest on Highway 1 for 58.5 miles (94.1 km), toward Bahía Concepción. Just north of Km 92, turn right onto the well-signed access road and head toward the campground; if you have trouble turning onto the access road from this direction, continue past the entrance, make a U-turn near Playa Buenaventura, and take the turn from the north.

Contact: Since there's no official contact person, mailing address, or phone number for Playa El Requesón, it's probably best to simply drive toward the campground and see which spots are available.

37 PLAYA LA PERLA

Scenic Rating: 9

on Bahía Concepción

See map page 164

Yet another in a string of primitive, RV-friendly campgrounds along the western shore of Bahía Concepción, Playa La Perla isn't one of the most popular options for overnight travelers. Still, like its neighboring locales, it offers proximity to a sandy beach, a sheltered cove, the rugged foothills of the Sierra de la Giganta, and, of course, the bay itself. While hikers, swimmers, snorkelers, divers, boaters, anglers, and wildlife enthusiasts will find plenty of reasons to stay here, kayakers might find this particular choice most ideal. After all, the protected cove is a wonderful place to practice (especially for beginners) before attempting breezier spots in the vast Bahía Concepción and the Sea of Cortez beyond.

RV sites, facilities: This primitive campground offers plenty of room for an indeterminate number of tents and small RVs (under 30 feet/9.1 meters long); camping is also possible north and south of the cove. Although there are no electric, water, or sewage hookups, Playa La Perla presents a few amenities, including easy access to the beach, some shady *palapas,* cold showers, and an outhouse with pit toilets. Only self-contained RVs and rugged tent campers should park here, preferably in pairs or groups, as there's no electricity, drinking water, dump station, laundry, or official security on the premises. Children and leashed pets are welcome, but the sandy terrain is not suitable for wheelchairs. Given the remote location of Playa La Perla, it's advisable to pick up groceries, purified water, gasoline, and other supplies in Mulegé or Loreto before heading down to the beach.

Reservations, fees: Reservations are not accepted; spaces are available on a first-come, first-served basis. RV and tent sites cost $7 per night. Credit cards are not accepted; cash (Mexican pesos or U.S. dollars) is the customary form of payment. This beachside campground is open all year.

Directions: From Mulegé, head southeast on Highway 1 for 27.4 miles (44.1 km), toward Bahía Concepción. Just south of Km 91, you'll see a sign for Playa La Perla. Turn left (east) onto the entrance road and drive 0.4 mile (0.6

km) toward the bay. Take care, as this sandy road is often quite rough to traverse, especially for more unwieldy rigs, and the bushes can scratch your rig on either side.

From Loreto, head northwest on Highway 1 for 57.8 miles (93 km), toward Bahía Concepción. Near Km 90.9, turn right onto the well-signed access road and head toward the campground. Note: Playa La Perla can also be accessed via Playa El Requesón, where a sandy road heads south from the beach and along the shore toward Playa La Perla (not an advisable route for large RVs without first surveying on foot).

Contact: Since there's no official contact person, mailing address, or phone number for Playa La Perla, it's probably best to simply drive toward the campground and see which spots are available.

38 PLAYA ARMENTA

Scenic Rating: 9

on Bahía Concepción

See map page 164

If you're headed south from Mulegé, then Playa Armenta will be the last campground (and one of the least crowded) that you'll reach along the western shore of Bahía Concepción, at least via the Carretera Transpeninsular. From Loreto, of course, it will be the first you'll encounter. As with most of the other *campos* and *playas* along this incredible bay, Playa Armenta offers access to rugged foothills; a sandy beach; a sheltered, crystalline cove; and the enormous Bahía Concepción.

Despite limited facilities, some travelers often find their way here—whether for solitude or for adventure. Hikers, swimmers, anglers, kayakers, wildlife-watchers, and other outdoor enthusiasts will appreciate this beautiful spot, which presents breathtaking views of the bay as well as the peninsula that has formed it. The only obvious drawbacks are that the beach is shorter and more exposed to the highway than most in this region; there is no sign for Playa Armenta; and the entrance road might be too tight for lengthy RVs. Just to be safe, you should probably not attempt this particular campground if you're driving anything longer than 30 feet (9.1 meters).

From Playa Armenta, you can explore the rough-hewn Península Concepción, a remote land of fish camps, lofty *cerros,* and isolated *puntas* along the Sea of Cortez. Be advised, however, that this rugged route should not be undertaken without a reliable, high-clearance, four-wheel-drive vehicle. If you're up for the challenge, simply head southeast on Highway 1, take the 5.7-mile (9.2-km) dirt road that skirts the southern shore of Bahía Concepción, and turn left onto the uneven 26.6-mile (42.8-km) dirt route that winds along the eastern shore of the bay, ending close to Punta Concepción at the northernmost tip of the peninsula.

Free beachside camping is possible all along this undeveloped coast; given the lack of amenities and official security, though, you should definitely travel with others and camp together. Despite the challenges of traversing this unique peninsula (including the tides), it can certainly be worth the trouble. If nothing else, it's an odd experience to face the western shore of Bahía Concepción and gaze at all the primitive campgrounds that line the other side.

RV sites, facilities: This primitive campground offers plenty of room for an indeterminate number of tents and RVs, preferably those under 30 feet/9.1 meters long. Although there are no electric, water, or sewage hookups, Playa Armenta presents a few amenities, including easy access to the beach, a few shady *palapas,* and some outhouses with pit toilets. Only self-contained RVs and rugged tent campers should park here, preferably in pairs or groups, as there's no electricity, drinking water, dump station, shower house, laundry, or official security on the premises. Children and leashed pets are welcome, but the sandy terrain is not suitable for wheelchairs. Given the remote location of Playa Armenta, it's advisable to pick up groceries, purified water, gasoline, and other supplies in Mulegé or Loreto before heading down to the beach.

Reservations, fees: Reservations are not accepted; spaces are available on a first-come, first-served basis. RV and tent sites cost $7 per night. Credit cards are not accepted; cash (Mexican pesos or U.S. dollars) is the customary form of payment. This beachside campground is open all year.

Directions: From Mulegé, head southeast on Highway 1 for 27.7 miles (44.6 km), toward Bahía Concepción. Between Km 91 and Km 90, you'll see an unmarked entrance road. Turn left (east) and drive 0.5 mile (0.8 km) toward the bay. Take care, as the entrance road can be tight for lengthy RVs. From Loreto, head northwest on Highway 1 for 57.5 miles (92.5 km), toward Bahía Concepción. Near Km 90.4, turn right onto the access road and head toward Playa Armenta.

Contact: Since there's no official contact person, mailing address, or phone number for Playa Armenta, it's probably best to simply drive toward the campground and see which spots are available.

LORETO, LA PAZ, AND SOUTHERN BAJA

BEST RV PARKS AND CAMPGROUNDS

Roughly 47 miles (76 km) south of Bahía Concepción, across the valley *ranchos* and steep *montañas* of the Sierra de la Giganta, lies the coastal community of Loreto, Baja's oldest continuously occupied town – despite a near-abandonment following a 19th-century hurricane. Founded in 1697 by Jesuit missionaries and named the first capital of the Californias, Loreto houses a museum devoted to Baja's history, including the Spanish missions. Aptly, the museum sits beside the Misión de Nuestra Señora de Loreto Conchó, and in the nearby mountains lies the restored Misión de San Francisco Javier, established in 1699.

With several restaurants, bars, shops, and campgrounds – even its own airport – Loreto is a burgeoning, hospitable village. Curious shoppers will especially enjoy the quaint downtown streets, where boutiques offer handmade *artes y oficios* (arts and crafts) from the Baja peninsula and Mexican mainland, including silver jewelry, fine textiles, and carved furniture.

Given its warm temperatures and proximity to the tranquil Sea of Cortez, it's no surprise that recreationists, from beachcombers to equestrians, flock here year-round. The view alone is stunning, especially at sunrise and sunset.

Separated from the arid desert by picturesque peaks, Loreto serves as the gateway to a chain of offshore islands. Part of the 513,000-acre (207,610-hectare) Parque Marino Nacional Bahía de Loreto, a World Heritage Site since 2005, the five closest islands entice snorkelers, kayakers, and sailors. Isla del Carmen is especially gorgeous, boasting secluded beaches, playful dolphins, and endangered sea turtles. Anglers, too, will delight in the bounty of marlin, dorado, and yellowtail. *Pangas* and fishing cruisers are available for charter, and local outfitters offer varied adventures, from scuba diving to whale-watching.

In the nearby canyons, hikers encounter palm tree oases, exotic birds and reptiles, and iridescent pools. Just a few miles south of town, in Nopoló, lies a family-friendly, government-built resort and sports complex, where visitors can enjoy sandy beaches, a tennis center, and a par-72 *campo de golf*.

Farther south along the coast, campers, yachters, and anglers head to the seaside town of Puerto Escondido, while others relish the nature hikes, massages, and island tours offered by two eco-retreat centers in

Ensenada Blanca. From here, Highway 1 turns inland toward the Valle de Santo Domingo and the irrigated farming region of Ciudad Constitución, colonized in 1940 and now the fourth largest city in Baja Sur, with supermarkets, RV parks, and crops of wheat, cotton, and produce.

Despite several pleasant detours – such as windsurfing in Puerto Agua Verde, visiting remote villages like San José Comondú, and watching *las ballenas gris* (the gray whales) in Bahía Magdalena – most travelers this far south have another destination in mind: La Paz, the capital of Baja Sur and home to one of the peninsula's most colorful Carnaval celebrations. Surprisingly less crowded than you might imagine, the La Paz area features numerous restaurants, sportfishing spots, tour operators, campgrounds, and white-sand beaches – from Playa El Coromuel to Playa El Tecolote.

Once known as Villa de la Santa Cruz, the area was first encountered by explorer Hernán Cortés in 1535, though it was Sebastián Vizcaíno who renamed it six decades later. Permanently settled by Europeans in 1811, the city now houses an anthropology museum, an international airport, a historic cathedral, libraries, art galleries, and an aquarium. From the port near Playa Pichilingue, ferries to the mainland are even offered.

Sun-seekers come here to fish for tuna, dive amid hammerhead sharks, swim with sea lions near Los Islotes, and explore Isla Espíritu Santo via kayak. But the sea isn't the only attraction. Whether on foot, bike, or all-terrain vehicle, you can venture into the rugged Sierra de la Laguna to tour prehistoric paintings or marvel at the endemic flora and fauna – from elephant trees to giant roadrunners. Visitors can also shop for handmade pottery, sample authentic Mexican cuisine, or stroll along the *malecón*, relishing fiery sunsets on the aquamarine bay.

Besides several RV parks and primitive campgrounds between Loreto and La Paz, you'll find no-frills boondocking sites alongside some restaurants, in hard-to-reach places like San Evaristo, on La Paz-area beaches such as Playa Coyote, and in towns like Puerto López Mateos and Puerto San Carlos – terrific spots to see migrating whales in winter. For safety reasons, solo camping isn't recommended in any of these primitive spots. But, if you enjoy "roughing it" in a more secure location, consider San Juanico, an isolated fishing village along the Pacific coast with its own beachside campground. Despite few amenities, it's fun to park atop the bluff and watch the surfers in Scorpion Bay – or test the waves, if you dare!

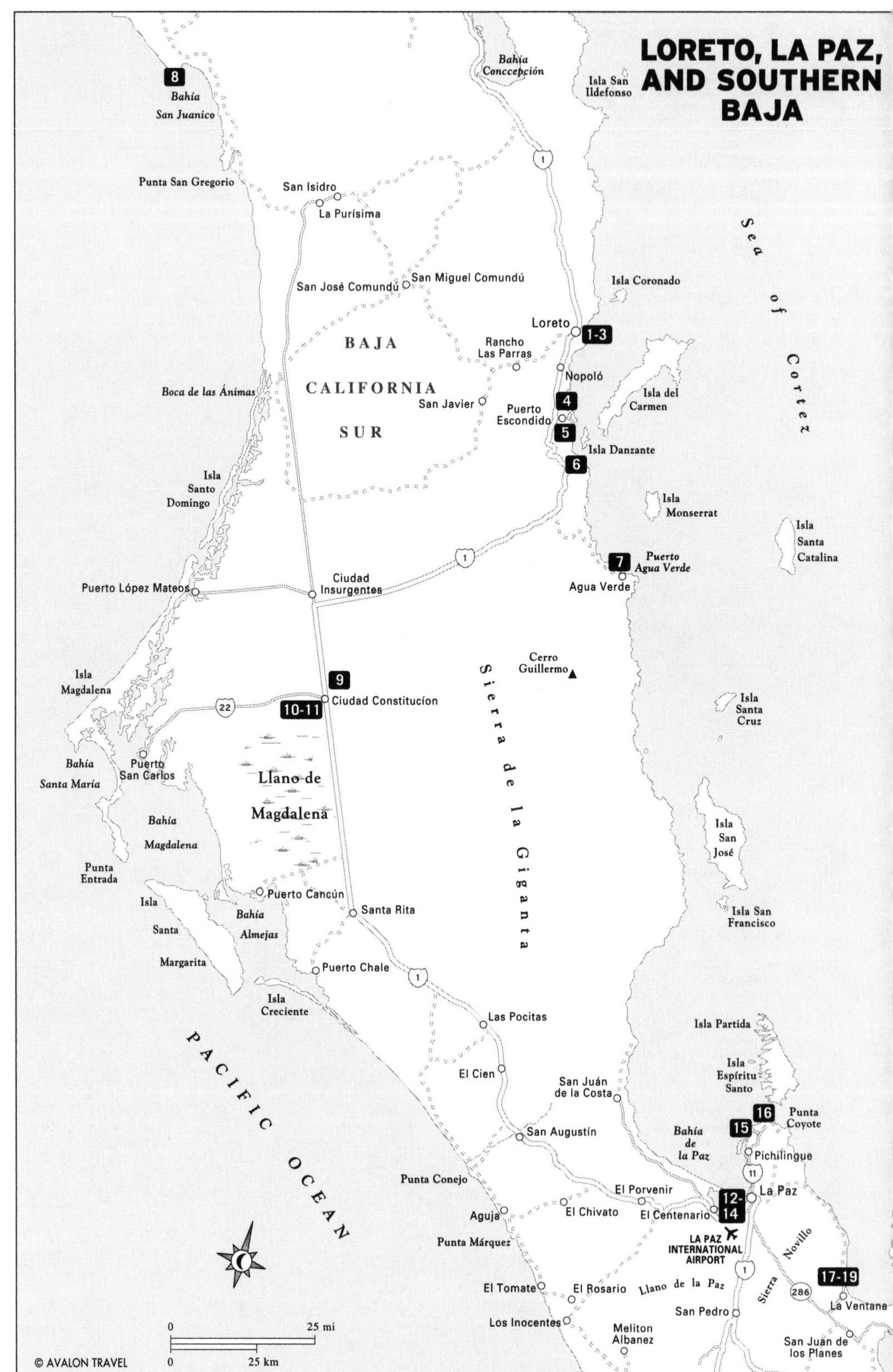
LORETO, LA PAZ, AND SOUTHERN BAJA
Bahía San Juanico
Bahía Conccepción
Isla San Ildefonso
Punta San Gregorio
San Isidro
La Purísima
Sea of Cortez
San José Comundú
San Miguel Comundú
Isla Coronado
Loreto
Rancho Las Parras
BAJA CALIFORNIA SUR
Nopoló
Boca de las Ánimas
San Javier
Puerto Escondido
Isla del Carmen
Isla Danzante
Isla Santo Domingo
Isla Monserrat
Isla Santa Catalina
Puerto Agua Verde
Agua Verde
Puerto López Mateos
Ciudad Insurgentes
Cerro Guillermo
Sierra de la Giganta
Isla Magdalena
Ciudad Constitucíon
Isla Santa Cruz
Bahía Santa María
Puerto San Carlos
Llano de Magdalena
Bahía Magdalena
Isla San José
Punta Entrada
Puerto Cancún
Santa Rita
Isla Santa Margarita
Bahía Almejas
Isla San Francisco
Puerto Chale
Isla Creciente
Las Pocitas
Isla Partida
PACIFIC OCEAN
El Cien
Isla Espíritu Santo
San Juán de la Costa
Punta Coyote
San Augustín
Bahía de la Paz
Pichilingue
Punta Conejo
El Porvenir
La Paz
El Chivato
El Centenario
Aguja
LA PAZ INTERNATIONAL AIRPORT
Punta Márquez
Sierra Novillo
El Tomate
El Rosario
Llano de la Paz
La Ventana
San Pedro
Los Inocentes
Meliton Albanez
San Juan de los Planes
0 25 mi
0 25 km
© AVALON TRAVEL

1 RIVERA DEL MAR RV PARK

Scenic Rating: 5

in Loreto

See map page 208 BEST

Situated in a relatively quiet residential area, beside the Café Sagitario Restaurant and Bar (a local favorite for casual courtyard dining), this modest campground has welcomed RVers for several years. Palm trees and flowering foliage pepper the small park, providing lots of shade. Since the fenced-in campground sits behind the home of its affable, accommodating owners, it is well supervised 24 hours a day, and its convenient location puts you within walking distance of the town center, beach, and marina.

A swim in the Sea of Cortez, a world-class catch on a sportfishing fleet, and a kayaking excursion amid pristine waters are literally just a hop, a skip, and a jump away. With towering mountains not far, it's also possible to spend the day hiking, biking, or horseback riding amid ancient cave paintings, hidden canyons, spring-fed oases, and diverse desert flora and fauna, ranging from ancient fig trees to black-collared lizards. Several tour operators are available for land or sea excursions. Arturo's Sport Fishing, for instance, offers guided fishing, scuba-diving, snorkeling, kayaking, and whale-watching tours, plus trips to the Misión de San Francisco Javier that lies within the Sierra de la Giganta to the west.

The only drawback to the park is the cramped quarters; the sites are narrow, there's little space for wide slide-outs, and RVs longer than 35 feet (10.7 meters) are usually out of luck. At times, however, the owners have permitted big rigs to park across multiple sites, allowing room for awnings and tow cars.

RV sites, facilities: All 25 of the back-in sites have full hookups (with 15-amp outlets, potable water, and sewage), but the lengths vary greatly. Small RVs (under 30 feet/9.1 meters long) will probably be most comfortable here. The park also contains a shady tent-camping area, a barbecue area, a coin laundry, a playground, and brand-new, thatched-roof restrooms, each with its own hot shower, toilet, and sink. There is, however, no dump station on the premises. Children and pets are welcome here, and the managers speak English. Restaurants, stores, and adventure outfitters are all within walking distance.

Reservations, fees: Space is limited, so reservations are recommended, especially in the milder months. Tent camping costs $7 per night year-round. From November to April, the daily RV

Loreto's history museum beside the Misión de Nuestra Señora de Loreto Conchó

rate is $14 for self-contained sites and $16 for full-hookup sites. From May to October, the daily prices are increased to $17 for self-contained sites and $19 for full hookups. Wireless Internet access is available for a nominal fee. Credit cards are not accepted; cash (Mexican pesos or U.S. dollars) is the customary form of payment. The park is open all year.

Directions: From north of Loreto, just before the Km 119 marker on Highway 1, turn left onto Paseo Pedro de Ugarte, pass the *glorieta,* and veer left onto Calle Salvatierra. Head toward the ocean and veer right onto Avenida Miguel Hidalgo. Turn left onto Calle de la Playa (also called Boulevard Adolfo López Mateos) and drive to the end of the waterfront street. Take the last left, turn right onto Calle Davis, take a left onto Calle La Pinta, and turn right again onto Calle Francisco I. Madero. The park is immediately on the left. From south of Loreto, head north on Highway 1, turn right onto Paseo Pedro de Ugarte, and follow the above directions to the campground.

Contact: Rivera del Mar RV Park, Calle Francisco I. Madero Norte #100, Loreto, Baja California Sur, C.P. 23880, Mexico, tel. 613/135-0718, www.riveradelmar.com. For more information about Arturo's Sport Fishing, visit www.arturosport.com.

2 EL MORO MOTEL AND RV PARK

Scenic Rating: 4

in Loreto

See map page 208 **BEST**

Fringed by palm trees and neighborhood dogs, the park is rather small—just a handful of spots behind a simple motel. Still, what it might lack in aesthetics (and quietude), it more than compensates for with its location. Equidistant to the sparkling beach and the bustling center square, this little campground allows you to swim in the sea, join a fishing charter, tour Loreto's historic downtown, shop for wooden sculptures and blown glass, taste everything from steak to tacos to seafood, and dance the night away—all within a few blocks of your RV.

The park even offers a special RV package that includes a seven-hour fishing trip with your overnight stay. In addition, the staff will clean, fillet, and freeze whatever you catch—which, depending on the season, could be dorado, marlin, sailfish, tuna, yellowtail, cabrilla, red snapper, grouper, or other sizable varieties.

Though the bountiful Sea of Cortez and the diverse islands of the Parque Marino Nacional Bahía de Loreto are mighty attractions for those staying here, it's hard to ignore the cultural sites in the other direction. Just a couple blocks inland, amid quaint cobblestone streets, stands the magnificent Misión de Nuestra Señora de Loreto Conchó, established by Spanish missionaries in 1697. Formed in the shape of a Greek cross, the Loreto mission was founded by Jesuit priest Juán María Salvatierra and his followers, over a decade after a similar attempt to establish a Spanish mission in La Paz, to the south, had failed miserably.

Eventually, the Loreto mission became the "mother" of all later missions founded in Baja California and Alta California (now a U.S. state). Despite suffering major damage in an 1829 hurricane, the mission has since been restored. Today, visitors can attend Catholic mass here or stop by the adjacent museum, which explains the fall of Baja's native society and honors the achievements of Spanish settlers and missionaries.

RV sites, facilities: There are 10 back-in RV sites, all with full hookups (including 30-amp outlets, water, and sewage). Each space can accommodate a midsized rig (up to 35 feet/10.7 meters long). Amenities include hot showers, individual restrooms, a pay phone, sportfishing charters, and a motel, offering a handful of air-conditioned rooms. There is, however, no dump station or laundry on the premises. Children, pets, and tent campers are welcome here, and the staff speaks limited English. Restaurants, stores, and tour operators are all within walking distance.

Misión de Nuestra Señora de Loreto Conchó

Reservations, fees: Space is extremely limited, so reservations are highly recommended. RV spaces cost around $15 per night, while tent sites cost $5 per night. The overnight fishing package costs $130. Yearly spaces are available for $2,000–2,400. Modest motel rooms are also available. Wireless Internet access is possible for a nominal fee. Credit cards are not accepted; cash (Mexican pesos or U.S. dollars) is the customary form of payment. The park is open all year.

Directions: From north of Loreto, just before the Km 119 marker on Highway 1, turn left onto Paseo Pedro de Ugarte, pass the *glorieta* (traffic circle), and veer left onto Calle Salvatierra. Head toward the ocean and veer right onto Avenida Miguel Hidalgo. Turn left onto Calle de la Playa (also called Boulevard Adolfo López Mateos), pass the pedestrian walkway, and turn left onto Calle Rosendo Robles. The park is on the left. From south of Loreto, head north on Highway 1, turn right onto Paseo Pedro de Ugarte, and follow the above directions to the campground.

Contact: El Moro Motel and RV Park, Calle Rosendo Robles #8, Loreto, Baja California Sur, C.P. 23880, Mexico, tel./fax 613/135-0542, www.loreto.com/elmoro.

3 LORETO SHORES VILLAS Y RV PARK

Scenic Rating: 8

in Loreto

See map page 208 **BEST**

With its highly prized waterfront location and plenty of room for longer rigs, this gated five-acre (two-hectare) RV park is the largest one in Loreto, and the only one situated directly beside the majestic Sea of Cortez—though permanent dwellings partially block the view. Also known as the Gulf of California, the Golfo de California, and the Mar de Cortés, this incredibly clear, biologically diverse sea beside the park once fascinated legendary marine explorer Jacques Cousteau, who alternately called it "the world's aquarium" and "the Galapagos of North America."

Since the mid-1990s, visitors to Loreto Shores have been able to see these beautiful waters any time of day, though they're particularly gorgeous at sunrise and sunset. Even better, you can immerse yourself in this marine playground, whether fishing for marlin and dorado with experts, kayaking amid dolphins and porpoises, or embarking upon a tour of the nearby islands. Part of the expansive, 513,000-acre (207,610-hectare) Parque Marino Nacional Bahía de Loreto, the five closest islands—Isla Coronado, Isla del Carmen, Isla Danzante, Isla Monserrat, and Isla Santa Catalina—provide a magnificent setting for scuba divers, snorkelers, swimmers, kayakers, and sailors. Established in 1996 and named a World Heritage Site of the United Nations in 2005, this national marine park protects over 800 species of marine life (some of which are endangered).

Although the entire park is stunning, Isla del Carmen, the largest and most complex of the five islands, is especially scenic, offering secluded white-sand beaches, sheltered anchorages, and the chance to spy sea lions, exotic birds, and whales at play. You can reach the island via kayak, private boat, or official tour operator; several outfitters and resorts offer such excursions. The RV park management can help you arrange fishing charters as well as tours of the Misión de San Francisco Javier in the nearby mountains.

RV sites, facilities: This fenced, gated park offers 34 pull-through spaces, all equipped with patios and full hookups (30-amp outlets, potable water, and sewage). Caravans especially favor this spacious park, despite the scarcity of shade. There is no maximum length or age restriction, and slide-outs are permitted, though wider rigs (with slide-outs on both sides) might require two adjacent spaces. Children and pets are welcome, though all dogs must be kept on a leash, and droppings must be picked up immediately. Tent campers are permitted in the designated tent-camping area.

You'll find new, clean restrooms; hot showers; a deluxe coin laundry; a large, *palapa*-roofed clubhouse with a bar, a kitchen, and tables; a public pay phone; a fish-cleaning station; a car/boat wash area; movie rentals (with popcorn); 24-hour security; and a bilingual park administrator, who can hail taxis, make restaurant reservations, and book fishing or sightseeing tours. RV storage, *casa* rentals, and shady *palapa* leases are also options. Wireless Internet access is available. The facilities are not wheelchair-accessible at this time, and there's no dump station on the premises. A swimming pool is scheduled to be completed by mid-2008. Though close to the gulf, the park is also within walking distance of downtown Loreto, including historic sites, restaurants, markets, and gas stations.

Reservations, fees: Reservations are recommended during peak season; a 50 percent deposit is required. You can expect a full refund if you cancel 30 days prior to arrival; otherwise, a credit for future stays is offered. Full-hookup RV spaces (including tax and wireless Internet access) cost $18.50 daily, $110 weekly, or $350 monthly (plus electricity usage). Tent camping (with a hot shower) costs $6 per night or $30 per week; wireless Internet access is available at an extra cost of $2 per day or $10 per month. Rates are subject to change when the pool is completed in mid-2008. Visitors can also store their vehicles, boats, RVs, and trailers for short or long-term periods; rates depend upon the unit's length, and all tires and batteries are checked weekly. For additional fees, guests can rent videos, purchase ice and beverages, and wash their boats and vehicles. Credit cards are not accepted; cash (Mexican pesos or U.S. dollars) and checks are the only acceptable forms of payment. The park is open all year.

Directions: From north of Loreto, just before the Km 119 marker on Highway 1, turn left onto Paseo Pedro de Ugarte, pass through the *glorieta,* and merge left onto Calle Salvatierra (which will become Avenida Miguel Hidalgo).

At the second stoplight, turn right onto Calle Francisco I. Madero and continue straight, across the Río Loreto *arroyo.* Six blocks after the *arroyo,* take a left onto Ildefonso Green. The RV park is directly ahead of you. From south of Loreto, head north on Highway 1, turn right onto Paseo Pedro de Ugarte, and follow the above directions to the campground.
Contact: Loreto Shores Villas y RV Park, Colonia Zaragoza, Apartado Postal #219, Loreto, Baja California Sur, C.P. 23880, Mexico, tel. 613/135-1513, fax 613/135-0711, www.loretoshoresvillasandrvpark.com.

4 PLAYA JUNCALITO

Scenic Rating: 8

south of Loreto

See map page 208 **BEST**

A few miles south of the FONATUR development scheme in Nopoló—where the public can enjoy tennis courts and an 18-hole, par-72 golf course for reasonable rates—several secluded beaches beckon tent campers and RV travelers. Playa Juncalito is one of the most popular of these primitive campgrounds, mostly due to the serene setting—and its relatively easy access from the highway. Here, you'll encounter palm oases, rocky reefs, a sandy beach, and turquoise waters, gently lapping ashore.

Travelers enjoy the peace and quiet of this secluded cove, where swimming, beachcombing, hiking, fishing, boating, and watching birds, reptiles, and marine mammals are favored pastimes. Boaters can anchor their crafts close to the beach, a terrific base for sportfishing and exploring the offshore islands in the Parque Marino Nacional Bahía de Loreto.

Although RVers will savor the relaxing environs, tent campers usually find it easier to park here. There's plenty of space for lengthy rigs, but, before heading in with a large motor home or unwieldy travel trailer, you should walk onto the beach to see if you'll fit. Getting stuck in the sand is no fun.

RV sites, facilities: There are no designated RV sites here—you can park wherever you like. Besides the sun, sand, rock, and sea, however, there's little in the way of amenities, just pit toilets and trash barrels. Only rugged tent campers and small, self-contained RVs (up to 30 feet/9.1 meters long) should park here, preferably in pairs or groups, as there's no drinking water, dump station, electricity, shower house, laundry, or security available. In addition, tools such as shovels, boards, and rope might be necessary for dislodging wheels that get stuck in the soft sand that abounds here. Children and pets are welcome, though the sandy terrain isn't suitable for wheelchairs. Groceries, purified water, gasoline, and other supplies can be purchased in Loreto to the northwest or Ciudad Constitución to the southwest. Remember to pack out all trash when you leave.
Reservations, fees: Reservations are not accepted; spaces are available on a first-come, first-served basis. Given its primitive status, the campground costs only $5 per night. Although perhaps no one will be available to collect the fee, you should have it ready just in case. Credit cards are not accepted; cash (Mexican pesos or U.S. dollars) is the customary form of payment. The beach is open all year.
Directions: Head south of Loreto on Highway 1 for 13.5 miles (21.7 km). Just south of the Km 98 marker, turn left and drive 0.5 mile (0.8 km) down a rough dirt road toward the beach. You'll see the small village of Juncalito along the northern waterfront. From Ciudad Insurgentes, drive northeast on Highway 1 for 56.2 miles (90.4 km), to the turnoff for the Tripui Vacation Park in Puerto Escondido. Continue another 1.7 miles (2.7 km) north and turn right onto the Juncalito access road.
Contact: Since there's no official contact person, mailing address, or phone number for Playa Juncalito, it's best just to drive down and see which spots are available. For more information about the Nopoló Sports Center, visit www.loreto.com/nopolo.htm. For details about the Loreto area, visit www.loreto.com.

5 TRIPUI VACATION PARK AND HOTEL TRIPUI

Scenic Rating: 9

in Puerto Escondido

See map page 208 BEST

Nestled between the Sierra de la Giganta and the Sea of Cortez, near the Marina Singlar, this hotel and RV park lures swimmers, hikers, anglers, boaters, equestrians, bird-watchers, and other nature lovers every season. Palm trees, cacti, and blossoming foliage grace the well-landscaped grounds. Only a 20-minute drive south of Loreto, the resort even has its own private beach, El Quemado (The Burnt)—in addition to a nearby launch ramp for those towing their own boats. Kayakers and anglers especially like this port because it provides easy access to the offshore waters and coastal areas stretching toward La Paz, which are difficult to reach via road.

Although the hotel is relatively new, the campground has existed for more than two decades. Caravans stop here often, especially those with large rigs. Not only does the park offer plenty of amenities, but visitors can also participate in official tours—fishing and scuba diving in the Parque Marino Nacional Bahía de Loreto, whale-watching in Puerto López Mateos on the western side of the peninsula, and touring ancient cave paintings and the Misión de San Francisco Javier in the mountains near Loreto.

RV sites, facilities: The park has 31 RV sites, a mixture of back-in and pull-through spaces. All sites have full hookups, benches, barbecue pits, and limited shade. There are no age or length restrictions for RVs; even lengthy rigs (up to 45 feet/13.7 meters long) will find room here. Besides a perimeter fence, a security gate, and nighttime surveillance, other amenities include a coin laundry, a playground, restrooms, hot showers, the hotel pool (which RV guests are welcome to use), the restaurant and bar, spa services, a grocery and liquor store, shuttle service, and wireless Internet access around the pool and inside the hotel's business center. There is, however, no dump station on the premises. The resident manager and many other staff members speak English (in addition to other languages). Children, pets, and tent campers are welcome, and the sites and facilities are wheelchair-accessible. Groceries, purified water, gasoline, and other supplies can be purchased in Loreto to the northwest or Ciudad Constitución to the southwest.

Reservations, fees: Reservations are recommended, though a 25 percent deposit is required. Cancellations should be made at least three weeks in advance. RV sites cost $18 nightly, $128 weekly, $519 monthly, $1,465 for three months, and $2,564 for six months. Tent spaces in the garden between the hotel and RV park cost $7 per person, per night. Hotel rooms are also available. Acceptable forms of payment include cash (Mexican pesos or U.S. dollars), personal checks, travelers checks, Visa, and MasterCard. The park is open all year.

Directions: If you're heading south from Loreto on Highway 1, drive 15.2 miles (24.5 km) to the Km 94 marker and take the exit to Puerto Escondido. Drive 0.6 mile (1 km) on the paved road, toward the ocean. The campground is on the right side. From Ciudad Insurgentes, drive northeast on Highway 1 for 56.2 miles (90.4 km), to the turnoff for the Tripui Vacation Park.

Contact: Tripui Vacation Park and Hotel Tripui, Apartado Postal #100, Loreto, Baja California Sur, C.P. 23880, Mexico, tel. 613/133-0814 or 613/133-0818, fax 613/133-0828, www.tripuihotel.com.mx or www.tripui.com.

6 PLAYA LIGUI

Scenic Rating: 8

south of Puerto Escondido

See map page 208

Within view of Isla Danzante, part of the Parque Marino Nacional Bahía de Loreto, this lovely beach is quite popular with RV enthusiasts and tent campers, headed to and from Loreto. With the exception of local anglers launching their boats from here, this primitive campground is extremely quiet and serene. Visitors can just relax on the beach, soaking up the ever-present sunshine and watching the ospreys, pelicans, and vultures circle the hills and offshore islands.

From the sandy beach, several routes lead to various campsites, some more private than others. Given the prevalence of thorny brush, soft spots, and dead-end roads, it's advisable to explore on foot and select a space before attempting the maze via RV. Once you've parked, other beaches can be reached in a four-wheel-drive vehicle.

Most travelers come here for simple outdoor pleasures—like swimming, hiking, fishing, diving, boating, and exploring secluded coves farther down the coast—but there are two other nearby attractions as well. Framed by the peaceful sea and rugged desert hills, the Danzante Destination Resort and El Santuario Eco-Retreat Center—both located in Ensenada Blanca a couple miles south—each offer guests a rejuvenating environment in which to pursue activities as diverse as yoga, massage, nature walks, island tours, snorkeling, and guided horseback riding.

RV sites, facilities: There are no designated RV sites here—you can park wherever you like. Big rigs (up to 40 feet/12.2 meters long) will have no trouble fitting somewhere, but slow, careful driving is advisable. In fact, tools such as shovels, boards, and rope might be necessary, for dislodging wheels that get stuck in the soft sand that abounds here. Despite the remarkable surroundings, the only amenities are pit toilets, trash barrels, and the white-sand beach. Only self-contained RVs and rugged tent campers should park here, preferably in pairs or groups, as there's no drinking water, dump station, electricity, shower house, laundry, or security available. Children and pets are welcome, but the sandy terrain is not suitable for wheelchairs. Groceries, purified water, gasoline, and other supplies can be purchased in Loreto to the northwest or Ciudad Constitución to the southwest. Remember to pack out all trash when you leave.

Reservations, fees: Reservations are not accepted; spaces are available on a first-come, first-served basis. The overnight camping fee is $5 (for RVs as well as tents). Although no one may be available to collect the fee, you should have it ready just in case. Credit cards are not accepted; cash (Mexican pesos or U.S. dollars) is the customary form of payment. The beach is open all year.

Directions: From Loreto, drive 21.4 miles (34.4 km) south, toward the Km 84 marker on Highway 1. Turn left onto the gravel road just south of the marker and drive about 0.9 mile (1.4 km) toward the beach. Take the last right turn and follow the signs marked "Playa." From Ciudad Insurgentes, drive northeast on Highway 1 for 50 miles (80.5 km), to the turnoff for Playa Ligui. Be aware that, beyond the highway, you'll see some private residences along this route—campers and anglers routinely ignore the "Propriedad Privada" (Private Property) sign at the fence, but remember to be respectful of your neighbors.

Contact: Since there's no official contact person, mailing address, or phone number for Playa Ligui, it's best just to drive down and see which spots are available. For more information about the two eco-resorts in Ensenada Blanca, visit www.danzante.com (Danzante Destination Resort) and www.el-santuario.com (El Santuario Eco-Retreat Center). For details about the Loreto area, visit www.loreto.com.

7 PUERTO AGUA VERDE

Scenic Rating: 9

between Loreto and Ciudad Insurgentes

See map page 208

At the end of a serpentine road, you'll find a beautiful rocky landscape, filled with palm trees and charming beaches. With impressive views of the Sea of Cortez and the eastern slope of the Sierra de la Giganta, this small, isolated village is a wonderful place to set up for the night. Tent campers and RV enthusiasts are both welcome in this primitive campground, but don't expect any amenities. Travelers come here for the low sandy beaches and beautiful sunrises and sunsets—not for luxuries.

The view of tranquil Agua Verde Cove is definitely worth the trip. Yachters have long used it as an anchorage, kayakers enjoy the calm waters, windsurfers find the breeze useful, and anglers come to these shores for grouper and barracuda, among other varieties. The only drawback perhaps is the road to the beach—worsened from storm damage, the narrow route traces steep cliffs as it descends toward the coast. In fact, it's probably best suited for four-wheel-drive vehicles with high clearance. No matter what you're driving, however, take the route slowly and use caution.

RV sites, facilities: There are no designated RV sites here—you can park wherever you like. Big rigs (up to 40 feet/12.2 meters long) will have no trouble fitting somewhere, but slow, careful driving is advisable. In fact, tools such as shovels, boards, and rope might be necessary, for dislodging wheels that get stuck in the soft sand that abounds here. Despite the lovely environs, there are no official amenities. Only self-contained RVs and rugged tent campers should park here, preferably in pairs or groups, as there's no drinking water, dump station, electricity, shower house, laundry, or security available. Children and pets are welcome, but the terrain is not suitable for wheelchairs. Groceries, purified water, gasoline, and other supplies can be purchased in Loreto to the northwest or Ciudad Constitución to the southwest. Remember to pack out all trash when you leave.

Reservations, fees: Reservations are not accepted; beachside spaces are available on a first-come, first-served basis. There is usually no cost for camping here, though you might be asked to pay a small fee (no more than $5 per night). Credit cards are not accepted; cash (Mexican pesos or U.S. dollars) is the customary form of payment. The beach is open all year.

Directions: About 34.2 miles (55 km) south of Loreto on Highway 1, turn left at the Km 63 marker and continue along the winding, graded dirt road toward Puerto Agua Verde, for roughly 25.4 miles (40.9 km). Be advised that this is an extremely bumpy, uncomfortable route—for RVs and jeeps alike—and it's only harder on the return trip uphill. From Ciudad Insurgentes, drive northeast for 37.2 miles (59.9 km) to Km 63 and turn right.

Contact: Since there's no official contact person, mailing address, or phone number for Puerto Agua Verde, it's best just to drive down and see which spots are available. For details about the Loreto area, visit www.loreto.com.

8 SCORPION BAY

Scenic Rating: 8

on Bahía San Juanico

See map page 208 **BEST**

Since San Juanico is an isolated fishing village, accessible by only two unpaved roads and situated far from Baja's main tourist centers, few RVers find themselves here by accident. Run by Americans in cooperation with the local *ejido,* the breezy campground at Scorpion Bay is the very definition of "primitive"—with no obvious sites along several hundred yards of cliffs, overlooking sandy beaches and rocky coasts. Although surfing is the prime reason to come, outdoor enthusiasts will delight in the variety of recreational activities available, including hiking, boating, fishing, swimming, and scuba diving.

In addition to the opportunities at Scorpion Bay, visitors can enjoy many sites en route to their destination. From Ciudad Insurgentes, RVers can head west to Puerto López Mateos to observe migrating California *ballenas gris* (gray whales) in the winter months. Headed north to San Juanico, you can take a northeasterly route along the Arroyo Comondú, into a fertile oasis, and tour the adjacent mountain villages of San Miguel Comondú and San José Comondú—terrific places for cyclists. Lastly, as you drive through the Valle de la Purísima, instead of turning left onto the unpaved turnoff toward Scorpion Bay, you can turn right, where two other hidden Baja gems, La Purísima and San Isidro, await.

RV sites, facilities: The campground offers space for an indeterminate number of RVs and tents. Lying along the coast, these primitive sites (65 feet, or 19.8 meters, from the mean high-tide line) present incredible views, but no hookups. Although there's plenty of room for lengthy rigs, the campground is best suited for small RVs (under 30 feet/9.1 meters long), especially given the long, slow-going, graded dirt road that travelers must take to reach this area. Nearby is a *palapa*-style restaurant and cantina, open year-round and serving inexpensive cuisine, from shrimp tacos to *carne asada.*

In addition, there's a boat launch area, three enclosed *palapas,* and a bath house, offering cold showers only. The manager and staff members speak English, but there is no laundry or dump station on the premises. Children and pets are welcome, though the terrain might not be suitable for wheelchairs. Although minimal supplies (such as ice, sunscreen, and hats) are available at the cantina, there are no other stores in this remote region. Consequently, you're advised to purchase extra groceries, purified water, gasoline, and other supplies in Ciudad Constitución to the southeast, before making the trip to San Juanico. Remember to pack out all trash when you leave.

Reservations, fees: Reservations are not accepted for campsites; spaces are available on a first-come, first-served basis. Primitive camping costs $10 per person, per night. *Palapas* can be reserved in advance and rented for $45 nightly (for up to two people); extra guests will be charged $15 per person, per night. Supplies, souvenirs, and hot showers cost extra, and there's also a rental house available for groups. Children can stay for free. Credit cards are not accepted; cash (Mexican pesos or U.S. dollars) and checks (received in advance by mail) are the only acceptable forms of payment. The campground is open all year.

Directions: From Ciudad Insurgentes on Highway 1, head northwest for 68.1 miles (109.6 km) on the paved road, turn left near La Purísima onto the graded dirt road, and drive 29.7 miles (47.8 km) along a winding, slow-going route to the coastal village of San Juanico. Follow the road above the bluff to the clearly marked entrance road, and head for the point south of town.

Contact: Scorpion Bay, c/o Promotora Punta Pequeña, 2952 Main Street, San Diego, CA 92113, tel. 619/239-1335, ext. 18 (U.S.), fax 619/235-6018 (U.S.), www.scorpionbay.net.

9 MISIONES RV PARK

Scenic Rating: 5

in Ciudad Constitución

See map page 208

Situated 89 miles (143.2 km) southwest of Loreto and 126.9 miles (204.2 km) north of La Paz along Highway 1, Ciudad Constitución is far different from those sumptuous seaside destinations, and yet it has a lot to offer as a base camp for other sights. Misiones RV Park is one of three convenient campgrounds in this farming community, and the closest one to Highway 22—pathway to the magnificent Bahía Magdalena, a popular spot for migrating California gray whales (and their human observers) in winter.

Peppered with hundreds of shrubs and trees, the RV park isn't terribly far from another popular whale-watching site, Puerto López Mateos, to the northwest. For history buffs, there are also several Spanish missions in the vicinity, including the Misión de San José Comondú, a shaded brick building in the mountainous village of the same name; the Misión de San Francisco Javier, which admittedly is less challenging to reach from Loreto; and the gleaming-white Misión de San Luis Gonzaga, located down a winding dirt road southeast of the Ciudad Constitución airport.

RV sites, facilities: Besides tent spaces, there are 30 roomy, pull-through RV sites, each with full hookups (15-amp electricity, potable water, and sewage drains) and space for lengthy rigs (up to 40 feet/12.2 meters long). Other amenities include a whirlpool spa, a swimming pool, Internet access via the owners' network, and two spotless restroom buildings with flush toilets and hot showers. In addition, the managers speak English. There is, however, no laundry or dump station on the premises. Children and pets are welcome. Limited groceries, water, fuel, and other supplies can be purchased in nearby Ciudad Constitución.

Reservations, fees: Space is limited, so reservations are recommended. RV and tent sites cost $15–20 nightly. Credit cards are not accepted; cash (Mexican pesos or U.S. dollars) is the only acceptable form of payment. The park is open all year.

Directions: Once you reach the northern city limits of Ciudad Constitución, the park isn't hard to find. From Ciudad Insurgentes, drive south on Highway 1, past Km 213. Misiones RV Park is on the left side, near the northern border of Ciudad Constitución. From the La Paz area, drive northwest on Highway 1, pass through Ciudad Constitución, and look for the RV park on your right, between Km 212 and Km 213.

Contact: Misiones RV Park, Km 213 de la Colonia Vargas, Ciudad Constitución, Baja California Sur, Mexico, tel. 613/132-1103, npso@hotmail.com.

10 CAMPESTRE LA PILA

Scenic Rating: 5

in Ciudad Constitución

See map page 208

The area around Ciudad Constitución is an irrigated farming region within the agricultural heart of the Valle de Santo Domingo, known for rich harvests of wheat, chickpeas, cotton, and citrus fruits. Still, most of the surrounding landscape is the same desert that Ciudad once was. So, in the height of summertime, RV travelers are grateful for the shady palm trees and pleasantly landscaped pool beside the spacious camping area.

If you ever tire of cooling off, however, you can take a walk through town, where stores, restaurants, and bars await. As an alternative, Puerto San Carlos is only a moderate drive to the west on Highway 22. Situated on Bahía Magdalena, beside the Pacific Ocean, San Carlos is a large commercial port, where hundreds of whale-watching visitors descend from January to March. During the off-season, ecotourists and sightseers can relish many other outdoor delights, including the white sand dunes of Isla Magdalena and Isla Santa Margarita; the gorgeous waters of Bahía Magdalena, Bahía Santa María, and Bahía Almejas; the colonies of migratory and native birds that frequent the estuary and mangrove trees; and the passing ships and cruisers within the bustling harbor.

RV sites, facilities: There are 18 back-in sites (with 15-amp outlets and potable water), separated by grassy areas. Lengthy rigs (up to 40 feet/12.2 meters long) will find room here. Amenities include hot showers, clean restrooms, a dump station, and a swimming pool. There is, however, no laundry on the premises. Children, pets, and tent campers are welcome. Groceries, water, fuel, and other supplies can be purchased in nearby Ciudad Constitución.

Reservations, fees: Space is limited, so reservations are recommended. RV and tent sites cost $10 per night (based on double occupancy); extra guests are charged $5 per night. Credit cards are not accepted; cash (Mexican pesos or U.S. dollars) is the only acceptable form of payment. The park is open all year.

Directions: Campestre La Pila is in the southern end of town. If you're driving from Ciudad Insurgentes, head south on Highway 1, turn right (west) just past the intersection of

© MEXICO TOURISM BOARD

aerial view of Bahía Santa María

the lateral main streets, and follow the high-tension electrical lines for 0.7 mile (1.1 km). The campground is on the left side of the access road, near the sign. From La Paz, drive northwest on Highway 1 to Km 208, just south of Ciudad Constitución, and turn left toward the campground.

Contact: Campestre La Pila, Apartado Postal #261, Ciudad Constitución, Baja California Sur, Mexico, tel. 613/132-0562.

11 PALAPA 206 RV PARK AND MOTEL

Scenic Rating: 6

in Ciudad Constitución

See map page 208

South of Ciudad Constitución, this campground has been owned and operated since 2002 by Michael and Bertha Gale, a friendly couple who know the area well and can help you experience the most out of this part of Baja Sur. Perhaps that's why it's become such a popular stop for large RVs and caravans—especially on fiesta nights, a celebration of Mexican cuisine, tropical drinks, and folkloric dancing.

To be fair, most RVers only use Ciudad Constitución as a pit stop en route to Loreto or La Paz. Although it's a good place to pick up supplies (like camera batteries, vehicle parts, and groceries), it isn't much of a destination. Usually, visitors have other side trips in mind, namely fishing in the Pacific Ocean to the west (on Highway 22), boarding a whale-watching *panga* in Bahía Magdalena, or taking the road southeast to the historic, gleaming-white Misión de San Luis Gonzaga. The park is a terrific base for such excursions—Michael is even willing to take visitors fishing. It's safe, too—the park is fenced-in, with a security gate and a red block wall facing the highway.

RV sites, facilities: The RV park has 23 pull-through sites, suitable for any size—even lengthy rigs (up to 45 feet/13.7 meters long). Luckily, there's plenty of room in which to maneuver. Twenty-two are full-hookup sites (including water, 20-amp electricity, and sewer access); one

Palapa 206 RV Park in Ciudad Constitución

has water and electricity only. Tents are permitted in the 1-acre (0.4-hectare) dry-camping area. There are no age or length restrictions for RVs. The restrooms have hot showers; wireless Internet service is available; and the managers speak both English and Spanish. Amenities also include a palm-roofed restaurant, a small motel (with air-conditioning and television), barbecue and picnic areas, and shady *palapas*. Sites are wheelchair-accessible, and security is provided by a perimeter fence and entrance gate. There is, however, no dump station or laundry on the premises. Children and pets are welcome in the park. Limited supplies, including purified water, can be purchased in Ciudad Constitución.

Reservations, fees: Space is limited, so reservations are recommended. Advance deposits aren't required, and you can cancel your reservation with just a phone call. Full-hookup RV sites cost $15 per night; tent and dry-docking RV spaces cost $7 per night; and $39 is the daily rate for motel rooms. Credit cards are not accepted; cash (Mexican pesos or U.S. dollars) is the only acceptable form of payment. The park is open all year.

Directions: As you leave the southern end of town on Highway 1, headed toward La Paz, drive roughly 1.4 miles (2.3 km) past the Ley supermarket to Km 206. The campground is on the right (west) side of the highway, opposite a large stand of trees. From La Paz, drive northwest on Highway 1 to Km 206 and turn left into the Palapa 206 RV Park.

Contact: Palapa 206 RV Park and Motel, Apartado Postal #186, Km 206 de la Carretera Transpeninsular, Ciudad Constitución, Baja California Sur, Mexico, tel. 613/132-3463, palapa206@prodigy.net.mx.

12 OASIS RV PARK

Scenic Rating: 5

in El Centenario

See map page 208

RV travelers headed from Loreto to La Paz will first encounter this little campground.

Located right on the beach in the town of El Centenario, roughly 8 miles (12.9 km) west of La Paz proper, the park offers quick access to an enclosed portion of Bahía de la Paz. A relatively old park, it's been fairly abandoned, following damage from a 2004 hurricane. Although the spaces are pretty basic—just sandy lots beside palm trees—its waterfront location is ideal, providing views of aquamarine waters and distant mountains.

The bay is shallow here, however; during low tide, mudflats take over the shore. Still, swimmers, beachcombers, hikers, cyclists, and wildlife-watchers will find the warm waters, year-round summertime temperatures, and quiet surroundings rewarding. If you miss the bustle of a city, there are other, better maintained RV parks farther east, which offer easier access to the shops, restaurants, bars, and sights of La Paz.

RV sites, facilities: There are 25 back-in RV sites situated on hard-packed sand, with full hookups (15-amp electricity, water, and sewer access) and direct access to the beach. Some of the sites are even partially shaded by wind-blown palm trees. Lengthy rigs (up to 40 feet/12.2 meters long) should be able to maneuver here. Prior to the hurricane damage, amenities included old restrooms with tiled floors, flush toilets, and hot showers; a swimming pool; a restaurant; a laundry room; and a security gate. Since 2004, however, amenities have been rather limited. Hopefully, there will be improvements in the near future. Only self-contained RVs and rugged tent campers should park here, preferably in pairs or groups, especially since there's not even a dump station available, much less official security. Children and pets are welcome, though the facilities are not wheelchair-accessible. Groceries, purified water, gasoline, and other supplies can be purchased in nearby La Paz.

Reservations, fees: Reservations are accepted. RV and tent sites cost $14 per night for two people ($2 for each extra person). In the past, weekly and monthly rates have been available, too. Credit cards are not accepted; cash (Mexican pesos or U.S. dollars) is the customary form of payment. The campground is open all year.

Directions: Headed toward La Paz from the north, take Highway 1 to the Km 15 marker. Halfway between the Km 15 and Km 14 markers, you'll see the campground on the left (north) side of the highway, toward the water. From downtown La Paz, head west on Highway 1; the campground will be on your right.

Contact: Oasis RV Park, Km 15 de la Carretera Transpeninsular al Norte, El Centenario, La Paz, Baja California Sur, Mexico, tel. 612/124-6090.

13 CAMPESTRE MARANATHA RV PARK

Scenic Rating: 6

east of El Centenario

See map page 208

With the recent loss of such popular La Paz–area haunts as Aquamarina RV Park (closed due to a land sale) and La Paz Trailer Park (now apparently reserved for RV caravans), this is one of only a few campgrounds left in this vibrant town. Established in the mid-1950s by missionaries, this quiet, safe, family-run park still hosts school groups and summer camps in addition to RV travelers and caravans. Close to several beaches, fishing outfitters, and assorted restaurants, Campestre Maranatha attracts outdoor enthusiasts and urbanites alike—not to mention a flock of pleasant regulars, who travel the Baja often and have plenty of tips to share with their neighbors, from the safest roads to the best beachside camping available on the peninsula. Swimming, fishing, boating, kayaking, wildlife-watching, and sightseeing are popular diversions here.

RV sites, facilities: There are eight full-hookup, angled, back-in RV sites (with 20/30-amp electricity and room for RVs up to 40 feet/12.2

meters in length). Although the lots are simply assigned spaces of dirt, trees provide some shelter from the sun. Amenities include a swimming pool, a coin laundry, a kitchen, restrooms and hot showers, communal rooms for larger groups, well-kept grounds, and, in general, immaculate facilities. There is, however, no dump station on the premises. The nearby coffee shop is owned and operated by the same family that owns the campground, so, any RVer who purchases coffee or a homemade pastry is entitled to free Internet service, including wireless access, and calls to Canada or the United States. Children, pets, and tent campers are welcome here, and the staff speaks English. Groceries, purified water, gasoline, and other supplies can be purchased in nearby La Paz.

Reservations, fees: Space is limited, so reservations are recommended. Full-hookup RV sites cost $18 per night, $110 per week, and $420 per month. Tent spaces (or dry camping for RVs) cost $15 per night. Long-distance phone calls and wireless Internet access are available at the nearby coffee shop. Credit cards are not accepted; cash (Mexican pesos or U.S. dollars) is the customary form of payment. The park is open all year.

Directions: Headed toward La Paz from the north, take Highway 1 past El Centenario. Now headed east, watch for the El Exquisito coffee shop on your right, near Km 11.3—about 2.5 miles (4 km) west of the whale's tail monument in La Paz. Turn right (south) onto the road that lies west of (just before) the coffee shop. Roughly 100 yards (91.4 meters) down the access road, you'll spy the park entrance on the left side. From the whale's tail monument in La Paz, head west on Highway 1 for 2.5 miles (4 km) and turn left onto the road just past the coffee shop.

Contact: Campestre Maranatha RV Park, Km 11 de la Carretera Transpeninsular al Norte, La Paz, Baja California Sur, Mexico, tel./fax 612/124-6275, maranatha@prodigy.net.mx. If you're interested in reserving a large space for an RV caravan, you might try contacting La Paz Trailer Park at 612/124-0830.

14 RV CASA BLANCA

Scenic Rating: 7

in La Paz

See map page 208 **BEST**

The gleaming white wall that surrounds this entire RV park, here since 1991, beckons weary travelers (especially large caravans) from the road and beneath the welcoming entrance bell. Although you can usually count on finding open spaces in this campground, its popularity means that you should call ahead. Tidy, roomy, and easy to find, the park provides a lovely place to rest between excursions into the bay and strolls into downtown La Paz. The refreshing pool is inviting, and the palm trees, cacti, and flowering bushes accentuate the clean facilities, though the high white concrete walls might be a bit too glaring on the region's hottest days.

The sites are somewhat close together, but, if you don't mind being so near your neighbors, this is an excellent place to use as a base camp. Then it's off to swim, surf, snorkel, hike, or picnic beside one of several pleasant beaches along the Bahía de la Paz. With the quaint, adobe-style pier and marina so near, fishing excursions and island tours are options, too. If you're looking to unwind from an active day, take a stroll along the nearby *malecón,* fringed with palm trees, dolphin statues, vendors, and historic architecture, including a lovely, storybook lighthouse. From here, you can sit on a bench at sunset and watch the passing yachts and sailboats against a gorgeous, rosy sky.

The park is also a good spot during Carnaval season; it puts you within walking distance of the food, music, costumes, games, and other holiday festivities. Just remember that the gate closes (but doesn't lock) every night at 10 P.M.—you're responsible for closing it again once you've passed through.

RV sites, facilities: There are 41 campsites with full hookups; some have 50-amp outlets, while others have 15-amp electricity. One is a pull-through space; the rest are back-ins. The entire camping area is hard-packed sand,

and the shaded spaces are separated by low concrete curbs, offering little room between neighbors. Tent campers are welcome, though this is primarily an RV park. Lengthy rigs (up to 45 feet/13.7 meters long), with slide-outs, are welcome, too. Park amenities include clean restrooms, flush toilets, hot showers, picnic tables, and barbecue pits. There's also a swimming pool, a tennis court, a communal *palapa,* a store, a coin laundry, a pay phone, a coffee shop and Internet café out front, and a hospital across the street. Guards near the gate offer 24-hour security, and the staff speaks English. There is, however, no dump station on the premises. Children are welcome here. Leashed, well-mannered pets are permitted in much of the park—save for the laundry, pool, and restroom areas. The facilities are not wheelchair-accessible. The park isn't far from restaurants, shops, and a hospital.

Reservations, fees: Reservations are accepted via email or phone. RV sites cost $20 per night for two people ($5 for each additional guest) and $400 per month. Tent sites are $15 per night. Credit cards are not accepted; cash (Mexican pesos or U.S. dollars) is the only acceptable form of payment. The park is open all year.

Directions: If you're driving into La Paz from the west, via Highway 1, veer left at the whale's tail monument, follow Abasolo for 1.2 miles (1.9 km), and turn right onto Avenida Delfines. It's hard to miss the distinctive white wall on the left side of the road—that's RV Casa Blanca. Turn into the driveway and stop by the coffee shop, which also doubles as the office. From the Los Cabos area, take Highway 1 north; when you reach La Paz, turn left onto Libramiento, turn right onto Abasolo, and follow the above directions to the park.

Contact: RV Casa Blanca, Km 4.5 de la Carretera Transpeninsular al Norte, Esquina Avenida Pez Vela, Fracc. Fidepaz, La Paz, Baja California Sur, C.P. 23090, Mexico, tel./fax 612/124-2477, rv.casablanca@gmail.com.

15 PLAYA BALANDRA

Scenic Rating: 10

north of La Paz

See map page 208 **BEST**

La Paz is certainly known for its beautiful beaches, and Playa Balandra, on Bahía de la Paz, is certainly the best. Warm, crystalline waters, plenty of glistening soft sand, and interesting rock formations—including the frequently photographed mushroom rock—are just some of the reasons that people come here to camp, swim, wade, sunbathe, and explore. More protected than Playa El Tecolote to the north, this secluded cove is less windy, which also means it has more stinging insects and tends to get hotter without the cooling sea breezes. Locals use this particular beach for picnics, but few RVers seem to utilize it for overnight camping. Although staying a night or two is acceptable, the local police have sometimes asked people to move along if they stay too long. Still, there's enough level parking for those hoping to escape the city for a while.

Although leaving the RV here for the day is probably inadvisable, given the lack of security, Balandra is a good base camp for the other beaches that stretch south to La Paz—including Playa Pichilingue north of the ferry terminal and Playa El Coromuel closer to town. Balandra itself is quite lovely, though—a pleasant stroll through the shallow waters, amid the shady rocks, can do much to rejuvenate even the most stressed-out traveler.

RV sites, facilities: There are no designated sites in this limited space—just rock and sand. Likewise, few amenities are available, save for pit toilets, trash cans, and Mother Nature herself. Lengthy rigs (up to 40 feet/12.2 meters long) will have no trouble fitting somewhere, but slow, careful driving is advisable. In fact, tools such as shovels, boards, and rope might be necessary, for dislodging wheels that get stuck in the soft sand that abounds in this area. Only self-contained RVs and rugged tent campers should park here, preferably in pairs or groups,

the often-photographed mushroom rock of Playa Balandra

as there's no drinking water, dump station, electricity, shower house, laundry, or security available. Children and pets are welcome, but the terrain is not suitable for wheelchairs. Groceries, purified water, gasoline, and other supplies can be purchased in nearby La Paz. Remember to pack out all trash when you leave.

Reservations, fees: Reservations are not accepted; spaces are available on a first-come, first-served basis. The overnight camping fee is $5 for RVs and tents. Credit cards are not accepted; cash (Mexican pesos or U.S. dollars) is the only acceptable form of payment. While the beach is open all year, long-term camping is not recommended.

Directions: From west of La Paz, take Highway 1 to the dove statue (whale's tail) at the entrance to town and follow the signs to Cabo San Lucas. After 2.7 miles (4.3 km), you'll reach a stoplight at a T junction. Turn left here, then take the first right at a sign for the Ruta de Camiones (Truck Route), a bypass around downtown La Paz. After 12.4 miles (20 km), turn right toward the Pichilingue ferry terminal, which you'll reach in 3.8 miles (6.1 km). Turn right at Pichilingue and continue straight for 4.1 miles (6.6 km), until the road forks. Go left toward Playa Balandra.

Contact: Since there's no campground manager, mailing address, or phone number for Playa Balandra, it's best just to drive up and see which spots are available. If you do require details about La Paz–area beaches, however, you can visit www.vivalapaz.com.

16 PLAYA EL TECOLOTE

Scenic Rating: 9

north of La Paz

See map page 208 **BEST**

Facing north, this lengthy beach presents a stunning view of Isla Espíritu Santo and its surrounding islands, across the 4-mile-wide (6.4-km-wide) Canal de San Lorenzo. Here, you'll find soft sand, fringed with dunes and flat plains, and heavy surf when the northerly winds are blowing, especially in winter. RV enthusiasts and tent campers can park along the beach to the right or behind the dunes, away from the restaurants, though some spots provide more shade and less obstructed island views than others. To the left, there's a large open area, often used by RV caravans. Just be careful where you park—there are soft spots, and many an RVer has gotten stuck in the sand here. Walk the route before you choose a spot.

Despite the lack of official security, there are often many campers here, especially during spring break and in the summertime. The biggest concern is theft of belongings left outside the RV at night or when owners are away, so keep an eye on your campsite.

Travelers can arrange fishing charters or rent personal watercraft and small boats for private explorations of the nearby islands. You can spend an entire day out there, picnicking in a secluded cove, viewing manta rays (if you're very fortunate) and swooping pelicans, snorkeling amid vibrant tropical fish, sea lions, and coral reefs, and diving in a number of popular spots. Swimming, beachcombing, hiking, and sunbathing are also favorite pastimes in this area. The golden sunsets and luminous starry skies are well worth the journey, too.

RV sites, facilities: There are no designated sites in this popular campground—you can park wherever you wish. There are few amenities, and they include several restaurants with primitive restrooms, trash cans, *pangas* and personal watercraft for rent, cold showers, and the glorious environs. Note that only customers of the restaurants can use the bathrooms. Lengthy rigs (up to 40 feet/12.2 meters long) will have no trouble fitting somewhere on this large open beach, but slow, careful driving is advisable. In fact, tools such as shovels, boards, and rope might be necessary, for dislodging wheels that get stuck in the soft sand that abounds in this area. Only self-contained RVs and rugged tent campers should park here, preferably in pairs or groups, as there's no drinking water, dump station, electricity, laundry, or security available. Children and pets are welcome, but the terrain is not suitable for wheelchairs. Groceries, purified water, gasoline, and other supplies can be purchased in nearby La Paz. Remember to pack out all trash when you leave.

Reservations, fees: Reservations are not accepted; spaces are available on a first-come, first-served basis. The overnight camping fee is $5 for RVs and tents. Credit cards are not accepted; cash (Mexican pesos or U.S. dollars) is the only acceptable form of payment. The beach is open all year.

Directions: From west of La Paz, take Highway 1 to the dove statue (whale's tail) at the entrance to town and follow the signs to Cabo San Lucas. After 2.7 miles (4.3 km), you'll reach a stoplight at a T junction. Turn left here, then take the first right at a sign for the Ruta de Camiones (Truck Route), a bypass around downtown La Paz. After 12.4 miles (20 km), turn right toward the Pichilingue ferry terminal, which you'll reach in 3.8 miles (6.1 km). Turn right at Pichilingue and continue straight for 4.1 miles (6.6 km), until the road forks. Go right toward Playa El Tecolote.

Contact: Since there's no campground manager, mailing address, or phone number for Playa El Tecolote, it's best just to drive up and see which spots are available. If you do require details about La Paz–area beaches, however, you can visit www.vivalapaz.com.

17 YOYO'S CAMPGROUND

Scenic Rating: 7

in La Ventana

See map page 208

The small seaside village of La Ventana is popular with windsurfers, especially in the windy winter season, so perhaps it's no surprise that there are three campgrounds in town. This one, named after local fishing guide and campground owner Gil Heleodoro Lucero Aviles ("YoYo"), is smaller than La Ventana Campground, but still visited often during the open winter season. Windsurfers and kiteboarders are the most frequent overnight guests to this gusty place, though swimmers and boaters find their way here, too. Despite the phone lines and lampposts along the highway, the view toward Bahía de la Ventana is stunning, with its aquamarine waters and distant islands almost distracting you from the highway noise.

RV sites, facilities: The fenced-in campground is relatively primitive. There are 20 RV and tent sites, with low-amp electrical hookups and potable water. Essentially a level sandy area behind the main building, the campground even has room for lengthy rigs (up to 40 feet/12.2 meters long), though slow, careful driving is still advisable. In fact, tools such as shovels, boards, and rope might be necessary for dislodging wheels from the soft sand that abounds here. The only amenities available include a dump station, restrooms with flush toilets and hot showers, access to the beach, and some scattered palm trees, providing limited shade. There is no laundry on the premises, and the management is fairly informal here. Children and pets are welcome. Given the lack of official security, it's probably best to park here in pairs or groups. Groceries, purified water, gasoline, and other supplies can be purchased in nearby La Paz. Remember to pack out all trash when you leave.

Reservations, fees: Reservations are not accepted; spaces are available on a first-come, first-served basis. The cost for overnight camping is inexpensive—$5–10 per night. Credit cards are not accepted; cash (Mexican pesos or U.S. dollars) is the only acceptable form of payment. The operating months are October–April, when the campground is filled with windsurfers and kiteboarders.

Directions: From La Paz, take the paved Highway 286 southeast toward the farming country around San Juán de los Planes. After 23.2 miles (37.3 km), you'll reach the turnoff for La Ventana. Turn left (north) at the T junction and drive north for about 4.4 miles (7.1 km). Near the entrance of La Ventana, look for YoYo's gate on the right, just south of the La Ventana Campground.

Contact: Although there's no mailing address or website for YoYo's Campground, you can call "YoYo" at 612/114-0015 or 612/348-0004 (cell) for details. Just remember to dial "1" before the cell phone number. If you're unable to reach the manager by phone, feel free to drive down and see which spots are available. For more information about La Ventana, visit www.bestoflaventana.com.

18 LA VENTANA CAMPGROUND

Scenic Rating: 7

in La Ventana

See map page 208

The breezy, southeastern neighbor of La Paz, La Ventana (which merges with El Sargento and El Teso to the north to become one town) is chiefly known among the windsurfing set, and the town's main campground is located on the key beach for windsurfers, beside the kiteboard beginners' launch area. Although the bay is gorgeous, the sand is soft, the swaying palm trees are restful, and the distant Isla Cerralvo serves as a majestic backdrop, the campground itself is pretty simple. Despite its proximity to the beach and the lovely Bahía de la Ventana, its roadside location also means a view of phone lines, lampposts, and asphalt—not to mention roadway noise.

The campground is only open during the winter season, when it's windier along the coast of La Ventana and more appealing to windsurfers and kiteboarders. Although the setting is lovely, travelers not interested in these sports might find the constant breeze a bit unbearable.

Still, some do come just to swim here and launch small fishing boats over the sand. If, during the popular winter season, the beach gets a bit crowded, there are two brush-covered *arroyos* north of this campground, where the services are scarce but the cost is free.

If you're looking for resort-style accommodations in the La Ventana area, you might consider renting a *casita* at Palapas Ventana, located between the villages of El Sargento and La Ventana. Surrounded by a wide array of desert flora and overlooking the Isla Cerralvo in the Sea of Cortez, these thatched-roof *palapas* offer year-round access to the ocean. Included in the price are meals in the on-site restaurant as well as the use of kayaks, sailboats, and snorkeling gear. In addition, there is an Internet café on the premises, and the staff offers diving instruction, kayak excursions, Spanish and cooking lessons, and tours to La Paz, Todos Santos, and other destinations in the Cape Region. Windsurfing, spear fishing, bird-watching, hiking, and beachcombing are other popular diversions here.

RV sites, facilities: The fenced, primitive lot offers plenty of camping space, but no utility hookups. RVs are welcome, though tents and vans seem to dominate; the space can accommodate 50–70 vehicles. Basically a large, flat sandy area adjoining the beach, the campground allows you to park not 20 feet (6.1 meters) from the water. Lengthy rigs (up to 40 feet/12.2 meters long) will probably have no trouble fitting somewhere, but slow, careful driving is advisable. In fact, tools such as shovels, boards, and rope might be necessary, for dislodging wheels that get stuck in the soft sand that abounds here. The only amenities available include restrooms, water faucets, cold showers, and some scattered palm and mesquite trees, providing limited shade. A store and restaurant sit across the street. Only self-contained RVs and rugged tent campers should park here, preferably in pairs or groups, as there's no drinking water, dump station, electricity, laundry, or security available. Children and pets are welcome here, though the terrain is unsuitable for wheelchairs. Groceries, purified water, gasoline, and other supplies can be purchased in nearby La Paz. Remember to pack out all trash when you leave.

Reservations, fees: Reservations are not accepted; spaces are available on a first-come, first-served basis. The cost for overnight camping is low: $8 per day for beachfront spots, $7 per day for other sites. Credit cards are not accepted; cash (Mexican pesos or U.S. dollars) is the only acceptable form of payment. The operating months are October–April, when the campground is filled with windsurfers and kiteboarders.

Directions: From La Paz, take the paved Highway 286 southeast toward the farming country around San Juán de los Planes. After 23.2 miles (37.3 km), you'll reach the turnoff for La Ventana. Turn left (north) at the T junction and drive north for about 5 miles (8 km). In La Ventana, look for the main campground and its chain-link fence on the right.

Contact: Since there's no campground manager, mailing address, or phone number for the La Ventana Campground, it's best just to drive down and see which spots are available. For details about the La Ventana area, visit www.bestoflaventana.com. For more information about Palapas Ventana, call 612/114-0198 or visit www.palapasventana.com.

19 KURT-N-MARINA

Scenic Rating: 9

in La Ventana

See map page 208 **BEST**

Regarded as one of the best windsurfing and kiteboarding locations in the world, the small Mexican fishing village of La Ventana has three beachfront campgrounds that cater to pursuers of such sports, including this relaxing spot. Situated southeast of La Paz, beside the turquoise waters of Bahía de la Ventana and within view of Isla Cerralvo, Kurt-n-Marina (named after the owners) definitely benefits from its location, a consistently windy place in season, from November to March. Besides the constant breezes, recreationists will encounter perfect temperatures, incredible vistas, riveting sunrises, and fiery sunsets—pleasing amenities for those who hope to swim or snorkel in the surf, take a boat ride in the bay, fish for dinner, hike or bike into the rugged hills, comb the beach for intriguing finds, watch soaring pelicans and other wildlife, relax in the nearby hot springs, or soak up the sunshine.

Although most travelers come here during the windy season, what many RVers don't know is that, from April to June (the off-season), La Ventana is a peaceful place, with fabulously mild weather. It's then that Kurt-n-Marina becomes a true paradise, especially for those who'd prefer smaller crowds.

RV sites, facilities: Only eight back-in RV sites are available, all with full hookups, benches, and space for lengthy rigs (up to 40 feet/12.2 meters long). In addition, you'll find lovely new *casitas,* with vivid decor, open-air patios, and blossoming foliage. Amenities include a centrally located bathroom with hot showers; a fish-cleaning station; windsurfing equipment; Internet access; and a communal kitchen beneath a huge *palapa,* equipped with a stove, sinks and barbecue grills, prep tables and fridges, and a brick oven. Children and pets are welcome here, and the staff is bilingual. The park is very secure, fenced-in and guarded by a guest-friendly watchdog named Sandy. There are no age restrictions for RVs and no special concessions made for visitors with disabilities. There's no laundry or dump station on the premises, and tent camping is no longer allowed.

Reservations, fees: Reservations are not accepted. Full-hookup RV spaces cost $15 per day, and guest rooms cost $55 nightly. Credit cards are not accepted; cash (Mexican pesos or U.S. dollars) is the only acceptable form of payment. The park is open all year.

Directions: From La Paz, take paved Highway 286 southeast for 23.2 miles (37.3 km), to the turnoff for La Ventana. At the bottom of a steep grade, you'll encounter a T junction. Turn left (north) onto the road marked "La Ventana, El Sargento" and drive north about 5 miles (8 km). In La Ventana, you'll see a pink house on the left and, farther north, a school on the right. Turn right onto this dirt road and head toward the water. Look for Kurt-n-Marina on the left side of the *arroyo.*

Contact: Kurt-n-Marina, Apartado Postal #308, Colonia Centro, La Paz, Baja California Sur, C.P. 23000, Mexico, tel. 612/114-0010 or 509/590-1409 (U.S.), www.kurtnmarina.com or www.ventanakiteboarding.com.

THE CAPE REGION

BEST RV PARKS AND CAMPGROUNDS

Even if you've never been to Baja before, you've probably heard of Cabo San Lucas – once a sleepy fishing town and now one of the peninsula's most visited cities. Most tourists see Cabo, situated within the Cape Region of Baja Sur, in one of two ways: after flying into the Los Cabos International Airport or disembarking from a cruise ship. RV enthusiasts might find the hectic, sun-kissed resort town a culture shock after experiencing miles of pristine deserts and secluded lagoons. But, if you've already come as far as La Paz, then Los Cabos (The Capes) – which includes Cabo San Lucas and San José del Cabo – is certainly worth a look.

From La Paz, you can take *la curva del sur* (the southern loop) around the Cape Region. Just south of San Pedro, along the western fringe of the Sierra de la Laguna, the main thoroughfare divides into two highways (19 and 1), which both cross the Tropic of Cancer and converge in Cabo San Lucas.

On the western side, Highway 19 leads past a 30-mile (48-km) stretch of *ranchos* to Todos Santos – a tranquil artists' colony, full of art galleries, crafts stores, and hidden gardens. Often called the "Pueblo Mágico" of Baja Sur, Todos Santos was founded in 1723 as a mission but, due to its warm climate and dependable spring, eventually became the heart of a thriving *caña de azúcar* (sugarcane) industry that fizzled in the 1950s. Tourists began discovering the area in the early 1980s, when the highway was finally paved.

Surrounded by lush groves of mango, papaya, avocado, and palm trees, Todos Santos offers numerous cultural and recreational pursuits. History buffs can stroll amid restored colonial-style buildings or view the ruins of several sugarcane mills. Culture lovers will appreciate the annual art festival, which highlights folk dancing and turtle conservation as much as Mexican artwork. Anglers can board a *panga* at Punta Lobos (Sea Lions' Point) and endure the choppy surf for a chance at snagging marlin and swordfish, while surfers can flock to the waves near El Pescadero (The Fishmonger).

South of Todos Santos, the highway traces the coast for nearly 50 miles (80 km) to Los Cabos itself – a well-developed area, rife with gorgeous hotels, exquisite restaurants, and world-class golf courses. In Cabo

San Lucas, you can board deep-sea fishing charters, watch lounging sea lions, tour the intriguing glass factory, and sip margaritas at Sammy Hagar's Cabo Wabo Cantina.

From here, Highway 1 heads east toward the more subdued San José del Cabo. This coastal stretch, called the Cabo Corridor, contains some of the peninsula's most popular beaches, known for sunbathing, surfing, and dramatic rock formations. Near Cabo San Lucas, swimmers appreciate the protected waters of Playa del Amor (Love Beach), on the eastern side of Finisterra (Land's End) and accessible by kayak or glass-bottom boat. Scuba divers favor the nearby sites, including a submerged shipwreck near El Punto and an underwater canyon of spectacular sandfalls. Around San José del Cabo lie several swimming beaches, plus a freshwater estuary that supports a variety of native flora and fauna.

Most RVers then take Highway 1 north – past the Picacho de San Lázaro and the Santiago Zoo – to Los Barriles on El Cabo Este (The East Cape), popular with anglers and windsurfers. More daring travelers, however, can follow the coastal road to La Ribera (The Shore), between the Sierra de la Trinidad and the Sea of Cortez. The seaside villages of Los Frailes and Cabo Pulmo offer some of Baja's best diving, surf fishing, and boondocking. The 17,300-acre (7,000-hectare) Parque Marino Nacional Cabo Pulmo is in fact home to one of the only coral reefs along the entire west coast of North and South America. Expert operators lead snorkelers down to these rocky reefs, which sustain vibrant fish species that can be found nowhere else in the world.

To complete the southern loop, head northwest from Los Barriles, through the towns of San Antonio, with its photogenic church, and El Triunfo, celebrated for its *artesanos de cestería* (basket makers). Soon afterward, you'll reach the Highway 19 junction, north of which lies the road to La Paz.

In the Cape Region, development has sadly overtaken several RV parks in the last few years, but some welcoming accommodations still exist, from dusty inland campgrounds in Todos Santos to resplendent hilltop parks in Los Cabos, to free, wide-open beaches between La Ribera and Cabo Pulmo. As always, your choice depends upon your interests, needs, and budget. Just be careful if you opt for primitive camping; in unsecured locations, it's always best to camp with others – and keep an eye on your belongings.

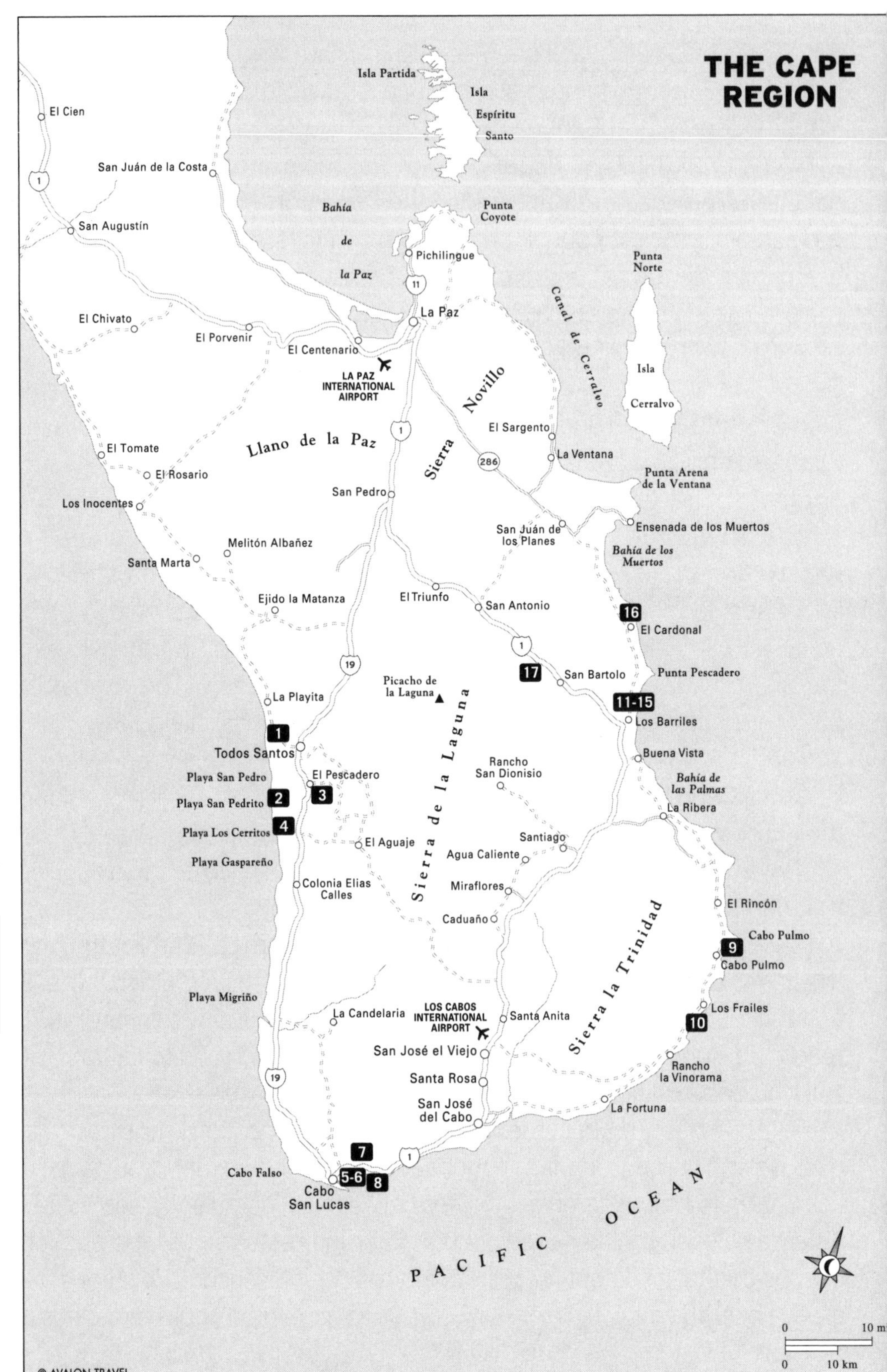
THE CAPE REGION
Isla Partida
Isla Espíritu Santo
El Cien
San Juán de la Costa
Bahía de la Paz
Punta Coyote
San Augustín
Pichilingue
Punta Norte
Canal de Cerralvo
La Paz
El Chivato
El Porvenir
El Centenario
LA PAZ INTERNATIONAL AIRPORT
Sierra Novillo
Isla Cerralvo
El Sargento
Llano de la Paz
El Tomate
La Ventana
El Rosario
Punta Arena de la Ventana
San Pedro
Los Inocentes
San Juán de los Planes
Ensenada de los Muertos
Melitón Albañez
Bahía de los Muertos
Santa Marta
Ejido la Matanza
El Triunfo
San Antonio
El Cardonal
San Bartolo
Punta Pescadero
Picacho de la Laguna
La Playita
Los Barriles
Todos Santos
Buena Vista
Playa San Pedro
El Pescadero
Rancho San Dionisio
Bahía de las Palmas
Playa San Pedrito
Sierra de la Laguna
La Ribera
Playa Los Cerritos
El Aguaje
Santiago
Agua Caliente
Playa Gaspareño
Colonia Elias Calles
Miraflores
El Rincón
Caduaño
Sierra la Trinidad
Cabo Pulmo
Playa Migriño
Los Frailes
La Candelaria
LOS CABOS INTERNATIONAL AIRPORT
Santa Anita
San José el Viejo
Rancho la Vinorama
Santa Rosa
San José del Cabo
La Fortuna
Cabo Falso
Cabo San Lucas
PACIFIC OCEAN
0 10 mi
0 10 km
© AVALON TRAVEL

1 EL LITRO TRAILER PARK

Scenic Rating: 4

in Todos Santos

See map page 232 **BEST**

As the only travel-oriented RV park left in the entire village of Todos Santos, this small campground certainly has a practical appeal, but there's little else to its advantage. Situated on a dusty back road at the southwestern end of town, the park has a tight (though passable) entrance. Once inside, you might be able to maneuver RVs longer than 30 feet (9.1 meters), but few travelers have attempted such a challenge.

Yet, what this simple spot lacks in amenities, it definitely compensates for in location, considering that it's positioned within walking distance of historic Todos Santos. Having become in recent years an artists' and writers' retreat, this small Mexican village, just south of the Trópico de Cáncer, still has the air of its colonial days, when *caña de azúcar* (sugarcane) ruled the local economy. In fact, curious travelers can tour the ruins of a few old mills. Also nearby are several fine art galleries, live music venues, boutiques, and restaurants. From October to May, you'll even find advertisements for a variety of classes, from cooking to yoga to drumming.

About a mile (1.6 km) from the Pacific Ocean, Todos Santos is a terrific base for those interested in surfing. Whether novice or pro, you'll find the waves to suit your desire and experience. For instance, Playa Las Pocitas, north of town, has a fairly strong undertow, favored by practiced surfers, while Playa Los Cerritos, south of Todos Santos, has gentler waves and a sandy bottom, better for swimmers and surfing beginners. For inexperienced surfers and sea kayakers, La Sirena (an eco-adventure outfitter based in Todos Santos) offers kayaking tours, snorkeling trips, and surfing instruction—in addition to whale-watching excursions, waterfall hikes, fishing packages, and lessons in sea turtle conservation.

As a bonus, anglers might enjoy watching the local *pangueros* negotiate the waters along Playa Punta Lobos. By early afternoon, they've usually returned with the day's catch, which might include marlin, swordfish, yellowtail, wahoo, dorado, even shark.

RV sites, facilities: There are 15 back-in spaces, each with 15-amp electricity, water service, and sewage drains, plus a few smaller RV sites, with only electrical hookups. Several spaces have patios, and some are shaded by *palapas*. There's also a shaded tent-camping area. The restrooms are simple, with flush toilets and hot showers. There's no dump station, laundry, or security gate, though an on-site manager is present 24 hours daily. Children and leashed pets are welcome, but the facilities are not designed for wheelchairs. Given that no supplies are available within the park, you'll need to pick up groceries, purified water, and other necessities in Todos Santos, where you'll find several convenient stores, in addition to a bank, post office, pharmacy, clinic, and police station.

Reservations, fees: Reservations are not accepted; spaces are available on a first-come, first-served basis. Since space is limited, it's advisable to get here early in the day. RV spaces cost $13 per night, and tent sites are available for $7 per night. Long-term rates are also available. Credit cards are not accepted; cash (Mexican pesos or U.S. dollars) is the only acceptable form of payment. The park is open all year.

Directions: From north of Todos Santos, head south on Highway 19 (which becomes Benito Juárez), take a sharp left (southeast) turn onto Avenida Santos Degollado (a continuation of Highway 19), and turn right (southwest) onto Calle Raúl A. Carrillo. From south of Todos Santos, head northwest on Highway 19 and turn left onto Calle Raúl A. Carrillo. The campground lies directly ahead, four blocks from the turn, at the intersection of Carrillo and Punta Abreojos—just east of the town's baseball stadium.

Contact: El Litro Trailer Park, Calle Raúl A. Carrillo, Todos Santos, Baja California Sur, C.P. 23305, Mexico, tel. 612/125-0121. For more information about La Sirena Kayak y Surf Aventuras, visit www.lasirenakayaksurf.com.

2 PLAYA SAN PEDRITO

Scenic Rating: 8

west of El Pescadero

See map page 232 BEST

For years, San Pedrito RV Park was a popular draw for surfers. The beachside property offered full hookup spaces, a swimming pool, a restaurant, and other amenities. When a 2003 hurricane damaged most of the buildings and flooded the roads, however, the park remained closed, until it was put up for sale in 2006, pending redevelopment.

Despite the park's closure, access to this lovely beach is still available, and many RV travelers and tent campers utilize it for sunbathing, hiking, mountain biking, surfing, sea kayaking, watching migratory whales in the winter months, and sleeping beneath the stars. Swimming is a frequent activity, too—though care must be taken at all times. The undertow and riptides are strong in this part of the Pacific Ocean, and there are no lifeguards on duty. In addition, the rocks that pepper the beach and distinguish the landscape can be nuisances for waders and swimmers; take care where you're stepping at all times. With caution, anglers can launch small boats from the shore.

Although RVers relish the tranquil environs, tent campers usually find it easier to park here. There's plenty of space for rigs longer than 30 feet (9.1 meters), but before heading in with a large motor home or unwieldy travel trailer, you should walk onto the beach to see if you'll fit. Travelers will find it easier to negotiate the road and sand with smaller rigs. No matter the size of your vehicle, take care when parking on the beach; be sure to have ropes, boards, and shovels handy in case your wheels get stuck.

Besides the glorious sunsets, another great aspect of this boondocking site is its proximity to other picturesque beaches, via Highway 19. Near Km 58, for instance, Playa San Pedro offers a gorgeous, relatively isolated beach, bordered by a lagoon, a grove of palm trees, and the ruins of an old sugarcane *rancho*—an excellent area for hiking and body surfing. Farther northwest, at Km 54, lies Playa Punta Lobos, the closest beach to Todos Santos, favored by local anglers. With its smooth sand and dramatic cliffs, Punta Lobos presents the perfect spot for enjoying a sunset, hiking beside a freshwater lagoon, exploring the ruins of a deserted cannery, and photographing playful sea lions.

As a note of caution, primitive camping areas throughout Baja have been closing at an alarming rate, mostly due to real-estate development and privatization plans. So, be sure to check with local residents before pulling onto Playa San Pedrito for the night, as it could be closed to the public at any time.

RV sites, facilities: There are no designated RV sites here—you can park wherever there's room. Besides the sun, sand, rocks, and sea, however, there's nothing in the way of amenities, not even pit toilets or trash barrels. Only self-contained RVs and rugged tent campers should park here, preferably in pairs or groups, as there's no drinking water, dump station, electricity, shower house, laundry, or security. Children and pets are welcome, but the terrain is not suitable for wheelchairs. In fact, it's advisable to bring your own shovels, boards, and rope, just in case your wheels get stuck in the sand. Groceries and other supplies can be purchased in nearby El Pescadero; of course, you'll find a greater selection in Todos Santos, to the north. Remember to pack out all trash when you leave.

Reservations, fees: Reservations are not accepted; spaces are available on a first-come, first-served basis. The fee for camping in this primitive area is roughly $5 per night. Although you might not find anyone to collect the fee, you should have it ready just in case. Credit cards are not accepted; cash (Mexican pesos or U.S. dollars) is the only acceptable form of payment. The beach is open all year.

Directions: From Todos Santos, drive 4.5 miles (7.2 km) southeast on Highway 19 to Km 59. Turn right (west) at the sign that marks the former San Pedrito RV Park. From El Pescadero, drive northwest on Highway 19 for 2 miles (3.2

km) to the turnoff for Playa San Pedrito; turn left (west) onto this access road and drive 1.9 miles (3.1 km) toward the ocean.

Contact: Since there's no official contact person, mailing address, or phone number for Playa San Pedrito, it's best just to drive down and see which areas are available on the beach. For details about the Todos Santos area, visit www.todossantos.cc or www.todossantos.com.

3 BAJA SERENA RV PARK

Scenic Rating: 3

in El Pescadero

See map page 232

Intimate and relatively new, this is the only RV park in the small farming town of El Pescadero, 6.5 miles (10.5 km) southeast of Todos Santos. The park is conveniently positioned beside a modest grocery store, the proprietors of which (Mayra and Dr. Hector Flores) also own the campground.

While the *playa* is the main attraction in this part of Baja California Sur, the town of El Pescadero has a laid-back charm of its own. Like an oasis in the *desierto,* the small *pueblo* is sandwiched between the Sierra de la Laguna to the east and the Pacific Ocean to the west. The temperature is mild year-round; ocean breezes keep this area cooler than other parts of the peninsula.

In the surrounding farmland, fields of basil leaves and cherry tomatoes are common sights, and while most of these crops are exported to gourmet markets in the United States, some of them find their way to roadside produce stands. You'll also find stores, restaurants, and bars in the center of town.

Of course, given the town's name (which literally means "The Fishmonger" in Spanish), it can come as little surprise that the Pacific Ocean lies only 1.3 miles (2.1 km) to the west. Besides hiking, beachcombing, bird-watching, swimming, kayaking, and other seaside diversions, this part of Baja's southern coast is popular among anglers—with or without a boat of their own.

RV sites, facilities: There are eight sandy back-in spaces, separated by small plants. Water and sewage hookups are available, but there is no electricity. Each spot can accommodate RVs up to 40 feet (12.2 meters) in length. Clean restrooms and hot showers are provided, but there is no dump station, laundry facility, or official security. Staff members speak both Spanish and English. Children and pets are welcome, though the facilities were not designed with wheelchairs in mind. Groceries and other supplies are available in the adjacent store; of course, you'll find a greater selection in Todos Santos, to the north.

Reservations, fees: Reservations are recommended; space is limited, so make your plans as early as possible. Sites for RVs and tents cost $11 per night. Long-term rates are also available. Credit cards are not accepted; cash (Mexican pesos or U.S. dollars) is the only acceptable form of payment. The park is open all year.

Directions: From Todos Santos, drive 6.5 miles (10.5 km) southeast on Highway 19 to Km 63. You'll notice a Pemex fueling station on the right (west) side. The campground, which has a well-marked sign, is beside a mini-supermarket (the Los Arcos) on the left (east) side—along the northern edge of El Pescadero.

Contact: Baja Serena RV Park, Carretera Transpeninsular (Highway 19), Colonia Única, El Pescadero, Baja California Sur, C.P. 23300, Mexico, tel. 612/130-3006, mayra_pithaya@yahoo.com.mx.

4 PLAYA LOS CERRITOS

Scenic Rating: 10

south of El Pescadero

See map page 232 **BEST**

Ringed by stark foothills, rocky formations, and occasional palm trees, Santa Lucia de los Cerritos—a 5-mile (8-km) expanse south of El Pescadero—is one of the most stunning, pristine beaches in all of Baja. With its gentle waves and sandy bottom, it's also one of the safest stretches for swimmers. Surfers, beginners and experts alike, have been enjoying the constant swells here for years. It's appropriate then that the Pescadero Surf Camp, which offers surfing instruction, group "surfaris," a swimming pool, and furnished *casitas,* is just north of here at Km 64.

Although the former Los Cerritos RV Park is no longer open, and is now being developed for permanent housing, that hasn't stopped tent and RV enthusiasts from camping on this beautiful beach. While here, travelers can take long strolls along the crescent-shaped coast, wade across the turquoise waters, comb the golden sand for seashells, enjoy the cool breezes and romantic sunsets, or watch for passing *ballenas gris* (gray whales) in the winter months. Other activities include surf fishing, mountain biking, sunbathing, bird-watching, hiking in the adjacent *desierto,* and relaxing at the nearby restaurant and bar.

RVers relish the tranquil environs, though tent campers usually find it easier to park here. There's plenty of space for rigs longer than 30 feet (9.1 meters), but before heading in with a large motor home or unwieldy travel trailer, you should walk onto the beach to see if you'll fit. Travelers will find it easier to negotiate the soft sand with smaller rigs. No matter the size of your vehicle, however, you should take care when parking on the beach. Be sure to have ropes, boards, and shovels handy in case your wheels get stuck. Also remember that, though you might be able to park on the beach, driving along the coast is not allowed.

As with many primitive camping areas along the Baja peninsula, Playa Los Cerritos may not remain open to RV enthusiasts for long. If in doubt about its status, consult the residents of Todos Santos or El Pescadero before pulling onto the beach for the night.

RV sites, facilities: There are no designated RV sites here—you can park wherever there's room. Besides the spectacular landscape, however, there's little in the way of amenities—just pit toilets, in fact. Only self-contained RVs and rugged tent campers should park here, preferably in pairs or groups, as there's no drinking water, dump station, electricity, shower house, laundry, or security. Children and pets are welcome, but the sandy terrain is not suitable for wheelchairs. Groceries, purified water, fuel, and other supplies, from sunblock to film, should be obtained in Todos Santos; limited goods are available in El Pescadero. Remember to pack out all trash when you leave.

Reservations, fees: Reservations are not accepted; spaces are available on a first-come, first-served basis. The fee for camping in this primitive area is roughly $5 per night. Although you might not find anyone to collect the fee, you should have it ready just in case. Credit cards are not accepted; cash (Mexican pesos or U.S. dollars) is the only acceptable form of payment. The beach is open all year.

Directions: From Todos Santos, drive about 7.8 miles (12.6 km) south on Highway 19 to Km 65, south of El Pescadero. Turn right (west) onto the gravel access road beside the highway. Drive 1.2 miles (1.9 km) toward the ocean, bypassing the now-defunct Los Cerritos RV Park.

Contact: Since there's no official contact person, mailing address, or phone number for Playa Los Cerritos, it's best just to drive down and see which areas are available on the beach. For details about the Todos Santos area, visit www.todossantos.cc or www.todossantos.com. For information about surfing lessons, rentals, and supplies at the nearby Pescadero Surf Camp, visit www.pescaderosurf.com.

5 CLUB CABO INN AND CAMP CABO

Scenic Rating: 7

east of Cabo San Lucas

See map page 232 **BEST**

Situated just east of downtown Cabo San Lucas, this pleasant, European-style park offers a

El Arco in Cabo San Lucas

peaceful, secluded setting within a bird-filled mesquite forest. Here, you'll awaken to the colorful sights and musical sounds of orioles, cardinals, morning doves, hummingbirds, warblers, woodpeckers, sea eagles, and snowy egrets. Exotic banana, mango, and coconut trees pepper the property, as do vibrant roses, bougainvillea, and hibiscus.

Operated by Dutch owners Irene and Martin Rozendaal since 1992, this lovely campground sits away from the beaten path and only a short stroll from the main swimming beach, Playa El Médano (The Dune Beach). Several other *playas* are within driving distance, offering secluded coves and excellent spots for sunbathing, beachcombing, hiking, snorkeling, scuba diving, surf fishing, boating, bird-watching, whale-watching, and kayaking. For those who fantasize about riding horses in Los Cabos, there are several stables between Cabo San Lucas and San José del Cabo, including the family-operated Cuadra San Francisco.

The Rozendaals are happy to arrange scooter and all-terrain-vehicle rentals, eco-conscious kayaking tours, guided snorkeling tours, sportfishing charters, and parasailing adventures. If surfing is your game (or you've always wanted to try it), the friendly owners can also advise you about the area's best surfing spots, including Playa Cabo Bello (Beautiful Cape Beach), Playa Buenos Aires (Good Air Beach), and Playa Costa Azul (Blue Coast Beach), among others. You can even rent a surfboard from nearby shops.

The location of this park is ideal, close to outdoor pleasures as well as the town itself. Not far from the marina, anglers can choose from several world-class sportfishing charters, including the Pisces Fleet, known for its consistent catch rates since 1980. Beyond the marina lies Baja's southernmost peninsula, at the end of which stands El Arco, a frequently photographed formation, and surrounding the peninsula are several popular scuba-diving spots. Visitors to Camp Cabo will also find a wide variety of restaurants and shops, from Señor

Greenberg's Mexicatessen and the El Faro Viejo Trailer Park (a favorite restaurant and long-term RV park) to the Golden Cactus Gallery. In addition, there's no end to the amusements available when the sun goes down, including live concerts at Sammy Hagar's Cabo Wabo Cantina, table-dancing at El Squid Roe, the "seafood orgy" at the Giggling Marlin Bar and Grill, and a Caribbean-style discotheque called the MamboCafé.

Another winning distraction is La Fábrica de Vidrio Soplado (The Blown Glass Factory), where recycled glass is used to make gorgeous vases, plates, bowls, and figurines. Most local tour agencies offer escorted visits with a bilingual guide, or you can explore the factory and on-site store on your own. Before midafternoon every day, the *taller* (shop) hums with activity; feel free to watch the artisans at work.

RV sites, facilities: There are 12 back-in campsites, half of which have full hookups, with water, sewage, and 15-amp electricity. The spaces are not made for large RVs; in fact, 25-foot (7.6-meter) motor homes are the longest that can easily maneuver within the park. Trees provide limited shade. Amenities include *palapas,* hammocks, tables, barbecues, a coin laundry, a trampoline, a swimming pool, a hot tub, a restaurant offering fresh International breakfasts, air-conditioned hotel suites and bungalows, and clean restrooms with flush toilets and hot showers. A shaded outdoor lounge contains a color television, barbecue grill, and clean-up station.

The walled, gated park is secured with motion-detecting floodlights, a chain across the entrance, and 24-hour security; in addition, the owners live on-site. Wireless Internet access and bilingual employees are also available, but there's no dump station or camp store in the park. Tent campers, children, and friendly leashed pets are welcome. The communal facilities are wheelchair-accessible. Groceries and supplies can be obtained in nearby Cabo San Lucas, and purified water is available on the premises (since the tap water isn't safe to drink).

Reservations, fees: Reservations are recommended; spaces must be prepaid during the high season. Full refunds, however, are only possible 30 days prior to the intended date of arrival. RV sites cost $25 per night, while tent spaces are $20 daily. All rates are based on double occupancy. Long-term rates are also available. Use of the pool and spa costs a little extra. Hotel suites and *cabañas* cost $55–95 daily. Credit cards are not accepted; cash (Mexican pesos or U.S. dollars) is the only acceptable form of payment. The park is open all year.

Directions: Club Cabo Inn is behind Vagabundos del Mar Trailer Park. From the junction of Highway 1 and Highway 19, 2 miles (3.2 km) east of downtown Cabo San Lucas, drive south 0.3 mile (0.5 km) on the unmarked street toward Club Cascadas, following the signs to Club Cabo. Turn left (east) onto the sandy road paralleling the beach and drive 0.2 mile (0.3 km) to a Y junction. Head straight to reach Club Cabo, 0.6 mile (1 km) down the dusty road. The RV park is on your left, northeast of the Villa del Palmar Beach Resort.

Contact: Club Cabo Inn and Camp Cabo, Apartado Postal #463, Cabo San Lucas, Baja California Sur, C.P. 23410, Mexico, tel./fax 624/143-3348, www.clubcaboinn.com. For details about Cuadra San Francisco, visit www.loscaboshorses.com. For more information about deep-sea fishing charters, contact Pisces Fleet Sportfishing, Cabo Maritime Center Marina 8-6, Suite #D-1, Cabo San Lucas, Baja California Sur, C.P. 23410, Mexico, tel. 624/143-1288, 624/143-9488, or 619/819-7983 (U.S.), www.piscessportfishing.com. For details about the El Faro Viejo Trailer Park, call 624/143-4211. For more information about other area attractions, visit the following websites: www.goldencactusgallery.com (Golden Cactus Gallery), www.cabowabo.com (Cabo Wabo Cantina), www.elsquidroe.com (El Squid Roe), www.gigglingmarlin.com (The Giggling Marlin), www.mambocafe.com.mx (MamboCafé), and www.glassfactorycabo.com (The Blown Glass Factory).

6 VAGABUNDOS DEL MAR TRAILER PARK

Scenic Rating: 8

east of Cabo San Lucas

See map page 232 **BEST**

Owned by José Arballo, a native of Baja's Cape Region, this park is one of the most attractive and well-maintained campgrounds on the entire peninsula. While there's no ocean view here, palm and mesquite trees provide natural beauty and refreshing shade. Despite the fact that Vagabundos del Mar isn't on the beach, the location is divine, close to downtown Cabo San Lucas and the launch ramps in the marina, so shoppers, partygoers, boaters, anglers, and swimmers will all find something to occupy their time. In addition, golfing enthusiasts will relish this spot, for several championship golf courses lie between Cabo San Lucas and San José del Cabo, including three Jack Nicklaus–designed courses at Cabo del Sol, Palmilla Golf Club, and El Dorado Golf & Beach Club. Equestrians won't be sorry either—a number of horse stables are available for those itching for a ride.

Los Cabos golf course

RV sites, facilities: There are 85 ample, gravel campsites, 30 of which are pull-throughs. All spaces have full hookups (water, sewage, and 15/30-amp electricity), concrete patio areas, shady trees, and picnic tables, and some spaces can accommodate lengthy motor homes (up to 40 feet/12.2 meters long). Many sites, especially along the outer edges of the park, are occupied by permanent RVs. Amenities include paved roadways, a coin laundry with new washers and dryers, a large heated swimming pool, a festive restaurant and bar, a meeting *palapa,* vehicle-washing facilities, a boat storage area, and clean, modern restrooms with flush toilets and hot showers.

A pay phone, wireless Internet service (for campsites near the office), bilingual staff members, and purified drinking water and ice are also available. Tent campers, children, and leashed pets are welcome, but the facilities are not suitable for wheelchairs. In addition, the tap water isn't safe to drink. The park is secured with a gate and 24-hour guard service; the manager lives on the premises. There's no dump station on-site. You'll have to obtain groceries and supplies in Cabo San Lucas, as there's no store in the park, but luckily the bus, which runs from one end of Los Cabos to the other, stops right out front, and taxis are always available.

Reservations, fees: Reservations are recommended; the required 25 percent deposit is refundable if the cancellation is made 30 days prior to arrival. RV and tent sites cost $22 per night, $130 per week, $530 per month, and $3,990–6,000 per year. The rates are based on a two-person occupancy; each additional guest will be charged $5 per day. Cash (Mexican pesos or U.S. dollars) and major credit cards are accepted. The park is open all year.

Directions: From Cabo San Lucas, head 1 mile (1.6 km) east on Highway 1. The park is at the Km 3 marker, on the south side of the road. It's only accessible from a lateral road, so eastbound vehicles (from Cabo San Lucas) should exit onto the eastbound lateral as soon as possible and turn right (south) into the park. Westbound vehicles (from San José del Cabo) will have to travel farther west and find a place to turn around in order to reach the eastbound lateral.

Contact: Vagabundos del Mar Trailer Park, Apartado Postal #197, Cabo San Lucas, Baja California Sur, C.P. 23410, Mexico, tel. 624/143-0290 or 800/474-2252 (U.S.), fax 624/143-0511, www.vagabundosrv.com. For more information about golf courses in the Los Cabos area, visit www.cabogolf.com.

7 EL ARCO RV PARK

Scenic Rating: 8

east of Cabo San Lucas

See map page 232

Overnight travelers relish the convenience of this large park, located on a scenic hillside just a few miles from the heart of Cabo San Lucas. Even more enticing, however, is the view. From here, you're guaranteed a spectacular look at the harbor and the rugged landscape of Finisterra (Land's End).

Despite Cabo's status as a tourist town, there's a surprising assortment of activities at your fingertips. Restaurants, cantinas, nightclubs, and boutiques abound within the city limits, but most travelers come for the outdoor pastimes, such as parasailing, kayaking, horseback riding, whale-watching, and glass-bottom boating. Given the area's reputation for world-class fishing, anglers will find many capable sportfishing fleets in the vicinity. Divers and snorkelers relish this area, too—there are numerous underwater sites worth exploring, from the sunken shipwreck near Land's End to the sandfalls beneath landmarks like The Chimney and Neptune's Finger.

Over the years, the only negative aspects of this park have alternately been its frequent popularity and its ongoing management issues. At times, it's crowded with permanent residents, and at other times it has an air of abandonment, especially given its run-down office and lounge area and its inconsistent staff, members of which you can count on seeing for perhaps a few hours on most days. Sadly, San José del Cabo no longer has any parks welcome to overnight travelers, and even those in Cabo San Lucas are gradually giving way to permanent housing, such as condominiums and long-term trailer parks. So, relish old parks like this one while you can—and don't be surprised if you soon find it closed.

RV sites, facilities: There are 50 back-in campsites and 40 pull-throughs; all 90 of them have patios and full hookups, with 15-amp electricity, water service, and sewage access. Some are arranged around a semicircular brick driveway, and others are farther up the hill. These upper sites accommodate lengthy RVs (up to 40 feet/12.2 meters long). Facilities include a coin laundry, a swimming pool, a restaurant, a public pay phone, and modest restrooms with flush toilets and hot showers. There is, however, no dump station on the premises. Tent campers, children, and leashed pets are welcome, but the facilities are not suitable for wheelchairs. The park is secured with a chain across the entrance, and at times the presence of numerous people can certainly help. You'll have to obtain groceries, purified water, ice, and other supplies in Cabo San Lucas, as there's no store in the park.

Reservations, fees: Reservations are accepted. RV spaces, with full hookups, cost $15 per night, and tent sites cost $8 daily. Monthly and annual rates are also available. Credit cards are not accepted; cash (Mexican pesos or U.S. dollars) is the customary form of payment. The park is open all year.

Directions: The entrance road to the park is on the north side of Highway 1, 3.4 miles (5.5 km) east of Cabo San Lucas. Eastbound

© MEXICO TOURISM BOARD

the El Dorado Golf & Beach Club

traffic (from Cabo San Lucas) will have to enter the eastbound lateral, pass the Km 5 marker, cross four lanes of highway traffic, and reverse direction on the westbound lateral. The park entrance is on the right (north). Westbound traffic (from San José del Cabo) can just use the westbound lateral. The park is on a hill, overlooking the ocean and Land's End.

Contact: El Arco RV Park, Km 5.5 de la Carretera Transpeninsular a San José del Cabo, Cabo San Lucas, Baja California Sur, C.P. 23410, Mexico. Since there's no official phone number, it might be best to drive toward the beach and see which spots are available.

8 VILLA SERENA RV PARK

Scenic Rating: 8

east of Cabo San Lucas

See map page 232 **BEST**

Relatively new and roomy enough for lengthy RVs, this is the closest park to the Cabo Corridor, en route to historic San José del Cabo, which no longer has any RV campgrounds of its own. So, it's a good spot to be if you plan to explore both of the towns that compose Los Cabos. RV caravans and tent campers flock here, especially in the milder winter months. With its proximity to the highway, the place is often used as a home base for exploring the Cape Region, including the area's eight stellar golf courses, three of which (the 18-hole ocean course at Cabo del Sol, the 18-hole semiprivate course at the Palmilla Golf Club, and the 18-hole course at the El Dorado Golf & Beach Club) were designed by golfing legend Jack Nicklaus.

For those who haven't come for the greens, the park offers full-day fishing packages on 23-foot (7-meter) *pangas* and 36-foot (11-meter) cruisers through Gaviota Sportfishing. Several horse stables lies in this vicinity as well. In addition, there are *playas* galore in Cabo San Lucas, San José del Cabo, and all along the 18-mile (29-km) Cabo Corridor in between.

© MEXICO TOURISM BOARD

aerial view of Los Cabos

Sadly, some of these relaxing playgrounds have fallen prey to developers, and others tend to get crowded on sunny days, but there are still plenty worth experiencing.

Northwest of Cabo San Lucas, Playa Migriño is a nesting area for sea turtles, popular with surfers and campers. Closer to town, Playa del Amor (Love Beach) offers a romantic nook facing the Sea of Cortez, only accessible by kayak, water taxi, and glass-bottom boat. The safest, most popular swimming beach in Cabo San Lucas, Playa El Médano (The Dune Beach), stretches from the eastern side of the harbor to Villa del Palmar. Along the tourist corridor lies a world-famous surf break on Playa Costa Azul (Blue Coast Beach), and, in San José del Cabo, you'll find El Estero (The Marsh), a famed freshwater lagoon with lush foliage and over 350 species of wildlife.

RV sites, facilities: The 54 large back-in campsites have full hookups, with water, sewage, and 40-amp electricity. Be advised, however, that the electric outlets are of the 15-amp variety, so bring an adapter. There are small trees here, but they haven't yet grown large enough to provide any useful shade. Some of the upper sites, however, do offer an ocean view. The facilities include a coin laundry with new washers and dryers, a swimming pool and rooftop spa, a restaurant and bar, a lounge area, a covered patio with tables, and tiled restrooms with flush toilets and hot showers. No dump station is on the premises, though a security guard is on duty at night. Children, leashed pets, and tent campers are welcome, but the facilities are not suitable for wheelchairs. You'll have to obtain purified drinking water, ice, groceries, and other supplies in Cabo San Lucas, as there's no store in the park.

Reservations, fees: Reservations are accepted. The fees for RVs and tents, based on a two-person occupancy, are $21 per night, $112 per week, $391 per month, $1,120 for three months, and $1,984 per half-year. Each extra person costs $2 per night. Extended stays and permanent accommodations can be arranged.

Cash (Mexican pesos or U.S. dollars) and major credit cards are accepted. The park is open all year.

Directions: Located 4.5 miles (7.2 km) east of Cabo San Lucas, the park is positioned on a lateral road south of Highway 1, opposite the Home Depot on the north side. Eastbound traffic (from Cabo San Lucas) should enter the eastbound lateral and, past the Km 7 marker, turn right (south) onto the entrance road of Villa Serena RV Park. Westbound traffic (from San José del Cabo) should enter the westbound lateral, pass the Km 5 marker, cross four lanes of highway traffic, and reverse direction on the eastbound lateral toward the park entrance. The park is on a hill, with a distant view of the ocean.

Contact: Villa Serena RV Park, Km 7.5 de la Carretera Transpeninsular Benito Juárez, Cabo San Lucas, Baja California Sur, C.P. 23410, Mexico, tel. 408/776-1806 (U.S.) or 888/522-2442 (U.S.), fax 408/778-1513 (U.S.), www.grupobahia.com. For more information about golf courses in Los Cabos, visit www.cabogolf.com.

9 CABO PULMO CAMPGROUND

Scenic Rating: 9

between La Ribera and San José del Cabo

See map page 232 BEST

Located in the Cabo del Este (East Cape), between the small coastal communities of La Ribera and Los Frailes, Cabo Pulmo boasts one of the most popular beaches in this region, especially known for its diving attributes. The campground here is very basic, just a roomy fenced area beside the beach, within a picturesque cove. The space beside the road is mostly sand, but RVs, vans, and tents can park on a layer of gravel and shrubs overlooking the sea. The surface is flat, and there's enough space for large motor homes to maneuver, though you should watch out for soft spots. Supposedly, the owner's house is on a hill across the road, farther from the beach.

The Parque Marino Nacional Cabo Pulmo is one of the only living *arrecifes de coral* (coral reefs) along the western side of the American continents. Scuba divers and snorkelers swarm here to explore the *arrecifes* that extend offshore in the diverse Sea of Cortez. Colorful fish and other marine life dwell amid the submerged coral, situated within water that ranges in depth from 15 to 80 feet (4.6 to 24.4 meters). Several dive shops, as well as a few restaurants, populate the nearby town of Cabo Pulmo. Although diving is the main focus here, hikers, swimmers, kayakers, and anglers also find their way to Cabo Pulmo, and the ever-present breezes attract windsurfers, too.

RV sites, facilities: There are no designated campsites here—you can park wherever there's room. Besides the sun, sand, and sea, however, there are few amenities—just pit toilets, cold showers, trash barrels, a nearby restaurant, and enough room to accommodate lengthy motor homes and travel trailers (up to 40 feet/12.2 meters long). Only self-contained RVs and rugged tent campers should park here, preferably in pairs or groups, as there's no drinking water, dump station, electricity, laundry, or security. Children and leashed pets are welcome, but the sandy terrain is not suitable for wheelchairs. In fact, it would be wise to bring shovels, boards, and rope with you, in case your vehicle gets stuck in the sand. You'll have to purchase purified water, ice, groceries, fuel, and other supplies in Cabo Pulmo, La Ribera, Los Barriles, or San José del Cabo, as there's no store on the beach.

Reservations, fees: Reservations are not accepted; spaces are available on a first-come, first-served basis. Given the primitive nature of this campground, the daily fee is minimal—$5 per RV or tent. Credit cards are not accepted; cash (Mexican pesos or U.S. dollars) is the only acceptable form of payment. The beach is open all year.

Directions: From Los Barriles, head south on Highway 1 for 10.9 miles (17.5 km). In the town of Las Cuevas, turn left (east) onto the paved road at Km 93. Drive for 6.7 miles (10.8 km) until you reach another paved road, just prior to La Ribera on the coast. Turn right and head southeast for 16.9 miles (27.2 km) to Cabo Pulmo. Be aware that the road is paved for only the first 10.4 miles (16.7 km), after which it becomes a gravel route—passable in any vehicle, though rather bumpy and unpleasant for an RV. The campground will appear on your left, 6.5 miles (10.5 km) after leaving the paved road.

From San José del Cabo, head east on the coastal road and drive 40.5 miles (65.2 km) to Cabo Pulmo. Be advised, however, that the road will be longer and more uncomfortable from this direction.

Contact: For more information about Cabo Pulmo Campground, call 612/125-5583. If no one answers, simply drive down to the campground and see which spots are available.

10 LOS FRAILES CAMPGROUND

Scenic Rating: 8

between La Ribera and San José del Cabo

See map page 232

Travelers from the north seem to love this remote area of the East Cape, even those with long, unwieldy rigs. Even in the winter months, you'll spot dozens of RVs parked in a large area on a gravel *arroyo* outwash near the beach. The waters here are gorgeous—fun for swimming, windsurfing, kayaking, deep-sea fishing, snorkeling, diving, and other water-related activities. The sunrises and sunsets here are just as magnificent.

However, this terrain changes every year after the fall storm season, a potentially dangerous time to be on this flood-sensitive beach. So, care must be taken to avoid soft spots in the winter, spring, and summer months; perhaps you should walk the path first before choosing a site. Remember to bring chains, boards, shovels, and other helpful tools in case your wheels get stuck in the sand. In addition, be prepared to pack out any trash, and feel free to pick up debris that others have left behind.

RV sites, facilities: There are no designated campsites here—you can park wherever there's room. Besides the sun, sand, and sea, however, there's little in the way of amenities—just a well from which water can be drawn via bucket. Remember to treat the water before washing or cooking with it. The large, open space can accommodate lengthy motor homes and travel trailers (up to 45 feet/13.7 meters long). Only self-contained RVs and rugged tent campers should park here, preferably in pairs or groups, as there's no drinking water, dump station, electricity, laundry, restroom, or security. Children and leashed pets are welcome, but the terrain is not suitable for wheelchairs. You'll have to purchase purified water, ice, groceries, fuel, and other supplies in Cabo Pulmo, La Ribera, Los Barriles, or San José del Cabo, as there's no store on the beach.

Reservations, fees: Reservations are not accepted; spaces are available on a first-come, first-served basis. Given the primitive nature of this campground, the daily fee is minimal—$5 per RV or tent. Credit cards are not accepted; cash (Mexican pesos or U.S. dollars) is the only acceptable form of payment. The beach is open all year.

Directions: From Los Barriles, head south on Highway 1 for 10.9 miles (17.5 km). In the town of Las Cuevas, turn left (east) onto the paved road at Km 93. Drive for 6.7 miles (10.8 km) until you reach another paved road, just prior to La Ribera on the coast. Turn right and head southeast for 16.9 miles (27.2 km) to Cabo Pulmo. Be aware that the road is paved for only the first 10.4 miles (16.7 km), after which it becomes a gravel route—passable in any vehicle, though rather bumpy and unpleasant for an RV. After leaving the paved road, you'll reach Cabo Pulmo in 6.5 miles (10.5 km). Continue through town and drive another 4.8 miles (7.7 km) to the *arroyo* in Los Frailes. The RV parking area is on the left (east) side.

From San José del Cabo, head east on the coastal road and drive 35.7 miles (57.4 km) to

© MEXICO TOURISM BOARD

Kayakers enjoy the lush waterways of Los Cabos.

Los Frailes. However, the road is longer and more uncomfortable from this direction.

Contact: Since there's no official contact person, mailing address, or phone number for the Los Frailes Campground, it's best just to drive down and see which areas are available on the beach.

11 MARTIN VERDUGO'S BEACH RESORT

Scenic Rating: 9

in Los Barriles

See map page 232 **BEST**

Adjacent to the sparkling Sea of Cortez, this waterfront resort is halfway between the tranquil beaches of La Paz and the festive atmosphere of Cabo San Lucas. Part of a complex that includes two air-conditioned hotel buildings, this long-running RV park is just steps from Los Barriles's restaurants, shops, and beautiful sandy beaches. Owned and operated by the Verdugo family—who have lived in Los Barriles for five generations—the property possesses modern amenities while still retaining the charm of old Mexico.

Popular activities here include sunbathing, beachcombing, hiking, mountain biking, birdwatching, swimming, snorkeling, kayaking, windsurfing, scuba diving, and sportfishing. Divers will relish the nearby shallow reefs, thrilling wall drop-offs, and underwater canyons, teeming with colorful fish and marine life. Anglers can climb aboard one of the resort's six diesel-powered cruisers, which are completely equipped, available for charter, and captained by experts that can take you to the best local spots for blue marlin, sailfish, dorado, yellowtail, grouper, amberjack, snapper, bonita, or roosterfish, depending on the season. In addition, visitors can keep their own small boats, kayaks, and canoes on the beach.

RV sites, facilities: All 65 sites have full hookups, with water, sewer access, and 15/30-amp outlets. Lengthy RVs (up to 45 feet/13.7 meters long) are welcome here, and tent campers will find 25 sites, some of which are equipped with water and electricity. The lots are sandy, and several spaces are shaded by palm trees. Guests also have access to clean bathrooms, hot showers, a coin laundry, a library, a boat launch, a refreshing pool, a rooftop restaurant and cocktail lounge, and a *palapa* bar overlooking the sea. A pay phone and an English-speaking staff are also present, and the park is secured by a guard and a perimeter fence. There is, however, no dump station on the premises. Children and leashed pets are welcome, but the facilities are not suitable for wheelchairs. Purified water, ice, groceries, and other supplies are available at a nearby *supermercado*.

Reservations, fees: Reservations are highly recommended. RV sites cost $15 per night, while tent spaces cost $11 per night. Long-term campsites and spacious motel rooms are also available. Cash (Mexican pesos or U.S. dollars) and major credit cards are accepted. The park is open all year.

Directions: From the southern end of La Paz, drive about 64.2 miles (103.3 km) south on Highway 1 to Los Barriles, which is between the Km 109 and Km 110 markers. Turn left and drive 0.3 mile (0.5 km) to the T junction. Turn left again and head northwest for 0.2 mile (0.3 km). The park is on the right, beside the beach. From San José del Cabo, head north on Highway 1 for 49.1 miles (79 km), turn right onto the main access road for Los Barriles, and follow the above directions.

Contact: Martin Verdugo's Beach Resort, Apartado Postal #17, Los Barriles, Baja California Sur, C.P. 23501, Mexico, tel. 624/141-0054, www.verdugosbeachresort.com.

12 EAST CAPE RV RESORT

Scenic Rating: 8

in Los Barriles

See map page 232 BEST

In the heart of Los Barriles, this roomy, increasingly popular campground is only a short walk from the beach. It's one of the nicest parks in all of Baja, with lots of palm trees, shrubs, and flowers—and a pamphlet to help amateur botanists identify them all. It's also the most ideal place for owners of large rigs, as the spots are spacious and the 30-amp electricity is consistent and strong.

As with many camping areas in the East Cape, favored pastimes include hiking, beachcombing, swimming, snorkeling, kayaking, windsurfing, scuba diving, fishing, and watching birds, whales, and other wildlife. Luckily, this well-managed park has a bilingual staff, willing and able to guide you around the area and offer advice about the many activities available. In addition, the campground owners operate two popular sportfishing boats, so it's easy to make arrangements for a deep-sea fishing trip in the bountiful Sea of Cortez. The only drawback here is the frequency of mosquitoes during the rainy season.

Besides enjoying nearby water sports, visitors and caravans often use this park as a home base for exploring the Sierra de la Laguna to the west. Animal lovers will delight in knowing that the only zoo in Baja Sur lies just 17.7 miles (28.5 km) south on Highway 1, toward Los Cabos. The Santiago Zoo houses several Mexican species, such as coyotes, deer, and bobcats, as well as fossils discovered in the mountainous region. Farther south, the quaint town of Miraflores, which is several hundred years old, offers shoppers the chance to peruse handmade leather goods; the village is also known for its sweet basil fields and natural *baños de agua caliente* (hot springs).

RV sites, facilities: There are 60 spaces, all of which have full hookups, including 30/50-amp electricity, water service, and sewage drains. Six of the sites are pull-throughs; the rest are backins. The spaces can accommodate lengthy motor homes and travel trailers (up to 40 feet/12.2 meters long). Palm trees provide some shade, and amenities include a new spa, a swimming pool, coin-operated washers and dryers, volleyball and horseshoe areas, wireless Internet access, bilingual employees, and clean, *palapa*-style restrooms with flush toilets and hot showers. There is, however, no dump station or official security on the premises. Children, leashed pets, and tent campers are welcome, and the campsites can accommodate wheelchairs. Since there's no store in the park, you should obtain supplies in Los Barriles; fortunately, groceries and restaurants are within walking distance. Internet access is also available in the nearby town.

Reservations, fees: Reservations are accepted. RV and tent spaces cost $25 per night, $150 per week, and $525 per month (though taxes do apply). Permanent rates are also available. Credit cards are usually accepted (when U.S.-based employees can process them), and cash (Mexican pesos or U.S. dollars) is always an acceptable form of payment. The park is open all year.

Directions: From the southern end of La Paz, drive about 64.2 miles (103.3 km) south on Highway 1 to Los Barriles, which is between the Km 109 and Km 110 markers. Turn left and drive 0.3 mile (0.5 km) to the T junction. Turn left again and head northwest along the coast for 0.4 mile (0.6 km). You'll see the park on the left-hand side. From San José del Cabo, head north on Highway 1 for 49.1 miles (79 km), turn right onto the main access road for Los Barriles, and follow the above directions.

Contact: East Cape RV Resort, 20 de Noviembre S/N, Los Barriles, Baja California Sur, Mexico, tel. 624/141-0231, tel./fax 208/726-1955 (U.S.), www.eastcaperv.com.

13 PARAISO DEL MAR RV RESORT

Scenic Rating: 8

north of Los Barriles

See map page 232

The East Cape is a year-round playground for a wide array of outdoor enthusiasts, including windsurfers, kiteboarders, deep-sea anglers, boaters, kayakers, scuba divers, snorkelers, hikers, horseback riders, and mountain bikers. With its gorgeous, somewhat deserted beaches and relatively calm waters, it's also a terrific place for a romantic stroll at sunset. Luckily, there are several primitive campgrounds and full-service RV parks in the area, so you can explore this diverse region for as long as you like.

This brand-new RV park, situated on a side road north of the East Cape RV Resort, offers relative proximity to Los Barriles as well as the beach. Despite its small size, this coastal town boasts several gift shops, Mexican restaurants, and festive cantinas; in addition, you'll find ATV rentals, guided tours, Spanish classes, Shakespearean plays, and seasonal art festivals.

Although Paraiso del Mar isn't directly beside the coast—which is the desire of most travelers to the East Cape—this 4-acre (1.6-hectare) property is extremely spacious, ideal for lengthy motor homes. In addition, while several small trees pepper the campground, most of the sites are wide-open and sunny.

RV sites, facilities: The park offers 90 spacious, full-hookup RV sites, each of which has electricity, a sewage drain, and purified, high-pressure water hookups. The spaces can easily accommodate lengthy motor homes and travel trailers (up to 40 feet/12.2 meters long). Other amenities include wireless Internet access, concierge service, a coin laundry, an on-site cafeteria, clean restrooms, and 24-hour security. Mountain bikes are also available for rent. There is no dump station on the premises. Children, leashed pets, and tent campers are welcome, but the sandy terrain might be unsuitable for wheelchairs. Groceries, gift shops, restaurants, medical clinics, and a bank are in nearby Los Barriles.

Reservations, fees: Reservations are accepted, via phone or through the website. Contact the park directly for details about daily, weekly, and long-term rates. Major credit cards and cash (Mexican pesos or U.S. dollars) are accepted. The park is open all year.

Directions: From the southern end of La Paz, drive about 63.7 miles (102.5 km) south on Highway 1 to Los Barriles. Just south of Km 111, turn left onto a dirt bypass road and head east toward the sea. At the end of the road, turn left again and cross the Buenos Aires Arroyo. After passing Km 1, you'll see a street sign that reads "El Camino del Jonathon." Turn left onto this dirt road, pass the first street, and turn left onto the second street. The park entrance is on the right-hand side. From San José del Cabo, head north on Highway 1 for 49.6 miles (79.8 km), turn right onto the dirt road south of Km 111, and follow the above directions.

Contact: Paraiso del Mar RV Resort, Los Barriles, Baja California Sur, Mexico, tel. 612/127-2558 (dial "1" first), www.eastcape rvresort.com.

14 PLAYA NORTE RV PARK

Scenic Rating: 9

north of Los Barriles

See map page 232 **BEST**

Situated directly on the beach, between the Buenos Aires and San Bartolo Arroyos, this well-landscaped, 25-acre (10-hectare) park has welcomed RV travelers and tent campers alike since the late 1990s. It's one of the last waterfront RV parks left in the East Cape, offering miles of open beach to explore. The nearest town, Los Barriles, is only five minutes away by car, and the corner grocery lies within walking distance.

As in many camping areas in this region, favored pastimes include watching the sunrise (or the starry nighttime sky), hiking, beachcombing, swimming, snorkeling, kayaking, scuba diving, and viewing birds, whales, and other wildlife. ATV rentals, fishing charters, guided tours, horseback riding, and windsurfing and kiteboarding lessons can also be arranged. In nearby Los Barriles, you'll find other operators that charter *pangas* and cruisers to fish the deep, blue waters of the Sea of Cortez, and surf fishing is terrific here, too.

Windsurfing and kiteboarding are especially popular along this beach, mostly because of the region's dependable occurrence of stout winter winds. Of course, while the breezy conditions are ideal for sail devices, they can make it challenging for kayakers and pleasure boaters. International windsurfing tournaments occur every winter, attracting enthusiasts from all over the world. Even for onlookers, it's an exciting time to visit, if only to watch the colorful sails as they whip across the water.

RV sites, facilities: There are 75 RV spaces with municipal water (from deep wells) and sewage hookups; 25 of them are private, dedicated pull-through sites intended for caravans. The remaining 50 are open to the public, and many of these are pull-through and/or waterfront spots, with individual 15/30/50-amp electricity, free wireless Internet access, and beautiful ocean views. Several sites measure 30 feet (9.1 meters) by 60 feet (18.3 meters), with plenty of room for 40-foot (12.2-meter) RVs. There is also a tent-camping area and a designated section for permanent RV residents. Sporadic trees provide some shade, and facilities include a dump station, a coin laundry, a pay phone, rustic showers (open to the sky and surrounded by walls of palm leaves), and tiled restrooms with flush toilets and hot showers (heated by gas or solar power). The park does not impose an age limit upon RVs.

Although there's no official security, a fence surrounds the entire property, and some members of the park's year-round staff dwell on the grounds. Children are welcome, and the sites and facilities are suitable for wheelchairs. Campfires are allowed in designated areas. Pets are permitted, but they must be kept on their site or taken for a run on the beach, and owners must collect and dispose of the pets' feces properly. The park has the only grooming center and animal clinic in a 60-mile (97-km) radius, with three licensed Mexican veterinarians managing the store. Many of the park employees speak Spanish and English. You should obtain purified water, ice, and other supplies in Los Barriles or the corner grocery, as there are no stores on the beach, and be advised that there is an on-site manager only during the wintertime. Shuttle services and medical clinics are available in town.

Reservations, fees: Reservations are accepted, accompanied by a deposit. The daily fee for a spot in the first two beachfront rows is $22, plus $3 for optional 15/30-amp power or $5 for 50-amp electricity. For a site in the remaining rows, the daily fee is $18, plus the same electric charges. Tent sites are $15 per night, including use of the water, restrooms, showers, parking, and wireless Internet access. The dump station is free for caravans and for customers who stay at least a week; otherwise, it's $5 per visit. Rates are based on double occupancy; extra guests are charged $5 per night. Suitable forms of payment include cash (Mexican pesos or U.S. dollars), major credit cards, and personal checks (when the site is reserved or prepaid). Permanent leases, long-term storage, monthly stays, and seasonal rates are also available. The park is open all year, though the office is only open during the busy winter season (November 15–March 15).

Directions: From the southern end of La Paz, drive about 64.2 miles (103.3 km) south on Highway 1 to Los Barriles, which is between the Km 109 and Km 110 markers. Turn left and drive 0.3 mile (0.5 km) to the T junction. Turn left again and head northwest along the coast for 1.8 miles (2.9 km). You'll see the campground entrance on the right-hand side. From San José del Cabo, head north on Highway 1 for 49.1 miles (79 km), turn right onto the main access road for Los Barriles, and follow the above directions.

Contact: Playa Norte RV Park, 4626 View Drive, Everett, WA 98203, tel. 624/142-8001 (Mexico) or 425/252-5952 (U.S.), fax 425/252-6171 (U.S.), www.playanortervpark.com.

15 QUINTA MARÍA

Scenic Rating: 8

north of Los Barriles

See map page 232

Although the principal accommodations along this picturesque beach are handsome bungalows atop a bluff overlooking the ocean, RV travelers and tent campers are welcome to dry-dock on the open lot between the rental cabins and the sea, and many choose to do so, especially in the cooler winter months. As with most camping areas in the East Cape, favored pastimes here include hiking, mountain biking, beachcombing, swimming, snorkeling, windsurfing, kayaking, horseback riding, and watching birds, whales, and other wildlife. To facilitate access to the Sea of Cortez (or Golfo de California), there's even a ramp that leads from the cliff to the beach.

Fishing is indeed one of the more popular activities in this region, especially during the mild winters. Nearby hotels charter *pangas* and cruisers to fish the deep, blue waters of Bahía de las Palmas and beyond, where anglers can potentially find every type of fish known to dwell in the Sea of Cortez, including marlin, sailfish, wahoo, amberjack, sea bass, pompano, snapper, giant needlefish, and many others.

Primitive camping areas throughout Baja have been closing at an alarming rate, mostly due to real-estate development and privatization plans, so be sure to check with local residents before pulling into the Quinta María campground for the night, as it could be closed at any time.

RV sites, facilities: There are no designated RV sites here—you can park wherever there's room on the sand, adjacent to the sea. There are no hookups, but there's enough room for any RV (even over 40 feet/12.2 meters long). Palm trees provide some shade, and minimal facilities include drinking water, a coin laundry, a swimming pool, and tiled restrooms with flush toilets and hot showers. Only tent campers and self-contained RVs should park here, as there's no dump station, electricity, or official security. Children and leashed pets are welcome, but the terrain is not suitable for wheelchairs. You should obtain groceries, ice, and supplies in Los Barriles, as there are no stores on the beach. There is, however, a restaurant nearby.

Reservations, fees: Reservations are not

accepted; spaces are available on a first-come, first-served basis. The daily fee is nominal—$5 per night. Credit cards are not accepted; cash (Mexican pesos or U.S. dollars) is the customary form of payment. The beach is open all year.

Directions: From the southern end of La Paz, drive about 64.2 miles (103.3 km) south on Highway 1 to Los Barriles, which is located between the Km 109 and Km 110 markers. Turn left and drive 0.3 mile (0.5 km) to the T junction. Turn left again and head northwest along the coast for 2.3 miles (3.7 km). At the fork in the road, veer to the right. Drive 0.7 mile (1.1 km) and turn right into the access road for the Quinta María bungalows. From San José del Cabo, head north on Highway 1 for 49.1 miles (79 km), turn right onto the main access road for Los Barriles, and follow the above directions.

Contact: Quinta María, Km 5.5 de la Carretera Los Barriles-El Cardonal, Municipio de La Paz, Baja California Sur, Mexico. Since there's no official phone number, it might just be best to drive toward the beach and see which spots are available.

16 EL CARDONAL'S HIDE-A-WAY

Scenic Rating: 9

in El Cardonal

See map page 232 **BEST**

A recently paved roadway north of Los Barriles has made this laid-back resort in the East Cape less of a secret, but it's still a charming, sandy oasis beside the sea—popular with RVers and tent campers alike. Adjacent to a small motel, the intimate beachfront campground, in existence since 1989, is accented by sculpted cacti, accessible via stone-lined paths, and not far from numerous water sports.

Besides swimming in the warm, aquamarine waters of the Sea of Cortez, outdoor enthusiasts can board a 23-foot (7-meter) *panga* for deep-sea fishing, take a scuba-diving trip with a master diver, snorkel at kaleidoscopic Coral Point, explore the sea in a rented kayak, or join a whale-watching excursion—all with the help of the resort's services and recommendations. Sunbathing, horseback riding, surf fishing for dorado and red snapper, watching birds and sea turtles, exploring nearby cave paintings, and strolling along the beach are also popular activities here.

Just be forewarned: Although the road from Los Barriles to El Cardonal has been paved, it's still rather steep and dangerous. Parts of the newer route were damaged by a 2006 hurricane. In fact, while some spaces in the campground accommodate lengthy rigs, probably only small RVs (especially heavy-duty pickup campers with high clearance) should make the journey on this uneven route.

RV sites, facilities: Three roomy, full-hookup RV sites offer potable water, drainage installations, and 15/30-amp electrical outlets; five more sites offer electricity and water only. All the spaces are back-ins or pull-ins, and all include shade, picnic tables, benches, and barbecue pits. Tent campers can pitch their tents on the beach or inside the formal camping area. Other facilities include a laundry room, a playground, a dump station, clean bathrooms with flush toilets and hot showers, and a colorful restaurant that serves seafood, vegetarian dishes, and Mexican cuisine. A full rental shop offers beach umbrellas, float tubes, kayaks, boats, wetsuits, and snorkeling equipment, and the staff offers guided fishing, scuba-diving, and whale-watching tours. Large RVs (up to 40 feet/12.2 meters long) are welcome, as are children and leashed pets (though no pit bulls are allowed). There are no age restrictions for visiting RVs. The park is secured by a fence and an entrance gate, and the employees have limited bilingual skills. The sites and facilities are not wheelchair-accessible. Groceries, purified water, and other supplies should be purchased in Los Barriles, to the south.

Reservations, fees: Reservations are highly recommended; if made online, a deposit is required. Full refunds (in the form of future credit) are possible only with a doctor's certificate proving your inability to travel. Full-hookup RV sites cost $13 per night, $86 per week, and $312 per month. Partial-hookup sites (with just water and electricity) cost $12 per night, $79 per week, and $288 per month. Primitive tent camping costs $10 per night, $66 per week, and $255 per month. For VIP camping—a unique service that ensures the setup and cleanup of park-owned tents, including air mattresses, stove and kitchen equipment, and electricity—the cost range is $20–45 per night and $133–299 per week. Deluxe hotel suites and long-term RV/tent rates are also available. All rates are based upon a two-adult occupancy; children stay for free, while extra adult guests are charged a daily fee of $2 each. Credit cards are not accepted; cash (Mexican pesos, U.S. dollars, or Canadian dollars) is the only acceptable form of payment. The park is open all year.

Directions: From Los Barriles, follow the somewhat paved road north for 5 miles (8 km). At the fork, you can continue straight on the upper route, though it's better to turn right onto the dirt road, drive 0.6 mile (1 km) to the coastal road, and follow it carefully for 8 miles (12.9 km) to the village of El Cardonal. When you pass the Hotel Punta Pescadero, continue for 4.4 miles (7.1 km). The campground sign is on the right. Note that, although the upper route is newer than the coastal road, you might find that recent storms have damaged parts of the higher path, making it fairly impassable for motor homes and travel trailers.

Contact: El Cardonal's Hide-a-Way, El Cardonal, Municipio de La Paz, Baja California Sur, C.P. 23330, Mexico, tel. 612/128-6859 or 612/100-3382, www.elcardonal.net.

17 RANCHO VERDE RV PARK

Scenic Rating: 7

between San Antonio and San Bartolo

See map page 232 BEST

Along the winding road between La Paz and Los Barriles lies this peaceful retreat, nestled high within the Sierra de la Laguna. Since 1994, this secluded park, which offers a carefree Mexican lifestyle amid the green wooded countryside of a 3,100-acre (1,250-hectare) ranch, has provided a pleasant change of scenery from Baja's typical deserts and beaches. Miles of hiking, horseback riding, bird-watching, and four-wheeler trails wind beside the cactus-strewn slopes and private *ranchos* of this mountainous region. While those are the most popular activities here, many visitors also enjoy touring the nearby villages of El Triunfo, an old gold and silver mining town, and San Antonio, which is situated within a farming valley and features an unusual, crimson-trimmed church with twin bell towers.

For those who miss the water, though, the park provides guided fishing tours in the Sea of Cortez and its own beachfront launch site in El Sargento on the Bahía de la Ventana, a 40-minute drive from the ranch. Even closer, Los Barriles, positioned beside the Bahía de las Palmas, is a favored windsurfing and kiteboarding spot.

If you really fall in love with the ranch, you can arrange for a 30-year lease of a 1-acre (0.4-hectare) plot, on which you can build a home, have utilities installed, or just park your RV. But, don't worry; despite its billing as a private RV destination community, there's no need to fear high-pressure sales tactics in this relaxed haven.

RV sites, facilities: There are 30 widely separated, back-in sites for tents and RVs. Each space has water and sewage hookups but no electricity. Most sites are spacious and able to accommodate large motor homes (up to

45 feet/13.7 meters long), though the entrance to the park is somewhat tight. Some spaces are shaded, with tables and barbecue pits. Simple, clean restrooms are within a *palapa*-style building, where flush toilets and hot showers are available, but there's no dump station or laundry on the premises. Other amenities include central recreation facilities, garbage disposal services, wireless Internet access, and semibilingual employees. The park is enclosed by a gated fence, and resident managers provide 24-hour security. Children and leashed pets are permitted on the property, though the facilities are not wheelchair-accessible. Given the park's remote location, it's best to obtain purified drinking water, ice, groceries, and fuel in La Paz; small markets in the nearby towns of San Antonio and El Triunfo also offer limited supplies.

Reservations, fees: Reservations are not required, and there is no cancellation policy. RV sites cost $12 per night and $72 per week, while tent spaces cost $8 per night. Long-term rates are also available. Credit cards are not accepted; only cash (Mexican pesos or U.S. dollars) will suffice. The park is open all year.

Directions: From La Paz, head south on Highway 1 for 17.2 miles (27.7 km). South of San Pedro, where the road divides into Highways 1 and 19, veer left (southeast) onto Highway 1. Continue for 27.1 miles (43.6 km), passing through the mountain towns of El Triunfo and San Antonio. The RV park is on the right (south) side of the highway at Km 142. From Los Barriles, head northwest on Highway 1 for 19.9 miles (32 km); from this direction, the park lies on the left (south) side of the road.

Contact: Rancho Verde RV Park, A-L Properties S.A. De C.V., c/o The Land Store, P.O. Box 1050, Eureka, MT 59917, tel. 888/516-9462 (U.S.), www.rancho-verde.com.

RESOURCES

The following pages provide a host of contact information and helpful suggestions regarding travel in Baja. Unless otherwise noted in parentheses, all phone numbers are based in Mexico.

If you're calling any of the following phone numbers from the United States, remember to dial "1" before the area code of any U.S. number (unless you happen to be within the same area code), "011-1" before the area code of any Canadian number, and "011-52" before the area code of any Mexican number. From Canada, you must dial "1" before any Canadian area code (unless you happen to be within the same area code), "001-1" before any U.S. area code, and "011-52" before any Mexican area code. If you're calling any of the following phone numbers from a Mexico-based phone, you must dial "001" before any U.S. or Canadian area code and "01" before any Mexican area code (unless you happen to be within the same area code).

RV RESOURCES

RV Rental Companies

Most U.S.-based RV rental companies forbid travelers to take their vehicles to Mexico. Luckily, however, the following two outfitters do permit such south-of-the-border travel. For more information, please contact them directly:

Cruise America RV Rental & Sales
11 West Hampton Avenue
Mesa, AZ 85210
tel. 480/464-7300 (U.S.) or
800/671-8042 (U.S.)
fax 480/464-7321 (U.S.)
www.cruiseamerica.com
Note: Cruise America, which offers Mexican liability insurance (required in Baja), only allows travel to the border zones of Mexico, defined as an area within 12.4–18.6 miles (20–30 km) south of the border, depending on the location. Ask for details.

El Monte RV Motorhome Vacations
12061 East Valley Boulevard
El Monte, CA 91732
tel. 562/483-4931 (U.S.) or
888/337-2214 (U.S.)
fax 626/443-6673 (U.S.)
www.elmonterv.com
Note: Mexican Auto Services (also called Auto Club of Mexico) provides emergency roadside assistance through some of El Monte RV's rental offices, including those based in Las Vegas and throughout Southern California.

Mexican Auto Insurance

No RV trip to Baja California is complete without first purchasing automobile insurance suitable for travel in Mexico. Most U.S.-based insurance policies are not valid in Baja and will, therefore, not cover you in the case of an accident or a collision. Since Mexican authorities will only recognize policies issued by companies that are licensed to sell automobile insurance in Mexico, it's imperative that motorists purchase separate insurance policies for their RVs and tow vehicles before crossing the U.S.-Mexico border (and carry said insurance at all times). You can apply at several Mexican-authorized insurance agencies on both sides of the border at Tijuana, Tecate, and Mexicali.

In addition, it's important to note that most (if not all) Mexican-authorized insurance providers expect you to report and file any insurance claims prior to leaving Mexico.

For more information, contact the following companies directly:

ACE Seguros S. A.
Calle Netzahualcoyotl #1660
Desp. 304
Colonia Zona Urbana Río Tijuana
1ª Sección
Tijuana, Baja California
C.P. 22320
Mexico
tel. 664/973-0507
fax 664/973-0504
www.acelatinamerica.com/acela
Note: You can also apply for this insurance provider through Baja Bound Insurance Services, Inc. (www.bajabound.com), Mexbound.com (www.mexbound.com), or DriveMex.com (www.drivemex.com).

ADA VIS Global Enterprises, Inc.
38790 Sky Canyon Drive
Murrieta, CA 92563
tel. 800/909-4457 (U.S.)
fax 800/909-1007 (U.S.)
www.adavisglobal.com

Adventure Mexican Insurance Services, Inc.
P.O. Box 1469
Soquel, CA 95073
tel. 831/477-0599 (U.S.) or
800/485-4075 (U.S.)
www.mexadventure.com
Note: Adventure Mexican Insurance has partnered with three Mexican insurance programs, including ACE Seguros, Genworth Seguros, and Mapfre Tepeyac.

Border Mexican Insurance Services
2004 Dairy Mart Road, Suite #103
San Ysidro, CA 92173
tel. 800/332-2118 (U.S.)
fax 619/428-0920 (U.S.)
www.mexborder.com

Caravan Insurance Services, L.L.C.
125 Promise Lane
Livingston, TX 77351
tel. 936/327-3428 (U.S.) or
800/489-0083 (U.S.)
fax 800/761-9821 (U.S.)
www.caravaninsuranceservices.net
Note: This insurance provider is affiliated with Adventure Caravans, Inc.

Genworth Seguros
Paseo de los Insurgentes #1701
Colonia Granada
León, Guanajuato
C.P. 37306
Mexico
tel. 477/710-4700 or 800/019-6000
www.gemexicoautoins.com
Note: You can also apply for this insurance provider through Baja Bound Insurance Services, Inc. (www.bajabound.com), Mexbound.com (www.mexbound.com), or DriveMex.com (www.drivemex.com).

Lewis & Lewis Insurance
8929 Wilshire Boulevard, Suite #220
Beverly Hills, CA 90211
tel. 310/657-1112 (U.S.) or
800/966-6830 (U.S.)
fax 310/652-5849 (U.S.)
www.mexicanautoinsurance.com

Mexico Insurance Online
121 East Birch Avenue, Suite #207
Flagstaff, AZ 86001
tel. 888/467-4639 (U.S.)
fax 928/213-8476 (U.S.)
www.mexicaninsuranceonline.com

Mexico Insurance Services
345-B Delaware Street
Imperial Beach, CA 91932
tel. 858/663-6453 (U.S.) or
800/004-9600 (from Mexico)
www.mexinsure.com

Oscar Padilla's MexicanInsurance.com
825 Imperial Avenue
Calexico, CA 92231
tel. 760/357-4883 (U.S.) or
800/466-7227 (U.S.)
fax 760/357-6114 (U.S.)
www.mexicaninsurance.com

Point South Insurance
11313 Edmonson Avenue
Moreno Valley, CA 92555
tel. 951/247-1222 (U.S.) or
888/421-1394 (U.S.)
fax 951/924-3838 (U.S.)
www.mexican-insurance.com

Sanborn's Mexico Auto Insurance
2009 S. 10th Street
McAllen, TX 78503
tel. 800/222-0158 (U.S.)
www.sanbornsinsurance.com

RV Clubs and Caravans

Many RV enthusiasts have discovered that traveling together to Baja, whether for the first time or for repeat visits, can be an incredibly rewarding experience—and infinitely safer than traveling alone. Here's a sampling of the RV clubs, caravans, and membership organizations available to those bound for Mexico:

Adventure Caravans, Inc.
125 Promise Lane
Livingston, TX 77351

tel. 936/327-3428 (U.S.) or
800/872-7897 (U.S.)
fax 936/327-3663 (U.S.) or
800/761-9821 (U.S.)
www.adventurecaravans.com

Baja and Back! RV Caravan Tours
#138-5751 Cedarbridge Way
Richmond, BC V6X 2A8
Canada
tel. 866/782-2252 (Canada)
fax 206/202-4650 (Canada)
www.bajaandback.com

Baja Winters RV Caravans
P.O. Box 166
Aguanga, CA 92536-0166
tel. 866/771-9064 (U.S.)
www.bajawinters.com

Discover Baja Travel Club
3089 Clairemont Drive
San Diego, CA 92117
tel. 619/275-4225 (U.S.) or
800/727-2252 (U.S.)
fax 619/275-1836 (U.S.)
www.discoverbaja.com
Note: Discover Baja also offers Mexican auto insurance (through Adventure Mexican Insurance Services, Inc.); you can even get a free online quote via the club website.

Fantasy RV Tours
111 Camino Del Rio
Gunnison, CO 81230
tel. 800/952-8496 (U.S.)
fax 970/642-4573 (U.S.)
www.fantasyrvtours.com

Good Sam Club
P.O. Box 6888
Englewood, CO 80155-6888
tel. 800/234-3450 (U.S.)
www.goodsamclub.com

Passport America
602 South Main Street
Crestview, FL 32536
tel. 800/681-6810 (U.S.)
www.passportamerica.com
Note: Occasionally, campgrounds in Baja will honor the Passport America daily discount (50 percent of the standard rate), but it's not a common practice.

Tracks to Adventure RV Tours
2811 Jackson Avenue
El Paso, TX 79930
tel. 800/351-6053 (U.S.)
www.trackstoadventure.com

Vagabundos Del Mar RV, Boat, and Travel Club
190 Main Street
Rio Vista, CA 94571
tel. 707/374-5511 (U.S.) or
800/474-2252 (U.S.)
fax 707/374-6843 (U.S.)
www.vagabundos.com
Note: Vagabundos also offers Mexican auto insurance via the club website.

MEXICO RESOURCES

Mexico Tourism Board

For more information about traveling along the Baja peninsula, consult the Mexico Tourism Board (Consejo de Promoción Turística de México) via telephone (800/446-3942) or website (www.visitmexico.com).

Regional Tourism Offices

Several tourism offices exist throughout Baja California Norte and Baja California Sur; many offer maps and brochures, and some even have bilingual staff members. For more information about specific regions and cities, contact the following organizations and websites.

Baja California Norte

To better explore the northern half of the Baja peninsula, you can contact the State Secretariat of Tourism of Baja California or one of several other tourism offices.

STATE SECRETARIAT OF TOURISM OF BAJA CALIFORNIA

For more information about Baja Norte, the main tourism board can be contacted directly, via either the main website (www.discoverbajacalifornia.com) or one of the following offices:

Central Office
Calle Juán Ruiz de Alarcón #1572
Edificio Río, Piso #3
Zona Río

Tijuana, Baja California
C.P. 22320
Mexico
tel. 664/682-3367
fax 664/682-9061 or 664/682-3331
amartineze@baja.gob.mx

Playas de Rosarito Office
Boulevard Benito Juárez #42
Esquina con Calle Magnolia
Zona Centro, Piso #2
Playas de Rosarito, Baja California
C.P. 22710
Mexico
tel. 661/612-5222
fax 661/612-0200
raragon@baja.gob.mx or rosaritotur@baja.gob.mx

Ensenada Office
Boulevard Lázaro Cárdenas y Calle Las Rocas #1477
Ensenada, Baja California
Mexico
tel. 646/172-5444, 646/172-3022, or 646/172-3000
fax 646/172-5372
jleonz@baja.gob.mx

Tecate Office
Callejón Libertad S/N
Zona Centro
Tecate, Baja California
Mexico
tel./fax 665/654-1095
ergarcia@baja.gob.mx

Mexicali Office
Boulevard Benito Juárez #1 y Francisco Montejano
Piso #2
Mexicali, Baja California
Mexico
tel. 686/566-1277, 686/566-1116, 686/566-1739, or 686/566-1705
egmoreno@baja.gob.mx

San Felipe Office
Avenida Mar de Cortez y Manzanillo #300
San Felipe, Baja California
Mexico
tel. 686/577-1865
fax 686/577-1115
rortizg@baja.gob.mx or sanfelipetur@baja.gob.mx

OTHER TOURISM OFFICES

For more information about Baja California Norte, you can also call the tourist assistance hotline at 078 (while in Mexico). In addition, you can contact the following tourism boards directly:

Tijuana Tourism Board
Boulevard Agua Caliente #4558
Piso #11, Oficina #1108
Colonia Aviación
Tijuana, Baja California
C.P. 22420
Mexico
tel. 664/686-1103, 664/686-1345, 800/025-0888 (in Mexico), or 888/775-2417 (from U.S.)
fax 664/686-1613
www.seetijuana.com

Rosarito Tourism Trust
Boulevard Benito Juárez #907, Int. 14
Centro Comercial Plaza Oceana
Playas de Rosarito, Baja California
C.P. 22710
Mexico
tel. 661/612-0396, 661/613-0710, 800/025-6288 (in Mexico), or 800/962-2252 (from U.S.)
fax 661/612-3078
www.rosarito.org

Ensenada Tourism Board
Boulevard Lázaro Cárdenas #609-5
Ensenada, Baja California
C.P. 22800
Mexico
tel. 646/178-8578, 800/025-3991 (in Mexico), or 800/310-9687 (U.S.)
fax 646/178-8588
www.enjoyensenada.com

Tecate Tourism Trust
Avenida Juárez #570
Zona Centro
Tecate, Baja California
Mexico
tel./fax 665/654-5892

Mexicali Tourism Board
Avenida Alvaro Obregon #1257
Local 12
Colonia Nueva
Mexicali, Baja California
Mexico
tel. 686/552-4401, 800/025-5887 (in Mexico), or 888/342-7323 (from U.S.)
fax 686/552-4402
www.mexicaliturismo.com

San Felipe Tourism Trust
Avenida Alvaro Obregon #1257
Local 11
Colonia Nueva
Mexicali, Baja California
Mexico
tel. 686/553-0100
www.visitsanfelipebc.com

Baja California Sur

For more information about the diverse regions, towns, and cities that compose the southern half of the Baja peninsula, visit www.bcs.gob.mx, the official website for the Gobierno del Estado de Baja California Sur. Just be advised that the content is only presented in Spanish.

In addition, you can contact the following tourism bureau directly:

Los Cabos Tourism Board
Lázaro Cárdenas S/N
Edificio Posada
Cabo San Lucas, Baja California Sur
Mexico
tel. 624/143-4777 or 866/567-2226 (from U.S.)
www.visitloscabos.org

Baja Parks and Preserves

The Baja California peninsula possesses a wide array of enchanting landscapes, some of which are even protected by the Mexican government. Unlike America's National Park Service (NPS), however—which maintains a well-organized system of parks, monuments, preserves, trails, seashores, and the like—Mexico's Comisión Nacional de Areas Naturales Protegidas (CONANP) makes it a little tougher to find out specific details about these protected areas prior to your trip. CONANP does, however, offer an informative website (if, that is, you can read Spanish). To find out more about Baja's national parks, biosphere reserves, and other protected areas, visit www.conanp.gob.mx/sig or contact the following destinations directly:

Tijuana and Northwest Baja

Parque Nacional Constitución de 1857

One of the oldest national parks on the Baja peninsula, this 28,000-acre (11,330-hectare) preserve has been protecting a unique landscape of elevated pine forests and shallow lakes, as well as an array of native fauna, since 1962. For more information, contact the Mexicali management office at 686/554-5470 or 686/554-4404.

Reserva de la Biósfera Isla Guadalupe

Established in 2005, this 1.18-million-acre (478,000-hectare) biosphere reserve protects a diverse island to the west of Baja Norte. For more information, contact the Ensenada management office at 646/152-1290.

Mexicali to San Felipe

Reserva de la Biósfera Alto Golfo de California y Delta del Río Colorado

Established in 1993, this 2.31-million-acre (935,000-hectare) biosphere reserve is nestled between the states of Baja California and Sonora (part of the Mexican mainland), where the Colorado River empties into the northern end of the Sea of Cortez (or Golfo de California). For more information, you can phone 653/536-3757 or 653/536-8131.

Central Pacific and the Sea of Cortez

Area de Protección de Flora y Fauna Valle de los Cirios

Consisting of Baja's central desert, which extends from El Rosario to the Baja Sur state line, this enormous area comprises 6.25 million acres (2.53 million hectares) of arid landscape, strange boulders, various cactus species, unique *cirio* plants, and an assortment of fascinating creatures. For more information, contact the Ensenada management office at 646/172-5583 or 646/176-4869.

Parque Nacional Archipiélago de San Lorenzo

A 2005 addition to Mexico's growing list of protected areas, this 144,400-acre (58,440-hectare) national park consists of a cluster of islands in the Sea of Cortez (Golfo de California), southeast of Bahía de los Ángeles. There is, unfortunately, no contact information.

Parque Nacional Sierra de San Pedro Mártir

Probably Baja's oldest national park, this 160,000-acre (64,750-hectare) preserve, established in 1947, offers cool forests and tall granite peaks amid a sea of desert terrain. For more information, contact the Ensenada management office at 646/172-3085 or 646/172-3080.

Reserva de la Biósfera Bahía de los Ángeles

This 959,000-acre (388,000-hectare) biosphere reserve, newly established in mid-2007, comprises the Canal de Ballenas and the Canal Salsipuedes, both of which are sandwiched between several islands in the Sea of Cortez and the coastline north and south, respectively, of Bahía de los Ángeles. There is, unfortunately, no contact information.

Guerrero Negro to Bahía Concepción

Reserva de la Biósfera Complejo Lagunar Ojo de Liebre

Originally established in 1972 and modified since then, this important 149,100-acre (60,340-hectare) biosphere reserve protects the wintertime breeding grounds of the California *ballenas gris* (gray whales). For more information, contact the management office in Guerrero Negro at 615/157-1777 or 615/157-0177.

Reserva de la Biósfera El Vizcaíno

One of Baja's most diverse biosphere reserves, this enormous 6.29-million-acre (2.55-million-hectare) area, established in 1988, includes the mountains, deserts, lagoons, and beaches surrounding Guerrero Negro and San Ignacio. For more information, contact the management office in Guerrero Negro at 615/157-1777 or 615/157-0177.

Loreto, La Paz, and Southern Baja

Area de Protección de Flora y Fauna Islas del Golfo de California

Comprising 53 islands in the Sea of Cortez (or Golfo de California), this 777,700-acre (314,700-hectare) biosphere reserve protects the isolated flora and fauna on these incredible islands, which stretch from Baja Norte to Baja Sur. There is, unfortunately, no contact information.

Parque Marino Nacional Bahía de Loreto

Established in 1996, this 513,000-acre (207,610-hectare) national park covers a large portion of the Sea of Cortez (including several islands), just east of Loreto in Baja California Sur. For more information, contact the Loreto management office at 613/135-1429 or 613/135-0477.

Parque Nacional Zona Marina del Archipiélago de Espíritu Santo

Recently established in May 2007, this 120,200-acre (48,650-hectare) national park protects the islands and waters north of La Paz. There is, unfortunately, no contact information.

Reserva de la Biósfera Sierra de la Laguna

This 277,830-acre (112,440-hectare) biosphere reserve, established in 1994, protects the mountainous region between La Paz, Todos Santos, and Los Cabos. For more information, contact the La Paz management office at 612/122-6890.

The Cape Region

Area de Protección de Flora y Fauna Cabo San Lucas

Established in 1993, this 9,880-acre (4,000-hectare) area protects the unique environs surrounding Cabo San Lucas in Baja California Sur. For more information, contact the management office in Cabo San Lucas at 624/172-0210.

Parque Marino Nacional Cabo Pulmo

This 17,540-acre (7,100-hectare) national park, established in 1995, comprises the fascinating *arrecifes de coral* (coral reefs) just east of Cabo Pulmo in Baja California Sur. For more information, contact the management office in Cabo San Lucas at 624/172-0210.

Reserva de la Biósfera Archipiélago de Revillagigedo

Established in 1994, this 1.6-million-acre (650,000-hectare) biosphere reserve protects a cluster of islands southwest of Los Cabos. For more information, contact the management office in Cabo San Lucas at 624/172-0210.

Medical Assistance

Although the only required vaccination for foreign travelers visiting Baja is the one for yellow fever (usually only applicable for residents of Africa and South America), travel insurance (which should include medical coverage) is highly recommended. SafeMex Travel Insurance & Assistance (www.safemex.com) is a good place to start for such protection.

There are hospitals in all of the major cities and towns, such as Tijuana, Ensenada, Mexicali, Guerrero Negro, Santa Rosalía, Ciudad Constitución, La Paz, and Cabo San Lucas. Medical and dental services abound as well, and Mexican pharmacies usually offer a greater variety of over-the-counter medications than their U.S. counterparts. Just remember that all hospitals and medical/dental offices will expect you to pay your bill in full before leaving the premises; be sure to save the receipt in order to pursue insurance reimbursement after your trip to Baja.

In the case of an emergency, eligible patients (which include insured U.S. residents traveling in Mexico, American expatriates living in Mexico, and international patients that can receive medical care in the United States) can contact the Sharp International Patient Transfer Program, based in San Diego, by phoning 888/265-1513 (from Mexico) or 858/499-4962 (in the U.S.). Sharp's Multicultural Department can assist you 24 hours daily. For more information, visit www.sharp.com.

In addition, you can always dial the Mexico-wide emergency number 066 (the equivalent to America's 911) if you need immediate medical assistance while in Baja. Other important 24-hour numbers (in Mexico) include:

Red Cross in Tijuana: 065
Police: 060
Fire: 068
Information: 040
State Tourist Assistance (in Baja Norte): 078 or 661/612-0200
Federal Highway: 664/682-5285

Mexican Road Signs

If you don't speak much (or any) Spanish, then encountering road signs in Baja can be a perplexing experience. Visual signs—such as those using international symbols to indicate steep downgrades, falling rocks, gasoline pumps, cattle crossings, railroad crossings, and the like—might seem rather obvious, but those that utilize Spanish words and phrases can be downright confusing, especially for first-timers to Mexico. To avoid dangerous driving conditions (or unnecessary confusion while traveling), it's best to familiarize yourself with many of these signs prior to your trip down the peninsula (and to bring along a Spanish phrasebook just in case).

For a detailed list of road signs in Mexico, visit www.ontheroadin.com/roadmarkings.htm. In the meantime, refer to this list of driving instructions—and the following visual representation of road signs—many of which you're likely to encounter often while in Baja:

Acceso a Playa: Beach Access
Acotamiento: Soft Shoulder
Area de Descanso: Rest Area
Calle Sin Salida: Dead End
Camino Cerrado: Road Closed
Carril Izquierdo Solo para Rebasar: Left Lane Only for Passing
Carril Lateral Solo por Vehículos Ligeros: Laterals Only for Light Vehicles
Caseta de Cobro: Tollbooth
Ciclopista: Bicycle Path
Circulación: Traffic
Con Lluvia Disminuya Su Velocidad: In Rain, Reduce Your Speed
Con Niebla (Neblina) Encienda Sus Luces: In Fog (Mist), Turn On Lights
Conserve (Guarde) Su Distancia: Keep Your Distance
Dirección Única: One Way
Disminuya Su Velocidad: Reduce Your Speed
En B.C.S. Es Obligatorio el Cinturón de Seguridad: In Baja California Sur, Seat Belts Are Mandatory
Entrada: Entrance
Entrada y Salida de Camiones: Truck Entrance and Exit
Entronque Peligroso: Dangerous Intersection

Entronque Próximo: Intersection Near
Esta Carretera No Es de Alta Velocidad: This Is Not a High-Speed Road
Estacionamiento Solo Para Emergencias: Emergency Parking Only
Evite Accidentes: Avoid Accidents
Gracias por Usar el Cinturón de Seguridad: Thanks for Using Your Seat Belt
Maneje con Precaución: Drive with Caution
Máquina Trabajando: Heavy Machines at Work
Mirador de Molinero: Viewpoint of Mill
No Adelantar: No Passing
No Circular por el Acotamiento: No Driving on the Shoulder
No de Frente: No Entry
No Estacionarse en Acotamiento: No Parking on the Shoulder
No Frene con Motor: No Braking with Engine
No Maltrate Las Señales: Do Not Disregard the Signs
No Rebase con Raya Continua: No Passing on a Continuous Line
No Rebase por el Acotamiento: No Passing on the Shoulder
Obedezca (Respete) Las Señales: Obey (Respect) the Signs
Peaje: Toll
Permita Rebasar Utilice Su Extrema Derecha: Allow Passing: Use Extreme Right
Plaza de Cobro: Tollbooth
Poblado Próximo: Town Near
Precaución Cruce de Peatones: Caution: Pedestrian Crossing
Precaución Curva Peligrosa: Caution: Dangerous Curve
Precaución Entrada y Salida de Maquinaria: Caution: Entrance and Exit of Machinery
Precaución Zona de Ganado: Caution: Livestock Zone
Precaución Zona de Tolvaneras: Caution: Wind Zone
Precaución Zona Escolar: Caution: School Zone
Prepare Su Cuota: Have Toll Ready
Principia Tramo en Reparación: Main Highway under Repair
Principia Zona de Derrumbes: Begin Rockslide Area
Principia Zona de Vados: Begin Area of Dips
Prohibido Aparcar: No Parking
Prohibido el Paso: No Entry
Prohibido Estacionarse: No Parking
Prohibido Tirar Basura (Multa o Cárcel): Throwing Garbage Prohibited (By Fine or Jail)
Reducción a Dos Carriles: Reduction to Two Lanes
Reducción de Acotamientosa: Reduction of Shoulders
Reductor de Velocidad: Speed Bump
Respete Límite de Velocidad: Respect the Speed Limit
Retorno: U-Turn
Ruta de Camiones: Truck Route
Salida: Exit
Semáforo en Operación: Stoplight in Operation
Se Usara Grua: Tow-Away Zone
Si (Cuando) Toma No Maneje: If (When) You Drink, Don't Drive
Termina Ampliación: End of Shoulders
Termina B.C./Principia B.C.S.: Leaving Baja California/Entering Baja California Sur
Termina Zona de Derrumbes: End Rockslide Area
Tráfico Pesado: Heavy Traffic
Tránsito Lento Carril Derecho: Slow Traffic: Use Right Lane
Trópico de Cancer: Tropic of Cancer
Un Solo Carril: Single Lane
Vado Peligroso: Dangerous Dip
Vehículos Ligeros: Light Vehicles
Vehículos Pesados: Heavy Vehicles
Vía Corta: Short Route
Vía Cuota: Toll Highway
Zona de Fallas: Landslide Area
Zona Escolar: School Zone
Zona Urbana Modere La Velocidad: Urban Zone: Slow Down

Note: In Mexico, all speed limits are expressed in kilometers, so don't be alarmed if you see a sign indicating a maximum speed of "100" (which is roughly equal to 62 miles per hour).

CURVA PELIGROSA–DANGEROUS CURVE

DESVIACIÓN–DETOUR

CONCEDA CAMBIO DE LUCES–DIM YOUR LIGHTS

VADO–DIP

PENDIENTE PELIGROSA–DANGEROUS INCLINE

ZONA DE DERRUMBES–FALLING ROCK AREA

GASOLINERA–GAS STATION

INSPECCIÓN–INSPECTION

CONSERVE SU DERECHA–KEEP TO THE RIGHT

DOBLE CIRCULACIÓN–TWO WAY

CAMINO SINUOSO–WINDING ROAD

CEDA EL PASO–YIELD

SOLO IZQ (IZQUIERDO)–
LEFT TURN ONLY

ZONA DE GANADO–
LIVESTOCK AREA

GRAVA SUELTA–
LOOSE GRAVEL

HOMBRES TRABAJANDO–
MEN WORKING

PUENTE ANGOSTO–
NARROW BRIDGE

NO TIRE BASURA–
NO LITTERING

NO ESTACIONARSE–
NO PARKING

NO REBASE–NO PASSING

ESTACIONAMIENTO–PARKING

CRUCE DE PEATONES–
PEDESTRIAN CROSSING

PRECAUCIÓN–CAUTION

CRUCE DE FERROCARRIL–
RAILROAD CROSSING

RESTAURANTE–RESTAURANT

NO HAY PASO–ROAD CLOSED

CRUCE DE ESCOLARES–
SCHOOL CROSSING

DESPACIO–SLOW

TOPE–SPEED BUMP

MAXIMA–SPEED LIMIT
IN KILOMETERS PER HOUR

SEMÁFORO–STOPLIGHT

ALTO–STOP

TELÉFONO–TELEPHONE

SANITARIOS–RESTROOMS

PELIGRO–DANGER

ESTACIONAMIENTO PARA
VEHÍCULOS RECREATIVOS–
RV PARKING

U.S.-Metric Conversion

Since Mexico adheres to the metric system of measurement, it's important to know the most common U.S.-metric conversions when traveling throughout Baja:

Length

1 inch = 2.54 centimeters (cm)
1 foot = 0.3048 meter
1 yard = 0.9144 meter
1 meter = 3.2808 feet
1 mile = 1.6093 kilometers (km)
1 kilometer = 0.6214 mile

Area

1 square foot = 0.0929 square meter
1 acre = 0.4047 hectare
1 hectare = 2.4709 acres
1 square mile = 2.5889 square kilometers
1 square kilometer = 100 hectares

Weight

1 ounce = 28.3495 grams
1 pound = 0.4536 kilogram (kg)
1 kilogram = 2.2046 pounds
1 short ton = 0.9072 metric ton
1 short ton = 2,000 pounds
1 long ton = 1.016 metric ton
1 long ton = 2,240 pounds
1 metric ton = 1000 kilogram (kg)

Volume

1 quart = 0.9464 liter
1 liter = 1.0567 quarts
1 U.S. gallon = 3.7856 liters
1 Imperial gallon = 4.5459 liters

Temperature

Americans typically express temperatures on the Fahrenheit (F) scale, while the metric system relies on the Celsius scale. To compute Celsius (C) temperatures, subtract 32 from the Fahrenheit temperature and divide by 1.8. To convert Celsius temperatures to Fahrenheit, multiply by 1.8 and add 32.

Some common temperature conversions include:

Freezing point
32°F = 0°C

Body temperature
98.6°F = 37°C

Boiling point
212°F = 100°C

Time

The metric system utilizes a 24-hour schedule for each calendar day. In other words, 1 A.M. equals 01:00, noon equals 12:00, 6 P.M. equals 18:00, and midnight equals 24:00.

Recommended Maps

A detailed map is an essential tool for any traveler to Baja California. While various websites, guidebooks, and tourism offices provide some useful choices, your best bet is to purchase a road map in advance of your trip to Baja. Just remember that road conditions and destinations can change at any time on the Baja peninsula, so when in doubt, consult local residents for more current information.

During your trip preparations, consider the following seven selections:

AAA: Baja California
Automobile Club of Southern California
P.O. Box 25001
Santa Ana, CA 92799-5001
tel. 800/400-4222 (in California) or 800/222-4357 (in U.S. and Canada)
www.aaa-calif.com or www.aaa.com
Note: AAA members can order this map for free; nonmembers will pay around $5 per copy (well worth the cost).

International Travel Maps: Baja California (Mexico)
ITMB Publishing, Ltd.
530 West Broadway
Vancouver, BC V5Z 1E9
Canada
tel. 604/879-3621 (Canada)
fax 604/879-4521 (Canada)
www.itmb.com

Baja California Almanac: Mexico's Land of Adventure
Baja Almanac Publishing
5130 East Charleston Boulevard, #5-52
Las Vegas, NV 89142-1003
www.baja-almanac.com

Esparza Editores: Baja California Road & Recreation Atlas
Esparza Editores
tel. 646/173-3727

Esparza Editores: Baja California Road & Recreation Map
Esparza Editores
tel. 646/173-3727

Ediciones Independencia: Baja California
Ediciones Independencia
www.mapasindependencia.com

Ediciones Independencia: Baja California Sur
Ediciones Independencia
www.mapasindependencia.com

MEXICAN EMBASSIES AND CONSULATES

Before heading to Baja, U.S. and Canadian citizens (and other foreign travelers preparing to cross the U.S.-Mexico border) can visit www.sre.gob.mx or contact any one of numerous Mexican embassies and consulates for last-minute questions.

United States

For more information about traveling in Baja, contact the following offices:

Mexican Embassy

Embajada de México en Estados Unidos de América
1911 Pennsylvania Avenue NW
Washington, D.C. 20006
tel. 202/728-1600 (U.S.)
http://portal.sre.gob.mx/usa

Consulates in Arizona

Consulado de Carrera de México
1201 F Avenue
Douglas, AZ 85607
tel. 520/364-3142 (U.S.)
fax 520/364-1379 (U.S.)
http://portal.sre.gob.mx/douglas

Consulado General de México
571 North Grand Avenue
Nogales, AZ 85621
tel. 520/287-2521 (U.S.) or 520/287-3381 (U.S.)
fax 520/287-3175 (U.S.)
www.sre.gob.mx/nogales

Consulado General de México
1990 West Camelback Road, Suite #110
Phoenix, AZ 85015
tel. 602/242-7398 (U.S.)
fax 602/242-2957 (U.S.)
www.sre.gob.mx/phoenix

Consulado de Carrera de México
553 South Stone Avenue
Tucson, AZ 85701
tel. 520/882-5595 (U.S.)
fax 520/882-8959 (U.S.)
http://portal.sre.gob.mx/tucson

Consulado de Carrera de México
600 West 16th Street
Yuma, AZ 85364
tel. 928/343-0066 (U.S.)
fax 928/343-0077 (U.S.)
www.sre.gob.mx/yuma

Consulate in Arkansas

Consulado de Carrera de México
3500 South University Avenue
Little Rock, AR 72204
tel. 501/372-6933 (U.S.)
fax 501/372-6109 (U.S.)
http://portal.sre.gob.mx/littlerock

Consulates in California

Consulado de Carrera de México
408 Heber Avenue
Calexico, CA 92231
tel. 760/357-3863 (U.S.)
fax 760/357-6284 (U.S.)
www.sre.gob.mx/calexico

Consulado de Carrera de México
2409 Merced Street
Fresno, CA 93721
tel. 559/233-0318 (U.S.)
fax 559/233-6156 (U.S.)
http://portal.sre.gob.mx/fresno

Consulado General de México
2401 West 6th Street
Los Angeles, CA 90057
tel. 213/351-6800 (U.S.)
fax 213/351-2114 (U.S.)
www.sre.gob.mx/losangeles

Consulado General de México
3151 West 5th Street, Suite #E-10
Oxnard, CA 93030
tel. 805/984-8738 (U.S.)
fax 805/984-8747 (U.S.)
http://portal.sre.gob.mx/oxnard

Consulado General de México
1010 8th Street
Sacramento, CA 95814
tel. 916/441-3287 (U.S.)
fax 916/441-3147 (U.S.)
http://portal.sre.gob.mx/sacramento

Consulado de Carrera de México
293 North D Street
San Bernardino, CA 92401
tel. 909/889-9836 (U.S.) or
909/889-9837 (U.S.)
fax 909/889-8285 (U.S.)
www.sre.gob.mx/sanbernardino

Consulado General de México
1549 India Street
San Diego, CA 92101
tel. 619/231-8414 (U.S.)
fax 619/231-4802 (U.S.)
http://portal.sre.gob.mx/sandiego

Consulado General de México
532 Folsom Street
San Francisco, CA 94105
tel. 415/354-1700 (U.S.)
fax 415/495-3971 (U.S.)
www.sre.gob.mx/sanfrancisco

Consulado General de México
540 North 1st Street
San José, CA 95112
tel. 408/294-3414 (U.S.)
fax 408/294-4506 (U.S.)
http://portal.sre.gob.mx/sanjose

Consulado de Carrera de México
828 North Broadway Street
Santa Ana, CA 92701
tel. 714/835-8578 (U.S.)
fax 714/835-3472 (U.S.)
http://portal.sre.gob.mx/santaana

Consulate in Colorado

Consulado General de México
5350 Leetsdale Drive, Suite #100
Denver, CO 80246
tel. 303/331-1110 (U.S.) or
877/575-5755 (U.S.)
fax 303/331-1110 (U.S.)
http://portal.sre.gob.mx/denver

Consulates in Florida

Consulado General de México
5975 Southwest 72nd Street, Suite #301-303
Miami, FL 33143
tel. 786/268-4900 (U.S.)
fax 786/268-4895 (U.S.)
www.sre.gob.mx/miami

Consulado de Carrera de México
100 West Washington Street
Orlando, FL 32801-2315
tel. 407/422-0514 (U.S.)
fax 407/422-9633 (U.S.)
http://portal.sre.gob.mx/orlando

Consulate in Georgia

Consulado General de México
2600 Apple Valley Road
Atlanta, GA 30319
tel. 404/266-2233 (U.S.)
fax 404/266-2302 (U.S.)
http://portal.sre.gob.mx/atlanta

Consulate in Illinois

Consulado General de México
204 South Ashland Avenue
Chicago, IL 60607

tel. 312/855-1380 (U.S.)
fax 312/491-9072 (U.S.)
http://portal.sre.gob.mx/chicago

Consulate in Indiana

Consulado de Carrera de México
39 West Jackson Place, Suite #103
Indianapolis, IN 46225
tel. 317/951-0005 (U.S.)
fax 317/951-4176 (U.S.)
www.sre.gob.mx/indianapolis

Consulate in Massachusetts

Consulado General de México
20 Park Plaza, Suite #506
Boston, MA 02116
tel. 617/426-4181 (U.S.) or 617/426-4942 (U.S.)
fax 617/695-1957 (U.S.)
www.sre.gob.mx/boston

Consulate in Michigan

Consulado de Carrera de México
645 Griswold Avenue, Suite #830
Detroit, MI 48226
tel. 313/964-4515 (U.S.)
fax 313/964-4522 (U.S.)
www.sre.gob.mx/detroit

Consulate in Minnesota

Consulado de Carrera de México
797 East 7th Street
Saint Paul, MN 55106
tel. 651/772-4084 (U.S.)
fax 651/772-4419 (U.S.)
http://portal.sre.gob.mx/saintpaul

Consulate in Missouri

Consulado de Carrera de México
1600 Baltimore Avenue, Suite #100
Kansas City, MO 64108
tel. 816/556-0800 (U.S.)
fax 816/556-0900 (U.S.)
http://portal.sre.gob.mx/kansascity

Consulate in Nebraska

Consulado de Carrera de México
3552 Dodge Street
Omaha, NE 68131
tel. 402/595-1841 (U.S.)
fax 402/595-1845 (U.S.)
info@consuladoomaha.org

Consulate in Nevada

Consulado de Carrera de México
330 South 4th Street
Las Vegas, NV 89101
tel. 702/383-0623 (U.S.)
fax 702/383-0683 (U.S.)
http://portal.sre.gob.mx/lasvegas

Consulate in New Mexico

Consulado de Carrera de México
1610 4th Street NW
Albuquerque, NM 87102
tel. 505/247-2147 (U.S.)
fax 505/842-9490 (U.S.)
www.sre.gob.mx/albuquerque

Consulate in New York

Consulado General de México
27 East 39th Street
New York, NY 10016
tel. 212/217-6400 (U.S.)
fax 212/217-6493 (U.S.)
www.sre.gob.mx/nuevayork

Consulate in North Carolina

Consulado de Carrera de México
336 East Six Forks Road
Raleigh, NC 27609
tel. 919/754-0046 (U.S.)
fax 919/754-1729 (U.S.)
www.sre.gob.mx/raleigh

Consulate in Oregon

Consulado de Carrera de México
1234 Southwest Morrison Street
Portland, OR 97205
tel. 503/274-1442 (U.S.)
fax 503/274-1540 (U.S.)
www.sre.gob.mx/portland

Consulate in Pennsylvania

Consulado de Carrera de México
111 South Independence Mall East
Bourse Building, Suite #310
Philadelphia, PA 19106
tel. 215/922-4262 (U.S.)
fax 215/923-7281 (U.S.)
www.sre.gob.mx/filadelfia

Consulates in Texas

Consulado General de México
800 Brazos Street, Suite #330
Austin, TX 78701
tel. 512/478-2866 (U.S.)
fax 512/478-8008 (U.S.)
www.sre.gob.mx/austin

Consulado de Carrera de México
301 Mexico Boulevard, Suite #F-2
Brownsville, TX 78520
tel. 956/542-4431 (U.S.)
fax 956/542-7267 (U.S.)
www.sre.gob.mx/brownsville

Consulado General de México
8855 North Stemmons Freeway
Dallas, TX 75247
tel. 214/252-9250 (U.S.)
fax 214/630-3511 (U.S.)
www.sre.gob.mx/dallas

Consulado de Carrera de México
2398 Spur 239
P.O. Box 1275
Del Rio, TX 78841-1275
tel. 830/775-2352 (U.S.)
fax 830/774-6497 (U.S.)
http://portal.sre.gob.mx/delrio

Consulado de Carrera de México
2252 East Garrison Street
Eagle Pass, TX 78852
tel. 830/773-9255 (U.S.)
fax 830/773-9397 (U.S.)
consulmxeag@sbcglobal.net

Consulado General de México
910 East San Antonio Avenue
El Paso, TX 79901
tel. 915/533-3644 (U.S.) or
915/533-3645 (U.S.)
fax 915/532-7163 (U.S.)
www.sre.gob.mx/elpaso

Consulado General de México
4506 Caroline Street
Houston, TX 77004
tel. 713/271-6800 (U.S.)
fax 713/779-0701 (U.S.)
www.sre.gob.mx/houston

Consulado General de México
1612 Farragut Street
Laredo, TX 78040
tel. 956/723-0990 (U.S.)
fax 956/723-1741 (U.S.)
www.sre.gob.mx/laredo

Consulado de Carrera de México
600 South Broadway Street
McAllen, TX 78501
tel. 956/686-0243 (U.S.)
fax 956/686-4901 (U.S.)
www.sre.gob.mx/mcallen

Consulado de Carrera de México
Juárez Avenue and 21 de Marzo Street
Presidio, TX 79845
tel. 432/229-2788 (U.S.)
fax 432/229-2792 (U.S.)
http://portal.sre.gob.mx/presidio

Consulado General de México
127 Navarro Street
San Antonio, TX 78205-2932
tel. 210/227-9145 (U.S.)
fax 210/227-1817 (U.S.)
http://portal.sre.gob.mx/sanantonio

Consulate in Utah

Consulado de Carrera de México
155 South 300 West, Suite #300
Salt Lake City, UT 84101
tel. 801/521-8502 (U.S.)
fax 801/521-0534 (U.S.)
www.sre.gob.mx/saltlake

Consulate in Washington

Consulado de Carrera de México
2132 3rd Avenue
Seattle, WA 98121
tel. 206/448-3526 (U.S.)

fax 206/448-4771 (U.S.)
http://portal.sre.gob.mx/seattle

U.S. Consulates in Baja

The Embassy of the United States of America (Embajada de los Estados Unidos de América) is located in Mexico City on the Mexican mainland. Detailed information can be found at www.usembassy-mexico.gov.

Luckily, there are three U.S. consular offices on the Baja peninsula. Before, after, or while traveling in Baja, U.S. citizens can direct any questions or concerns to these three offices:

Consulate General in Baja Norte
Avenida Tapachula #96
Colonia Hipódromo
Tijuana, Baja California
C.P. 22420
Mexico
tel. 664/622-7400
fax 664/681-8592
http://tijuana.usconsulate.gov

Consular Annex in Baja Norte
Diego Rivera #2
Zona Río
Tijuana, Baja California
C.P. 22010
Mexico
tel. 664/634-3045
http://tijuana.usconsulate.gov

Consular Agency in Baja Sur
Boulevard Marina
Local C-4
Plaza Nautica
Colonia Centro
Cabo San Lucas, Baja California Sur
C.P. 23410
Mexico
tel. 624/143-3566
fax 624/143-6750
usconsulcabo@yahoo.com

Note: To reach the U.S. Consulate from Baja, you can also write to: American Consulate General, P.O. Box 439039, San Diego, CA 92143-9039, U.S.A. In case of a general emergency (even after hours), you can also phone 619/692-2154 (U.S.).

Canada

For more information about traveling in Baja, contact the following offices:

Consulate in Alberta

Consulado de Carrera de México
833 4th Avenue SW, Suite #1100
Calgary, AB T2P 3T5
Canada
tel. 403/264-4819 (Canada)
fax 403/264-1527 (Canada)

Consulate in British Columbia

Consulado General de México
710-1177 West Hastings Street
Vancouver, BC V6E 2K3
Canada
tel. 604/684-3547 (Canada) or
604/684-1859 (Canada)
fax 604/684-2485 (Canada)
http://portal.sre.gob.mx/vancouver

Consulates in Ontario

Consulado de Carrera de México
36 Erie Street South
Leamington, ON N8H 3A7
Canada
tel. 519/325-1460 (Canada)
fax 519/325-1464 (Canada)

Consulado General de México
Commerce Court West
199 Bay Street, Suite #4440
Toronto, ON M5L 1E9
Canada
tel. 416/368-2875 (Canada)
fax 416/368-8342 (Canada)
www.consulmex.com

Consulate in Québec

Consulado General de México
2055 Rue Peel, Suite #1000
Montréal, QC H3A 1V4
Canada
tel. 514/288-2502 (Canada)
fax 514/288-8287 (Canada)
www.sre.gob.mx/montreal

Canadian Consulates in Baja

The Embassy of Canada (Embajada de Canadá en México) is located in Mexico City on the Mexican mainland. Detailed information can be found at www.dfait-maeci.gc.ca/mexico-city.

Luckily, there are two Canadian consulates on the Baja peninsula, one in each state. So, before, after, or while visiting Baja, Canadian travelers are welcome to address any questions or concerns to these two offices:

Consulate in Baja Norte
Germán Gedovius #10411-101
Condominio del Parque
Zona Río
Tijuana, Baja California
C.P. 22320
Mexico
tel. 664/684-0461
fax 664/684-0301
tijuana@canada.org.mx

Consulate in Baja Sur
Plaza José Green
Local 9
Boulevard Mijares S/N
Colonia Centro
San José del Cabo, Baja California Sur
C.P. 23400
Mexico
tel. 624/142-4333
fax 624/142-4262
loscabos@canada.org.mx

Other Foreign Embassies in Mexico

All major foreign embassies are located in Mexico City, the capital of Mexico. While traveling in Baja, foreign citizens can contact the following phone numbers and websites with questions and concerns:

Embassy of Australia
tel. 55/1101-2200
www.mexico.embassy.gov.au

Embassy of Austria
tel. 55/5251-0806
www.embajadadeaustria.com.mx

Embassy of France
tel. 55/9171-9700
www.ambafrance-mx.org

Embassy of Germany
tel. 55/5283-2200
www.embajada-alemana.org.mx

Embassy of Israel
tel. 55/5201-1500
http://mexico-city.mfa.gov.il

Embassy of Italy
tel. 55/5596-3655

Embassy of New Zealand
tel. 55/5283-9460
www.mfat.govt.nz

Embassy of the People's Republic of China
tel. 55/5616-0609
www.embajadachina.org.mx

Embassy of Spain
tel. 55/5282-2974 or 55/5282-2271

Embassy of United Kingdom
tel. 55/5242-8500
www.embajadabritanica.com.mx

ADVENTURE OUTFITTERS

Some of Baja's campgrounds, such as the Estero Beach Hotel/Resort south of Ensenada, offer outdoor activities like guided scuba-diving trips and deep-sea fishing excursions. In addition, several independent outfitters invite travelers to explore the Baja peninsula and its surrounding waters.

Here's a sampling of the options available:

Activity-Oriented Campgrounds

The following campgrounds and RV resorts either offer guided activities or can arrange them for you:

Tijuana and Northwest Baja

Estero Beach Hotel/Resort
Scuba diving, kayaking, deep-sea fishing, whale-watching, and horseback riding south of Ensenada.
www.hotelesterobeach.com

Mexicali to San Felipe

Guadalupe Canyon Hot Springs & Campground
Cave-painting tours via jeep, southwest of Mexicali.
www.guadalupe-canyon.com

Papa Fernández Restaurant and Camping
Sportfishing on Bahía San Luis Gonzaga.
www.papafernandez.com

Central Pacific and the Sea of Cortez

Coyote Cal's
Hiking and mountain biking west of San Vicente.
www.coyotecals.com

Daggett's Campground
Boating, sportfishing, scuba diving, snorkeling, and kayaking on Bahía de los Ángeles.
www.campdaggetts.com

Guillermo's Sportfishing, Hotel, & Restaurant
Sportfishing charters on Bahía de los Ángeles.
www.guillermos.net

Puerto Santo Tomás Resort
Sportfishing, whale-watching, scuba diving, snorkeling, and kayaking west of Santo Tomás.
www.puertosantotomas.com

Villa Vitta Hotel Resort
Sportfishing charters on Bahía de los Angeles.
www.villavitta.com

Guerrero Negro to Bahía Concepción

Campo Rene
Kayaking, sportfishing, and whale-watching beside Estero El Coyote.
www.camporene.com

Ecoturismo Kuyimá
Whale-watching and cave-painting excursions, based in San Ignacio.
www.kuyima.com

Hotel Serenidad
Sportfishing, kayaking, diving, and snorkeling in Mulegé.
www.serenidad.com

Malarrimo Restaurant, Motel y RV Park
Whale-watching and cave-painting excursions, based in Guerrero Negro.
www.malarrimo.com

Mario's Tours and Restaurant
Whale-watching and cave-painting excursions, based in Guerrero Negro.
www.mariostours.com

Loreto, La Paz, and Southern Baja

Kurt-n-Marina
Windsurfing, kiteboarding, sportfishing, and mountain biking in La Ventana.
www.ventanakiteboarding.com or www.kurt-nmarina.com

Tripui Vacation Park and Hotel Tripui
Sportfishing, diving, snorkeling, and whale-watching south of Loreto.
www.tripui.com

The Cape Region

Club Cabo Inn and Camp Cabo
Kayaking, snorkeling, scuba diving, and sport-fishing in Cabo San Lucas.
www.clubcaboinn.com

East Cape RV Resort
Sportfishing charters in Los Barriles.
www.eastcaperv.com

El Cardonal's Hide-a-Way
Kayaking, sportfishing, scuba diving, snorkeling, and whale-watching in El Cardonal.
www.elcardonal.net

Martin Verdugo's Beach Resort
Sportfishing, windsurfing, and scuba diving in Los Barriles.
www.verdugosbeachresort.com

Rancho Verde RV Park
Guided sportfishing tours in El Sargento.
www.rancho-verde.com

Villa Serena RV Park
Sportfishing charters through Gaviota Sport-fishing, based in Cabo San Lucas.
www.gaviotasportfishing.com

Independent Outfitters

The following shops and outfitters either provide the necessary equipment for self-guided activities or lead charters, tours, and classes for visiting adventurers:

Tijuana and Northwest Baja

Alisitos K-58 Board Shop
Surfing equipment and instruction west of La Misión.
www.alisitosk58.com

Dale's Dive Shop
Scuba diving, snorkeling, and whale-watching on the Punta Banda peninsula.
www.labufadoradive.com

Mexicali to San Felipe

Alfonsina's
Fishing charters on Bahía San Luis Gonzaga.
tel. 555/150-2825

Tony Reyes Fishing Tours
Sportfishing in San Felipe.
www.tonyreyes.com

Central Pacific and the Sea of Cortez

Baja Surf Adventures
Surfing instruction at a full-service resort near Punta San Jacinto.
www.bajasurfadventures.com

Castro's Fishing Place
Sportfishing charters west of San Vicente.
tel. 646/176-2897

Guerrero Negro to Bahía Concepción

Cortez Explorers
Scuba-diving instruction in Mulegé.
www.cortez-explorers.com

Instituto Nacional de Antropología e Historia (INAH)
Guided cultural tours around San Ignacio.
www.inah.gob.mx

Isla San Marcos SportFishing
Fishing near Isla San Marcos, between Santa Rosalía and Mulegé.
www.islasanmarcos.com

Loreto, La Paz, and Southern Baja

Arturo's Sport Fishing
Sportfishing charters, whale-watching trips, kayaking, scuba diving, and cultural excursions near Loreto.
www.arturosport.com

Club Cantamar Resort & Sports Centre
Scuba diving, kayaking, and whale-watching in La Paz.
www.clubcantamar.com

The Cape Region

Cuadra San Francisco
Horseback riding in Los Cabos.
www.loscaboshorses.com

La Sirena Kayak y Surf Aventuras
Kayaking, surfing, whale-watching, and sea turtle ecotours near Todos Santos.
www.lasirenakayaksurf.com

Pescadero Surf Camp
Surfing rentals and instruction near El Pescadero.
www.pescaderosurf.com

Pisces Fleet Sportfishing
Variety of fishing and yacht charters near Cabo San Lucas.
www.piscessportfishing.com

Wide Open Baja
High-speed Baja driving, with trips leaving Cabo San Lucas.
www.wideopenbaja.com

SPANISH PHRASEBOOK

Your Mexico adventure will be more fun if you use a little Spanish. Mexican folks, although they may smile at your funny accent, will appreciate your halting efforts to break the ice and transform yourself from a foreigner to a potential friend.

Spanish commonly uses 30 letters—the familiar English 26, plus four straightforward additions: ch, ll, ñ, and rr, which are explained in *Consonants.*

Pronunciation

Once you learn them, Spanish pronunciation rules—in contrast to English—don't change. Spanish vowels generally sound softer than in English. (*Note:* The capitalized syllables below receive stronger accents.)

Vowels

a like ah, as in "hah": ***agua*** AH-gooah (water), ***pan*** PAHN (bread), and ***casa*** CAH-sah (house)

e like ay, as in "may": ***mesa*** MAY-sah (table), ***tela*** TAY-lah (cloth), and ***de*** DAY (of, from)

i like ee, as in "need": ***diez*** dee-AYZ (ten), ***comida*** ko-MEE-dah (meal), and ***fin*** FEEN (end)

o like oh, as in "go": ***peso*** PAY-soh (weight), ***ocho*** OH-choh (eight), and ***poco*** POH-koh (a bit)

u like oo, as in "cool": ***uno*** OO-noh (one), ***cuarto*** KOOAHR-toh (room), and ***usted*** oos-TAYD (you); when it follows a "q," the u is silent; when it follows an "h" or has an umlaut, it's pronounced like "w"

Consonants

b, d, f, k, l, m, n, p, q, s, t, v, w, x, y, z, and ch—pronounced almost as in English; **h** occurs, but is silent—not pronounced at all.

c like k as in "keep": ***cuarto*** KOOAR-toh (room), ***Tepic*** tay-PEEK (capital of Nayarit state); when it precedes "e" or "i," pronounce c like s, as in "sit": ***cerveza*** sayr-VAY-sah (beer), ***encima*** ayn-SEE-mah (atop).

g like g as in "gift" when it precedes "a," "o," "u," or a consonant: ***gato*** GAH-toh (cat), ***hago*** AH-goh (I do, make); otherwise, pronounce g like h as in "hat": ***giro*** HEE-roh (money order), ***gente*** HAYN-tay (people)

j like h, as in "has": ***Jueves*** HOOAY-vays (Thursday), ***mejor*** may-HOR (better)

ll like y, as in "yes": ***toalla*** toh-AH-yah (towel), ***ellos*** AY-yohs (they, them)

ñ like ny, as in "canyon": ***año*** AH-nyo (year), ***señor*** SAY-nyor (Mr., sir)

r is lightly trilled, with tongue at the roof of your mouth like a very light English d, as in "ready": ***pero*** PAY-doh (but), ***tres*** TDAYS (three), ***cuatro*** KOOAH-tdoh (four).

rr like a Spanish r, but with much more emphasis and trill. Let your tongue flap. Practice with ***burro*** (donkey), ***carretera*** (highway), and Carrillo (proper name), then really let go with ***ferrocarril*** (railroad).

Note: The single small but common exception to all of the above is the pronunciation of Spanish **y** when it's being used as the Spanish word for "and," as in "Ron y Kathy." In such case, pronounce it like the English ee, as in "keep": Ron "ee" Kathy (Ron and Kathy).

Accent

The rule for accent, the relative stress given to syllables within a given word, is straightforward. If a word ends in a vowel, an n, or an s, accent the next-to-last syllable; if not, accent the last syllable.

Pronounce ***gracias*** GRAH-seeahs (thank you), ***orden*** OHR-dayn (order), and ***carretera*** kah-ray-TAY-rah (highway) with stress on the next-to-last syllable.

Otherwise, accent the last syllable: ***venir*** vay-NEER (to come), ***ferrocarril*** fay-roh-cah-REEL (railroad), and ***edad*** ay-DAHD (age).

Exceptions to the accent rule are always marked with an accent sign: (á, é, í, ó, or ú), such as ***teléfono*** tay-LAY-foh-noh (telephone), ***jabón*** hah-BON (soap), and ***rápido*** RAH-pee-doh (rapid).

Basic and Courteous Expressions

Most Spanish-speaking people consider formalities important. Whenever approaching anyone for information or some other reason, do not forget the appropriate salutation—good morning, good evening, etc. Standing alone, the greeting *hola* (hello) can sound brusque.

Hello. *Hola.*
Good morning. *Buenos días.*
Good afternoon. *Buenas tardes.*
Good evening. *Buenas noches.*
How are you? *¿Cómo está usted?*
Very well, thank you. *Muy bien, gracias.*
Okay; good. *Bien.*
Not okay; bad. *Mal* or *feo.*
So-so. *Más o menos.*
And you? *¿Y usted?*
Thank you. *Gracias.*
Thank you very much. *Muchas gracias.*
You're very kind. *Muy amable.*
You're welcome. *De nada.*
Goodbye. *Adios.*
See you later. *Hasta luego.*
please *por favor*
yes *sí*
no *no*
I don't know. *No sé.*
Just a moment, please. *Momentito, por favor.*
Excuse me, please (when you're trying to get attention). *Disculpe* or *Con permiso.*
Excuse me (when you've made a boo-boo). *Lo siento.*
Pleased to meet you. *Mucho gusto.*
What is your name? *¿Cómo se llama usted?*
Do you speak English? *¿Habla usted inglés?*
Is English spoken here? (Does anyone here speak English?) *¿Se habla inglés?*
I don't speak Spanish well. *No hablo bien el español.*
I don't understand. *No entiendo.*
How do you say... in Spanish? *¿Cómo se dice... en español?*
My name is... *Me llamo...*
Would you like... *¿Quisiera usted...*
Let's go to... *Vamos a...*

Terms of Address

When in doubt, use the formal *usted* (you) as a form of address.

I *yo*
you (formal) *usted*
you (familiar) *tu*
he/him *él*
she/her *ella*
we/us *nosotros*
you (plural) *ustedes*
they/them *ellos* (all males or mixed gender); *ellas* (all females)
Mr., sir *señor*
Mrs., madam *señora*
miss, young lady *señorita*
wife *esposa*
husband *esposo*
friend *amigo* (male); *amiga* (female)
sweetheart *novio* (male); *novia* (female)
son; daughter *hijo; hija*
brother; sister *hermano; hermana*
father; mother *padre; madre*
grandfather; grandmother *abuelo; abuela*

Transportation

Where is... ? *¿Dónde está... ?*
How far is it to... ? *¿A cuánto está... ?*
from... to... *de... a...*
How many blocks? *¿Cuántas cuadras?*
Where (Which) is the way to... ? *¿Dónde está el camino a... ?*
the bus station *la terminal de autobuses*
the bus stop *la parada de autobuses*
the taxi stand *la parada de taxis*
the train station *la estación de ferrocarril*
the boat *el barco*
the launch *lancha; tiburonera*
the dock *el muelle*
the airport *el aeropuerto*
the entrance *la entrada*
the exit *la salida*
the ticket office *la oficina de boletos*
Where is this bus going? *¿Adónde va este autobús?*
I'd like a ticket to... *Quisiera un boleto a...*
first (second) class *primera (segunda) clase*
roundtrip *ida y vuelta*
reservation *reservación*
baggage *equipaje*
Stop here, please. *Pare aquí, por favor.*
(very) near; far *(muy) cerca; lejos*
to; toward *a*
by; through *por*
from *de*
the right *la derecha*
the left *la izquierda*
straight ahead *derecho; directo*
in front *en frente*
beside *al lado*
behind *atrás*
the corner *la esquina*
the stoplight *la semáforo*
a turn *una vuelta*
right here *aquí*

somewhere around here *por acá*
right there *allí*
somewhere around there *por allá*
road *el camino*
street; boulevard *calle; bulevar*
block *la cuadra*
highway *carretera*
kilometer *kilómetro*
bridge; toll *puente; cuota*
address *dirección*
north; south *norte; sur*
east; west *oriente (este); poniente (oeste)*

Accommodations

hotel *hotel*
Is there a room? *¿Hay cuarto?*
May I (may we) see it? *¿Puedo (podemos) verlo?*
What is the rate? *¿Cuál es el precio?*
Is that your best rate? *¿Es su mejor precio?*
Is there something cheaper? *¿Hay algo más económico?*
a single room *un cuarto sencillo*
a double room *un cuarto doble*
double bed *cama matrimonial*
twin beds *camas gemelas*
with private bath *con baño*
hot water *agua caliente*
shower *ducha*
towels *toallas*
soap *jabón*
toilet paper *papel higiénico*
blanket *frazada; manta*
sheets *sábanas*
air-conditioned *aire acondicionado*
fan *abanico; ventilador*
key *llave*
manager *gerente*

Food

I'm hungry *Tengo hambre.*
I'm thirsty. *Tengo sed.*
menu *carta; menú*
order *orden*
glass *vaso*
fork *tenedor*
knife *cuchillo*
spoon *cuchara*
napkin *servilleta*
soft drink *refresco*
coffee *café*
tea *té*
drinking water *agua pura; agua potable*
bottled carbonated water *agua mineral*
bottled uncarbonated water *agua sin gas*
beer *cerveza*
wine *vino*
milk *leche*
juice *jugo*
cream *crema*
sugar *azúcar*
cheese *queso*
snack *antojo; botana*
breakfast *desayuno*
lunch *almuerzo*
daily lunch special *comida corrida* (or *el menú del día* depending on region)
dinner *comida* (often eaten in late afternoon); *cena* (a late-night snack)
the check *la cuenta*
eggs *huevos*
bread *pan*
salad *ensalada*
fruit *fruta*
mango *mango*
watermelon *sandía*
papaya *papaya*
banana *plátano*
apple *manzana*
orange *naranja*
lime *limón*
fish *pescado*
shellfish *mariscos*
shrimp *camarones*
meat (without) *(sin) carne*
chicken *pollo*
pork *puerco*
beef; steak *res; bistec*
bacon; ham *tocino; jamón*
fried *frito*
roasted *asada*
barbecue; barbecued *barbacoa; al carbón*

Shopping

money *dinero*
money-exchange bureau *casa de cambio*
I would like to exchange traveler's checks. *Quisiera cambiar cheques de viajero.*
What is the exchange rate? *¿Cuál es el tipo de cambio?*
How much is the commission? *¿Cuánto cuesta la comisión?*
Do you accept credit cards? *¿Aceptan tarjetas de crédito?*
money order *giro*
How much does it cost? *¿Cuánto cuesta?*
What is your final price? *¿Cuál es su último precio?*
expensive *caro*
cheap *barato; económico*
more *más*
less *menos*
a little *un poco*
too much *demasiado*

Health

Help me please. *Ayúdeme por favor.*
I am ill. *Estoy enfermo.*
Call a doctor. *Llame un doctor.*
Take me to... *Lléveme a...*
hospital *hospital; sanatorio*
drugstore *farmacia*
pain *dolor*
fever *fiebre*
headache *dolor de cabeza*
stomachache *dolor de estómago*
burn *quemadura*
cramp *calambre*
nausea *náusea*
vomiting *vomitar*
medicine *medicina*
antibiotic *antibiótico*
pill; tablet *pastilla*
aspirin *aspirina*
ointment; cream *pomada; crema*
bandage *venda*
cotton *algodón*
sanitary napkins use brand name, e.g., Kotex
birth control pills *pastillas anticonceptivas*
contraceptive foam *espuma anticonceptiva*
condoms *preservativos; condones*
toothbrush *cepilla dental*
dental floss *hilo dental*
toothpaste *crema dental*
dentist *dentista*
toothache *dolor de muelas*

Post Office and Communications

long-distance telephone *teléfono larga distancia*
I would like to call... *Quisiera llamar a...*
collect *por cobrar*
station to station *a quien contesta*
person to person *persona a persona*
credit card *tarjeta de crédito*
post office *correo*
general delivery *lista de correo*
letter *carta*
stamp *estampilla, timbre*
postcard *tarjeta*
aerogram *aerograma*
air mail *correo aereo*
registered *registrado*
money order *giro*
package; box *paquete; caja*
string; tape *cuerda; cinta*

At the Border

border *frontera*
customs *aduana*
immigration *migración*
tourist card *tarjeta de turista*
inspection *inspección; revisión*
passport *pasaporte*
profession *profesión*
marital status *estado civil*
single *soltero*
married; divorced *casado; divorciado*
widowed *viudado*
insurance *seguros*
title *título*
driver's license *licencia de manejar*

At the Gas Station

gas station *gasolinera*
gasoline *gasolina*
unleaded *sin plomo*
full, please *lleno, por favor*
tire *llanta*
tire repair shop *vulcanizadora*
air *aire*
water *agua*
oil (change) *aceite (cambio)*
grease *grasa*
My... doesn't work. *Mi... no sirve.*
battery *batería*
radiator *radiador*
alternator *alternador*
generator *generador*
tow truck *grúa*
repair shop *taller mecánico*
tune-up *afinación*
auto parts store *refaccionería*

Verbs

Verbs are the key to getting along in Spanish. They employ mostly predictable forms and come in three classes, which end in *ar, er,* and *ir,* respectively:

to buy *comprar*
I buy, you (he, she, it) buys *compro, compra*
we buy, you (they) buy *compramos, compran*
to eat *comer*
I eat, you (he, she, it) eats *como, come*
we eat, you (they) eat *comemos, comen*
to climb *subir*
I climb, you (he, she, it) climbs *subo, sube*
we climb, you (they) climb *subimos, suben*

Here are more (with irregularities indicated):

to do or make *hacer* (regular except for *hago,* I do or make)
to go *ir* (very irregular: *voy, va, vamos, van*)
to go (walk) *andar*
to love *amar*

to work *trabajar*
to want *desear, querer*
to need *necesitar*
to read *leer*
to write *escribir*
to repair *reparar*
to stop *parar*
to get off (the bus) *bajar*
to arrive *llegar*
to stay (remain) *quedar*
to stay (lodge) *hospedar*
to leave *salir* (regular except for *salgo*, I leave)
to look at *mirar*
to look for *buscar*
to give *dar* (regular except for *doy*, I give)
to carry *llevar*
to have *tener* (irregular but important: *tengo, tiene, tenemos, tienen*)
to come *venir* (similarly irregular: *vengo, viene, venimos, vienen*)

Spanish has two forms of "to be":
to be *estar* (regular except for *estoy*, I am)
to be *ser* (very irregular: *soy, es, somos, son*)
Use *estar* when speaking of location or a temporary state of being: **"I am at home."** *"Estoy en casa."* **"I'm sick."** *"Estoy enfermo."* Use *ser* for a permanent state of being: **"I am a doctor."** *"Soy doctora."*

Numbers

zero *cero*
one *uno*
two *dos*
three *tres*
four *cuatro*
five *cinco*
six *seis*
seven *siete*
eight *ocho*
nine *nueve*
10 *diez*
11 *once*
12 *doce*
13 *trece*
14 *catorce*
15 *quince*
16 *dieciseis*
17 *diecisiete*
18 *dieciocho*
19 *diecinueve*
20 *veinte*
21 *veinte y uno* or *veintiuno*
30 *treinta*
40 *cuarenta*
50 *cincuenta*
60 *sesenta*
70 *setenta*
80 *ochenta*
90 *noventa*
100 *ciento*
101 *ciento y uno* or *cientiuno*
200 *doscientos*
500 *quinientos*
1,000 *mil*
10,000 *diez mil*
100,000 *cien mil*
1,000,000 *millón*
one-half *medio*
one-third *un tercio*
one-fourth *un cuarto*

Time

What time is it? *¿Qué hora es?*
It's one o'clock. *Es la una.*
It's three in the afternoon. *Son las tres de la tarde.*
It's 4 A.M. *Son las cuatro de la mañana.*
six-thirty *seis y media*
a quarter till eleven *un cuarto para las once*
a quarter past five *las cinco y cuarto*
an hour *una hora*

Days and Months

Monday *lunes*
Tuesday *martes*
Wednesday *miércoles*
Thursday *jueves*
Friday *viernes*
Saturday *sábado*
Sunday *domingo*
today *hoy*
tomorrow *mañana*
yesterday *ayer*
January *enero*
February *febrero*
March *marzo*
April *abril*
May *mayo*
June *junio*
July *julio*
August *agosto*
September *septiembre*
October *octubre*
November *noviembre*
December *diciembre*
a week *una semana*
a month *un mes*
after *después*
before *antes*

(Spanish phrasebook is courtesy of Bruce Whipperman, author of *Moon Pacific Mexico.*)

GLOSSARY

The following Spanish words and phrases are used throughout *Baja RV Camping*. Learning their definitions will facilitate your trip to Mexico:

abarrotería grocery store
agua purificada purified water
alacrán scorpion
alfarerías pottery and tile works
alto stop
apartado postal post office box
arrecifes de coral coral reefs
arroyo brook
artesanos de cestería basket makers
artes y oficios arts and crafts
avenida avenue
bahía bay
ballenas gris gray whales
balneario swimming resort
baños de agua caliente hot springs
bodega winery
cabaña cabin
cabo cape
calle street
camino road
campo camp
campo de béisbol baseball stadium
campo de golf golf course
caña de azúcar sugarcane
canódromo greyhound racetrack
cardón world's largest cactus
carnicería butcher's shop
carretera highway
casa house
casita cottage
cerro hill
chubasco storm
cirio candle
ciudad fantasma ghost town
coctelería cocktail bar
codorniz quail
curva del sur southern loop
desierto desert
ejido government-supported farming cooperative
erizo de mar sea urchin
estero marsh
fresa strawberry
frutería produce store
gas butano propane
glorieta traffic circle
gringo foreign
hielo ice
hora oficial de las montañas mountain standard time
hora oficial del Pacífico Pacific standard time
iglesia church
isla island
laguna small lake
langosta lobster
lonchería casual eatery
malecón waterfront promenade
mercado market
mestizos people of Spanish and American Indian descent
misión mission
molino viejo old mill
montaña mountain
muelle viejo old pier
museo museum
museo de cera wax museum
observatorio astronómico nacional national astronomical observatory
oliva olive
palapa open, thatched-roof shade structure
panadería bakery
panga small fiberglass fishing boat
panguero fishing operator
parque nacional national park
pescadería fish market
pimiento pepper
piñata a colorful, suspended figure filled with toys and candy
piñon pine tree
pinturas rupestres cave paintings
playa beach
plaza de toros bull ring
potrero pasturing place
Propriedad Privada Private Property
pueblo town
puerto port
punta point
ramada open shade structure
rancho ranch
río river
salinas salt flats or salt mines
salsipuedes leave if you can
serpiente de cascabel rattlesnake
sin número (S/N) street address without a specific number
sol sun
sombra shade
supermercado supermarket
taller shop
tarántula tarantula
tienda small store
tierras de labranza farmland
tomate tomato
tortillaría tortilla shop
turista tourist
vidrierías glassworks

SUGGESTED READING

Baja is a fascinating, complicated place, with a rich history, a variety of ecosystems, and a wealth of intriguing sights. For centuries, this unique peninsula has been luring hordes of curious travelers, biologists, historians, writers, and others—many of whom have recorded their observations and experiences in the form of travel guides, cookbooks, novels, and the like. Before embarking upon your own Baja adventure, take a moment to peruse the advice of those who have already been there (and be sure to bring a Spanish phrasebook along for the journey).

Here's just a sampling of the titles available.

Activity Guides

With or without an RV, outdoor enthusiasts will find several books geared toward adventuring in the Baja.

Amey, Ralph. *Wines of Baja California: Touring and Tasting Mexico's Undiscovered Treasures.* South San Francisco: The Wine Appreciation Guild Ltd., 2003. Amey's guide provides details about Baja's winemaking history, notable wineries, specific vintages, and annual wine festivals.

Dreisbach, Carl. *50 Hikes in the Cape Region, Baja Sur.* Seattle: Big Raven Book, 2007. This illustrated guide describes short trips and multiday excursions from La Paz to the Sierra de la Laguna.

Gatch, Tom. *Hooked on Baja: Where & How to Fish Mexico's Legendary Waters.* Woodstock, VT: The Countryman Press, 2007. Gatch, a popular recreational columnist, blends travel information with real-life adventures, authentic recipes, useful maps, and real-estate advice.

Graham, Gary. *Guide to Fly Fishing Southern Baja.* Tucson, AZ: No Nonsense Fly Fishing Guidebooks, 2004. With equipment advice, detailed maps, and a Spanish glossary, this expert guide helps you plan a variety of saltwater fly-fishing trips to Baja Sur.

Johnson, Markes E. *Discovering the Geology of Baja California: Six Hikes on the Southern Gulf Coast.* Tucson, AZ: The University of Arizona Press, 2002. This accessible guide explores the natural history of the Punta Chivato region, north of Mulegé.

Kelly, Neil, and Gene Kira. *The Baja Catch: A Fishing, Travel & Remote Camping Manual for Baja California.* 3rd ed. Valley Center, CA: Apples & Oranges, Inc., 1997. Though a bit outdated, this guide offers helpful advice about camping equipment, fishing techniques and regulations, RV boondocking, and off-highway driving on the Baja peninsula.

Parise, Mike. *The Surfer's Guide to Baja.* 3rd ed. Los Angeles: SurfPress Publishing, 2007. Parise, a California-based advertising executive and avid surfer, has assembled the most detailed guide for Baja-bound surfers, complete with break descriptions, wave charts, and travel tips.

Peterson, Walt. *The Baja Adventure Book.* 3rd ed. Berkeley, CA: Wilderness Press, 1998. Peterson's guide covers a wide spectrum of activities, from fishing and scuba diving to bicycling and backpacking.

Peterson, Walt. *Diving & Snorkeling Baja California.* Hawthorn, Victoria, Australia: Lonely Planet Publications, 1999. With helpful maps, color photos, and driving directions, this guide describes over 50 of the peninsula's best dive sites, including kelp forests, historic shipwrecks, and coral reefs.

Romano-Lax, Andromeda. *Adventure Kayaking: Baja.* 2nd ed. Berkeley, CA: Wilderness Press, 2001. Included with each paddling route is a map, a trip summary, and specific directions; details about climate, campgrounds, and regulations are also provided.

Salvadori, Clement. *Motorcycle Journeys Through California & Baja.* 2nd ed. Conway, NH: Whitehorse Press, 2007. Filled with photos, maps, and travel tips, this guide also devotes a portion to traversing the Baja peninsula.

Speck, Susan, and Bruce Williams. *Diving and Snorkeling the Sea of Cortez: The Most Complete Guide to Baja California's Best Sites.* Bloomington, IN: AuthorHouse, 2006. Ideal for veteran divers or novice snorkelers, this guide explores over 90 underwater dive sites; photos, maps, directions, accommodations, and marine life descriptions are included.

Cookbooks

One of the most convenient aspects of RV travel is having round-the-clock access to your very own kitchen, and, luckily, a few offerings exist for those interested in Baja cuisine.

Hazard, Ann. *Cooking with Baja Magic: Mouth-Watering Meals from the Enchanted Kitchens & Campfires of Baja.* Solana Beach, CA: Renegade Enterprises, 1997. A collection of more than 170 recipes, from salsas to burritos.

Hazard, Ann. *Cooking with Baja Magic Dos: More Mouth-Watering Meals from the Kitchens and Campfires of Baja.* San Diego: Renegade Enterprises, 2005. The follow-up to Hazard's first scrumptious cookbook.

Kennedy, Diana. *The Essential Cuisines of Mexico.* New York: Clarkson Potter Publishers, 2000. Combining Kennedy's first three cookbooks, this collection boasts over 300 recipes from the Mexican mainland.

Schneider, Deborah M. *Baja! Cooking on the Edge.* New York: Rodale Books, 2006. Schneider's offering tantalizes gourmands with colorful photos and innovative twists on traditional Mexican cooking.

Fiction

Though no replacement for well-researched guidebooks, fictional tales set upon the Baja California peninsula can definitely give travelers a sense of the cultural and natural diversity of this unique place.

Campbell, Flores. *Tijuana Noir: A Long Short Story.* Bloomington, IN: AuthorHouse, 2006. A dark modern thriller about the investigation of a murdered Catholic cardinal in Tijuana's airport.

Hazard, Ann. *Cartwheels in the Sand: Baja California, Four Women and a Motor Home.* Solana Beach, CA: Renegade Enterprises, 1999. A rollicking month-long road trip for four unlikely female travelers—an executive chef, an ecotravel guide, a sassy songwriter, and a prim businesswoman.

Kira, Gene. *King of the Moon.* Valley Center, CA: Apples & Oranges, Inc., 1996. A vivid, haunting novel about life in a Baja fishing village.

Nordhoff, Walter. *The Journey of the Flame.* Berkeley, CA: Heyday Books, 2003 (originally published in 1933). Based on meticulous research, this historical novel tells the story of a man who, in 1810, accompanied the Spanish viceroy of Baja California on a journey across the entire peninsula and beyond.

Nunn, Kem. *Tijuana Straits.* New York: Scribner, 2004. Nunn's fifth novel, a literary thriller, focuses on the lawless U.S.-Mexico border and its affect on an ex-con, an environmental activist, and a grieving father.

Pérez-Reverte, Arturo. *The Queen of the South.* Trans. New York: Penguin Group, Inc., 2004. In Pérez-Reverte's sixth thriller, the author explores the gritty world of drug trafficking in Mexico, Spain, and Morocco.

Reveles, Daniel. *Enchiladas, Rice, and Beans.* New York: Ballantine Books, 1994. Filmmaker and screenwriter Reveles offers several novellas about life in Tecate.

Reveles, Daniel. *Guacamole Dip: From Baja... Tales of Love, Faith—and Magic.* San Diego: Sunbelt Publications, Inc., 2008. Tecate-based tales of intrigue and humor from a California-born Mexican author.

Reveles, Daniel. *Salsa and Chips: Tales from Tecate, the Little Baja Border Town Where Ordinary Life Is Spiced with Magic...* New York: Ballantine Books, 1997. Stories about the taco men, flower girls, witches, and scoundrels that define laid-back Tecate.

Reveles, Daniel. *Tequila, Lemon, and Salt: From Baja... Tales of Love, Faith—and Magic.* San Diego: Sunbelt Publications, Inc., 2005. More magical stories about Tecate and life on the border.

Stanton, Larry. *Arriba! Baja: More of the Best Stories of Baja.* Templeton, CA: Templeton Publishing, 1999. A follow-up to Stanton's first collection of historical fiction on the Baja peninsula.

Stanton, Larry. *Best Stories of Baja: Coyote, Cactus, Mosquitos and Mud...* Templeton, CA: Templeton Publishing, 1998. Honest, humorous stories about the "last frontier" and its memorable inhabitants.

Steinbeck, John. *The Pearl.* London, England: Penguin Books Ltd., 2002 (originally published in 1947). Steinbeck's famous novel about the trials of a Mexican pearl diver.

Historic and Social Accounts

History buffs and amateur sociologists will find a varied selection of books about Baja's intriguing (and, at times, surprising) past, present, and future.

Crosby, Harry W. *Antigua California: Mission and Colony on the Peninsular Frontier, 1697–1768.* Albuquerque: University of New Mexico Press, 1994. The definitive study of Jesuit activities on the Baja peninsula.

Crosby, Harry W. *The Cave Paintings of Baja California: Discovering the Great Murals of an Unknown People.* 2nd ed. El Cajon, CA: Sunbelt Publications, Inc., 1998. Expanded from a 1975 book, Crosby's latest edition reveals his undeniable passion for these stunning ancient art forms, some of the finest in the world.

Fiolka, Marty. *1000 Miles to Glory: The History of the Baja 1000.* Phoenix: David Bull Publishing, 2005. Written by an off-road racer, this colorful tribute to the challenging Baja 1000 chronicles each year of this dusty, world-famous endurance contest.

Hundley, Jr., Norris. *The Great Thirst—Californians and Water: A History.* Revised ed. Berkeley, CA: University of California Press, 2001. The definitive examination of California's water-policy issues, including their effect on Baja's northern region.

Laylander, Don, and Jerry D. Moore. *The Prehistory of Baja California: Advances in the Archaeology of the Forgotten Peninsula.* Gainesville, FL: University Press of Florida, 2006. An archaeologist and an anthropology professor have collaborated to produce the first comprehensive book-length study of Baja's ancient past.

Martínez, Oscar J. *Troublesome Border.* Revised ed. Tucson, AZ: The University of Arizona Press, 2006. In concise language, Martínez explores the troubled history of the U.S.-Mexico border and offers possible resolutions.

Niemann, Greg. *Baja Legends: The Historic Characters, Events, and Locations that Put Baja California on the Map.* El Cajon, CA: Sunbelt Publications, Inc., 2002. An accessible history of the people, resorts, and other elements that helped to create today's Baja.

O'Neil, Ann, and Don O'Neil. *Loreto, Baja California: First Mission and Capital of Spanish California.* Studio City, CA: Tio Press, 2001. With rare photos and illustrations, this comprehensive book presents the 300-year-old history of Baja's former capital.

Urrea, Luis Alberto. *By the Lake of Sleeping Children: The Secret Life of the Mexican Border.*

New York: Anchor Books, 1996. At times funny, poignant, and shocking, this book examines the impoverished, yet resourceful, garbage pickers that live just south of Tijuana's border.

Vernon, Edward W. *Las Misiones Antiguas: The Spanish Missions of Baja California.* Santa Barbara, CA: Viejo Press, 2002. Enhanced by the oral history of area residents, this photographic study chronicles each and every mission on the Baja peninsula.

Nature and Conservation Guides

Several books aim to familiarize visitors with Baja's unique flora and fauna—as well as the preservation of both.

Dedina, Serge. *Saving the Gray Whale: People, Politics, and Conservation in Baja California.* Tucson, AZ: The University of Arizona Press, 2000. A cautionary tale, written by an ecologist, about the potential threat of Baja's tourism and fishing industries on the once-endangered California gray whale.

Eder, Tamara. *Whales and Other Marine Mammals of California and Baja.* Edmonton, Alberta, Canada: Lone Pine Publishing, 2002. Illustrations and detailed descriptions assist marine lovers traveling to the Baja peninsula.

Gotshall, Daniell W. *Sea of Cortez Marine Mammals: A Guide to the Common Fishes and Invertebrates, Baja California to Panama.* Monterey, CA: Sea Challengers, 1998. A helpful reference guide for boaters, kayakers, anglers, snorkelers, and scuba divers.

McPeak, Ron H. *Amphibians and Reptiles of Baja California.* Monterey, CA: Sea Challengers, 2000. The only photographic resource of its kind.

Minch, John, Edwin Minch, and Jason Minch. *Roadside Geology and Biology of Baja California.* Santa Barbara, CA: John Minch & Associates, Inc., 1998. Photographs, sketches, detailed directions, and an illustrated glossary enhance this expert examination of Baja's ecosystems and geologic history.

Peterson, Roger Tory, and Edward L. Chalif. *A Field Guide to Mexican Birds.* Revised ed. New York: Houghton Mifflin Company, 1999 (originally published in 1973). Though not one of the better Peterson Field Guides, this ornithological catalog includes illustrations and descriptions for more than 1,000 bird species in Mexico, Guatemala, Belize, and El Salvador.

Roberts, Norman C. *Baja California Plant Field Guide.* Revised ed. La Jolla, CA: Natural History Publishing Co., 1989. A complete revision of Baja's first botanical field guide, now including over 400 native plants.

Thomson, Donald A., Lloyd T. Findley, and Alex N. Kerstitch. *Reef Fishes of the Sea of Cortez: The Rocky-Shore Fishes of the Gulf of California.* Revised ed. Austin, TX: University of Texas Press, 2000. First published in 1979, this updated edition has become the definitive resource for scuba divers and scientists alike.

Regional and City Guides

Mainstream travel guides offer details about Baja's cities, attractions, restaurants, and shops, with useful maps and contact information.

Clampet, Jason. *The Rough Guide to Baja California.* London, England: Rough Guides Ltd., 2006.

Cummings, Joe, and Nikki Goth Itoi. *Moon Baja: Tijuana to Cabo San Lucas.* 7th ed. Berkeley, CA: Avalon Travel Publishing, 2007.

Cummings, Joe, and Nikki Goth Itoi. *Moon Cabo: Including La Paz and Todos Santos.* 6th ed. Berkeley, CA: Avalon Travel Publishing, 2007.

Franz, Carl, and Lorena Havens. *The People's Guide to Mexico.* 13th ed. Berkeley, CA: Avalon Travel Publishing, 2006.

Harris, Richard. *Hidden Baja.* 5th ed. Berkeley, CA: Ulysses Press, 2007.

Makabe, Lori. *Best Places Baja: The Best Restaurants, Lodgings, and Outdoor Adventure.* Seattle: Sasquatch Books, 2002.

Palmerlee, Danny. *Lonely Planet: Baja California & Los Cabos.* 7th ed. Footscray, Victoria, Australia: Lonely Planet Publications Ltd., 2007.

Quinn, Emily Hughey. *Frommer's Los Cabos & Baja.* 2nd ed. Hoboken, NJ: Wiley Publishing, Inc., 2008.

Stallings, Douglas. *Fodor's In Focus Los Cabos.* New York: Fodor's Travel, 2008.

Williams, Jack, Patty Williams, and Barbara Williams. *The Magnificent Peninsula: The Comprehensive Guidebook to Mexico's Baja California.* 7th ed. Redding, CA: H. J. Williams Publications, 2002.

Travel Journals

Memoirs and travelogues—written by experienced, passionate travelers of Baja—can evoke a tantalizing sense of place.

Berger, Bruce. *Almost an Island: Travels in Baja California.* Tucson, AZ: The University of Arizona Press, 1998. Berger's travelogue illustrates his three-decade passion for Baja's diverse landscapes, towns, and people.

Gardner, Erle Stanley. *The Hidden Heart of Baja.* New York: William Morrow, 1962. An account of the peninsula's most significant archaeological aspect—the ancient Indian caves found throughout its interior.

Gardner, Erle Stanley. *Hovering Over Baja.* New York: William Morrow, 1961. The author's breathtaking helicopter adventure over the palm-lined canyons of Baja.

Gardner, Erle Stanley. *Hunting the Desert Whale.* New York: William Morrow, 1960. Gardner's first account of his adventures in Baja.

Gardner, Erle Stanley. *Off the Beaten Track in Baja.* New York: William Morrow, 1967. Gardner's lively retelling of high adventure in Baja's remote regions.

George, Taggart. *Baja Bound: To Cabo and Back.* Pollock Pines, CA: Far and Away Publications, 2006. A couple's captivating 16-day journey across the Baja peninsula.

Krutch, Joseph Wood. *The Forgotten Peninsula: A Naturalist in Baja California.* Tucson, AZ: The University of Arizona Press, 1986. Though outdated nowadays, this famous travelogue offers helpful information about Baja's natural history.

Mackintosh, Graham. *Into a Desert Place: A 3000-Mile Walk Around the Coast of Baja California.* 3rd ed. New York: W. W. Norton & Company, Inc., 1995. An "unadventurous" Englishman's rugged 500-day journey across a perilous landscape.

Mackintosh, Graham. *Journey with a Baja Burro.* San Diego: Sunbelt Publications, Inc., 2000. Mackintosh's account of his second, sweat-inducing marathon across the forgotten peninsula.

Mackintosh, Graham. *Nearer My Dog to Thee: A Summer in Baja's Sky Island.* Lemon Grove, CA: Baja Detour Press, 2003. The third Baja-related memoir from an armchair traveler turned real-life adventurer.

Mayo, C. M. *Miraculous Air: Journey of a Thousand Miles Through Baja California, the Other Mexico.* 2nd ed. Minneapolis: Milkweed Editions, 2007. A dual resident of Mexico and the United States, Mayo offers a unique perspective on the dichotomy that is Baja—a land of remote desert and fertile farmland, rich developers and poor villagers, modern cities and crumbling missions.

Niemann, Greg. *Baja Fever: Journeys into Mexico's Intriguing Peninsula.* La Crescenta, CA: Mountain N' Air Books, 1998. From camping to beachcombing, this travelogue covers a wide range of experiences, courtesy of the author's longtime love affair with Baja.

Romano-Lax, Andromeda. *Searching for Steinbeck's Sea of Cortez: A Makeshift Expedition Along Baja's Desert Coast.* Seattle: Sasquatch Books, 2002. Inspired by John Steinbeck's legendary journey, the author and her family complete a two-month, 4,000-mile boating excursion in the Gulf of California.

Steinbeck, John. *The Log from the Sea of Cortez.* London, England: Penguin Books Ltd., 1995 (originally published in 1951). Driven by his interest in marine biology, the famed American novelist chronicled his 1930s exploration of the Gulf of California, as part of a larger collaborative effort called *The Sea of Cortez.*

INTERNET RESOURCES

The Internet offers a wealth of information about Baja California, RV travel, and other subjects related to traveling in Mexico. Just be aware that conditions in Baja can change quickly, rendering some websites out-of-date. When in doubt about the status of a destination or the validity of online information, contact businesses in advance or consult local residents.

Here's just a sampling of the websites available to the savvy Baja traveler:

General Baja Travel

Several websites cover the entire Baja peninsula. Here are just a handful:

Baja.com—www.baja.com
BajaInsider—www.bajainsider.com
Baja Life Online—www.bajalife.com
BajaLinks—www.bajalinks.com
Baja Nomad—www.bajanomad.com
Baja Quest—www.bajaquest.com
Baja Traveler—www.bajamagazine.com
Baja Web—www.baja-web.com
Tour by Mexico—www.tourbymexico.com

Regional Baja Travel

Many of Baja's towns and cities have at least one devoted website (if not more). Here are just some of the more localized websites that exist:

Bahía de los Ángeles—www.bahiadelosangeles.info
Ensenada—www.ensenada.com
La Paz—www.vivalapaz.com or www.vivalapaz.net
La Ventana—www.bestoflaventana.com
Loreto—www.loreto.com
Los Cabos—www.loscabos.net or www.loscabosguide.com
Mexicali—www.controlservers.com/cotuco
Mulegé—www.mulege.net
Playas de Rosarito—www.rosarito.com
San Felipe—www.sanfelipe.com.mx
Tijuana—www.tijuanaonline.org or www.tijuana.com
Todos Santos—www.todossantos.cc or www.todossantos.com

RV and Adventure Travel

The following websites include information specific to RV travelers and/or those journeying in Baja:

GORP.com—www.gorp.com
Go RVing—www.gorving.com
Mexico's Baja Camping—www.ontheroadin.com/baja/thebaja.htm
RV.Net—www.rv.net

Miscellaneous

The following websites offer tools, such as medical advice and currency conversions, that could prove useful on any trip to Baja:

International Calls—www.countrycodes.com
MD Travel Health—www.mdtravelhealth.com
Spanish-English Dictionary—www.wordreference.com
U.S. Department of State—www.travel.state.gov
U.S.-Metric Conversion—www.onlineconversion.com

Index

Page numbers in **bold** indicate maps.

AB

C

DEF

GH

IJK

Acknowledgments

It would be impossible to thank each and every person who contributed to the production of this guide. During the past seven years, my husband and I have traveled often to Baja, and on every trip, we've encountered a myriad of friendly, helpful residents, always willing to point us in the right direction—for the perfect margarita, the quietest beach, the luckiest fishing spot, the finest furniture, or whatever else we sought at the time. So, thanks to everyone who made each of our journeys into Mexico—even those fraught with wrong turns, RV troubles, and lost items—a memorable experience. Thanks, too, to those who have previously traveled to and written about Baja—they'll never know how much their journals and guidebooks helped us over the years.

Of course, there are a few folks to whom I'm particularly grateful. First, I offer a special thanks to the campground owners and managers who made the job of compiling this directory a little easier. In addition, I appreciate the assistance of four helpful residents: Victor Hugo García of Rosarito, Kat Hammontre and Dr. Tony Colleraine of San Felipe, and Arnaud Vuillermet of La Ventana. Thanks also to those who provided photographs for this book—most notably, Rob Williams, Ken Wright, Mike Gale, Jonathan Soto, and the Mexico Tourism Board. Thanks, too, to the patient editors of Avalon Travel Publishing, who offered valuable assistance during the preparation of this guide.

Moreover, thanks to my friends and family, all of whom have supported me during each of my frenzied writing projects. Most of all, I'd like to thank my husband, Daniel, who encouraged me to accept the monumental task of writing this guide and who supported me at each and every turn, especially as seemingly impossible deadlines approached. He's the best traveling companion a girl could ask for.

And thanks to you, the reader. May your next RV trip to Baja be as magical as ours have been.

Notes